Colonialism and Antarctica

Manchester University Press

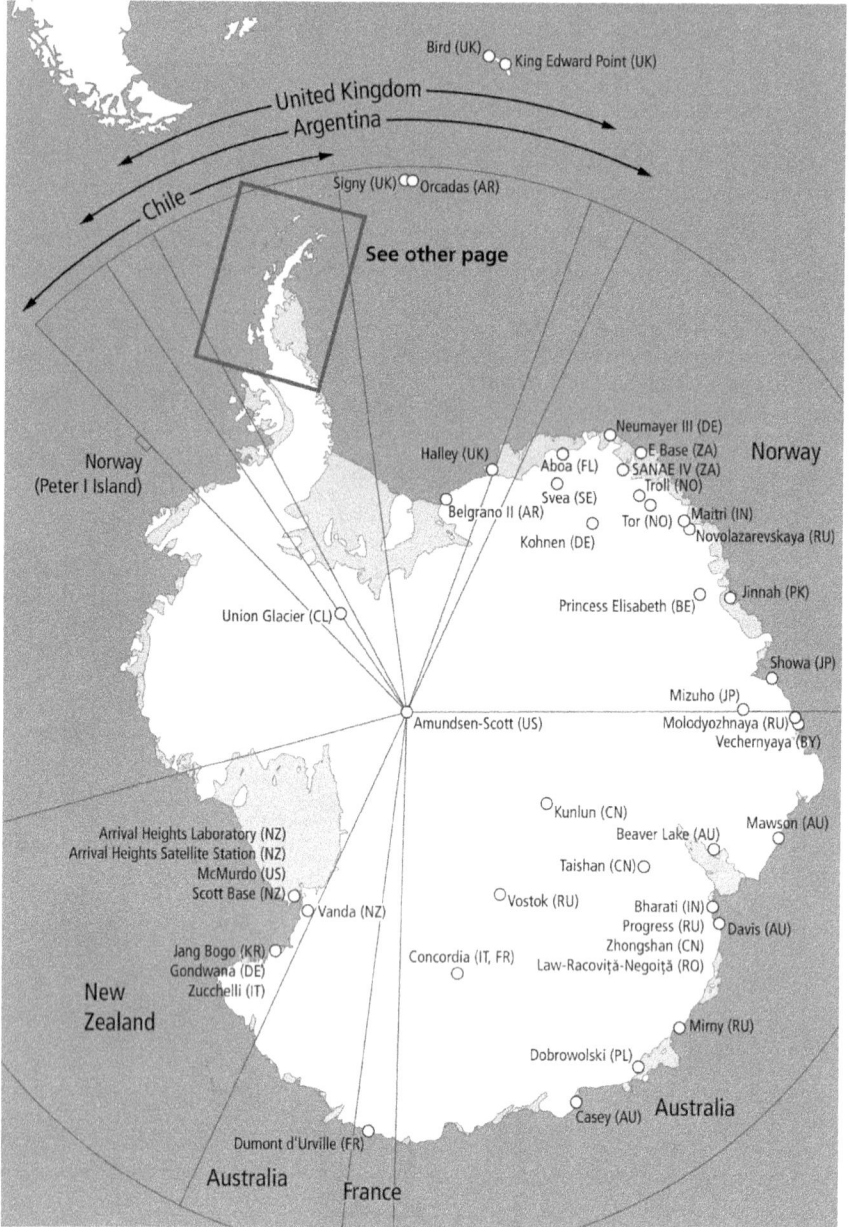

Frontispiece Key locations mentioned in the book

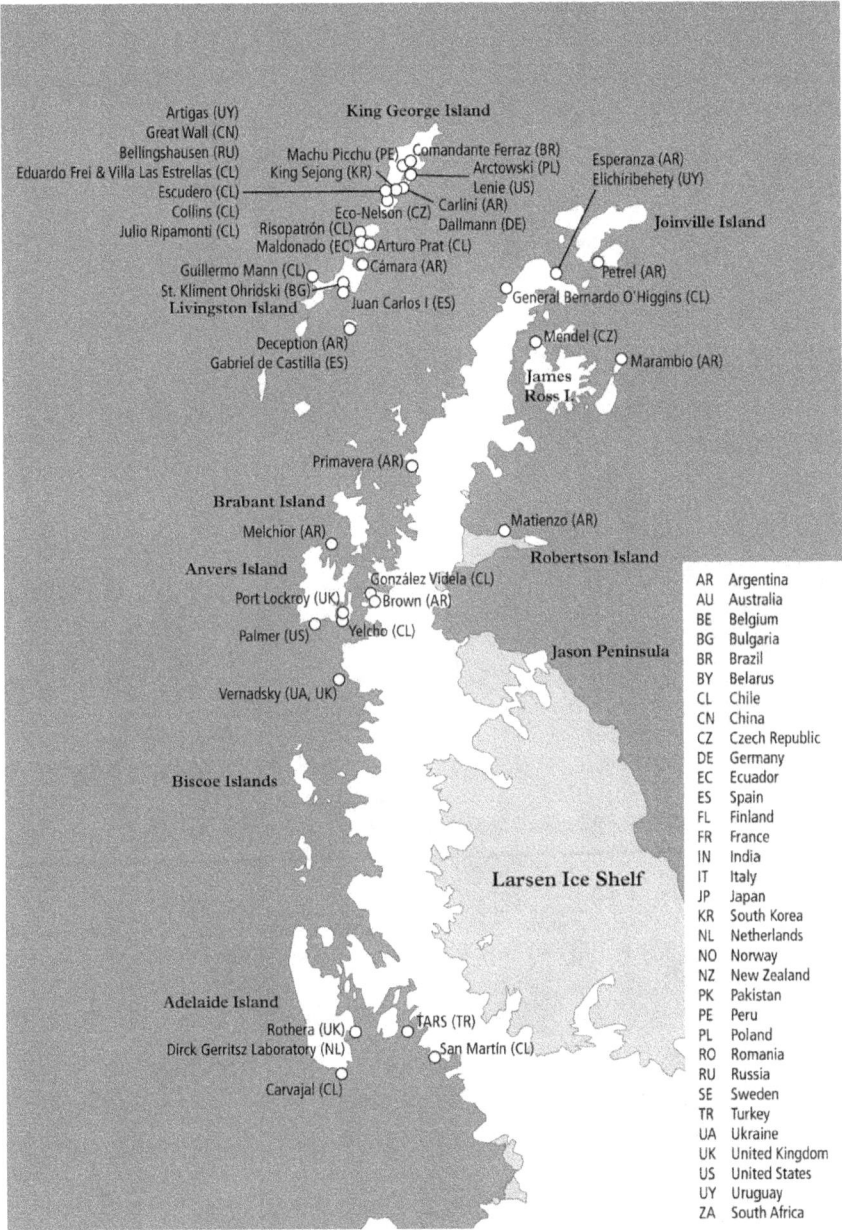

King George Island

Artigas (UY)
Great Wall (CN)
Bellingshausen (RU)
Eduardo Frei & Villa Las Estrellas (CL)
Escudero (CL)
Collins (CL)
Julio Ripamonti (CL)

Machu Picchu (PE)
King Sejong (KR)

Comandante Ferraz (BR)
Arctowski (PL)
Lenie (US)
Carlini (AR)

Esperanza (AR)
Elichiribehety (UY)

Eco-Nelson (CZ)
Risopatrón (CL)
Maldonado (EC)

Dallmann (DE)
Arturo Prat (CL)
Cámara (AR)

Joinville Island

Guillermo Mann (CL)
St. Kliment Ohridski (BG)
Livingston Island

Juan Carlos I (ES)

Petrel (AR)
General Bernardo O'Higgins (CL)

Deception (AR)
Gabriel de Castilla (ES)

Mendel (CZ)

Marambio (AR)

James
Ross I.

Primavera (AR)

Brabant Island

Melchior (AR)

Matienzo (AR)

Anvers Island

Robertson Island

Port Lockroy (UK)

González Videla (CL)
Brown (AR)

Palmer (US)

Yelcho (CL)

Jason Peninsula

Vernadsky (UA, UK)

Biscoe Islands

Larsen Ice Shelf

Adelaide Island

Rothera (UK)
Dirck Gerritsz Laboratory (NL)

TARS (TR)
San Martín (CL)

Carvajal (CL)

AR	Argentina
AU	Australia
BE	Belgium
BG	Bulgaria
BR	Brazil
BY	Belarus
CL	Chile
CN	China
CZ	Czech Republic
DE	Germany
EC	Ecuador
ES	Spain
FL	Finland
FR	France
IN	India
IT	Italy
JP	Japan
KR	South Korea
NL	Netherlands
NO	Norway
NZ	New Zealand
PK	Pakistan
PE	Peru
PL	Poland
RO	Romania
RU	Russia
SE	Sweden
TR	Turkey
UA	Ukraine
UK	United Kingdom
US	United States
UY	Uruguay
ZA	South Africa

Frontispiece (Continued)

Colonialism and Antarctica

Attitudes, logics and practices

Edited by

Peder Roberts and Alejandra Mancilla

MANCHESTER UNIVERSITY PRESS

Published by Manchester University Press
Oxford Road, Manchester, M13 9PL

www.manchesteruniversitypress.co.uk

British Library Cataloguing-in-Publication Data
A catalogue record for this book is available from the British Library

ISBN 978 1 5261 7063 7 hardback
ISBN 978 1 5261 8217 3 paperback

First published 2024

The publisher has no responsibility for the persistence or accuracy of URLs for any external or third-party internet websites referred to in this book, and does not guarantee that any content on such websites is, or will remain, accurate or appropriate.

Typeset by Newgen Publishing UK

Contents

Figures

Maps

Contributors

Ignacio Javier Cardone is Professor of International Relations at the Academic Department of Social Sciences, Pontificia Universidad Católica del Perú. His research explores Antarctic politics, covering the role of science, South American politics and Antarctic governance. He is the author of *The Antarctic Politics of Brazil: Where the Tropic Meets the Pole* (2022), and has contributed to *The Polar Journal* and *Defence Strategic Communications*, amongst others.

María Jimena Cruz is an archaeologist and postdoctoral researcher at the Multidisciplinary Institute of History and Human Sciences (National Scientific and Technical Research Council – IMHICIHU, CONICET, Argentina). She studies the nineteenth-century presence of sealers in Antarctica, focusing on food practices, zooarchaeology, memory and production processes. Her work has been published as chapters in contributory volumes and articles in several leading journals.

Rebecca Herman is Associate Professor of History at the University of California, Berkeley. She is the author of *Cooperating with the Colossus* (2022), and is currently at work on a new book about Antarctica in the 1970s and 1980s. Her articles and essays have appeared in the journals *Environmental History*, *American Historical Review*, *Diplomatic History* and *Gender & History*.

Adrian Howkins is Reader in Environmental History at the University of Bristol, and Codirector of the Centre for Environmental Humanities. He has published extensively on the history of Antarctica and is currently completing a book on the environmental history of the McMurdo Dry Valleys. Adrian is the co-editor with Peder Roberts of the *Cambridge History of the Polar Regions*.

Katarzyna Jarosz holds a PhD in archaeology. She works as an associate professor at the University of Logistics in Wrocław, Poland. Her research interests cover the history of science and museum studies in post-Soviet space. She has published articles and chapters in, among others, the *Journal of Community Archaeology & Heritage*, and *Global Environment*.

Roman Khandozhko holds a PhD in history. His research interests lie in the field of the history of science, technology and the environment, with a focus on the USSR during the Cold War period. His work on the history of the Soviet Antarctic programme was part of the European Research Council project 'Greening the Poles: Science, the Environment, and the Creation of the Modern Arctic and Antarctic'.

Kati Lindström is Associate Professor of the History of Science, Technology and Environment at KTH Royal Institute of Technology, Stockholm, Sweden, researching the protection and non-protection of Antarctic environment and heritage from a transnational perspective. She is an expert member of the ICOMOS International Polar Heritage Committee and the Polar Research Committee of the Estonian Academy of Sciences, and serves as the Estonian contact point to the Antarctic Treaty System.

Alejandra Mancilla is Professor of Philosophy at the Faculty of Humanities, University of Oslo. She is the author of *The Right of Necessity* (2016), and coeditor of *Theories of Justice* (2012). Her work on the foundations of basic human rights, global justice, territorial rights and resource rights has been published in leading journals such as *The Journal of Political Philosophy* and *Social Philosophy and Policy*, among others.

Germana Nicklin is Honorary Research Associate at Massey University, New Zealand. Her research on Antarctic borders, New Zealand borders, maritime security and public policy has been published in journals such as *The Polar Journal*, *The Anthropocene Review* and the *International Review of Public Policy*. She is coeditor of *Indo-Pacific Security: US–China Rivalry and Regional States' Responses* (2023).

Alice E. Oates is a geographer specialising in the historical geographies of Antarctica and histories of Antarctic science. Her doctoral research at the University of Cambridge focused on Halley research station, Antarctica, investigating the people, places, politics and science that have shaped British Antarctic science in the latter half of the twentieth century. Her current work investigates the experiences of people with disabilities within Antarctic research. Her chapter is informed by research funded by an AHRC Collaborative Doctoral Award.

Luís Guilherme Resende de Assis is Associate Professor of Social Anthropology at the Interdisciplinary Center for the Humanities, Citizenship and the Environment, University of the Federal District, Brasília. He is also a federal expert on social anthropology at the National Expertise Center, Federal Prosecution Service of Brazil. He is a member of the Committee for Professional Anthropology, Brazilian Anthropological Association, and was a member of the Executive Committee of the Association of Polar Early Career Scientists. He has performed pioneering ethnographic fieldwork research in the Antarctic in 2010–11, together with archaeologists, oceanographers, glaciologists, biologists, and military and civil logistic staff.

Peder Roberts is Associate Professor of Modern History at the University of Stavanger, Norway. His main research interests are the history of the science and the politics of environmental management in the polar regions. In addition to writing *The European Antarctic: Science and Strategy in Scandinavia and the British Empire* (2011) he has coedited a number of volumes, including the *Handbook of the Politics of Antarctica* (2017) and *The Cambridge History of the Polar Regions* (2023).

Melisa A. Salerno is an archaeologist and researcher at the Multidisciplinary Institute of History and Human Sciences (National Scientific and Technical Research Council – IMHICIHU, CONICET, Argentina). Her research on the historical archaeology of the South Shetland Islands focuses on sealers' practices, identities, exploitation strategies and cultural construction of the landscape. She is the coauthor of *Archaeology in Antarctica* (2023). Her work has also been published in leading journals including *Polar Record, Historical Archaeology* and the *Journal of Contemporary Archaeology*, among others.

Katherine Mariko Sinclair is a PhD candidate at Rutgers University in New Brunswick, New Jersey. She specialises in environmental history and the history of science in the nineteenth- and twentieth-century French empire. She is currently completing a dissertation examining the changing dimensions of French sovereignty claims to the sub-Antarctic Kerguelen Islands.

Yelena Yermakova holds a PhD in philosophy and is a postdoctoral research associate at the Princeton Institute for International and Regional Studies. She works in political philosophy, with a special interest in global governance and institutional legitimacy. Her work on the polar regions has been published in *The Polar Journal* and *The Yearbook of Polar Law.*

Andrés Zarankin is an archaeologist and full professor at the Universidade Federal de Minas Gerais (Brazil). He is the director of the Laboratório de Estudos Antárticos em Ciências Humanas at the same University, and he leads the international project Landscapes in White, focusing on the incorporation of Antarctica into the modern world. His research interests include archaeological theory and the use of new technologies in the discipline. He is the main author of *Archaeology in Antarctica* (2023) and *Historias de un Pasado en Blanco: Arqueología Histórica Antártica* (2007). He has also published numerous articles in leading journals such as the *International Journal of Historical Archaeology* and the *Journal of Contemporary Archaeology*.

Introduction: What colonialism tells us about Antarctica, and what Antarctica tells us about colonialism

Alejandra Mancilla and Peder Roberts

As exceptional as Antarctica is when compared to the rest of the earth in terms of its physical geography, it is often regarded as even more exceptional for its political geography. The Antarctic Treaty and its associated instruments, often known collectively as the Antarctic Treaty System (ATS), have become emblematic of an innovative approach to governance.[1] In the standard telling, the International Geophysical Year (IGY) (1957–58) marked a decisive shift because its provision that scientific activities would not have consequences for sovereignty claims paved the way for the successful negotiation of the Antarctic Treaty in 1959, which entrenched the continent as a space for science and peace with sovereignty claims frozen (though definitely not extinguished).[2]

Today, such 'Antarctic exceptionalism' no longer stands up to scrutiny. Declaring that Antarctica is not and has never been isolated from the social, political and economic contests that shaped the rest of the world has fortunately become uncontroversial. James Cook's circumnavigation of the continent in the late eighteenth century took place in the context of British naval imperialism; the brutally effective harvesting of Antarctic fur seals at the start of the nineteenth century made sense only in the context of international capitalism; the Protocol on Environmental Protection at the end of the twentieth century responded to concerns over political, as well as environmental, injustice through the potential effects of mining; and the current failure to agree on the designation of new Marine Protected Areas in the Southern Ocean reflects wider geopolitical tensions, with Russia and China repeatedly blocking proposals.[3] Even the Treaty itself is now recognised as in many ways a product of its political circumstances rather than being wholly exceptional to them.[4] Setting aside a portion of the earth from militarisation dovetailed neatly with the overarching aims of the superpowers – to establish a space where prior claims to supremacy (sovereignty) would be negated, and the dominant currency of prestige would be science, which in turn was a function of financial resources and political will.

Klaus Dodds and Christy Collis have called for a development of 'critical Antarctic studies' that denies the Antarctic exceptionality thesis and examines Antarctica through the same analytical tools employed by the social sciences and humanities beyond Antarctica.[5] This call has resonated with a growing scholarly community that recognises Antarctica as a site of race, gender and class discrimination, as well as a site of capitalism, imperialism, nationalism and many of the other -isms that characterise the modern world.[6] No intellectual equivalent of biosecurity exists that strips humans of their political, social, economic and cultural commitments once they cross 60 degrees south. There is, however, one category whose application to the southern continent remains particularly controversial: when it comes to colonialism (as readers will see in the chapters that follow), there is disagreement as to whether it took place in Antarctica or not, what shape it took (if it did), and what analytic purpose is ultimately served by examining Antarctica through its lens.

Part of the reason for that controversy is that Antarctica lacks any people to be wronged. Violence in the Belgian Congo or the American West had no counterpart in Antarctica. But are there commonalities between conceptions of domination over Antarctica and those over inhabited spaces elsewhere? As legal scholar and historian Martti Koskenniemi has shown, the role of international law in legitimising colonialism during the era of the 'Scramble for Africa' and beyond reflected the politically negotiated norms of control over territory and resources that permeated European conceits of civilisation.[7] The paternalism embodied in the 'white man's burden' and the French 'civilizing mission' persisted as a positive concept well into the twentieth century.[8] Colonial powers from Denmark (in Greenland) to Australia (in the Pacific), Portugal (in Africa) and many more claimed to be acting in the spirit of longstanding principles rooted in benevolent tutelage, principles that many regarded as a convincing argument for administration of 'backward' peoples even as opposition grew during the early years of the twentieth century.[9] These attitudes are now generally regarded as wrong, an inescapable conclusion given the genocidal violence (cultural as well as physical) that often followed. We agree in centring the systemic violence against subjugated humans that today is regarded as the most defining feature of colonialism. Our contention is nevertheless that colonialism as an analytical category can help to illuminate Antarctica's place in the world – and the world's place in Antarctica.

While the Cold War was the dominant frame both then and now for understanding the origins of the ATS, we suggest that colonisation and decolonisation might also be foregrounded. The territorial claims of seven countries that were also founding members of the Antarctic Treaty were frozen, but not extinguished, by virtue of its Article IV. This has allowed them to retain their sovereignty claims while actively participating in the ATS. Decisions made about Antarctica are deeply influenced by domestic policies and aspirations, often grounded in a conviction that a particular nation has a privileged claim to Antarctica based on exploration and possession of territory, and maintaining permanent settlements. The co-existence of these claims with the functioning of the ATS is the strongest example of the 'constructive ambiguity' that defines the governing of Antarctica, an agreement to disagree to avoid disrupting the system as a whole.[10] But they are also a reminder that the structural features of political geographies past still linger in the present.

The aim of this introduction – and of this book, ultimately – is to argue that it makes sense to analyse Antarctica through a colonial lens because doing so illuminates our understanding of both colonialism and Antarctica. Colonialism pushes us to ask questions not only about the practices of humans in Antarctica and the power relations established between them, but also about the overarching logics and attitudes that have governed both specific human activities in Antarctica and larger human schemes to govern Antarctica. At the same time, Antarctica pushes us to ask where the limits of colonialism as an analytic category might lie, and how far the concept's utility extends for providing insight not available through other tools. What follows, then, is an exploration of what colonialism can do for Antarctica, and what Antarctica can do for colonialism.

The chapter begins by noting that, while imperialism has been a comparatively uncontroversial concept when describing Antarctica's history and politics, it is much more contentious whether colonialism took place in Antarctica and, if it did, in what form. We then examine different definitions of colonialism and different accounts of the specific moral wrong embedded within it, noting that a common feature in the definitions is the domination of one group of people by another. In the next section, we discuss what analytic use the term could then have in Antarctica, where there were no people to subjugate. The aim here is less to provide a narrowly defined tool with which Antarctica will be analysed, and more to demarcate the contours of the space which colonialism can usefully illuminate. We suggest that, while there was no subjugation of people in Antarctica, the colonial logics, attitudes and – to a certain extent – practices underlying it were present here as elsewhere. We suggest, moreover, that what happened and happens in Antarctica might entrench colonial structures still present at the international level. The chapter then considers decolonisation as a concept and how it may expand the scope of the analysis in Antarctica, particularly in considering the structural legacies of colonialism worldwide.

Imperialism, yes – but colonialism?

Imperialism, broadly understood, refers to a system of state expansion and domination 'through settlement, sovereignty or other indirect mechanisms of control'.[11] In the case of Antarctica, what was central was the acquisition of territory and the administration of power over it, reflected – among other things – in the production of instruments of authority such as cartography and scientific knowledge. Shirley Scott has suggested that there have been not one, but three distinct imperialist waves in Antarctica. The first was led by Spain in the fifteenth century when, by virtue of the Treaty of Tordesillas signed with Portugal, it considered itself entitled to claim lands yet to be discovered in the 'New World' all the way to the South Pole. The second was the European imperial wave that took place roughly from 1830 to 1914, when the last bits and pieces of what was considered global *terra nullius* (including Antarctica) were sought after and claimed. The third wave is still ongoing, according to Scott, led by the United States in the form of an informal empire ruled by science and multilateral negotiations.[12]

The basic thought here is that imperialism does not require a conquered population in a conquered territory. Antarctica would then constitute a 'pure' case study of imperialism, undistracted by the presence of people: the imperial state projected power over territory without any form of local resistance. On the contrary, a common reaction to the question of whether colonialism took place in Antarctica is to deny it, on the grounds that colonialism consists in the subjugation of one group of people over another, and that in Antarctica there were no people to subjugate. Colonialism is standardly theorised as a 'thick' concept, namely a concept that is evaluative but at the same time descriptive (like 'courage', 'injustice' and 'generosity').[13] In terms of description, most definitions of colonialism foreground the presence of people. In terms of evaluation, they refer to some problematic trait in the treatment of people. To give some examples from different disciplinary fields, anthropologist Ronald J. Horvath defines colonialism as 'the form of intergroup domination in which settlers in significant numbers migrate permanently to the colony from the colonising power'.[14] Political scientists Margaret Kohn and Kavita Reddy consider it 'a practice of domination, which involves the subjugation of one people to another ... the practice of colonialism usually involved the transfer of population to a new territory, where the arrivals lived as permanent settlers while maintaining political allegiance to their country of origin'.[15] Historian Dane Kennedy defines colonialism as 'the imposition by a foreign power of direct rule over another people', while historian Frederick Cooper stresses 'the institutionalisation of a set of practices that both defined and reproduced over time the distinctiveness and subordination of particular people in a differentiated space'.[16] Philosopher Daniel Butt proposes that three traits emerge when describing colonialism. First, there is domination of one group over another, where that domination implies denying the self-determination of the colonised and locating the rulers in a separate political jurisdiction. Second, there is cultural imposition, inspired by a belief that the customs of the colonisers are superior or that the colonising process is part of a religious mission, or simply because controlling the local culture serves to consolidate political control. Third, there is exploitation in diverse forms, paradigmatically through enslavement and through the misappropriation of cultural heritage and natural resources.[17] The creation of structural inequality between people could thus be regarded as a hallmark of colonialism, although there are different ways of rendering its distinctive wrong.

And indeed, the past generation (and more) has seen a flourishing of studies on colonialism, postcolonialism and decolonisation that stress colonialism's enduring structural presence in contemporary societies. Responding to this surge, as well as to the growing number of theories seeking to justify the territorial rights of nation-states from a moral standpoint, political theorists have in the last decade attempted to pin down the essential evil of colonialism. None of these theories, taken literally, seems to apply to the Antarctic case. Lea Ypi proposes that the wrong of colonialism lies in 'the embodiment of an objectionable form of political relation ... the establishment of a form of association that fails to offer equal and reciprocal terms of interaction to all its members'.[18] As such, colonialism belongs together with all other associations that deny equality and reciprocity to their members, but its specific procedural injustice is that it applies to territorially distinct political agents. Relatedly, Anna Stilz proposes that the specific wrong of colonialism lies in the fact that the colonised could not identify with the colonising practices and institutions imposed on them, therefore affecting their freedom as makers of their own rules.[19] Because there were no political agents living in Antarctica at the time when it was claimed, Ypi's and Stilz's definitions would have no bearing on Antarctic history.

Another candidate for the essential wrong of colonialism is violence as a means to the end of control. Rather than considering torture, murder, destruction of settlements, enslavement and all other evils associated with colonial practices as contingent, philosopher Vittorio Bufacchi singles out the systematic use of arbitrary violence aimed at domination.[20] Such violence, we suggest, might also take the form of the erasure of a culture, a practice that has increasingly been recognised as a form of genocide (notably with regard to Indigenous peoples in Canada).[21] Historian Ben Maddison seems to confirm this way of understanding colonialism when he claims that the explorers who first came to Antarctica 'found the prospect of a vast uninhabited landmass profoundly unsettling to their prevailing understandings and procedures of colonial possession'.[22] These prevailing understandings were inevitably associated with violent practices, to the point where their absence broke a mental mould. Here, instead, as the French Second Officer Dubouzet expressed in taking possession of Adélie Land, 'it was ... "a wholly pacific conquest" undertaken with none of the "abuse which has been born of such acts" in many places, because they "dispossessed none, and our titles were incontestable"'.[23] In a similar spirit, when New Zealand accepted Britain's request that it administer the Ross Sea Dependency in the early 1920s, reaction among public servants included laughter that it would be an easier task than administering a territory populated largely by indentured labourers.[24] There were of course animals present, and as Peder Roberts and Kati Lindström discuss in this volume, their treatment by human visitors to Antarctica might be regarded as echoing colonial practices. But the penguins were unlikely to resist.

Focusing on settler colonialism, philosopher Margaret Moore highlights that its characteristic wrong was the taking of land by a dominant group (the settlers), aimed at reproducing their own culture on the land.[25] That process for Moore necessarily involved the domination and erasure of pre-existing Indigenous cultures, robbed of the possibility of constructing their life as a self-determining collective in a space to which they had strong affective attachments and in which they constructed their life plans and projects. From this standpoint, again, it is hard to see how colonialism could be meaningfully applied to the Antarctic case. Exerting epistemic authority, the right to classify and to map – and even to erase – was central to the exercise of centralised power over distant spaces and peoples under European imperialism.[26] But, if there were no social relations to be recast, no converts to be won, no local labour to be exploited, no land from which Indigenous populations were displaced, then what function might colonialism serve as an analytical category when looking to Antarctica? Our answer is in part to return to Dubouzet's example and switch attention from actions to ambitions, and to ask whether a commonality of purpose and intent linked Antarctica with other sites of colonisation.

Colonial practices, logics and attitudes in Antarctica

The connotations of imperialism and colonialism are often regarded as similar to the point where some Antarctic actors and scholars have used them interchangeably. The United Kingdom initially used the language of 'dependencies' rather than 'colonies' to refer to the South Atlantic and Ross Sea areas, but when it changed the name of the Falkland Islands Dependencies to the 'British Antarctic Territory' in 1962, the new entity was described as a 'colony' in formal diplomatic correspondence.[27] (Chilean newspapers promptly protested that this new British 'colony' insulted Chile's own claim to that space.)[28] Scholars have often acted similarly. To give just one example, Scott moves between describing Antarctica as a site of imperialism and describing it as a site that 'has always been infused with artefacts of colonialism' (like the idea of establishing a trusteeship arrangement, echoing a concept from the League of Nations mandate system, and the application in Antarctica of the international law doctrine of territorial acquisition).[29]

One way of responding to these usages is to say that they are misplaced: the fact that the terms are used almost interchangeably does not mean that they should be. A more charitable response is to consider whether the use of the term 'colonialism' in Antarctica brings to light other features that its closest cognate, imperialism, does not, even if both are sufficiently close that they possess meaningful overlap.

If one revisits the characterisations of colonialism provided in the previous section, it is worth noting that they all refer to a practice or set of practices that were morally problematic because of some specific feature or features that had a direct impact on other humans: non-reciprocal treatment, domination through the imposition of rules, display of arbitrary violence and territorial displacement. We suggest there are three additional ways in which colonialism might be more directly useful to thinking about Antarctica. First, there may be problematic features in the practice of colonialism that do not refer directly to the treatment of people. Second, and relatedly, maybe the wrongs of colonialism are also connected to an underlying logic and attitude. And third, even if one denies that colonialism occurred in Antarctica, one could still accept that a class of people (i.e. those from 'non-Antarctic states') were entrenched in institutionalised positions of structural disadvantage and oppression because of decisions made around Antarctica.

Regarding the first point, historian Adrian Howkins refers to Antarctica as the site for an idealised form of settler colonialism, promising economic wealth without having to deal with any Indigenous populations.[30] The thought here is that what grounds the settler colonial project is the desire to accumulate space and resources: to take as much as possible at the expense of others – where the presence of Indigenous populations is considered a complication rather than an essential part of the enterprise. This position necessarily operates at the level of idealisation because it lacks the replacement and erasure that Moore, historian Lorenzo Veracini and others regard as central to settler colonialism.[31] In a similar vein, Elizabeth Leane and Hanne Nielsen explore the United States explorer Richard Byrd's practices and statements related to his 1933–35 expedition to West Antarctica. Leane and Nielsen pay particular attention to the three Guernsey cows that Byrd brought along, inscribing a particular form of American identity upon a continent that Byrd deemed ripe for colonisation – with himself as the heroic agent of that process.[32] But they qualify their argument by describing this as 'symbolic settler colonialism', and we agree that such a qualification is necessary, given that Byrd's work was of inscription rather than erasure and replacement. Even granting Stephen Pyne's claim that Byrd consciously regarded himself as inaugurating a more enduring form of presence than previous expeditions, with echoes of settlement, we agree with Leane and Nielsen that Byrd's actions were provocations to future settlement rather than acts of settlement in their own right.[33]

Byrd was not alone in wanting to recreate agricultural settlement on the continent, with its attendant connotations of permanence and improvement – hallmarks of earlier justifications of settler colonialism.[34] As Alejandra Mancilla's contribution to this volume notes, the Chilean military stationed at O'Higgins base in 1947 brought with them chickens, sheep and dogs. Decades later, both Chileans and Argentinians brought whole families to live, respectively, in Villa Las Estrellas and Base Esperanza, a vanguard of *colonos* who, in the same vein as those who had been sent to inhabit Patagonia before, would lay the ground for permanent settlement and occupation. These Latin American bases were depicted in their national media as organic extensions of the homeland, and those who lived there were considered to be fulfilling a patriotic role that those who remained on the mainland did not.[35]

One might ask why this should be characterised as 'colonialism' rather than 'imperialism' or the more morally neutral 'colonisation' (which might simply describe the practice of appropriating and occupying natural spaces, common both to humans and non-humans). While recognising that these categories lie along a spectrum, rather than pointing to qualitatively different phenomena, in line with our second point above we suggest that what these scholars are illuminating is an underlying logic and attitude of colonialism, laid bare in a place where there are no humans to dominate. What Howkins calls 'settler colonialism' can perhaps be redescribed as 'resource colonialism' or 'extractive colonialism', driven by the assumption that everything in the non-human natural world is a potential resource for humans to use, control and possess – and where the definition of 'human' is such that many fall out of it and end up being treated also as resources.[36] Scholars in postcolonial studies and ecocriticism have highlighted this dimension of colonialism, emphasising the continuum from the exploitation of nature to non-humans to 'other' humans. As postcolonial studies scholar Helen Tiffin puts it, 'human slavery and environmental damage are connected because human – and, more specifically, Western – exploitation of other peoples is inseparable from attitudes and practices in relation to *other species* and the extra-human environment generally'.[37] Connecting imperialism with colonialism as its armed force, historian Richard Grove made a similar point when he claimed that: 'In many ways the business of empire, for most of the colonised, had far more to do with the impact of different modes of colonial resource control and colonial environmental concepts, than it had to do with the direct impact of the military or political structures.'[38] To the question 'What is colonisation?' (which he took to be synonymous with colonialism), Martinican poet and politician Aimé Césaire also underlined the focus on resource extraction: 'the decisive actors here are the adventurer and the pirate, the wholesale grocer and the ship owner, the gold digger and the merchant, appetite and force'.[39] As much as Césaire was concerned with the brutalisation of the coloniser in the process of brutalising the colonised, he recognised this dimension of colonialism without people, for the sole purpose of accumulation and enrichment – which, as a communist, he connected to capitalism specifically.

Capitalism was indeed integral to European imperial expansion and the colonies created within that context. Lenin famously argued that acquisition of dominion over territory and peoples was a necessary consequence of the evolution of capitalism, and that the acquisition of territory rather than the achievement of national self-determination was the most important factor in the First World War. This view, formed against the backdrop of the Scramble for Africa and the second industrial revolution, established an enduring notion that colonialism and capitalism were linked in a way that is not just incidental, but necessary.[40]

While recognising the link between imperialism and capitalism, we reject the notion that capitalism is the sole root from which colonialism can grow. Although communist regimes provided vital material and ideological support for anti-colonial national liberation movements from South Africa to Vietnam during the Cold War, the USSR forcibly remade societies and economies in eastern Europe and elsewhere. Moreover, rapacious occupation and accumulation were as characteristic of Soviet whalers in Antarctic waters as of their western, capitalist competitors.[41] And the USSR and its satellites' eagerness to extract value from Antarctic krill or minerals (as Roman Khandozhko persuasively shows in his contribution to this volume) was also present as in any other western capitalist state at the time. It is this logic that turns everything in the non-human natural world into a mere resource that comes to the fore when looking at colonialism in Antarctica – and it is arguably also this attitude that justified the treatment of other humans as resources rather than as equals in the colonies elsewhere. Extractive conceptions of the world as a store of treasure to be found and conquered were equally present in capitalist and communist worldviews.[42]

For those who remain sceptical about the analytical utility of extending the definition of colonialism along the lines suggested above, one could still grant that colonial practices and attitudes were perpetuated and deep-ened *through* Antarctica, if not *in* Antarctica. A range of works identify colonialism as a crucial ingredient in ongoing injustice around the world, from pollution to asylum seekers to consumerism, all drawing important attention to how structural inequality derived from colonialism continues to facilitate inequality in the present.[43] Colonialism could thus be seen as a background against which to make sense of Antarctic history and politics. This is one way of interpreting Maddison's historical analysis of nineteenth-century Antarctic exploration, as an expression of the same (mainly British and French) impulse to colonial rule, dependent upon colonial infrastruc-ture and strengthening the power of colonial empires. Furthermore, giving a twist to Ypi's definition of colonialism as a practice of domination of one territorial group over another, one could also interpret the origin and main-tenance of the Antarctic Treaty as deepening the more general structures of domination entrenched by international law at the global level.[44] The con-nection between domination and colonialism is explored further in Yelena Yermakova's contribution to this volume.

If one accepts that colonialism is connected with Antarctica in any (or all) of these three ways, the next question is how decolonisation may function as a meaningful category of analysis in Antarctica. To this point we now turn.

Decolonisation in Antarctica and through Antarctica

The processes of rolling back the social, political and economic structural inequalities associated with colonialism are often given the blanket name of decolonisation. In the wave of changes that brought independence to states in Africa, Asia and the Caribbean during the 1960s, political decolo-nisation was equated with the acquisition of sovereignty, and equality was measured through participation in international forums such as the United Nations (UN). Persistent economic inequality, meanwhile, led to calls for structural reform through the New International Economic Order (NIEO), adopted by the UN in 1974.[45] Central to the NIEO was the argument that the newly independent states were voiceless during the earlier period when the economic structures governing the world were created and solidified. Decolonisation may thus have granted political sovereignty, but it had not erased the entrenched economic inequalities inherent in the global economy.

A serious objection to decolonisation as it would pertain to Antarctica derives from the work of Eve Tuck and K. Wayne Yang, who have criticised the blanket use of decolonisation as a term for addressing social justice and inequality.[46] In their view, such a broad usage decentres the defining wrong of colonialism – the theft of Indigenous lands and the erasure of Indigenous cultures and lives. Their analysis is focused on settler colonialism, which in their view (correctly, we think) represents the most urgent theatre for the work of decolonisation. The external colonialism that Tuck and Yang note as part of the wider architecture of colonialism includes the appropriation of Indigenous flora, fauna and space in addition to human lives. Can that process of appropriation still be regarded as colonial if the objects of appropriation are not initially possessed by another culture but the appropriation serves to perpetuate injustice linked to colonialism? We argue that this may be possible. If one goes back to the analysis of how colonialism is manifested in or through Antarctica, we suggest that there are – analogously – at least three ways in which decolonisation can have conceptual relevance for thinking about the continent's history and politics and, through it, about decolonisation processes happening beyond it.

If one considers Antarctica as a clear-cut case of resource colonialism and as a site where the logics and attitudes underlying it acquired full expression, then an obvious way to decolonise the continent would be to recognise the colonial origin of the territorial claims and give them up.[47] This could be regarded as decolonisation in that it relinquishes the authority of a select group of states whose privilege derived from acts of discovery and occupation, and thus removes a structural advantage over states excluded from such acts. It may be objected that the unjust authority rests not with the claimant states but with the ATS consultative parties as a whole, the group of states that hold decision-making power within the ATS by virtue of their scientific activity and/or their pre-1959 engagement with Antarctica. Relinquishing claims would not therefore solve the problem, given that consultative party status is not predicated upon claimant status. This is true, but the persistence of territorial claims means that those states believe they are in continued possession of a trump card that grants rights to object to decisions over the territory in question. The response that such claims are not in themselves colonial – a position articulated by a number of scholars, including Ignacio Cardone in this volume – is however worth exploring in further detail.

Furthermore, the wider definition of decolonisation as a set of practices aimed at reversing the broader legacies of colonialism seems appropriate in the case of Antarctica, especially if one looks at international law itself as being shaped by colonial logics and attitudes.[48] For states such as Malaysia, the club-like nature of the ATS (which was in the midst of an opaque process of negotiating an agreement on minerals exploitation in the 1980s) reflected the colonial power structures of the past.[49] In a well-known speech to the United Nations General Assembly, Malaysian Prime Minister Mahathir Mohamad acknowledged that 'those countries [the members of the ATS at the time] are not depriving any natives of their lands, and they are therefore not required to decolonise [Antarctica]'.[50] Instead, what required changing for Mahathir was the very mindset that allowed the colonisers to appropriate uninhabited lands for themselves, just as they had appropriated populated territories before, with the aim of enhancing their own wealth and power. Against the view that effective prior occupation granted privileged rights in Antarctica, Mahathir suggested that 'like the seas and the seabed, those uninhabited lands belong to the international community'.[51] Ensuring that all the world's states had a say in the governance of Antarctica's mineral resources was thus part of the larger project of decolonising international power structures. In short, decolonisation was not to happen *in* Antarctica, but *through* Antarctica.

It is important to stress the context within which Mahathir spoke. By the 1980s the structural economic advantages of coloniser over colonised were widely acknowledged, and their redress was sought through the NIEO, adopted at the behest of the Group of 77, a coalition of 'developing' states at the United Nations. The heart of the NIEO was recognition that political sovereignty did not produce economic equality: colonialism had locked in economic dependency on the former colonial periphery.[52] When the United Nations Convention on the Law of the Sea (UNCLOS) concluded negotiations in 1982, an additional concept emerged: that of 'common heritage of mankind' over areas of the earth not subject to the sovereignty of states (in this case, the seabed of the deep oceans).[53] When negotiations began in the early 1980s on a regime for administering minerals exploitation in Antarctica, initially as a closed process conducted by the ATS consultative parties, states such as Malaysia immediately linked it to a wider process of entrenching unequal access to resources – for which an alternative model now existed, a designation of common heritage of mankind under the United Nations. It might of course be noted that common heritage itself presupposes the same logic of appropriation of the non-human natural world that, as argued above, is a problematic feature of colonialism. As the term makes clear, its intent was not to move the non-human world out of the category of potentially exploitable resources, but more to ensure that all humans were entitled to do the exploiting.

The ATS states rejected any attempt to undermine their privileged status. Richard Woolcott, Australian ambassador to the UN and leader of the ATS opposition to the Malaysian initiative, argued that 'emotional rhetoric about the New International Economic Order and residual colonialism in the debate on Antarctica' would be unlikely to attract support from 'moderate countries', implying that drawing those broader connections was an extreme position.[54] Woolcott's position comes across at best as patronising. Emotionality was contrasted to rationality, echoing the logic through which colonising powers justified their authority over colonised peoples and lands, their superior capacity to govern (and to know what was best) legitimising their power. But the global process of decolonisation, to which the NIEO was central, had to include Antarctica because the persistence of a structure that excluded most of the world's poorest countries from decision-making over one of the world's last potential major stores of natural resources was unjust.

Among the advocates of the opposing view – that the privileged status of the ATS consultative parties was just and appropriate – was the historian Stephen Pyne. Writing in 1986, he characterised their privileged position as a legitimate consequence of 'national heritages of which they are properly proud'. To question that status was to bring 'to Antarctic discussions an anticolonial rhetoric as inappropriate as the colonial cant that was applied to Africa a century earlier'.[55] The real wrong would come from states that hitherto had not been engaged with the continent's being granted authority at the expense of those currently in charge. States that had earned their place through the worthy sacrifice of exploration and science, and who had since administered the continent in a responsible manner (as even Malaysia acknowledged), ought not to be pushed aside by states whose interest in Antarctica had been non-existent until mineral exploration became an issue.

Pyne's category of 'national heritages' evoked a blank field upon which noteworthy acts had been inscribed without their overriding previous ownership – there were no Indigenous peoples whose presence could be erased. The wrong of erasure would be committed by denying those legacies and instead imposing a common heritage of mankind on the continent. Yet legacies of national achievement through science and exploration have been intertwined with colonialism elsewhere in the world. The distinction here rested partly on the absence of people, but also – in our view – on the result, that national actions led to an international treaty and not to a mutually recognised parcelling out of sovereign territory. This fails to address a more fundamental issue: namely that regardless of how well they have ruled Antarctica, the fundamental assumption that a certain group of states ought to hold that power remains debatable, independent of the specific actions they discharge as self-appointed trustees.

The question of science

The Antarctic Treaty is often cited as an open instrument that may be ratified by any state, which may then rise to the status of a consultative party. But in practical terms the costs of earning that status make it impossible (or at least very difficult) for many of the world's states.[56] And the reason for that economic disadvantage, in the great majority of cases, may be linked to the systematic structural inequalities of colonialism. One way to respond is to suggest that specific reforms should be made to the system. Dropping the requirement to perform 'substantial research activity' as a prerequisite for consultative party status could remove a structural barrier to full participation in Antarctic decision-making, for instance.[57]

Another is to say that science in Antarctica should itself be decolonised, by defining research with value within the ATS as including alternative knowledge systems, thereby ending the hegemony of western science (on this point, see Germana Nicklin's chapter in this volume). The projects of 'decolonising methodology' and 'decolonising science' have particular importance in spaces where the hegemony of European knowledge systems over pre-existing systems of Indigenous knowledge has been a central component of enforcing state power.[58] Analogously, insofar as Antarctic science served to legitimise and strengthen the authority of colonial power structures more generally, a more inclusive approach to knowledge-making in Antarctica that reflects voices structurally silenced by colonialism may also serve to further the decolonisation of the states that make that knowledge. Along these lines, Priscilla Wehi and her collaborators have called for *matauranga Māori* (Māori traditional knowledge) to be incorporated into Antarctic research.[59] Much of the attention of their article focused on the group's findings regarding Māori knowledge of Antarctica preceding European contact. But the more ambitious claim is that, as part of the work of decolonising Aotearoa/New Zealand, the hegemony of colonial-era intellectual structures in Antarctic research should itself be challenged. This could mean including Māori cosmologies that posit human–non-human relationships in terms of kinship rather than dominion, and emphasise reciprocity and responsibility, thus reshaping the practices of the national Antarctic programme itself.[60]

It could be objected that there are legitimate practical reasons to privilege certain knowledge-making practices over others, even if they are the fruit of colonialist trees. The IGY embodied an assumption of universality with its network of World Data Centres in which information collected by different national expeditions could be made accessible by all scientists – which in turn presumed commensurability.[61] This was by and large successful, even if the IGY itself (and indeed science under the ATS regime more generally) reflected international co-ordination more than collaboration. Nor is there dispute that scientific research, from the breeding cycle of penguins to the history of Antarctic climate as measured through ice cores, may be considered valuable for humanity at large. What is at stake in decolonising science is not the fate of such research, but rather the acknowledgement that research conducted from other perspectives and traditions may also be accorded the status of legitimate knowledge. Researchers in the natural sciences already collaborate with researchers in the social sciences and humanities in Antarctica.[62] We suspect that the issue is less the difference of the backgrounds and more the willingness (and ability) of the researchers to work collaboratively with mutual respect for the different traditions from which they come.[63]

Might the point be extended not just to Indigenous knowledge systems that exist within the borders of many consultative parties, but to those that lack the Māori claim to Antarctic relevance, and whose knowledge keepers reside in states unconnected to the ATS? Just as including Māori knowledge systems in Antarctic research would help to reconfigure the relations between scientists and their objects of study, considering other perspectives would be valuable too. After all, the very rationale of excluding from political decision-making those who do not have the means to conduct traditional science in Antarctica is what a decolonising process should target.

The stake of Indigenous communities in Antarctica may be regarded as real from another perspective. The term 'green colonialism' is increasingly used to describe how transitions toward a lower-carbon global economy shift environmental, economic and health-related burdens to the peoples already structurally disadvantaged through colonialism.[64] Indigenous homelands from Sápmi in northern Fennoscandia to northern Nevada are redesignated as spaces where extractive industry supporting green transitions is justified, even needed, to support continued high-energy lifestyles among the rich. A ban on mining in Antarctica is thoroughly justified both on environmental grounds (the scale of damage that could result, and the cost and difficulty of remediation) and on what might be termed security grounds, as it removes a potential source of conflict. But could mining in Antarctica be regarded as preferable to mining elsewhere on the grounds that it might spare the lands of Indigenous and formerly colonised peoples elsewhere in the world? While the question is complex, it points to an important issue: restricting the authority to take decisions over Antarctica to a group of states who claim to act on the continent's behalf is no guarantee that such actions will be in the best interests of humanity. Sacrificing Indigenous homelands on the altar of the green transition while preserving Antarctica as a space free of mining is, to say the least, a situation that invites reflection on the structural power dynamics involved. As long as Indigenous peoples remain structurally discriminated against within global political and economic systems – legacies of colonialism – decisions on the future of Antarctica will continue to sideline their interests.

Conclusion

Analysing Antarctica through a colonial lens helps to connect the continent with world history and politics. It shows that, despite its remoteness and lack of human inhabitants, Antarctica remains part and parcel of global social, economic and political processes in the last two centuries, especially – but not exclusively – connected to the western world. More interestingly, we think, analysing colonialism through an Antarctic lens helps to bring out certain problematic features that tend to be clouded when the focus is put on the wrongs directly done to colonised peoples. The accumulation of space and resources with the purpose of eventual exploitation – what we have called 'resource colonialism' – is at the heart of the Antarctic enterprise, attended by a logic and attitude where the non-human natural world is placed at humanity's disposal (and where sometimes even particular humans are labelled as belonging in that category, thus allowing for their exploitation). Furthermore, the way in which decisions have been made and are still made around Antarctica – through the Antarctic Treaty – might reinforce structural inequalities at the global level that were rooted in colonialism. Malaysia's complaint in the 1980s brought this to the fore, but the Protocol on Environmental Protection and other legal instruments geared to the protection of the Antarctic environment could also be questioned along these lines.

What is at stake is not the content of these arrangements, which may be laudable, but the procedure through which they were established: excluding from the negotiating table three-quarters of the world's states (and, within them, the vast majority of Europe's former African, Asian and Caribbean colonies). This distinction between content and the procedure might be more relevant today than at any point in the history of the Antarctic Treaty. In a context where one of the Treaty members has invaded another, and where flexing muscles in Antarctica has become a way to mark increased presence on the global political stage more generally, the need for the ATS to be accepted as just and legitimate is greater than ever.

We have chosen to err on the side of being provocative in this volume. The contributors come from a range of disciplinary backgrounds, and their interests – while including Antarctica – range geographically from western Europe to Latin America, Oceania to the USSR. Collectively we hope that the result is a stimulating cacophony rather than a reassuring harmony. Our overarching question (why think about colonialism in connection with Antarctica?) does not have an obvious or easy answer, but we trust that readers will follow our contention that the process of answering it will provide illumination to compensate for the lack of neatly packaged conclusions.

Structure of the book

This volume is divided into two parts. In the first, we collect a series of chapters that deal with the question of Antarctic colonialism from the perspective of specific countries, especially claimants and potential claimants. Whether Argentina, Chile, France, Poland, China and the Soviet Union enacted or enact colonial practices, and to what extent their actions were or are infused by the attitudes and logic of colonialism elsewhere, are the central questions around which their arguments revolve.

Against standard accounts, historian Roman Khandozhko suggests that Soviet Antarctic politics may be interpreted as colonial if one grants that an important dimension of colonialism is resource extraction. Despite its official anti-imperialist and anti-colonialist rhetoric, the Soviet Union engaged in a process of expansion where Antarctica appeared as a promised land of valuable mineral resources and even as a potential site for future settlers. 'Extractive socialism', Khandozhko claims, thus followed the same underlying logic of 'extractive capitalism', no matter how much the Soviet authorities tried to distance themselves from it. 'Rational' or not, it nonetheless concerned the conquest and exploitation of nature.

Katherine Sinclair compares three French colonial sites that, despite their differing geographies and histories, all served one common purpose: the furthering of French power and prestige in the second half of the twentieth century against the backdrop of decolonisation. Algeria, French Guiana, Terre Adélie and the Kerguelen Islands were all sites for the development of the French sounding rocket programme, and also became part of a network of satellite tracking stations, through which France aimed to become a space power at a time when its terrestrial power was in decline.

Katarzyna Jarosz looks at the institution of Historic Sites and Monuments within the ATS and asks to what extent these help to foster and maintain colonial narratives in the continent. Provocatively, Jarosz suggests that Poland, China and the Soviet Union can be interpreted as engaging in colonial practices not qualitatively different from those of the original claimants, based on their attempts to show priority and superiority over others, and therefore a sense of entitlement to territory.

Ignacio Cardone defends Argentina and Chile against the charge that they engaged in colonial and/or imperial practices in Antarctica, and suggests instead that their actions must be understood in the context of their being young nations in the process of consolidating their sovereign territories against foreign powers. The way in which these two countries perform science in Antarctica is, for Cardone, indicative of their distinct approach to the continent as a permanent national commitment, as well as their understanding of their Antarctic territories as continuous and integral components of state territories (rather than separate units).

Alejandra Mancilla, on the contrary, argues that the position of the South American claimants in Antarctica was based on colonial assumptions that were not questioned, but embraced. Their claims should thus be seen as following a similar logic to the claims of the others, including the United Kingdom – even if this logic was rarely made explicit. This would be a step forward in the recognition that these countries behaved in a colonial and imperial manner as they expanded to the south, and would help to see the history of their Antarctic territories in continuity with what happened in their southern continental territories.

The second half of the book takes a more thematic view, focusing upon concepts or practices that cut across national boundaries. Adrian Howkins considers the role of religion in Antarctica as an expression of values linked to colonialism: a firm Christian faith that linked missionaries in the Scramble for Africa to the first heroic explorers of the Antarctic continent, and later became institutionalised through chaplaincies associated with national programmes. Official expressions of faith have also strengthened Latin American and more recently Bulgarian presence in Antarctica, further inscribing national values upon Antarctic spaces.

Germana Nicklin focuses on border-making as a means to mediate human conceptualisations of Antarctic space. For Nicklin, the demarcation of an 'inside' and an 'outside' through the ATS cuts across the relationships that claimant states continue to maintain with settlements and stations upon their slices of Antarctica. Her characterisation of this as a fluid form of 'extra-colonialism' invites reflection upon how borders serve to create as well as reflect political and social imaginaries.

María Jimena Cruz, Melisa A. Salerno and Andrés Zarankin look at the Antarctic sealing era to discuss the connections between capitalism and colonialism during the early history of Antarctica. While the capitalist aspects of the Antarctic sealing industry have been widely acknowledged, the colonial aspects of the activity have been downplayed. Resorting to historical and archaeological evidence, the authors shed light on the potential colonial dynamics behind sealers' interests, their ways of establishing presence and their power relationships.

Peder Roberts and Kati Lindström explore how a focus on colonialism may help illuminate human–animal relationships in Antarctica. While cautious about equating Antarctic animals to human victims of colonialism elsewhere in the world, they ask whether colonial mindsets encouraged a view of animals as ersatz subjects, and whether the actions of Greenpeace in mobilising penguins within its campaigns to protect the Antarctic environment itself bore echoes of colonialism.

Alice Oates focuses on the British Halley VI station as a site of ongoing British colonial engagement with Antarctica. In particular, Oates argues that the mindset of settler colonialism has contributed to a distinctive local identity rooted in collective experience of a place. Her thought-provoking intervention pushes the concept of settler colonialism beyond its traditional bounds, stressing the domination of space as the first step toward the creation of a settler identity.

Yelena Yermakova points to the problem of domination in the Antarctic Treaty, manifested in a two-tiered system where consultative parties who perform 'substantial science' have decision-making power, while non-consultative parties may observe and speak, but not partake in the actual decision-making process. Yermakova suggests that this hierarchical system is a result of the colonial genesis of the Treaty, and that it reflects the colonial structures present at the time of its signature. The Treaty may thus be decolonised by moving toward a more equitable arrangement, where all parties have the same influencing power.

Luís Guilherme Resende de Assis concludes the section with a reorientation of colonialism itself, contrasting the metropolitan colonialism of European empires with the 'autochthonous colonisation' through which humans know and change the spaces they inhabit – including Antarctica. De Assis thus shifts from lines on a map drawn by politicians to acts in the field performed by scientists – practices whereby human presence becomes materialised through everything from instruments to organic waste. Antarctica has been colonised not by the words of states, but through the concrete culture of polar research.

The volume concludes with an afterword from Rebecca Herman that circles back to the main themes of the chapters. Words matter. Can colonialism without direct subjugation best be described with other terminology? Can states such as Argentina and Chile that emerged from European empires, and which were active in pushing the NIEO, still be placed on one side of a ledger at least partially defined by colonialism? These are questions that are easier to pose than to answer – but as Herman notes, the possibility of arguing in different ways is perhaps evidence of their importance.

Acknowledgements

For their thoughtful feedback on earlier versions of this text, we would like to thank Patrik Baard, Ben Etherington, Andrea Foss, Zsofia Korosy, Anna Wienhues, the participants at the 2022 workshop of the Norwegian Network of Practical Philosophy, participants at seminars held at the University of New South Wales and Western Sydney University, and the participants at the workshop 'Rights of Nature and Antarctica: Historical, Legal and Philosophical Perspectives', Lysebu, Oslo. We would also like to thank Fabian Stenhaug for his excellent research assistance.

This chapter received funding from the European Research Council (ERC) under the European Union's Horizon 2020 research and innovation programme (grant agreement nos 948964 and 716211) and the Research Council of Norway (grant agreement no. 267692).

Notes

1 See amongst many others Paul Berkman, Michael A. Lang, David W. H. Walton and Oran Young (eds), *Science Diplomacy: Science, Antarctica, and the Governance of International Spaces* (Washington, DC: Smithsonian, 2011); Christopher C. Joyner, *Governing the Frozen Commons: The Antarctic Regime and Environmental Protection* (Columbia: University of South Carolina Press, 1998).

2 For an overview of this historiographic position and the surrounding debates, see Klaus J. Dodds, 'The International Geophysical Year and the Antarctic Treaty', in Adrian Howkins and Peder Roberts (eds), *The Cambridge History of the Polar Regions* (Cambridge: Cambridge University Press, 2023), pp. 536–62. The International Geophysical Year (inspired by the earlier International Polar Years) was an international scientific initiative where 67 countries collaborated between July 1957 and December 1958, in which Antarctica was one of the key research sites.

3 Ben Maddison, *Class and Colonialism in Antarctic Exploration, 1750–1920* (London: Pickering & Chatto, 2014); Andrés Zarankin and Melisa Salerno, 'So Far, So Close: Approaching Experience in the Study of the Encounter between Sealers and the South Shetland Islands (Antarctica, Nineteenth Century)', in Peder Roberts, Lize-Marié van der Watt and Adrian Howkins (eds), *Antarctica and the Humanities* (New York: Palgrave Macmillan, 2016), pp. 79–104; Robert J. Headland and Bryan J. Lintott, *Historical Antarctic Sealing Industry: Proceedings of an International Conference in Cambridge 16–21 September 2016* (Cambridge: Scott Polar Research Institute, 2018); Andrew Jackson, *Who Saved Antarctica? The Heroic Age of Antarctic Diplomacy* (Basingstoke: Palgrave Macmillan, 2021); Cassandra M. Brooks, 'Geopolitical Complexity at the Bottom of the World: CCAMLR's Ongoing Challenge of Adopting Marine Protected Areas', in Nengye Liu, Cassandra M. Brooks and Tianbao Qin (eds), *Governing Marine Living Resources in the Polar Regions* (Cheltenham: Edward Elgar Publishing, 2019), pp. 43–65.

4 Dodds, 'The International Geophysical Year'; Adrian Howkins, *Frozen Empires: An Environmental History of the Antarctic Peninsula* (Oxford: Oxford University Press, 2016); Peder Roberts, *The European Antarctic: Science and Strategy in Scandinavia and the British Empire* (New York: Palgrave Macmillan, 2011), Chapter 7.

5 Klaus J. Dodds and Christy Collis, 'Post-Colonial Antarctica', in Klaus J. Dodds, Alan D. Hemmings and Peder Roberts (eds), *Handbook on the Politics of Antarctica* (New York: Edward Elgar Publishing, 2017), pp. 50–68 (p. 53).

6 On racism, see Lize-Marié van der Watt and Sandra Swart, 'The Whiteness of Antarctica: Race and South Africa's Antarctic History', in Peder Roberts, Lize-Marié van der Watt and Adrian Howkins (eds), *Antarctica and the Humanities* (London: Palgrave Macmillan, 2016), pp. 126–50. On gender discrimination, see Lisa Bloom, *Gender on Ice: American Ideologies of Polar Expeditions*, Vol. X (Minneapolis: University of Minnesota Press, 1993).

On class, see Maddison, *Class and Colonialism*. On capitalism, see Andrés Zarankin and María Ximena Senatore, 'Archaeology in Antarctica: Nineteenth-Century Capitalism Expansion Strategies', *International Journal of Historical Archaeology* 9:1 (2005), 43–56. On imperialism, see Adrian Howkins, 'Appropriating Space: Antarctic Imperialism and the Mentality of Settler Colonialism', in Tracey Banivanua Mar and Penelope Edmonds (eds), *Making Settler Colonial Space* (London: Palgrave Macmillan, 2010), pp. 29–52; Shirley V. Scott, 'Ingenious and Innocuous? Article IV of the Antarctic Treaty as Imperialism', *The Polar Journal*, 1:1 (2011), 51–62 (p. 55); Shirley V. Scott, 'Three Waves of Antarctic Imperialism', in Klaus J. Dodds, Alan D. Hemmings and Peder Roberts (eds), *Handbook on the Politics of Antarctica* (Cheltenham: Edward Elgar Publishing, 2017), pp. 37–49. On nationalism, see Alan Hemmings, Sanjay Chaturvedi, Elizabeth Leane, Daniela Liggett and Juan Francisco Salazar, 'Nationalism in Today's Antarctic', *The Yearbook of Polar Law* 7 (2015), 531–55.

7 Martti Koskenniemi, *The Gentle Civilizer of Nations: The Rise and Fall of International Law 1870–1960* (Cambridge: Cambridge University Press, 2001).

8 See, amongst many others, Miguel B. Jerónimo, *The 'Civilizing Mission' of Portuguese Colonialism* (New York: Palgrave Macmillan, 2015); Michael Adas, *Dominance by Design: Technological Imperatives and America's Civilizing Mission* (Cambridge, MA: Harvard University Press, 2006); Alice L. Conklin, *A Mission to Civilize: The Republican Idea of Empire in France and West Africa, 1895–1930* (Stanford, CA: Stanford University Press, 1997).

9 Susan Pedersen, *The Guardians: The League of Nations and the Crisis of Empire* (Oxford: Oxford University Press, 2015).

10 For a thorough discussion of constructive ambiguity and the ATS, see James Roberts, 'Flexibility, Ambiguity and the Construction of the Antarctic Treaty System' (Postgraduate Certificate in Antarctic Studies thesis, University of Canterbury, 2011).

11 Margaret Kohn and Kavita Reddy, 'Colonialism', in Edward N. Zalta (ed.), *Stanford Encyclopedia of Philosophy*, fall 2017 edn, https://plato.stanford.edu/archives/fall2017/entries/colonialism/ (accessed 14 February 2022).

12 Scott, 'Three Waves'.

13 Debbie Roberts, 'Thick Concepts', *Philosophy Compass* 8:8 (2013), 677–88.

14 Ronald J. Horvath, 'A Definition of Colonialism', *Current Anthropology* 13:1 (1972), 45–57.

15 Kohn and Reddy, 'Colonialism'.

16 Dane K. Kennedy, *Decolonization: A Very Short Introduction* (Oxford: Oxford University Press, 2016), p. 1; Frederick Cooper, *Colonialism in Question: Theory, Knowledge, History* (Berkeley: University of California Press, 2005), p. 26.

17 Daniel Butt, 'Colonialism and Postcolonialism', in Hugh LaFollette (ed.), *The International Encyclopedia of Ethics* (Malden, MA: Blackwell, 2013), pp. 892–8 (p. 893).

18 Lea Ypi, 'What's Wrong with Colonialism', *Philosophy & Public Affairs* 41:2 (2013), 158–91 (pp. 162, 178).

19 Anna Stilz, 'Decolonization and Self-Determination', *Social Philosophy and Policy* 32:1 (2015), 1–24, DOI: 10.1017/S0265052515000059.

20 Vittorio Bufacchi, 'Colonialism, Injustice, and Arbitrariness', *Journal of Social Philosophy*, 48:2 (2017), 197–211 (p. 201).

21 We stress that the term 'genocide' has also been regarded as appropriate because cultural erasure caused the deaths of Indigenous individuals, from residential schools to the murders of Indigenous women and girls. For a thorough analysis see National Inquiry into Missing and Murdered Indigenous Women and Girls, 'A Legal Analysis of Genocide: Supplementary Report of the National Inquiry into Missing and Murdered Indigenous Women and Girls' (2019), www.mmiwg-ffada.ca/wp-content/uploads/2019/06/Supplementary-Report_Genocide.pdf (accessed 21 February 2024).

22 Maddison, *Class and Colonialism*, p. 52.

23 Quoted in Maddison, *Class and Colonialism*, p. 52.

24 Malcolm Templeton, *A Wise Adventure: New Zealand and Antarctica 1920–1960* (Wellington: Victoria University Press, 2000), p. 24.

25 Margaret Moore, 'Justice and Colonialism', *Philosophy Compass* 11:8 (2016), 447–61 (p. 455), DOI: 10.1111/phc3.12337.

26 On erasure, see Londa Schiebinger, *Plants and Empire: Bioprospecting in the Atlantic World* (Cambridge, MA: Harvard University Press, 2004).

27 Oslo, Riksarkivet, RA/S-6794/D/Da/Dab/L1739:0003, folder Britiske interesser i Antarktis bind III, 'British Embassy in Oslo to Foreign Ministry of Norway', 17 March 1962.

28 *Guardian*, 'New Colony "Insults" Chile', *Guardian* (5 March 1962).

29 Scott, 'Three Waves', p. 37.

30 Howkins, 'Appropriating Space', p. 31.

31 Lorenzo Veracini, *Settler Colonialism: A Theoretical Overview* (New York: Palgrave Macmillan, 2010); Moore, 'Justice and Colonialism'.

32 Elizabeth Leane and Hanne E. F. Nielsen, 'American Cows in Antarctica: Richard Byrd's Dairy as Symbolic Settler Colonialism', *Journal of Colonialism and Colonial History* 18:2 (2017), 1–13.

33 Leane and Nielsen, 'American Cows in Antarctica', pp. 4–5. See also Stephen J. Pyne, *The Ice: A Journey to Antarctica* (Iowa City: University of Iowa Press, 1986), pp. 101–2.

34 See, amongst many others, Jonathan Hart, *Empires and Colonies* (Cambridge: Polity, 2008); Gershon Shafir, 'Settler Citizenship in the Jewish Colonization of Palestine', in Caroline Elkins and Susan Pedersen (eds), *Settler Colonialism in the Twentieth Century* (London: Routledge, 2005), pp. 41–58.

35 See also Pablo Fontana, *La pugna Antártica: El conflicto por el sexto continente 1939–1959* (Buenos Aires: Guazuvirá, 2018); Nelson Llanos, 'Populating Antarctica: Chilean Families in the Frozen Continent', in Elizabeth Leane and Jeffrey McGee (eds), *Anthropocene Antarctica: Perspectives from the Humanities, Law and Social Sciences* (Abingdon: Routledge, 2019), pp. 156–71.

36 While we have drawn inspiration from the work of Per Högselius, Hanna Vikström, Dag Avango and David Nilsson's conceptualisation of resource

colonialism, theirs differs in stressing the participation of states and actors that do not exercise political control over the space in which the resources are found – such as Swedes in Turkey and the Caucasus. See for instance Hanna Vikström, Per Högselius and Dag Avango, 'Swedish Steel and Global Resource Colonialism: Sandviken's Quest for Turkish Chromium, 1925–1950', *Scandinavian Economic History Review* 65:3 (2017), 307–25.

37 Helen Tiffin, *Five Emus to the King of Siam: Environment and Empire* (Leiden: Brill, 2007), pp. xii, emphasis in the original.

38 Richard H. Grove, *Ecology, Climate and Empire: Colonialism and Global Environmental History, 1400–1940* (Cambridge: White Horse Press, 1997), p. 3.

39 Aimé Césaire, *Discourse on Colonialism*, trans. Joan Pinkham (New York: New York University Press, 2000 [1955]), p. 33.

40 Vladimir I. Lenin, *Imperialism: The Highest Stage of Capitalism* (London: Penguin, 2010 [1917]).

41 Ryan T. Jones, *Red Leviathan: The Secret History of Soviet Whaling* (Chicago: University of Chicago Press, 2022).

42 See also Bathsheba Demuth, *Floating Coast: An Environmental History of the Bering Strait* (New York: W. W. Norton, 2019). It is perhaps worth remembering that the United States under Woodrow Wilson and later Franklin Delano Roosevelt irritated the European imperial powers with its opposition to colonialism, even against a backdrop of US colonial rule in the Philippines. See for instance William R. Louis, 'American Anti-Colonialism and the Dissolution of the British Empire', *International Affairs* 61:3 (1985), 395–420; Caroline Elkins, *Legacy of Violence: A History of the British Empire* (New York: Knopf, 2022); Julian Go and Anne L. Foster (eds), *The American Colonial State in the Philippines: Global Perspectives* (Durham, NC: Duke University Press, 2003).

43 See for instance Max Liboiron, *Pollution Is Colonialism* (Durham, NC: Duke University Press, 2021); Lucy Mayblin, *Asylum after Empire: Colonial Legacies in the Politics of Asylum Seeking* (London: Rowman and Littlefield, 2017); Aja Barber, *Consumed: The Need for Collective Change: Colonialism, Climate Change, and Consumerism* (London: Brazen, 2021).

44 Alejandra Mancilla, 'Decolonising Antarctica', in Alan D. Hemmings and Dawid Bunikowski (eds), *Philosophies of Polar Law* (Abingdon: Routledge, 2020), pp. 49–61.

45 On the NIEO, see for instance Craig Murphy, *The Emergence of the New International Economic Order* (Boulder, CO: Westview, 1984).

46 Eve Tuck and K. Wayne Yang, 'Decolonization Is Not a Metaphor', *Decolonization, Indigeneity, Education & Society* 1:1 (2012), 1–40.

47 Mancilla, 'Decolonising Antarctica'.

48 See, amongst others, Antony Anghie, 'Finding the Peripheries: Sovereignty and Colonialism in Nineteenth-Century International Law', *Harvard International Law Journal* 40:1 (1999), 1–80; Koskenniemi, *The Gentle Civilizer of Nations*.

49 This was CRAMRA, the Convention on the Regulation of Antarctic Mineral Resource Activities, negotiated during the 1980s and ditched at the last minute, to be replaced by the Protocol on Environmental Protection.

50 United Nations General Assembly, 37th Session, 10th Plenary Meeting, 1982, UN Doc A/37/Pv.10, pp. 129–55 (p. 132), https://documents.un.org/doc/undoc/gen/nl8/603/49/pdf/nl860349.pdf?token=Y25U33si0wiSdv39rp&fe=true (accessed 20 March 2024).

51 United Nations General Assembly, UN Doc A/37/Pv.10, p. 132.

52 On dependency theory, see notably Andre Gunder Frank, *Dependent Accumulation and Unequal Development* (New York: New York University Press, 1979).

53 For a thorough discussion of the common heritage of mankind and its application in Antarctica, see for instance Giovannina Sutherland Condorelli and Gisselle Gajardo Flores, 'Antártica y el patrimonio común de la humanidad: Inviabilidad jurídica y desafíos geopolíticos' (BA thesis, University of Chile, 2019).

54 Richard Woolcott in Rüdiger Wolfrum and E. A. Michos-Ederer (eds), *Antarctic Challenge III: Conflicting Interests, Cooperation, Environmental Protection, Economic Development. Proceedings of an Interdisciplinary Symposium July 7th–12th, 1987* (Berlin: Duncker & Humblot, 1988), p. 239. See also Richard W. Woolcott, *The Hot Seat: Reflections on Diplomacy from Stalin's Death to the Bali Bombings* (Sydney: HarperCollins, 2003), especially pp. 209–18.

55 Pyne, *The Ice*, p. 372.

56 See for instance Aant Elzinga, 'Antarctica: The Construction of a Continent by and for Science', in Elisabeth Crawford, Terry Shinn and Sverker Sörlin (eds), *Denationalizing Science: The Contexts of International Scientific Practice* (Dordrecht: Klüwer, 1993), pp. 73–96.

57 See for example Mancilla, 'Decolonising Antarctica'; Yelena Yermakova, 'Governing Antarctica: Assessing the Legitimacy and Justice of the Antarctic Treaty System' (PhD dissertation, University of Oslo, 2021).

58 See notably Linda Tuiwhai Smith, *Decolonizing Methodologies: Research and Indigenous Peoples* (London: Zed Books, 1999).

59 Priscilla M. Wehi, Vincent van Uitregt, Nigel J. Scott *et al.*, 'Transforming Antarctic Management and Policy with an Indigenous Māori Lens', *Nature Ecology & Evolution*, 5 (2021), 1055–9.

60 Relational cosmologies of this kind are central features of many Indigenous cultures. See, amongst many others, Rachel A. Qitsuarlik, 'Innumarik: Self-Sovereignty in Classic Inuit Thought', in Scot Nickels, Kren Kelly, Carrie Grable, Martin Lougheed and James Kuptana (eds), *Nilliajuit: Inuit Perspectives on Security, Patriotism and Sovereignty* (Ottawa: Inuit Quajisarvingat, 2013); Enrique Salmón, 'Kincentric Ecology: Indigenous Perceptions of the Human–Nature Relationship', *Ecological Applications* 10:5 (2000), 1327–32; Paul Nadasdy, 'The Gift in the Animal: The Ontology of Hunting and Human–Animal Sociality', *American Ethnologist* 34:1 (2007), 25–43.

61 On the centres, see Elena Aronova, 'Geophysical Datascapes of the Cold War: Politics and Practices of the World Data Centers in the 1950s and 1960s', *Osiris* 32:1 (2017), 307–27.

62 For a good example, see the McMurdo Dry Valleys Long Term Ecological Project (https://mcm.lternet.edu (accessed 23 February 2024), which in recent years has included historian Adrian Howkins as a principal investigator.

63 For an example of this going wrong in practice, see Paul Nadasdy, *Hunters and Bureaucrats: Power, Knowledge, and Aboriginal–State Relations in the Southwest Yukon* (Vancouver, University of British Columbia Press, 2003).

64 For an overview of how the concept has been mobilised in contemporary political actions around the world, see Earth.org, 'Explainer: What Is Green Colonialism?' (25 May 2021), https://earth.org/green-colonialism/ (accessed 21 February 2024).

Bibliography

Adas, Michael. *Dominance by Design: Technological Imperatives and America's Civilizing Mission*. Cambridge, MA: Harvard University Press, 2006.

Anghie, Antony. 'Finding the Peripheries: Sovereignty and Colonialism in Nineteenth-Century International Law'. *Harvard Inernational Law Journal* 40, no. 1 (1999): 1–80.

Aronova, Elena. 'Geophysical Datascapes of the Cold War: Politics and Practices of the World Data Centers in the 1950s and 1960s'. *Osiris* 32, no. 1 (2017): 307–27.

Barber, Aja. *Consumed: The Need for Collective Change. Colonialism, Climate Change, and Consumerism*. London: Brazen, 2021.

Berkman, Paul A., Michael A. Lang, David W. H. Walton and Oran Young (eds). *Science Diplomacy: Science, Antarctica, and the Governance of International Spaces*. Washington, DC: Smithsonian, 2011.

Bridge, Gavin. 'Material Worlds: Natural Resources, Resource Geography, and the Material Economy'. *Geography Compass* 3, no. 3 (2009): 1217–44.

Bufacchi, Vittorio. 'Colonialism, Injustice, and Arbitrariness'. *Journal of Social Philosophy* 48, no. 2 (2017): 197–211.

Bloom, Lisa. *Gender on Ice: American Ideologies of Polar Expeditions*. Vol. X. Minneapolis: University of Minnesota Press, 1993.

Brooks, Cassandra M. 'Geopolitical Complexity at the Bottom of the World: CCAMLR's Ongoing Challenge of Adopting Marine Protected Areas'. In *Governing Marine Living Resources in the Polar Regions*, ed. Nengye Liu, Cassandra M. Brooks and Tianbao Qin, pp. 43–65. Cheltenham: Edward Elgar Publishing, 2019.

Butt, Daniel. 'Colonialism and Postcolonialism'. In *The International Encyclopedia of Ethics*, ed. Hugh LaFollette, pp. 892–8. Malden, MA: Blackwell, 2013.

Césaire, Aimé. *Discourse on Colonialism*, trans. Joan Pinkham. New York: New York University Press, 2000 [1955].

Conklin, Alice L. *A Mission to Civilize: The Republican Idea of Empire in France and West Africa, 1895–1930*. Stanford, CA: Stanford University Press, 1997.

Cooper, Frederick. *Colonialism in Question: Theory, Knowledge, History*. Berkeley: University of California Press, 2005.

Demuth, Bathsheba. *Floating Coast: An Environmental History of the Bering Strait*. New York: W. W. Norton, 2019.

Dodds, Klaus J. 'The International Geophysical Year and the Antarctic Treaty'. In *The Cambridge History of the Polar Regions*, ed. Adrian Howkins and Peder Roberts, pp. 536–62. Cambridge: Cambridge University Press, 2023.

Dodds, Klaus J. and Christy Collis. 'Post-Colonial Antarctica'. In *Handbook on the Politics of Antarctica*, ed. Klaus J. Dodds, Alan D. Hemmings and Peder Roberts, pp. 50–68. New York: Edward Elgar Publishing, 2017.

Earth.org. 'Explainer: What Is Green Colonialism?', 25 May 2021. https://earth.org/green-colonialism/. Accessed 21 February 2024.

Elkins, Caroline. *Legacy of Violence: A History of the British Empire*. New York: Knopf, 2022.

Elzinga, Aant. 'Antarctica: The Construction of a Continent by and for Science'. In *Denationalizing Science: The Contexts of International Scientific Practice*, ed. Elisabeth Crawford, Terry Shinn and Sverker Sörlin, pp. 73–96. Dordrecht: Klüwer, 1993.

Fontana, Pablo. *La pugna Antártica: El conflicto por el sexto continente 1939–1959*. Buenos Aires: Guazuvirá, 2018.

Frank, Andre Gunder *Dependent Accumulation and Unequal Development*. New York: New York University Press, 1979.

Go, Julian and Anne L. Foster (eds). *The American Colonial State in the Philippines: Global Perspectives*. Durham, NC: Duke University Press, 2003.

Grove, Richard H. *Ecology, Climate and Empire: Colonialism and Global Environmental History, 1400–1940*. Cambridge: White Horse Press, 1997.

Guardian. 'New Colony "Insults" Chile'. *Guardian*, 5 March 1962.

Hart, Jonathan. *Empires and Colonies*. Cambridge: Polity, 2008.

Headland, Robert J. and Bryan Lintott. *Historical Antarctic Sealing Industry: Proceedings of an International Conference in Cambridge 16–21 September 2016*. Cambridge: Scott Polar Research Institute, 2018.

Hemmings, Alan, Sanjay Chaturvedi, Elizabeth Leane, Daniela Liggett and Juan Francisco Salazar. 'Nationalism in Today's Antarctic'. *The Yearbook of Polar Law* 7 (2015): 531–55.

Howkins, Adrian. 'Appropriating Space: Antarctic Imperialism and the Mentality of Settler Colonialism'. In *Making Settler Colonial Space*, ed. Tracey Banivanua Mar and Penelope Edmonds, pp. 29–52. London: Palgrave Macmillan, 2010.

Howkins, Adrian. *Frozen Empires: An Environmental History of the Antarctic Peninsula*. Oxford: Oxford University Press, 2016.

Horvath, Ronald J. 'A Definition of Colonialism'. *Current Anthropology* 13, no. 1 (1972): 45–57.

Jackson, Andrew. *Who Saved Antarctica? The Heroic Age of Antarctic Diplomacy*. Basingstoke: Palgrave Macmillan, 2021.

Jerónimo, Miguel B. *The 'Civilizing Mission' of Portuguese Colonialism*. New York: Palgrave Macmillan, 2015.

Jones, Ryan T. *Red Leviathan: The Secret History of Soviet Whaling*. Chicago: University of Chicago Press, 2022.

Joyner, Christopher C. *Governing the Frozen Commons: The Antarctic Regime and Environmental Protection*. Columbia: University of South Carolina Press, 1998.

Kennedy, Dane K. *Decolonization: A Very Short Introduction*. Oxford: Oxford University Press, 2016.

Kohn, Margaret and Kavita Reddy. 'Colonialism'. In *Stanford Encyclopedia of Philosophy*. Fall 2017 edn, ed. Edward N. Zalta. https://plato.stanford.edu/archives/fall2017/entries/colonialism/. Accessed 14 February 2022.

Koskenniemi, Martti. *The Gentle Civilizer of Nations: The Rise and Fall of International Law 1870–1960*. Cambridge: Cambridge University Press, 2001.

Leane, Elizabeth and Hanne E. F. Nielsen. 'American Cows in Antarctica: Richard Byrd's Dairy as Symbolic Settler Colonialism'. *Journal of Colonialism and Colonial History* 18, no. 2 (2017): 1–13.

Lenin, Vladimir I. *Imperialism: The Highest Stage of Capitalism*. London: Penguin, 2010 [1917].

Liboiron, Max. *Pollution Is Colonialism*. Durham, NC: Duke University Press, 2021.

Llanos, Nelson. 'Populating Antarctica: Chilean Families in the Frozen Continent'. In *Anthropocene Antarctica: Perspectives from the Humanities, Law and Social Sciences*, ed. Elizabeth Leane and Jeffrey McGee, pp. 156–71. Abingdon: Routledge, 2019.

Louis, William R. 'American Anti-Colonialism and the Dissolution of the British Empire'. *International Affairs* 61, no. 3 (1985): 395–420.

Maddison, Ben. *Class and Colonialism in Antarctic Exploration, 1750–1920*. London: Pickering & Chatto, 2014.

Mancilla, Alejandra. 'Decolonising Antarctica'. In *Philosophies of Polar Law*, ed. Alan D. Hemmings and Dawid Bunikowski, pp. 49–61. Abingdon: Routledge, 2020.

Mayblin, Lucy. *Asylum after Empire: Colonial Legacies in the Politics of Asylum Seeking*. London: Rowman and Littlefield, 2017.

Moore, Margaret. 'Is Canada Entitled to the Arctic?' *Canadian Journal of Philosophy* 50, no. 1 (2020): 98–113. DOI: 10.1017/can.2019.8.

Moore, Margaret. 'Justice and Colonialism'. *Philosophy Compass* 11, no. 8 (2016): 447–61. DOI: 10.1111/phc3.12337.

Murphy, Craig. *The Emergence of the New International Economic Order*. Boulder, CO: Westview, 1984.

Nadasdy, Paul. 'The Gift in the Animal: The Ontology of Hunting and Human–Animal Sociality'. *American Ethnologist* 34, no. 1 (2007): 25–43.

Nadasdy, Paul. *Hunters and Bureaucrats: Power, Knowledge, and Aboriginal–State Relations in the Southwest Yukon*. Vancouver: University of British Columbia Press, 2003.

National Inquiry into Missing and Murdered Indigenous Women and Girls. 'A Legal Analysis of Genocide: Supplementary Report of the National Inquiry into Missing and Murdered Indigenous Women and Girls', 2019. www.mmiwg-ffada.ca/wp-content/uploads/2019/06/Supplementary-Report_Genocide.pdf. Accessed 21 February 2024.

Pedersen, Susan. *The Guardians: The League of Nations and the Crisis of Empire*. Oxford: Oxford University Press, 2015.

Pyne, Stephen J. *The Ice: A Journey to Antarctica*. Iowa City: University of Iowa Press, 1986.

Qitsualik, Rachel A. 'Innumarik: Self-Sovereignty in Classic Inuit Thought'. In *Nilliajuit: Inuit Perspectives on Security, Patriotism and Sovereignty*, ed. Scot Nickels, Kren Kelly, Carrie Grable, Martin Lougheed and James Kuptana, pp. 23–34. Ottawa: Inuit Quajisarvingat, 2013.

Roberts, Debbie. 'Thick Concepts'. *Philosophy Compass* 8, no. 8 (2013): 677–88.

Roberts, James. 'Flexibility, Ambiguity and the Construction of the Antarctic Treaty System'. Postgraduate Certificate in Antarctic Studies thesis. University of Canterbury, 2011.

Roberts, Peder. *The European Antarctic: Science and Strategy in Scandinavia and the British Empire*. New York: Palgrave Macmillan, 2011.

Salmón, Enrique. 'Kincentric Ecology: Indigenous Perceptions of the Human–Nature Relationship'. *Ecological Applications* 10, no. 5 (2000): 1327–32.

Schiebinger, Londa. *Plants and Empire: Bioprospecting in the Atlantic World*. Cambridge, MA: Harvard University Press, 2004.

Scott, Shirley V. 'Ingenious and Innocuous? Article IV of the Antarctic Treaty as Imperialism'. *The Polar Journal* 1, no. 1 (2011): 51–62.

Scott, Shirley V. 'Three Waves of Antarctic Imperialism'. In *Handbook on the Politics of Antarctica*, ed. Klaus J. Dodds, Alan D. Hemmings and Peder Roberts, pp. 37–49. Cheltenham: Edward Elgar Publishing, 2017.

Shafir, Gershon. 'Settler Citizenship in the Jewish Colonization of Palestine'. In *Settler Colonialism in the Twentieth Century*, ed. Caroline Elkins and Susan Pedersen, pp. 41–58. London: Routledge, 2005.

Stilz, Anna. 'Decolonization and Self-Determination'. *Social Philosophy and Policy* 32, no. 1 (2015): 1–24. DOI: 10.1017/S0265052515000059.

Sutherland Condorelli, Giovannina and Gisselle Gajardo Flores. 'Antártica y el patrimonio común de la humanidad: Inviabilidad jurídica y desafíos geopolíticos'. BA thesis. University of Chile, 2019.

Templeton, Malcolm. *A Wise Adventure: New Zealand and Antarctica 1920–1960*. Wellington: Victoria University Press, 2000.

Tiffin, Helen. *Five Emus to the King of Siam: Environment and Empire*. Leiden: Brill, 2007.

Tuck, Eve and K. Wayne Yang. 'Decolonization Is Not a Metaphor'. *Decolonization, Indigeneity, Education & Society* 1, no. 1 (2012): 1–40.

Tuiwhai Smith, Linda. *Decolonizing Methodologies: Research and Indigenous Peoples*. London: Zed Books, 1999.

United Nations General Assembly. 37th Session, 10th Plenary Meeting, 1982. UN Doc A/37/Pv.10, pp. 129–55. https://documents.un.org/doc/undoc/gen/nl8/603/49/pdf/nl860349.pdf?token=Y25U33si0wiSdv39rp&fe=true. Accessed 20 March 2024.

Van der Watt, Lize-Marié and Sandra Swart. 'The Whiteness of Antarctica: Race and South Africa's Antarctic History'. In *Antarctica and the Humanities*, ed. Peder Roberts, Lize-Marié van der Watt and Adrian Howkins, pp. 126–50. London: Palgrave Macmillan, 2016.

Veracini, Lorenzo. *Settler Colonialism: A Theoretical Overview*. New York: Palgrave Macmillan, 2010.

Vikström, Hanna, Per Högselius and Dag Avango. 'Swedish Steel and Global Resource Colonialism: Sandviken's Quest for Turkish Chromium, 1925–1950'. *Scandinavian Economic History Review* 65, no. 3 (2017): 307–25.

Wehi, Priscilla M., Vincent van Uitregt, Nigel J. Scott *et al.* 'Transforming Antarctic Management and Policy with an Indigenous Māori Lens'. *Nature Ecology & Evolution* 5 (2021): 1055–9.

Wolfrum, Rüdiger and E. A. Michos-Ederer (eds). *Antarctic Challenge III: Conflicting Interests, Cooperation, Environmental Protection, Economic Development. Proceedings of an Interdisciplinary Symposium July 7th–12th, 1987*. Berlin: Duncker & Humblot.

Woolcott, Richard W. *The Hot Seat: Reflections on Diplomacy from Stalin's Death to the Bali Bombings*. Sydney: HarperCollins, 2003.

Yermakova, Yelena. 'Governing Antarctica: Assessing the Legitimacy and Justice of the Antarctic Treaty System'. PhD thesis. University of Oslo, 2021.

Ypi, Lea. 'What's Wrong with Colonialism'. *Philosophy & Public Affairs* 41, no 2 (2013): 158–91.

Zarankin, Andrés and Melisa Salerno. 'So Far, So Close: Approaching Experience in the Study of the Encounter between Sealers and the South Shetland Islands (Antarctica, Nineteenth Century)'. In *Antarctica and the Humanities*, ed. Peder Roberts, Lize-Marié van der Watt and Adrian Howkins, pp. 79–104. London: Palgrave Macmillan, 2016.

Zarankin, Andrés and María Ximena Senatore. 'Archaeology in Antarctica: Nineteenth-Century Capitalism Expansion Strategies'. *International Journal of Historical Archaeology* 9, no. 1 (2005): 43–56.

1

Antarctic minerals for the Soviet Bloc? Imagining the South Pole frontier of extractive socialism

Roman Khandozhko

Soviet Antarctic politics is rarely interpreted in terms of colonialism, for several reasons. Colonial and postcolonial framing in general has found rather limited application in the historical studies of Antarctica, given the lack of both an Indigenous population and a stable population of colonists.[1] At the same time, territorial claims, creation of long-term infrastructures of Antarctic stations and allocation of various kinds of special zones can be considered quasi-colonial practices. No less important, the suppressed colonialist imaginaries of the engaged countries latently influenced their Antarctic politics even at times of an avowed consensus on the need for 'extra-colonial' governance. Amongst other Antarctic nations, this certainly applies to the Soviet Union and Russia. Soviet Russia itself largely fell beyond the view of postcolonial criticism, both because of its 'left' genesis during the Cold War, and because of the specifics of Russian terrestrial colonialism, which differed from the overseas models typical of the West. Russia lacked experience in governing overseas colonial possessions, focusing on its 'internal colonisation' and peripheral expansion – and this makes it even more astonishing that in the twentieth century it became so eagerly involved in exploring and exploiting the continent on the opposite side of the globe.[2]

The USSR is often seen as a 'postcolonial and avowedly non-imperial empire', despite its continuous territorial expansion through invasion or subversion.[3] Thinking about Soviet Russia in colonial terms gets even more complicated because anti-colonial and postcolonial criticism had been heavily employed in ideological discourses on both sides of the Iron Curtain, at least from the mid-1950s.[4] The Soviet Union supported anti-colonial movements in cases where it led to the weakening of capitalist countries, and Soviet Marxists' anti-imperialist rhetoric facilitated the emergence of the 'communist third world'. At the same time, from the eve of the Second World War onwards, the Soviet Union itself experienced a lot of colonialist momentum that manifested itself in the expansion of its borders to the west and the east (Karelia, Baltics, Sakhalin, Kuril islands) and in various forms of indirect domination (for instance, in the Arctic). This discrepancy between expansionist activity and anti-imperialist discourse also profoundly affected Soviet Antarctic endeavour.

Official Soviet discourse celebrated the emancipation of people, yet colonisation (or conquest) of nature was an integral part of state ideology.[5] In parallel with western 'extractive capitalism', one can talk of Soviet 'extractive socialism', where withdrawal of natural resources from the imperial outskirts in favour of the centre has become the cornerstone of the state's existence.[6] Neurotic greed for more and more resources that could be extracted to serve the metropolis had been the driving force behind Russian colonial expansion in Eurasia across the centuries and constituted the core of her colonial mindset. In the twentieth century, minerals and fossil fuels took centre stage in this resource obsession, proving to be one of the driving forces behind Antarctic exploration.

In this chapter, I will show how the giant machine of extractive socialism proved itself in the special conditions of Antarctica, and how its activity was infused by Soviet/Russian colonialist thinking. Following the idea of *neuere Kolonialgeschichte* – namely, that 'colonialist thinking is deeply embedded in the mindset of colonising nations' – and Adrian Howkins's insight that Antarctic imperialism represented 'an idealised version of the colonial mentality' and 'the "highest stage" of settler colonialism', I will focus on the appropriation of nature and space in the Soviet Antarctic programme, showing how Antarctica, together with its resources, was symbolically framed, discussed and fantasised about in the post-Second World War Soviet Union, and what role minerals played in this vision.[7]

The Cold War and the race for Antarctic minerals

The unique international legal position of Antarctica – its status as a 'continent of science' – against the background of increasing interest in resource frontiers in the second half of the twentieth century, made Antarctic geology a complex intertwining of science and politics, where fundamental knowledge about the structure of the earth's crust turned out to be directly related to the realm of international relations. During the first three decades of research and negotiations within the framework of the Antarctic Treaty System (ATS), the minerals and hydrocarbons of Antarctica had not been extracted or even properly prospected, yet they were actively co-produced in the sense proposed by critical resource studies.[8] In the Antarctic environment, geologists had to rely mainly on indirect methods of discovering

deposits, which left considerable room for speculation and political manipu-
lation. In a way, during the Cold War Antarctic minerals played a much
more significant role not in their natural occurrence, but as a construct of the
collective imagination, co-created at the intersection of various technoscien-
tific goals, personal ambitions, institutional lobbies, public discourses and
diplomatic games. Practices of 'resource-making' were distributed across
multiple actors, which determined directions for reconnaissance geological
surveys, organised fieldwork and cameral data processing; produced scientific articles and official memos; decided on sharing information on minerals activity; and speculated about exploitation potentials.[9] Although these
practices had been implemented in the unique environment of Antarctic
collective governance, their colonial origin profoundly impacted the way
Antarctica was studied and imagined in the twentieth century.

Geological research conducted by various Antarctic explorers from the
late nineteenth century fuelled a belief that the icy continent and its shelf
might contain economically valuable mineral resources. The first Antarctic
boom of the interwar period had been mainly driven by whaling, but as
the scramble for the South Pole escalated in the late 1940s, an obsession
with minerals began to affect all the key Antarctic players. Scientific exploration of Antarctic terrain was boosted by the International Geophysical
Year (IGY) of 1957–58 – a crucial event both for the internationalisation of
environmental science and for the establishment of science diplomacy as a
side-track for releasing Cold War tensions.[10] When the Antarctic Treaty was
signed in 1959, the minerals issue was not incorporated, let alone formally
discussed, but all the engaged countries started *de facto* to develop their
own geological research programmes in Antarctica.[11] These programmes
had a dual purpose: to obtain scientific knowledge about the structure
of the earth's crust and to identify the presence and location of valuable
mineral deposits.

The mining issue was first raised in 1970 by the UK and New Zealand,
whose governments had been approached by mining companies interested
in exploration in the Southern Ocean.[12] A possible legal framework for
Antarctic minerals exploitation became a focal point of heated international
debates that also touched on the technical and economic feasibility and environmental impact of future mining.[13] The Antarctic Treaty countries had
been working for more than 10 years to set a legal framework in advance
of any future mining, but the resulting Convention on the Regulation of
the Antarctic Mineral Resource Activity (CRAMRA) never came into force.

Up to the mid-1950s, Soviet presence in Antarctica was limited to the
Slava whaling flotilla, which began operating in Antarctic waters in January
1947.[14] After the USA had initiated negotiations toward the establishment
of an international condominium over the continent in 1950, the Soviet

Union joined the battle for Antarctica on a diplomatic front, issuing a memorandum stating that 'any decision on the Antarctic regime taken without its participation' would be illegitimate.[15] Thus, Antarctica was recognised by the Soviets as a potential battlefield of the incipient Cold War. At this time, the Soviet leadership was mostly concerned with the military-strategic importance of the continent and its possible employment in the USA's preparations for a new world war.

Soviet propagandistic narratives at the beginning of the Cold War represented Antarctica as the last piece of no man's land that could soon become the target of an imperialist invasion. This vision was reproduced, for instance, by experts of the Initiative group for organisation of Antarctic research under the auspices of the USSR Academy of Sciences, which lobbied for more active involvement of the USSR in Antarctic affairs in the early 1950s. In their notes prepared for the Soviet leadership, experts from the Initiative group blamed the imperialist nature of western involvement in Antarctica and warned that the USA was preparing to join the ranks of the states that had already claimed Antarctic sectors. Since US territorial intentions in the Antarctic had not yet been publicly clarified, Soviet observers carefully monitored media signals in this regard. Thus, the initiative of the American senators Thor Tollefson and Francis Case to invest $200,000 in an Antarctic expedition in 1954 attracted close attention. Experts from the Initiative group highlighted this expedition's intentions to validate the territorial claims of the United States and to explore the mineral resources of Antarctica, noting suspiciously that the Americans denied their plans deliberately in order to search for uranium and other fissionable elements.[16] In her 'Historical reference' on Antarctica, L. M. Nikolaeva of the Institute of Geography summed up this 'anti-imperialist' Antarctic rhetoric using a quote from Lenin's *Imperialism: The Highest Stage of Capitalism*:

> finance capital in general strives to seize the largest possible amount of land of all kinds in all places, and by every means, taking into account potential sources of raw materials and fearing to be left behind in the fierce struggle for the last remnants of independent territory, or for the repartition of those territories that have been already divided. [17]

In 1956, the first Complex Antarctic Expedition of the USSR landed in Antarctica in order to begin preparations for Soviet participation in the IGY programme. It included two geologists. Starting from this point, the Soviet Union had been developing 'one of the largest and most obviously resource-oriented geological research programmes in Antarctica', being spurred by constant fears of lagging behind and being outperformed by the Americans and other western countries.[18] In parallel to geological research, minerals occupied an important place in the Soviet Antarctic discourse, thus connecting a new icy frontier to a broader realm of the Soviet extractivist imagination.

In terms of raw materials, the Soviet Union was one of the richest countries in the world. The discovery of large oil and gas fields in Siberia and the far north between the 1950s and the 1970s, as well as diamonds, phosphates and strategic metals, became a determining factor in the development of the Soviet and Russian economies for many decades. At the same time, it is not quite accurate to say that the USSR enjoyed total raw materials self-sufficiency.[19] In the postwar period it began to explore and exploit minerals in foreign territories – not least because of real demand for strategic minerals, which was not possible (or not easy) to meet using only domestic reserves. Thus, experiencing a shortage of its own uranium reserves for the nuclear race, the USSR actively exploited the uranium deposits of Czechoslovakia and the German Democratic Republic (GDR) in the 1940s and 1950s, and Mongolia in the 1980s.[20] Control over resources was also an important motive for Soviet expansion into the Third World, using diplomatic and military manoeuvres.[21] In 1964, a special research institute, Zarubezhgeologiya, was created to prospect for mineral wealth outside the USSR. Besides that, in the 1970s and 1980s, the USSR developed costly programmes to search for minerals on the deep seabed and offshore territories (for example, in the Caribbean and Svalbard). This expanding resource activity, which did not promise short-term economic rewards, was part of the Soviet project's deep obsession with 'securing the future' and long-term planning. A number of scholars speak of a specific rationality behind the Soviet state's global resource ambitions, driven by the cult of self-sufficiency and longstanding fears of shortage. An anonymous commentator from Moscow's Institute of United States Studies put it this way: 'The Soviet government behaves like an ordinary Soviet consumer. He grabs anything which happens to be on the counter, even if he doesn't need it, knowing that tomorrow it may no longer be available.'[22] The resource-oriented Antarctic geological programme of the USSR can certainly be considered one concrete outcome of this logic.

In its propaganda narratives, the Soviet Union distinguished between a 'good' socialist way of 'rational utilisation of resources' and 'bad' capitalist exploitation. Throughout its Antarctic epic, despite close scientific ties with the West and common interests within the framework of the ATS, the USSR exploited anti-imperialist rhetoric to strengthen its position of moral authority on the global stage. As the parting words to the participants of the second Soviet Antarctic expedition said: 'Striving for expansion is alien to the Soviet people. Our scientists landed on the coast of Antarctica not with the aim of seizing new territories, but solely for reasons of the development of science for peaceful purposes.'[23] One of the components of this discourse was to accuse the West of resource-centrism, and to attempt to depict the Soviet Union as a leader in fundamental science, the main defender of the environment and a guardian of peace on earth. Even in professional books, such as *Geology and Mineral Resources of Antarctica*, published in 1990, authors routinely condemned the 'resource ideology' that caused the 'spirit of unhealthy competition' in geological research in the 1970s and 1980s.[24]

The level of interest of the Soviet government in Antarctic minerals fluctuated along with the dynamics of the Cold War. For the first time it peaked on the eve, and immediately after the end, of the IGY, when the future outlines of Antarctic governance were still to be decided upon and the Soviet Union was preparing for a possible territorial division of the continent. In the first half of the 1960s, the USSR lowered the priority of its Antarctic programme in general, and its geological part in particular. At that time, however, geologists even more actively promoted the importance of their field to the party leadership, using a Cold War discourse of rivalry between the two systems to justify their claims for more funding. One of the main arguments in favour of increasing investment in polar geology was the growing lag behind the United States, New Zealand and Australia.[25] Cold War ideology was instrumentalised in the same way in many other fields of cutting-edge science on both sides of the Iron Curtain – for instance, in high-energy physics and space science.[26] In the case of Antarctic geology, however, in addition to the common rhetoric of scientific prestige and national priority, there was an idea of direct competition with the West for valuable resources that could be exploited in the future.

In the 1970s, when the minerals issue was raised within the ATS, the Soviet Union again increased investment in geological studies of Antarctica. A preoccupation with resources became the *Zeitgeist* of the epoch: a resource scarcity narrative was spreading around the globe and fossil fuel prices were peaking. The Club of Rome report *Limits to Growth* (1972) triggered a discussion about limits for the exploitation of the global environment, and the Soviet authors supported something of a 'pro-grow' position in these debates, arguing for 'rational utilisation of resources' as a main remedy for upcoming resource scarcity. Soviet authors such as Evgenii K. Fedorov (head of the state hydrometeorological service between 1962 and 1974) campaigned for exploration of hard-to-reach resource frontiers, including the ocean floor and nearby planets.[27] This atmosphere favoured the field of Antarctic geological research, which flourished during the 1970s and 1980s, in terms of funding, geographic coverage and scientific complexity. At the same time, because of the raised sensitivity of the minerals issue within the ATS, most of the geological explorations of the time were officially framed as pursuing purely scientific, but not economic, goals.

While, in the 1960s, Soviet geologists were mainly engaged in reconnaissance work in close proximity to the active Antarctic stations, in the 1970s the Soviet Union switched to large projects that covered significant areas. Thus, as a result of 'Operation Amery' in 1971–74, mapping of an area of about 500,000 km², mostly covered by glacier, was carried out using various geophysical methods on the MacRobertson, Princess Elizabeth and Wilhelm II lands.[28] Among the important achievements of the Soviet Antarctic programme was the discovery of iron deposits in the Prince Charles Mountains and coal deposits in East Antarctica. At the same time, in the early 1970s the USSR was noticeably lagging behind in research on the Antarctic shelf and in the search for hydrocarbons. In contrast to mainland deposits, which during this period were considered unexploitable for economic reasons, off-shore oil and gas were perceived as the main prize in the race for Antarctic minerals amid the oil crisis of the 1970s. Against the backdrop of scientific détente and the Agreement on Joint Activities in the Study of the World Ocean with the United States, the Soviet Union joined some international Antarctic shelf research projects in the 1970s. One of the most important was the expedition of the research vessel *Glomar Challenger*, which discovered traces of natural gas in the Ross Sea as a result of offshore drilling in 1973.[29] On the other hand, the USSR launched its own project to undertake a geological and geophysical study of the Weddell Sea, which lasted from the mid-1970s to the late 1980s, establishing a series of seasonal stations on the ice shelf for this purpose. The peak of activity by Soviet geologists in Antarctica occurred in the mid-1980s, after the release of the Decree of the Council of Ministers of the USSR '[o]n a sharp expansion of geological and geophysical research in the Antarctic and strengthening the material and technical base of the work'. At that time the geological and geophysical activity of the Soviet Antarctic expeditions covered to a greater or lesser degree all regions of the continent and its shelf.[30]

The race for imaginary Antarctic minerals unfolded at this time not only on the scientific but also on the diplomatic front. From the mid-1970s, the Soviet Union was actively involved in debates on the elaboration of a regime for the exploitation of Antarctic mineral resources. In 1975, the USSR helped instigate an initiative for a moratorium on mining in the Antarctic, fearing that the United States and other countries would benefit from their advantages in offshore mining technologies.[31] According to reports from western diplomats, once the negotiation process for the mineral convention began, the USSR dragged its feet in the negotiations and insisted upon the adoption of strict environmental restrictions on mineral extraction.[32] This position changed in 1982, when the question of Antarctica began to be actively discussed at the United Nations, and the exclusive right of members of the ATS to decide the fate of Antarctic resources was questioned by the non-aligned countries. From then on, the Soviet Union began to advocate a 'simple convention with details to be delivered later'.[33] As the USSR Minister of Geology Yevgenii A. Kozlovsky noted in his speech at the Academy of Sciences in 1983:

> We consider it of principal importance to work out such a regime for development of Antarctic mineral resources that would be a further strengthening of the Antarctic Treaty of 1959 and would exclude extension of the Common Heritage of Mankind's concept to the areas covered by this treaty, since its main provisions correspond most to the long-term economic, political and defense interests of the USSR.[34]

In 1979–80, the Soviet Union initiated consultations with scientific and party officials of the GDR on the possibility of the creation of an East German Antarctic station as a precondition for obtaining consultative status in the ATS. One of the important motives in these negotiations was the potential benefits of exploiting the Antarctic mineral resources for the Socialist Bloc. The Soviet proposal recommended that the East Germans build a station with a strong geological programme on the Larsemann Hills in eastern Antarctica, on territory that in 2014 received the status of a Specially Protected Area because of its mineral diversity.[35] The German side initially agreed with the Soviet proposal, but, after collecting different expert opinions, revisited its decision, becoming sceptical about possible economic returns from the station in the foreseeable future. Ultimately, the Soviet Union created its own 'Progress' station in the area. Apparently, one of the reasons why the USSR was interested in the creation of the East German station was the opportunity to represent not the Soviet Union itself, but the Socialist Bloc as a whole, as the agent of future mineral extraction, which could help to avoid possible accusations of 'Soviet imperialism'. Thus, Antarctic mineral potential not only became a focal point of Russian imperialist imagination and a driving force for geopolitical rivalry between East and West, but was also used to empower collaboration between the USSR and its east European satellite states. The Soviet Union tried to use assumptions and speculations about Antarctic minerals in order to mobilise support within the Eastern Bloc for its geopolitical ambitions in the region of the South Pole, and to seize control over an important 'resource frontier' of the world.

The interpolar space of Soviet colonialism

Justina Dahl, Peder Roberts and Lize-Marié van der Watt have drawn attention to the phenomenon of the 'polar identity' of the states of the Northern Hemisphere, whose Arctic and Antarctic programmes often turn out to be a continuation of each other, forming a single field of geopolitics of the poles.[36] Following this logic, I argue that the Soviet Antarctic project inherited colonial programmes and practices deployed in the Russian far north. That manifested itself in the transfer of people, institutions and technologies from the Soviet Arctic to the Antarctic – as well as in the use of the similar colonialist lexicon, and in the common spirit of the chase for resources, which determined the Soviet polar imagination.[37]

The main link between the Soviet Arctic and Antarctic was constituted by the Main Administration of the Northern Sea Route (Glavsevmorput) and its subordinate institution, the Arctic Research Institute, which co-ordinated and organised all the Soviet Antarctic expeditions from 1956 to 1963. Glavsevmorput was thrown to the Antarctic front mainly because it already had an experience of the forced deployment of colonial infrastructure in the Arctic and of organising scientific expeditions to the North Pole, being *de facto* the main colonial agent of the Soviet power in the Arctic region. As Paul Josephson put it, Glavsevmorput 'acquired responsibility to organise, administer, extract, smelt, transport, and explore the entire vast region from Murmansk to Kamchatka and to modernise the people within it'.[38] The golden age of the Glavsevmorput empire ended in the late 1930s.[39] After the war, and especially after the death of Stalin, it steadily lost its influence. In 1953, from an independent administration under the Council of Ministers, Glavsevmorput was transformed into a subdivision of the Ministry of the Navy. Nevertheless, it retained control over a significant material base, and above all ships, as well as the Arctic Research Institute and many specialists who were experienced in working in polar conditions.[40]

A peculiarity of Glavsevmorput as a colonial agent is that its mission was not so much the colonisation of vast land areas, but naval colonisation of the coast and islands of the Arctic Ocean. The context of this colonisation was the struggle for Soviet dominance in the north polar region. On 29 September 1916, the Russian empire declared its sovereignty over the islands of the Arctic Ocean, which 'constituted the northern continuation of the Siberian part of the continent'.[41] In 1926, Soviet territorial claims in the Arctic were announced by the decree 'On the Declaration of Lands and Islands Located in the Arctic Ocean as the Territory of the USSR', which declared all discovered and non-discovered islands in the sector from the borders of the Soviet mainland up to the North Pole as territorial possessions of the USSR. The sectoral concept in the Arctic was borrowed from Canada, which had adopted a similar act a year earlier. Almost immediately, Soviet lawyers began to discuss extension of the sectoral principle not only to solid land, but also to drift-ice and ice-free waters, as well as airspace.[42] Although the Soviet leadership never defended such a radical understanding of the sector concept in practice, the 'symbolic colonisation' of vast expanses of ice became an important purpose of Soviet Arctic politics from the 1930s. One of its key elements was extensive investments in scientific programmes and, above all, the launch of the North Pole drifting stations, which criss-crossed the Arctic Ocean, entering the sectors of all Arctic states.[43]

Thus, along with the more traditional 'internal colonisation', Glavsevmorput was also engaged in inventing new forms of external expansion. It was a specific model of hybrid colonisation that relied less on military force and legal claims, but used emphatically peaceful scientific initiatives as a tool to ensure the effective presence of the Soviet Union in the North Pole. This strategy was associated, among other things, with the claims of the USSR to leadership in the world anti-capitalist movement, which made it more problematic to use classical forms of territorial expansion, labelled by Soviet propaganda as 'imperialist aggression'.

After the war, the experience of Glavsevmorput in the colonisation of the Arctic was transposed to the opposite part of the globe. The choice of Glavsevmorput for the organisational support of Antarctic expeditions signalled that the Soviet leadership perceived Antarctica as another space for potential resource colonisation. The 'conquerors of the north', whose talents had proved themselves in the Arctic, were moved to a new frontier. For example, Mikhail M. Somov, who headed a drift-ice station North Pole-2 in 1951–52, became the commander of the first Soviet Antarctic Expedition. The second expedition was headed by Alexey F. Tryoshnikov, the head of the North Pole-3 drifting station.

Here one can speak not only about the transfer of people, institutions and technologies from the Arctic to the Antarctic, but also about the transfer of discourses. The key concept of the Soviet colonial lexicon was *osvoenie* – a word that combines the connotations 'to incorporate' and 'to make your own', and at the same time the motives of utilisation and exploitation. This concept intertwines two colonial patterns: colonisation as economic development and 'cultivation' of a region, and colonisation as extraction of resources in favour of the metropolis. Film historian Emma Widdis writes of *osvoenie* as a grand Stalinist project of gaining control over vast remote areas through a variety of practices, including mapping, infrastructure and geological surveys.[44] The Antarctic project in the 1950s had been developed at the junction of this romantic Stalinist rhetoric of incorporating the periphery within a more modern technological and technocratic paradigm aimed primarily at controlling the material (natural) environment through scientific research; quantification; and, not least, the assessment and extraction of fossils.

Documents show that before the signing of the Antarctic Treaty, one of the goals of the Soviet presence in Antarctica was to prepare the ground for possible territorial claims.[45] Following the same logic that applied to

Soviet investments in drifting stations at the North Pole, scientific research in Antarctica served as a geopolitical tool to mark the Soviet presence in various parts of the continent. At one of the meetings of the Arctic and Antarctic Reseach Institute (AARI) Academic Council in 1958, Mikhail M. Somov expressed it this way:

> Antarctica is still a no-man's land. Sooner or later, the question of her future fate will arise. It is quite natural that when deciding this issue, our country should have open eyes ... considering the funding [for the expeditions], the government agreed with the main task – to recognise the need for a general study [of Antarctica] in order to sit with open eyes at a round table where the boundaries of possessions of states will be determined.[46]

Although these conversations were conducted behind closed doors, at some point the prospect of Antarctic colonisation even appeared in the Soviet public discourse. In a publication of the Soviet popular science magazine *Tekhnika – molodezhi* (*Technology to the Youth*) of 1956, one of the leaders of the Soviet Antarctic programme, geologist and member of the Academy of Sciences Dmitry I. Shcherbakov, suggested that 'in the future, the colonisation [*zaselenie*] and development [*osvoenie*] of Antarctica will undoubtedly begin, and this will be done pretty much in the same way as in our far north: first, meteorological and radio stations will be created, and small villages around them, then the construction of ports and airfields will begin'.[47] Thus, Shcherbakov imagined Antarctica becoming a colony in a classical sense, in which settlers migrate from the colonising group to the colonised land, also arguing for the relevance of the Russian Arctic colonial experience for Antarctica.

The chief of Glavsevmorput, Vasilii F. Burhanov, and deputy chief, Evgenii I. Tolstikov, reacted to this article in their note to the Central Committee of the Communist Party of the Soviet Union and criticised it on the basis that it might lead to a distorted view of Soviet Antarctic policy overseas. Nevertheless, ambitions of territorial domination were constantly articulated in the meetings of the Scientific Council of the AARI and Glavsevmorput leadership in 1957–59. Protocols of the meetings show that both scientists and bureaucrats perceived the development of the network of the Soviet Antarctic stations after the IGY as a colonial enterprise. Here again, the interest in resource extraction, and particularly in the minerals, played one of the central roles. Towards the end of the IGY it was suggested that the primary purpose of the new Antarctic stations should be securing the territories of the continent with the highest resource potential for Soviet power. Director of the AARI, Vyacheslav V. Frolov, at a meeting with the Deputy Minister of the Navy, assessed the results of the IGY for the USSR as follows: 'There is nothing to hold on to in the Mirny area; we made our contribution, we were "used" for this purpose, being sent to the most unpromising area ... It is necessary, if possible, to reclaim land, and not thousands of metres of bare ice.'[48] According to Frolov, geology was supposed to play one of the major roles in this process, since it could help to search and take hold of the most strategically important and resource-rich territories of Antarctica. In the 'Prospective Work Plan in Antarctica for 1959–65', prospective geological investigations of mountainous areas was justified by the need 'to determine the economic potential and opportunities for the development [*osvoenie*] of the territory.[49] The authors of the plan also highlighted the necessity of transferring the main Soviet station from Mirny 'to a new geologically promising place in Antarctica'.[50] Another Arctic institute – the Research Institute of Arctic Geology (NIIGA) – should play a decisive role in the formulation and implementation of these plans.

The history of NIIGA goes back to the geology department of the All-Union Arctic Institute and the Special Geological and Mining Department of Glavsevmorput, within which the institute was established in 1948. A new chapter in the history of NIIGA began in 1953, when it was transferred from Glavsevmorput to the Ministry of Geology. In fact, heroic efforts of the employees of this institute made resource extraction from the Russian far north an integral part of Soviet economic development after the Second World War. During the Cold War period, the Institute was gradually expanding its zone of competence, first to Antarctica and later on to the oceanic floor, thus following the logic of expanding resource frontiers. Throughout the history of the Institute, Antarctica has not been the leading area of its activity, but a number of researchers had successfully lobbied and further expanded the activities of its Antarctic Division. The deputy director of NIIGA, leader of the Institute's geological research programme in Antarctica Mikhail G. Ravich (1912–78), played a decisive role in this process. Ravich graduated as a mining geologist from Leningrad Mining Institute in 1936, and in 1947–49 worked on the Taimyr Expedition, where he discovered uranium ore on the Chelyuskin Peninsula. Another key figure of Soviet Antarctic geology was Dmitry S. Soloviev (1926–74), who in the 1950s was one of the discoverers of Yakut diamonds. An important characteristic feature of the Institute is that it combined scientific activity with applied work in the field of geological exploration. NIIGA was supposed to assess mineral reserves and to contribute to the state's five-year plans with the analysis of the prospects for the economic development of mineral deposits. The material well-being, medals and state awards of the Institute's employees were directly related to the success of the subsequent exploitation of the found deposits. That is why they also actively pushed forward the so-called 'resource aspect' of the Soviet geological programme in Antarctica.

The role of geological arguments in the development of the Soviet Antarctic programme can be illustrated by the discussion regarding the choice of site for a new Antarctic station in 1958. One of the proposed options was the Bellingshausen Sea coast. According to polar geographer Yakov Ya. Gakkel, who took part in the discussion, 'The Bellingshausen Sea is the Russian Sea, where Antarctica was discovered by the Russians ... The Bellingshausen Sea is located in the sector for which the countries of Latin America have made claims, but if we create our stations there, we will have more grounds for securing this territory for the Soviet Union.'[51] On the other hand, Ravich and the Institute of Arctic Geology insisted on the creation of the Lazarev station on Queen Maud Land, which, in their opinion, was of more significant geological interest.[52] The decisive argument in favour of 'Lazarev' was the fact that geological expeditions of several western countries had already begun to work in this area, and the Soviet Union did not want to be left behind.

The same logic continued in the 1960s, 1970s and 1980s, until the end of the Soviet Union. It was the typical Cold War situation of 'catching up and overtaking', which in this case resembled a struggle among several colonial powers for dominance over territory. The rhetoric of division of spheres of influence was still present in Soviet documents well after the conclusion of the Antarctic Treaty. For example, after the prospect of developing Antarctic oil and gas was discussed at an expert meeting held at the Norwegian Nansen Foundation in 1973, the USSR began to reconsider the priorities of its geological programme, fearing that the marine geology and geophysics materials available to it '[did] not permit the claiming, in the case of an economic division of the Antarctic shelf, of a priority in developing any part of it'.[53] Although the ATS formally froze existing territorial claims and effectively prevented the emergence of new ones, it did not cancel the possibility of future exploitation of mineral resources and the related possible assignment of certain areas of Antarctic territories to individual states and commercial enterprises representing them. In this respect, the Spitsbergen regime, where the USSR was simultaneously actively invested in oil and other mineral prospecting, could be a model.[54]

Conclusion

Although colonialism was a main point of Soviet criticism of western Antarctic policies, the Soviet Union itself clearly followed colonialist patterns and shared a resource-oriented approach toward the continent, using as a model its expansion in the Arctic. At the same time, the transfer of the Arctic discourse and development practices was not complete, since, under the conditions of the ATS, the USSR had to adapt to the regime of collective governance and participate in the formation of new environmental regulations.

To a great extent, Antarctica is still perceived in Russia through the prism of resources and potential future territorialisation. Thus, even though Russian Foreign Minister Sergei Lavrov referred to the Antarctic issue as 'an example of complete unanimity between Moscow and Washington' in a 2019 television interview, the presenters of the TV programme considered it necessary to mention 'creepy-crawly sovereignisation', thus actualising the narrative of territorial division of the icy continent.[55] At the same time, the modern Russian Antarctic programme openly declares one of its goals as assessing the mineral resource potential of Antarctica, sparking international debate about its violation of the provisions of the 1998 Madrid Protocol.[56]

The Antarctic regime that emerged by the end of the Cold War was a multilayered combination of various models, and one of its deepest layers was constituted by the 'colonial subconscious'. During and after the Cold War, even countries such as Chile and Argentina appropriated a colonialist approach to Antarctica in the guise of anti-colonial slogans.[57] But for Russia, the Antarctic epic of the twentieth century was a direct continuation of the colonial patterns formed long before the Soviet era. In 2023, amidst the full-scale invasion and occupation of Ukraine by Russia, the significance of discourses and practices of territorial domination in Russian/Soviet history is difficult to overestimate. While we have in one case an uninhabited territory on the furthest part of the globe and, in the other, a densely populated neighbouring country, these stories have more in common than it seems at first glance.

Notes

1　The utility of a postcolonial lens in the studies of Antarctic history is discussed in Klaus J. Dodds, 'Post-Colonial Antarctica: An Emerging Engagement', *Polar Record* 42:1 (2006), 59–70; Shirley V. Scott, 'Ingenious and Innocuous? Article IV of the Antarctic Treaty as Imperialism', *The Polar Journal* 1:1 (2011), 51–62. For the interpretation of Antarctica as part of a 'settler colonial project', see Adrian Howkins, 'Appropriating Space: Antarctic Imperialism and the Mentality of Settler Colonialism', in Tracey Banivanua Mar and Penelope Edmonds (eds), *Making Settler Colonial Space: Perspectives on Race, Place and Identity* (London: Palgrave Macmillan, 2010), pp. 29–52. For the colonial spatialities of Antarctic stations, see Christy Collis and Quentin Stevens, 'Cold Colonies: Antarctic Spatialities at Mawson and McMurdo Stations', *Cultural Geographies* 14:2 (2007), 234–54.

2 Alexander Etkind, *Internal Colonization: Russia's Imperial Experience* (Cambridge: Polity, 2011).

3 Andy Bruno, *The Nature of Soviet Power: An Arctic Environmental History* (Cambridge: Cambridge University Press, 2016), p. 138. On the problems of interpreting the USSR as a colonial power, see, for example, Epp Annus, 'The Problem of Soviet Colonialism in the Baltics', *Journal of Baltic Studies* 43:1 (2012), 21–45, DOI: 10.1080/01629778.2011.628551.

4 On the western interpretation, see Władysław W. Kulski, 'Soviet Colonialism and Anti-Colonialism', *The Russian Review* 18:2 (1959), 113–25; M. A. Heiss, 'Exposing "Red Colonialism": U.S. Propaganda at the United Nations, 1953–1963', *Journal of Cold War Studies*, 17:3 (2015), 82–115, DOI: 10.2307/126807.

5 Alla Bolotova, 'Colonization of Nature in the Soviet Union: State Ideology, Public Discourse, and the Experience of Geologists', *Historical Social Research* 29:3 (2004), 104–23, DOI: 10.12759/hsr.29.2004.3.104-123.

6 The concept of extractivism and its criticism have their origins primarily in the social struggles of South and Central America. It denotes a neocolonial situation of large-scale resource exploitation, mainly for export from the 'Global South' to the 'Global North'. See, for instance, James Petras and Henry Veltmeyer, *Extractive Imperialism in the Americas: Capitalism's New Frontier* (Leiden/Boston, MA: Brill, 2014). In the case of the Soviet Union, in place of the 'Global South' there was the entire complex of imperial margins, including Central Asia, Siberia, the Far East and the Arctic, and instead of multinational corporate monopolies, the process was led by powerful governmental agencies. However, the consequences of 'extractive socialism' and 'extractive capitalism' are not particularly different. They include intensive and long-term destructive impacts on the affected communities and their environments, as well as on the non-inhabited areas.

7 Sara Friedrichsmeyer, Sara Lennox and Susanne Zantop, 'Introduction', in Sara Friedrichsmeyer, Sara Lennox and Susanne Zantop (eds), *The Imperialist Imagination: German Colonialism and Its Legacy* (Ann Arbor: University of Michigan Press, 1998), pp. 1–29 (p. 18); Howkins, 'Appropriating Space', pp. 48–9.

8 As defined by Sheila Jasanoff, the concept of 'co-production' shows how scientific knowledge both embeds and is embedded in social identities, institutions, representations and discourses; Sheila Jasanoff, 'The Idiom of Co-Production', in Sheila Jasanoff (ed.), *States of Knowledge: The Co-Production of Science and the Social Order* (Abingdon: Routledge, 2004), p. 3.

9 On the conceptualisation of the collective practices of 'resource-making', see, for instance, E. E. Ferry and M. E. Limbert (eds), *Timely Assets: The Politics of Resources and Their Temporalities* (Santa Fe, NM: School for Advanced Research Press, 2008).

10 Dian Olson Belanger, *Deep Freeze: The United States, the International Geophysical Year, and the Origins of Antarctica's Age of Science* (Boulder: University Press of Colorado, 2006); Klaus J. Dodds, Irina Gan and Adrian

Howkins, 'The IPY-3: The International Geophysical Year (1957–1958)', in Susan Barr and Cornelia Luedecke (eds), *The History of the International Polar Years (IPYs)* (Heidelberg: Springer, 2010), pp. 239–58.

11 E. V. Mikhal'skii, E. N. Kamenev and A. S. Mikhal'skaya, 'Geologicheskoe izuchenie Antarktidy: Istoricheskie aspekty i sovremennoe sostoyanie ['Geological Study of Antarctica: Historical Aspects and Current State'], *Problemy Arktiki i Antarktiki [Arctic and Antarctic Problems]* 88:2 (2011), 97–112; C. Kehrt, 'Gondwana's Promises: German Geologists in Antarctica between Basic Science and Resource Exploration in the Late 1970s', *Historical Social Research* 40:2 (2015), 202–21.

12 Alessandro Antonello, *The Greening of Antarctica: Assembling an International Environment* (Oxford: Oxford University Press, 2019), pp. 77–8.

13 See, for instance, Francisco Orrego Vicuña, *Antarctic Mineral Exploitation: The Emerging Legal Framework* (Cambridge: Cambridge University Press, 1988); Gerry Nagtzaam, *The Making of International Environmental Treaties: Neoliberal and Constructivist Analyses of Normative Evolution* (Cheltenham: Edward Elgar, 2009), pp. 80–155; Rudiger Wolfrum, *Convention on the Regulation of Antarctic Mineral Resource Activities: An Attempt to Break New Ground* (Berlin: Springer, 2012).

14 Irina Gan, ' "The First Practical Soviet Steps towards Getting a Foothold in the Antarctic": The Soviet Antarctic Whaling Flotilla *Slava*', *Polar Record* 47:1 (2011), 21–8, DOI: 10.1017/S003224740999043X.

15 S. V. Molodtsov, *Sovremennoe mezhdunarodno-pravovoe polozhenie Antarktiki [The Current International Legal Situation of Antarctica]* (Moscow: Gosyurizdat, 1954), p. 45.

16 Archive of the Russian Academy of Sciences (ARAN), f. 653, op. 2, d. 3, ll. 1–4. Letter to Khrushchev from Nesmeyanov, Bakaev, Ishkov and Ivanov, 1954.

17 ARAN, f. 653, op. 2, d. 1, l. 145. Historical reference by L. M. Nikolaeva, 1954.

18 Barbara Mitchell and Richard Sandbrook, *The Management of the Southern Ocean* (London: International Institute for Environment and Development, 1980), p. 78.

19 On the limitations of Soviet mineral self-sufficiency, see, for instance, Daniel S. Papp, 'Soviet Non-Fuel Mineral Resources: Surplus or Scarcity?', *Resources Policy* 8:3 (1982), 155–76, DOI: 10.1016/0301-4207(92)90034-7; Philip R. Ballinger, 'Probability of Continued Soviet Mineral Self-Sufficiency', *Resources Policy* 12:3 (1985), 160–76, DOI: 10.1016/0301-4207(85)90054-6.

20 Rainer Karlsch, *Uran für Moskau: Die Wismut – eine populäre Geschichte* (Berlin: Links Christoph Verlag, 2007); Zbynek Zeman and Rainer Karlsch, *Uranium Matters: Central European Uranium in International Politics, 1900–1960* (Budapest: Central European University Press, 2008); Grégory Delaplace, 'Neighbours and Their Ruins: Remembering Foreign Presences in Mongolia', in Franck Billé, Grégory Delaplace and Caroline Humphrey (eds), *Frontier Encounters: Knowledge and Practice at the Russian, Chinese and Mongolian Border* (Cambridge: Open Book Publishers, 2012), pp. 211–33.

21 On the resource motives for the Soviet invasion of Afghanistan, see John F. Shroder, 'Afghanistan Resources and Soviet Policy in Central and South Asia', in Milan Hauner and Robert L. Canfield (eds), *Afghanistan and the Soviet Union: Collision and Transformation* (New York: Routledge, 2019), pp. 101–19. On the USSR's attention to Africa's resource potential, see, for example, Elena Kochetkova , David Damtar, Lilia Boliachevets, Polina Slyusarchuk and Julia Lajus, 'Soviet Technological Projects and Technological Aid in Africa and Cuba, 1960s–1980s', *SSRN Electronic Journal* (January 2017), 1–16 (p. 6).

22 Cited in Shroder, 'Afghanistan Resources', p. 105.

23 ARAN, f. 653, op. 2, d. 4, l. 147. Address to the participants of the second voyage of the Complex Antarctic Expedition of the USSR Academy of Sciences, 1956.

24 V. L. Ivanov and E. N. Kamenev (eds), *Geologiya i mineral'nye resursy Antarktidy* [*Geology and Mineral Resources of Antarctica*] (Moscow: Nedra, 1990), p. 13.

25 For instance, the director of the Research Institute of Arctic Geology, Boris V. Tkachenko, stressed in a report to the Deputy Head of the State Hydrometeorological Service, Evgenii I. Tolstikov, that 'American scientists are investigating … the economic prerequisites for mining in Antarctica.' Report from 24 October 1964 on the main results of Soviet geological research in Antarctica for 1956–64, Russian State Archive of Economics (RGAE), f. 8061, op. 9, d. 1189, ll. 40–3. Materials on the state and prospects of Soviet research in Antarctica, 1964.

26 Roman Khandozhko, 'Quantum Tunneling through the Iron Curtain: The Soviet Nuclear City of Dubna as a Cold War Crossing Point', *Cahiers du monde russe* 2:2–3 (2019): 369–96, DOI: 10.4000/monderusse.11222.

27 Julia Lajus, 'Soviet Official Critiques of the Resource Scarcity Prediction by Limits to Growth Report: The Case of Evgenii Fedorov's Ecological Crisis Rhetoric', *European Review of History/Revue européenne d'histoire* 27:3 (2020), 321–41, DOI: 10.1080/13507486.2020.1737654.

28 S. V. Popov and A. V. Kiselev, 'Otechestvennye aerogeofizicheskie issledovaniya na zemlyakh Mak-Robertsona, Printsessy Elizavety i Vil'gel'ma II, Vostochnaya Antarktida' ['Russian Airborne Geophysical Surveys on the MacRobertson, Princess Elizabeth and Wilhelm II lands, East Antarctica'], *Kriosfera Zemli* 22:1 (2018), 3–13 (pp. 4–5).

29 David J. Drewry, 'Deep-Sea Drilling from *Glomar Challenger* in the Southern Ocean', *Polar Record* 18:112 (1976), 47–71 (pp. 62–3).

30 G. E. Grikurov, G. L. Leichenkov, V. V. Lukin and V. N. Masolov, 'Rossiiskie geologo-geofizicheskie issledovaniya v Antarktide: Dostizheniya, sostoyanie, perspektivy' ['Russian Geological and Geophysical Research in Antarctica: Achievements, Status, Prospects'], in V. L. Ivanov (ed.), *60 let v Arktike, Antarktike i Mirovom okeane* [*60 Years in the Arctic, the Antarctic and the World Ocean*] (St Petersburg: VNIIOkeangeologiya, 2008), pp. 313–28 (p. 314).

31 Nagtzaam, *The Making of International Environmental Treaties*, p. 101.

32 According to a report by British diplomat John Heap, 'the Soviet delegation consistently argued that … the ecological impact of any exploitation should be assumed to be unacceptable until scientific research proved otherwise'. Foreign and Commonwealth Office Archives (FCO), EG 14/62, 'Antarctic Minerals: Delegation Report on Two Antarctic Treaty Meetings on the Eco/ Technical and the Legal/Political Aspects', 23 July 1979, p. 1.

33 Andrew Jackson, *Who Saved Antarctica? The Heroic Era of Antarctic Diplomacy* (Basingstoke: Palgrave Macmillan, 2021), p. 72.

34 ARAN, f. 2, op. 1, d. 890, l. 50. Speech by the Minister of Geology of the USSR, Yevgenii A. Kozlovsky, at a meeting of the Presidium of the Academy of Sciences of the USSR on the issue of the Antarctic, 10 November 1983.

35 Diedrich Frietzsche, 'Geowissenschaftliche Forschung der DDR in der Antarktis', in *Schriftenreihe für Geowissenschaften 18: Zur Geschichte der Geowissenschaften in der DDR – Teil II* (Ostklüne: Verlag Störr, 2011), pp. 303–17; Jessica O'Reilly, 'Tectonic History and Gondwanan Geopolitics in the Larsemann Hills, Antarctica', *PoLAR: Political and Legal Anthropology Review* 34:2 (2011), 214–32, DOI: 10.1111/j.1555-2934.2011.01163.x.

36 Justina Dahl, Peder Roberts and Lize-Marié van der Watt, 'Is There Anything Natural about the Polar?', *Polar Record* 55:5 (2019), 326–9, DOI: 10.1017/ S0032247419000652.

37 The first attempt to connect the Soviet Arctic and Antarctic programmes (although without references to the colonialist paradigm) was made in Christopher C. Joyner, 'A Comparison of Soviet Arctic and Antarctic Policies', in Lawson W. Brigham (ed.), *The Soviet Maritime Arctic* (Annapolis, MD: Naval Institute Press, 1991), pp. 284–300. Similarly, the frontier mentality of Wild West exploration influenced the American Antarctic programme; Adrian Howkins, 'The Significance of the Frontier in Antarctic History: How the US West Has Shaped the Geopolitics of the Far South', *The Polar Journal* 3:1 (2013), 29–52 (pp. 9–30).

38 Paul Josephson, *The Conquest of the Russian Arctic* (Cambridge, MA: Harvard University Press, 2014), p. 66.

39 Linda Trautman, 'Stalin's Last Frontier: Soviet Arctic in the 1930s, Glavsevmorput' and the Northern Sea Route', PhD thesis (University of London, 2004).

40 In 1958 rebranded into the Arctic and Antarctic Research Institute.

41 Viatcheslav V. Gavrilov, 'Legal Status of the Northern Sea Route and Legislation of the Russian Federation: A Note', *Ocean Development & International Law* 46:3 (2015), 256–63 (p. 258).

42 Leonid Timtchenko, 'The Russian Arctic Sectoral Concept: Past and Present', *Arctic* 50:1 (1997), 29–35 (pp. 30–2), DOI: 10.14430/arctic1088.

43 William F. Althoff, *Drift Station: Arctic Outposts of Superpower Science* (Washington, DC: Potomac, 2007), pp. 33–63.

44 Emma Widdis, *Visions of a New Land: Soviet Film from the Revolution to the Second World War* (New Haven, CT: Yale University Press, 2003), pp. 7–13.

45 Bolesław A. Boczek, 'The Soviet Union and the Antarctic Regime', *American Journal of International Law* 78:4 (1984), 834–58 (pp. 842–3), DOI: 10.2307/2202198.

46 Central State Archive of Scientific and Technical Documentation, St. Petersburg (TsGANTD SPb), f. r-369, op. 11, d. 1247, l. 273. Minutes of the Academic Council meeting, 24 May 1958.

47 V. Polushkin and S. Ushakov, '44 voprosa po Antarktide' ['44 Questions on Antarctica'], *Tekhnika – molodezhi* 3 (1956), 2–9.

48 TsGANTD SPb, f. r-369, op. 11, d. 1292, l. 66. Minutes of the meeting with the Deputy Minister of the Navy, 18 October 1958.

49 TsGANTD SPb, f. r-369, op. 11, d. 1361, l. 35. 'Prospective Work Plan in Antarctica for 1959–65'.

50 TsGANTD SPb, f. r-369, op. 11, d. 1361, l. 11. Prospective work plan in Antarctica for 1959–65.

51 TsGANTD SPb, f. r-369, op. 11, d. 1247, l. 130. Minutes of the Academic Council meeting, 24 May 1958. On the Soviet construction of the narrative of the discovery of the Antarctic by the Bellingshausen and Lazarev expedition, see Rip Bulkeley, *The Historiography of the First Russian Antarctic Expedition, 1819–21* (Basingstoke: Palgrave Macmillan, 2020), pp. 65–77.

52 TsGANTD SPb, f. r-369, op. 11, d. 1292, l. 64. Minutes of meeting with the Deputy Minister of the Navy, 18 October 1958.

53 RGAE, f. 9571, op. 8, d. 2725, l. 5. Report note 'On the Project of Geological-Geophysical Research by "Sevmorgeo" in the Antarctic in 1976–1980', 7 March 1974.

54 According to the Mining Charter attached to the Svalbard Treaty, any country could conduct geological exploration and claim areas for exclusive rights to mineral prospecting and commercial mining on Svalbard. Similar rules were discussed during the CRAMRA convention negotiations, although the overlapping claims made the UK, Argentina and Chile very sceptical about it from the beginning.

55 VESTI.ru, 'Lavrov privel primer polnogo edinodushija Moskvy i Vashingtona' ['Lavrov Gave an Example of Complete Unanimity between Moscow and Washington'], 30 November 2019, VESTI.ru, www.vesti.ru/article/1289873 (accessed 17 November 2022).

56 Tiara Walters, " 'Gentleman's Agreement": Despite Mining Ban, Russia Scours Antarctica for Massive Fossil Fuel Deposits', *Daily Maverick*, 17 May 2022, www.dailymaverick.co.za/article/2022-05-17-gentlemans-agreement-despite-mining-ban-russia-scours-antarctica-for-massive-fossil-fuel-deposits/ (accessed 2 September 2023).

57 See Alejandra Mancilla's chapter in this volume.

Bibliography

Althoff, William F. *Drift Station: Arctic Outposts of Superpower Science*. Washington, DC: Potomac, 2007.

Annus, Epp. 'The Problem of Soviet Colonialism in the Baltics'. *Journal of Baltic Studies* 43, no. 1 (2012): 21–45. DOI: 10.1080/01629778.2011.628551.

Antonello, Alessandro. *The Greening of Antarctica: Assembling an International Environment*. Oxford: Oxford University Press, 2019.

Ballinger, Philip R. 'Probability of Continued Soviet Mineral Self-Sufficiency'. *Resources Policy* 12, no. 3 (1985): 160–76. DOI: 10.1016/0301-4207(85)90054-6.

Belanger, Dian Olson. *Deep Freeze: The United States, the International Geophysical Year, and the Origins of Antarctica's Age of Science*. Boulder: University Press of Colorado, 2006.

Boczek, Bolesław A. 'The Soviet Union and the Antarctic Regime'. *American Journal of International Law* 78, no. 4 (1984): 834–58. DOI: 10.2307/2202198.

Bolotova, Alla. 'Colonization of Nature in the Soviet Union: State Ideology, Public Discourse, and the Experience of Geologists'. *Historical Social Research* 29, no. 3 (2004): 104–23. DOI: 10.12759/hsr.29.2004.3.104-123.

Bruno, Andy. *The Nature of Soviet Power: An Arctic Environmental History*. Cambridge: Cambridge University Press, 2016.

Bulkeley, Rip. *The Historiography of the First Russian Antarctic Expedition, 1819–21*. Basingstoke: Palgrave Macmillan, 2020.

Collis, Christy and Quentin Stevens. 'Cold Colonies: Antarctic Spatialities at Mawson and McMurdo Stations'. *Cultural Geographies* 14, no. 2 (2007): 234–54. DOI: 10.1177/1474474007075356.

Dahl, Justiina, Peder Roberts and Lize-Marié van der Watt. 'Is There Anything Natural about the Polar?'. *Polar Record* 55, no. 5 (2019): 326–9. DOI: 10.1017/S0032247419000652.

Delaplace, Grégory. 'Neighbours and Their Ruins: Remembering Foreign Presences in Mongolia'. In *Frontier Encounters: Knowledge and Practice at the Russian, Chinese and Mongolian Border*, ed. Franck Billé, Grégory Delaplace and Caroline Humphrey, pp. 211–33. Cambridge: Open Book Publishers, 2012.

Dodds, Klaus J. 'Post-Colonial Antarctica: An Emerging Engagement'. *Polar Record* 42, no. 1 (2006): 59–70. DOI: 10.1017/S0032247405004857.

Dodds, Klaus J., Irina Gan and Adrian Howkins. 'The IPY-3: The International Geophysical Year (1957–1958)'. In *The History of the International Polar Years (IPYs)*, ed. Susan Barr and Cornelia Luedecke, pp. 239–58. Heidelberg: Springer, 2010.

Drewry, David J. 'Deep-Sea Drilling from *Glomar Challenger* in the Southern Ocean'. *Polar Record* 18, no. 112 (1976): 47–71. DOI: 10.1017/S0032247400028710.

Etkind, Alexander. *Internal Colonization: Russia's Imperial Experience*. Cambridge: Polity, 2011.

Ferry, Elizabeth Emma and Mandana E. Limbert (eds). *Timely Assets: The Politics of Resources and Their Temporalities*. Santa Fe, NM: School for Advanced Research Press, 2008.

Friedrichsmeyer, Sara, Sara Lennox and Susanne Zantop. 'Introduction'. In *The Imperialist Imagination: German Colonialism and Its Legacy*, ed. Sara Friedrichsmeyer, Sara Lennox and Susanne Zantop, pp. 1–29. Ann Arbor: University of Michigan Press, 1998.

Frietzsche, Diedrich. 'Geowissenschaftliche Forschung der DDR in der Antarktis'. In *Schriftenreihe für Geowissenschaften 18: Zur Geschichte der Geowissenschaften in der DDR – Teil II*, pp. 303–17. Ostklüne: Verlag Störr, 2011.

Gan, Irina. '"The First Practical Soviet Steps towards Getting a Foothold in the Antarctic": The Soviet Antarctic Whaling Flotilla *Slava*'. *Polar Record* 47, no. 1 (2011): 21–8. DOI: 10.1017/S003224740999043X.

Gavrilov, Viatcheslav V. 'Legal Status of the Northern Sea Route and Legislation of the Russian Federation: A Note'. *Ocean Development & International Law* 46, no. 3 (2015): 256–63. DOI: 10.1080/00908320.2015.1054746.

Grikurov, G. E., G. L. Leichenkov, V. V. Lukin and V. N. Masolov. 'Rossiiskie geologo-geofizicheskie issledovaniya v Antarktide: Dostizheniya, sostoyanie, perspektivy' ['Russian Geological and Geophysical Research in Antarctica: Achievements, Status, Prospects']. In *60 let v Arktike, Antarktike i Mirovom okeane* [*60 Years in the Arctic, the Antarctic and the World Ocean*], ed. V. L. Ivanov, pp. 313–28. St Petersburg: VNIIOkeangeologiya, 2008.

Heiss, Mary Ann. 'Exposing "Red Colonialism": U.S. Propaganda at the United Nations, 1953–1963'. *Journal of Cold War Studies* 17, no. 3 (2015): 82–115. DOI: 10.1162/JCWS_a_00562.

Howkins, Adrian. 'Appropriating Space: Antarctic Imperialism and the Mentality of Settler Colonialism'. In *Making Settler Colonial Space: Perspectives on Race, Place and Identity*, ed. Tracey Banivanua Mar and Penelope Edmonds, pp. 29–52. London: Palgrave Macmillan, 2010.

Howkins, Adrian. 'The Significance of the Frontier in Antarctic History: How the US West Has Shaped the Geopolitics of the Far South'. *The Polar Journal* 3, no. 1 (2013): 9–30. DOI: 10.1080/2154896X.2013.768417.

Ivanov, V. L. and E. N. Kamenev (eds). *Geologiya i mineral'nye resursy Antarktidy* [*Geology and Mineral Resources of Antarctica*]. Moscow: Nedra, 1990.

Jackson, Andrew. *Who Saved Antarctica? The Heroic Era of Antarctic Diplomacy*. Basingstoke: Palgrave Macmillan, 2021.

Jasanoff, Sheila. 'The Idiom of Co-Production'. In *States of Knowledge: The Co-Production of Science and the Social Order*, ed. Sheila Jasanoff, pp. 1–12. Abingdon: Routledge, 2004.

Josephson, Paul. *The Conquest of the Russian Arctic*. Cambridge, MA: Harvard University Press, 2014.

Joyner, Christopher C. 'A Comparison of Soviet Arctic and Antarctic Policies'. In *The Soviet Maritime Arctic*, ed. Lawson W. Brigham, pp. 284–300. Annapolis, MD: Naval Institute Press, 1991.

Karlsch, Rainer. *Uran für Moskau: Die Wismut – eine populäre Geschichte*. Berlin: Links Christoph Verlag, 2007.

Kehrt, Christian. 'Gondwana's Promises: German Geologists in Antarctica between Basic Science and Resource Exploration in the Late 1970s'. *Historical Social Research* 40, no. 2 (2015): 202–21. DOI: 10.12759/hsr.40.2015.2.202-221.

Khandozhko, Roman. 'Quantum Tunneling through the Iron Curtain: The Soviet Nuclear City of Dubna as a Cold War Crossing Point'. *Cahiers du monde russe* 2, nos 2–3 (2019): 369–96. DOI: 10.4000/monderusse.11222.

Kochetkova, Elena, David Damtar, Lilia Boliachevets, Polina Slyusarchuk and Julia Lajus. 'Soviet Technological Projects and Technological Aid in Africa and Cuba, 1960s–1980s'. *SSRN Electronic Journal* (January 2017): 1–16.

Kulski, Władysław W. 'Soviet Colonialism and Anti-Colonialism'. *The Russian Review* 18, no. 2 (1959): 113–25. DOI: 10.2307/126807.

Lajus, Julia. 'Soviet Official Critiques of the Resource Scarcity Prediction by Limits to Growth Report: The Case of Evgenii Fedorov's Ecological Crisis Rhetoric'. *European Review of History/Revue européenne d'histoire* 27, no. 3 (2020): 321–41. DOI: 10.1080/13507486.2020.1737654.

Mancilla, Alejandra. 'South American Claims in Antarctica: Colonial, Malgré Tout'. *The Polar Journal* 12, no. 1 (2022): 22–41. DOI: 10.1080/2154896X.2022.2062558.

Mikhal'skii, E. V., E. N. Kamenev and A. S. Mikhal'skaya. 'Geologicheskoe izuchenie Antarktidy: Istoricheskie aspekty i sovremennoe sostoyanie ['Geological Study of Antarctica: Historical Aspects and Current State']. *Problemy Arktiki i Antarktiki* [*Arctic and Antarctic Problems*] 88, no. 2 (2011): 97–112.

Mitchell, Barbara and Richard Sandbrook. *The Management of the Southern Ocean.* London: International Institute for Environment and Development, 1980.

Molodtsov, S. V. *Sovremennoe mezhdunarodno-pravovoe polozhenie Antarktiki* [*The Current International Legal Situation of Antarctica*]. Moscow: Gosyurizdat, 1954.

Nagtzaam, Gerry. *The Making of International Environmental Treaties: Neoliberal and Constructivist Analyses of Normative Evolution.* Cheltenham: Edward Elgar, 2009.

O'Reilly, Jessica. 'Tectonic History and Gondwanan Geopolitics in the Larsemann Hills, Antarctica'. *PoLAR: Political and Legal Anthropology Review* 34, no. 2 (2011): 214–32. DOI: 10.1111/j.1555-2934.2011.01163.x.

Papp, Daniel S. 'Soviet Non-Fuel Mineral Resources: Surplus or Scarcity?'. *Resources Policy* 8, no. 3 (1982): 155–76. DOI: 10.1016/0301-4207(92)90034-7.

Petras, James and Henry Veltmeyer. *Extractive Imperialism in the Americas: Capitalism's New Frontier.* Leiden/Boston, MA: Brill, 2014.

Polushkin, V. and Ushakov, S. '44 voprosa po Antarktide' ['44 Questions on Antarctica']. *Tekhnika – molodezhi* 3 (1956): 2–9.

Popov, S. V. and A. V. Kiselev. 'Otechestvennye aerogeofizicheskie issledovaniya na zemlyakh Mak-Robertsona, Printsessy Elizavety i Vil'gel'ma II, Vostochnaya Antarktida' ['Russian Airborne Geophysical Surveys on the MacRobertson, Princess Elizabeth and Wilhelm II Lands, East Antarctica']. *Kriosfera Zemli* 22, no. 1 (2018): 3–13.

Scott, Shirley V. 'Ingenious and Innocuous? Article IV of the Antarctic Treaty as Imperialism'. *The Polar Journal* 1, no. 1 (2011): 51–62. DOI: 10.1080/2154896X.2011.568787.

Shroder, John F. 'Afghanistan Resources and Soviet Policy in Central and South Asia'. In *Afghanistan and the Soviet Union: Collision and Transformation,* ed. Milan Hauner and Robert L. Canfield, pp. 101–19. New York: Routledge, 2019.

Timtchenko, Leonid. 'The Russian Arctic Sectoral Concept: Past and Present'. *Arctic* 50, no. 1 (1997): 29–35. DOI: 10.14430/arctic1088.

Trautman, Linda. 'Stalin's Last Frontier: Soviet Arctic in the 1930s, Glavsevmorput' and the Northern Sea Route'. PhD thesis (University of London, 2004).

VESTI.ru. 'Lavrov privel primer polnogo edinodushija Moskvy i Vashingtona' ['Lavrov Gave an Example of Complete Unanimity between Moscow and Washington'], 30 November 2019. VESTI.ru. www.vesti.ru/article/1289873. Accessed 17 November 2022.

Vicuña, Francisco Orrego. *Antarctic Mineral Exploitation: The Emerging Legal Framework.* Cambridge: Cambridge University Press, 1988.

Walters, Tiara. '"Gentleman's Agreement": Despite Mining Ban, Russia Scours Antarctica for Massive Fossil Fuel Deposits'. *Daily Maverick,* 17 May 2022. www.dailymaverick.co.za/article/2022-05-17-gentlemans-agreement-despite-mining-ban-russia-scours-antarctica-for-massive-fossil-fuel-deposits/. Accessed 2 September 2023.

Widdis, Emma. *Visions of a New Land: Soviet Film from the Revolution to the Second World War*. New Haven, CT: Yale University Press, 2003.

Wolfrum, Rudiger. *Convention on the Regulation of Antarctic Mineral Resource Activities: An Attempt to Break New Ground*. Berlin: Springer, 2012.

Zeman, Zbynek and Rainer Karlsch. *Uranium Matters: Central European Uranium in International Politics, 1900–1960*. Budapest: Central European University Press, 2008.

2

Imperial rockets, colonial geographies: Algeria, Antarctica, Guiana and the French space programme, 1959–74

Katherine Mariko Sinclair

Legal analogy often links the Antarctic region to outer space, especially within the earth–moon system.[1] Both are relatively inaccessible areas with no permanent population; both are governed by careful international accords. Human endeavours on the Antarctic continent and in outer space also share a similar history. The construction of Antarctic research stations and their permanent occupation was motivated by the wide-ranging goals of the International Geophysical Year (IGY), from 1957 to 1959. Similarly, IGY activities included the launch of some 200 rockets around the globe, and eventually the launch of the first artificial satellite, the USSR's *Sputnik*, in 1957.[2] Histories of both 'the scramble for the poles' and 'the space race' often focus on the participation of the United States and the Soviet Union, and how these scientific endeavours defined and were defined by Cold War geopolitical concerns.[3] But these activities also took place in a period fraught with colonial conflict as European empires broke apart and formerly colonised nations came together in solidarity through the Non-Aligned Movement. Nations such as France, lacking great power status, faced with a long and difficult cultural and economic recovery after the devastation of the Second World War, and fighting through escalating colonial conflicts in Vietnam (then Indochina) and Algeria, clung to the possibilities offered by expansion into Antarctica and outer space during the IGY and beyond. French officials pushed for scientific and technological achievements that aimed to implement Charles de Gaulle's goal of spreading the 'radiance' of France around the world, even as the physical scope of the French empire was shrinking.[4]

Moving beyond metaphor or comparison, this chapter examines how France's Antarctic territories became key sites in the experimental rock-etry programme that grew to define the French space agency, the Centre national d'études spatiales (National Centre for Space Studies (CNES)). In doing so, the chapter puts Antarctic rocketry experiments in the context of the French space programme's other colonial ventures, at Hammaguir in the Algerian Sahara and in the city of Kourou on French Guiana. Each of these locations served as a testing and launch site in the French sounding rocket programme, in which relatively small rockets carrying scientific instruments surveyed and experimented in the earth's upper atmosphere. Sounding rocket experiments in the French empire not only allowed French scientists and engineers to 'conquer' the challenges of going to space; they also contributed to conquering, or in some cases reconquering, imperial territory, erasing, ignoring or destroying existing habitations in the regions where they worked. The people displaced from these sites, whose movement was restricted based on launch schedules and trajectories, then became objects for the scientific gaze of French rocketry personnel, who analysed 'alien' peoples with much of the same dispassionate interest they used for rocket telemetry. Rocket launches from each of these territories served to demonstrate French activity and geopolitical power in the region – to bring French science and technology to the remotest outposts of the French empire and, in doing so, strengthen and reaffirm France's colonial power across the world. In all three cases, continued sovereignty over imperial territory was necessary for French scientific and technological achievement. Rather than replacing colonialism, expansion into Antarctica and exploration of outer space *required* it.

Historians often put decolonisation and technological progress in a dialectical relationship – the growing 'radiance' of France's progress at the cutting edge of nuclear and space science compensates for the dimming radiance of its empire; the 'interior colonisation' of French life by technology responds to 'exterior' decolonisation in the violent conflicts of Vietnam and Algeria.[5] In some ways, this historiographical tendency follows the thinking of Charles de Gaulle, who warned of the 'colonisation' of France if the government did not pursue a top-down strategy of technological development.[6] Close attention to the development of the French rocketry programme, however, reveals that although the anxious investment in science and technology may have been motivated by the loss of much of France's overseas empire, the advances brought about by this investment depended on continued French colonial occupation of various territories around the globe. French achievements in rocketry and geophysical science became possible through colonisation of the Sahara, Terre Adélie, the Kerguelen Islands and French Guiana. In turn, close attention to the history of French research in the Antarctic region demonstrates that the French government and French space scientists viewed this territory not as a separate and exceptional space so much as a necessary, contiguous part of the frontier of French empire.

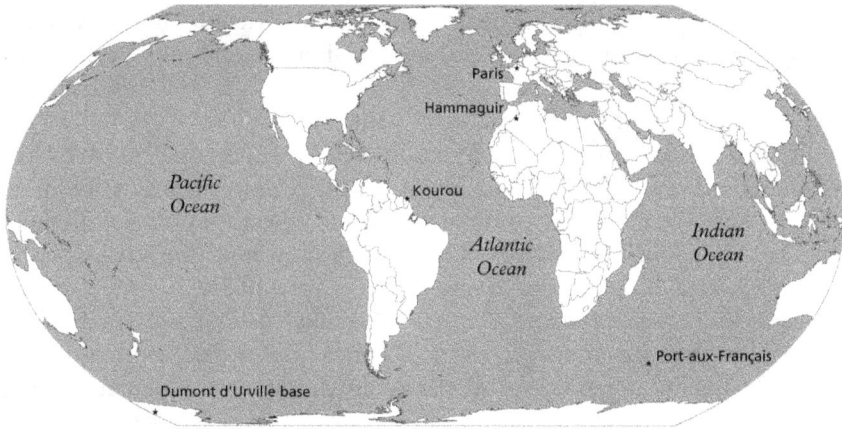

Map 2.1 Key locations mentioned in the chapter

'The twentieth century in all its splendor': Hammaguir, Algeria

On 12 March 1959, the young and ambitious physics professor Jacques Blamont, joined by his team of technicians and engineers, squinted up at the clear predawn sky over France's Hammaguir rocket launching base. A Véronique sounding rocket had launched seconds before, bearing an experiment that would define the French space programme. This was the first civilian project carried out at the Hammaguir site, which until then had served as a highly classified testing range for the French missile programme. The 12 March launch was also the third launch in a series of aeronomy experiments that involved ejecting a sodium vapour cloud into the upper atmosphere to observe air turbulence in various vertical zones.[7] The first launch had failed, the rocket only ascending to and altitude of 35 km; the second had been a success. This final launch was also a success, ejecting a 'magic, enchanting' arabesque of sodium that shone among the stars in the predawn light.[8] This simple experiment proved the existence of the 'turbopause', the altitude beyond which atmospheric particles are no longer evenly mixed and are instead separated by their chemical composition and atomic weight.[9] It also proved the value and feasibility of using French-made sounding rockets for civilian science, ultimately leading to the creation of the French space programme. And, finally, it jump-started Jacques Blamont's career – Blamont would eventually become the first scientific and technical director of the CNES. But this climactic moment in French space history did not occur in metropolitan France. Instead, the rocket was launched from the heart of colonised Algeria, even as Algeria was embroiled in a bitter struggle for independence from France. Attention to the imperial context of the Hammaguir base shows the colonial assumptions and experiences that made up the fabric of daily life at the base, and informed the scope, size and nature of the sounding rocket programme.

Hammaguir and the nearby settlement of Colomb-Béchar (100 km away) had long been a site for imperial activity in the region.[10] It was a southern military base for the Oran region and a hub of France's system of disciplinary battalions for refractory soldiers.[11] With the end of the Spanish Civil War, thousands of Spanish refugees fled to France and North Africa, where the right-leaning governments decided to put their labour to 'rational use' on infrastructure projects such as the construction of the Mediterranean–Niger railway line, intended to link the Maghreb to France's colonial territories at the centre of Africa. The Groupes de Travailleurs Etrangers (Foreign Workers' Groups (GTE)) laboured in concentration camps in brutal, unsanitary and often deadly conditions that only worsened under the Vichy regime.[12] When French officials sought a space to test the missiles and rockets developed for them by German scientists involved in the Nazi V-2 programme, it was not only the open spaces around Hammaguir that attracted them but also the region's well-developed road and rail network, built by forced labour in the preceding years (much as the V-2 rocket programme had also been built up through forced labour). The Centre interarmées d'essais d'engins spéciaux (Inter-Army Centre for Special Engine Tests (CIEES)) – the precursor to the CNES – was inaugurated at Hammaguir in 1947, and the tents of enlisted soldiers were soon replaced by metal buildings housing power plants; tracking antennae; hangars; launch pads; and, as the base and its programmes expanded, the necessary accommodation and administrative offices for hundreds of personnel involved in rocket testing and launches.[13] Between 1954 and 1967, the Hammaguir testing sites saw 158 rocket launches, and the scientific experiments performed at Hammaguir had an important institutional, as well as scientific, purpose. As Jacques Blamont later recalled, 'The aeronomy studied by sounding rockets was the formative discipline of the men who became directors of the European space programmes.'[14] According to Blamont, Hammaguir, both as a physical territory and as a metonym for the nascent French rocketry programme, 'represented the twentieth century in all its splendor'.[15]

French observers associated with the rocketry programme made much of the 'isolation' of Hammaguir, drawing parallels between the landscape's supposed emptiness and the emptiness of outer space. Describing the landscape, Blamont evoked 'the absolute solitude of that flat plain extending to the horizon in all directions, offering nothing but sand and stones'.[16] The view of Hammaguir as unpopulated *terra nullius* and the futuristic surroundings of the rocketry programme made scientists and engineers think of themselves as colonists on another planet. But the programme's location on occupied and inhabited territory was fundamental to the experience of early rocket scientists and engineers. In memoirs of rocket programme participants, encounters between the scientific and military personnel working at Hammaguir and the Arab and Amazigh locals around them took on the tone of science fiction. Marius Le Fèvre, launch director at the CIEES in Hammaguir from 1957 to 1960, assumed the role of ethnographer in his memoirs as he reminisced about taking part in an official ceremony for opening a well in the desert: a ceremony attended, on one side, by a French minister, a general and representatives of the CIEES, and, on the other side, by Tuareg locals – exoticied by Le Fèvre as the 'blue men' of the desert.[17] He recalled that 'they invited me to join them and dance with them, me in my uniform', dwelling on his own role in the ceremony as both observer and participant, and highlighting the encounter between the 'space age' and the 'Stone Age'.[18] Marcel Lebaron, a former soldier who also worked on the sounding rocket programme, referred to his meeting with a Tuareg encampment as 'a "lunar" encounter with someone from another world'.[19] In the futuristic atmosphere of Hammaguir, the colonial encounter was transposed into an extraterrestrial setting, emphasising not only the space-centred dreams of Hammaguir's scientists and soldiers, but also the perceived alienness of the peoples that surrounded them.

Looming large over the French rocketry programme at Hammaguir was the spectre of the Algerian War, a conflict with deep roots and a long afterlife that lasted officially from 1954 to 1962. Recollections from rocketry programme personnel echo the 'politics of concealment' that mark both the public and private memory of the *guerre d'Algérie*.[20] In her article about French nuclear testing in the Sahara (at Reganne, some 600 km south of the Hammaguir rocket launch sites), Roxane Panchasi points out the 'historiographic tendency to segregate' the history of the French nuclear programme and the history of the Algerian War.[21] This tendency is also visible in the recollections of those who took part in the French space programme. Jacques Blamont recalled that 'if we passed through the Algerian War, it was almost without noticing, because it never touched the region of Colomb-Béchar, even situated as it was on a hostile frontier'.[22] But rocket testing on occupied land 'participated in war's theatre even if it was not, strictly speaking, a theatre of war', to borrow Panchasi's excellent phrasing.[23] Ballistics tests and rocket launches from Hammaguir, visible from a great distance in the clear desert air, were a powerful symbol of French presence in the Sahara. Hammaguir's location on occupied territory also informed decisions about the nature of the rocketry tests that took place on its launch sites. The vast Saharan desert offered two possible long trajectories for rocket tests: a range of 1,000 km toward the Algerian city of

Tindouf in the southwest, and a range of 3,000 to the east, toward the Chad border.[24] But there was not much room for error in other directions. In 1960, launch personnel remotely destroyed a Véronique rocket moments after its test launch, because its wobbly trajectory was taking it in the direction of the Moroccan border, only 20 km away.[25] The decision, made in an abundance of caution, was greeted with frustration by observers such as Colonel Robert Genty, mission leader for that launch cycle – the 'political situation' had interfered with scientific achievement once again. Beyond its effect on rocket launches, the ongoing Algerian War and the beginnings of Algerian independence also put an expiration date on the Hammaguir testing centre. Although the secret 'military clauses' of the Evian Accords ending the Algerian War in 1962 allowed French use of the Hammaguir launch site for five years, officials stopped investing in expansions to the site by 1960.[26] Instead, the base became an interim site to perform rocket tests and upper-atmosphere experiments while various governmental organisations searched for alternative launch locations. Attention to Hammaguir's location on contested imperial territory reveals the colonial roots of the twentieth century's 'splendor', to quote Blamont once more. It shows that even as the French state was in the process of losing, or 'decolonising', Algeria, it was using occupied Algerian land to test and refine the sounding rockets that would become the foundation for the scientific and technical advances of the CNES. While rocketry programme members no doubt thought they were using space-age metaphors to describe the 'lunar' landscape and 'alien' peoples they encountered, they drew from a long tradition of exoticising and othering French colonial subjects. Yet the 'alien' peoples they encountered troubled sounding rocket launches through their fight for independence, and as such, the next destination for the French rocketry programme involved unpopulated territories where French control was simultaneously more certain and more tenuous: France's Antarctic territories.

'That beautiful adventure': Antarctica and the Kerguelen Islands

The CNES was created by law in December 1961, only three months before the Evian Accords officially ended the Algerian War. As the CNES lacked a permanent launch base, in order to maintain a strong French presence in the space race, its rocketry division orchestrated a series of launches around the globe using innovative 'mobile launch units' that allowed for sounding rocket launches even in places that lacked permanent launch infrastructure.[27] Jacques Blamont referred to the mobile launch campaigns as one of the organisation's 'claims to fame'.[28] Mobile launches, and the rigorous organisation they required, created professionalised, close-knit teams that would become the core of the French space programme and its future leadership for years to come. The mobile launch unit also allowed French scientists to perform upper-atmosphere and ionosphere experiments with large sounding rockets. Rocketry teams for the CNES privileged France's allies and existing French imperial territory in selecting launch sites, to take advantage of existing infrastructure for transport and supplies. In order to investigate the earth's magnetic field, therefore, the newly formed CNES worked with the administration of the *Terres australes et antarctiques fran-çaises* (French Southern and Antarctic Lands (TAAF)) to launch sounding rockets in Terre Adélie and on the Kerguelen Islands, two locations with unique magnetic and ionospheric properties. Long-term French occupation in both of these regions facilitated the installation of temporary launch bases and the gathering and interpretation of experimental data. At the same time, French scientists' ability to transport and to launch rockets from French Antarctic territories demonstrated not only French skill in rocketry but also France's continued control over these far-flung pieces of empire.

For the architects of the rocketry programme, who had positioned themselves so clearly as explorers of the new frontier of space, voyaging to a twentieth-century terrestrial frontier was a golden opportunity – and an opportunity that was only possible because Antarctica was already within the political and logistical boundaries of the French empire. An Antarctic imaginary infused the mobile launch units from their inception. As an organisation, the CNES took inspiration for its structure from the TAAF administration, established in 1955.[29] Officials of the CNES sought the advice of Paul-Emile Victor, charismatic founder of the organisation Expéditions Polaires Françaises (French Polar Expeditions (EPF)), on their first mobile launches in the Northern Hemisphere (in Iceland and Norway). Paul-Emile Victor, or 'PEV' to his friends and followers, was a celebrated French ethnographer and polar explorer whose organisation worked with the French government and TAAF administration to staff and supply Dumont d'Urville base in Antarctica.[30] His collaboration with the CNES would continue in 1966 and 1967 as CNES rocketry teams prepared for their Antarctic expedition. Travelling with the CNES team aboard the cargo ship *Thala Dan* en route from Hobart, Tasmania, to Terre Adélie, Victor would capture the attention and imagination of the rocketry scientists, engineers and technicians with his 'Antarctic University' or 'Université Paul-Emile Victor': shipboard seminars where he lectured about life in Antarctic conditions, and where participants in the 'seventeenth expedition' could present their experiments to the rest of the team.[31] Even the structure and organisation of the mobile launch units themselves drew inspiration from earlier Antarctic voyages. Marius Le Fèvre was inspired by the organisational ethos of Norwegian polar explorer Roald Amundsen and his use of the 'simplest and surest' materials and techniques, which influenced Le Fèvre's own work as launch director leading teams of engineers and technicians on rocketry campaigns from Iceland to Terre Adélie.[32] Le Fèvre and others involved in the French sounding rocket programme, like many space scientists and engineers, consciously placed themselves within a genealogy of primarily white and male explorers of Euro-American colonial mythology.[33] And like the work of the white, male explorers who had come before them, the mobile launch unit's scientific achievements also served to inscribe French power on the landscape, colonising it for French science while reaffirming not only France's Antarctic sovereignty claims but also the 'radiance' of France.

The 1967 launch of four Dragon-type rockets from France's Dumont d'Urville base in Terre Adélie, Antarctica, was perhaps the most emblematic campaign for the mobile launch unit, hailed by French officials as the first sounding rocket launches from the icy continent.[34] The purpose of the rocket launches was to investigate how particles from solar wind interacted with charged particles in the ionosphere, and how that interaction corresponded to magnetic lines of force.[35] Understanding the effects of solar wind on the upper atmosphere was vital for work with radiocommunications, satellite launches and functionality, and more ambitious rocketry programmes (such as the goal of launching humans into space). Such ionospheric activity is particularly evident in the atmosphere above the Dumont d'Urville base, thanks to its proximity to the magnetic South Pole. Participants in the expedition and state officials alike made much of the specificity of the magnetosphere above Terre Adélie. In his account of his work in the Antarctic launch campaign, engineer Pierre Simon was delighted that 'the magnetic South Pole is French ... so that we can experiment in our home, with French equipment!'.[36] Preparing a presentation for the eighth conference of the Scientific Committee on Antarctic Research (SCAR) in 1964, TAAF Chief Administrator Pierre Rolland wrote 'In Terre Adélie, the simple presence of the magnetic pole near the French base suffices, if it is necessary, to justify the base's existence on the international scale.'[37]

But Terre Adélie was not entirely French. Eight years prior to the Antarctic launch campaign, Article IV of the 1959 Antarctic Treaty had 'frozen' all territorial sovereignty claims on the Antarctic continent, pausing but not solving the dispute among claimant nations (France, Argentina, Australia, Chile, New Zealand, Norway and the United Kingdom) and non-claimant nations, including the United States and USSR. The Antarctic Treaty allowed for free circulation of personnel and free construction of bases, regardless of whether these bases were constructed on territory claimed by another nation. Much of France's Antarctic policy, therefore, and the state's primary motivation for continuing to fund a costly Antarctic base, was to prevent other nations from infringing upon the relatively small French claim and to keep France's Antarctic presence under the control of the French Overseas Ministry. As an official wrote, and underlined, in an analysis of the Antarctic Treaty for the French cabinet, 'It is evident that if France does not maintain a scientific station in Terre Adélie that responds to the needs of researchers, it will be, in fact as in law, impossible to object to the installation of foreign bases.'[38] The project of launching French rockets from a French base in the French Antarctic functioned as an expensive but showy attempt to maintain France's position as an Antarctic scientific leader while simultaneously reaffirming its occupation of Antarctic territory. To a certain extent, both goals were achieved. Data from the Antarctic launches proved valuable in refining the results of earlier experiments and creating new models for charged particle interactions in the magnetosphere. And the rockets earned Dumont d'Urville Base a visit by helicopter from military personnel on the icebreaker USCGC *Eastwind*, involved in the United States' Operation Deep Freeze of 1967 – verifying, presumably, that the launches had involved no nuclear testing, and looking into French launch infrastructure in Terre Adélie.[39]

Like the Antarctic experiments, French sounding rocket launches on the Kerguelen Islands took advantage of the islands' unique geophysical and political situation. Located just above the 60° latitude line, which forms the border of the Antarctic Treaty's jurisdiction, the Kerguelen Islands are a small, uninhabited archipelago claimed by France with varying degrees of intensity since 1772.[40] The archipelago is a geomagnetic conjugate with the town of Sogra in Arkanghelsk, Russia, meaning that Sogra and the Kerguelen Islands are located at opposite ends of the same magnetic field line. It is rare for conjugate points in each hemisphere to be located on land, and the uniqueness of the Kerguelen Islands served to justify continued funding for geophysical research there.[41] The geomagnetic link to Arkanghelsk also provided a clear structure for scientific collaboration with the Soviet Union. Multiple collaborative experiments occurred, but the crowning achievement of the CNES mobile launch units was Project Araks, or 'Artificial Radiation and Aurora between Kerguelen and Sogra', in 1974/75. In this experiment, teams from CNES, Intercosmos (the USSR's space agency) and NASA worked together to launch two Eridan sounding rockets from the Kerguelen Islands. Each rocket was equipped with an electron 'gun' to shoot a stream of electrons along the magnetic field line, as well as sophisticated measuring equipment designed by both French and Soviet laboratories.[42] Measurements were taken on the Kerguelen Islands, at the conjugate point in Arkhangelsk and at various other stations along the magnetic field line. The results obtained from the multiple experiments aboard the rockets created a flurry of scientific publications in Russian, French and English, and provided a basis for further experimentation within earth's magnetosphere.[43]

Institutional histories laud the mobile launch campaigns as 'the spear-head of the CNES' for international scientific collaboration.[44] Through rocket launches on the Kerguelen Islands, France cultivated diplomatic and scientific ties to the USSR, as CNES became the first international partner of Intercosmos.[45] Meanwhile, participants in the Terre Adélie and Kerguelen Island launch campaigns primarily remembered the singularity of both locations: their remoteness, their inaccessibility and the difficult terrain and weather conditions that launch officials had to take into account, along with the rarity of their own experience. Thus CNES rocketry team member Claude Salmon recalled 'What luck to have participated in that beautiful adventure!'.[46] But officials in administration of the French Southern and Antarctic Lands also highlighted how that 'beautiful adventure' depended on a continued French presence in the Antarctic and Southern Ocean region. In his 1976 report on scientific research in the French Southern and Antarctic Lands, Professor Michel Alliot praised French rocketry teams' 'remarkable' work in launching from the Kerguelen Islands. He went on to link France's achievement in space science with its imperial holdings in the Antarctic and Southern Ocean region, noting that these possessions offered 'a non-negligible asset that permits France to participate in large international programmes'.[47] France's role as a producer of internationally significant scientific research was predicated on its existing imperial claims and infrastructure. Even as the French state dealt with the aftermath of the Algerian War and widespread decolonisation, the continued occupation of Terre Adélie and the Kerguelen Islands facilitated the scientific achievement so lauded by De Gaulle and his successors as a form of 'radiance' that would make up for lost grandeur on the imperial stage. As new and different as they seemed, the extremely visible and highly publicised display of rocket launches on the Antarctic continent relied on the existing political and logistical infrastructure of the French empire, and was inflected with many of the same dynamics that characterised French colonialism.

'Europe's Spaceport': Kourou, French Guiana

Back in Algeria, the imminent closure of the CIEES led to a search for alternative rocket launch and testing sites that began as soon as the Evian Accords were signed. The list of possible equatorial launch sites reads like a tour of the twentieth-century French empire, with locations in French Guiana, Madagascar, Guadeloupe, Somalia, Mauritania, Sri Lanka and French Polynesia, as well as alternatives in Australia, Trinidad, the Seychelles and Brazil.[48] The winning candidate, after officials tallied up the positive 'points' for each possible base, was French Guiana. In addition to features such as a deepwater port, multiple possible launch trajectories and an existing air-field, CNES officials prioritised locations with a 'stable political situation' so that the base would not be compromised by 'a change of local political regime'.[49] French officials preferred an equatorial launch site to a metropolitan one for both practical and political reasons. Launching rockets from the Equator allows the rocket to take advantage of the higher velocity of earth's orbit at the Equator, adding up to 460 metres per second to the initial launch velocity and facilitating travel through the upper atmosphere and into orbit. In addition, officials predicted that building a launch facility in a less developed area would cause less social unrest than building a rocket testing site in metropolitan France, where resistance was all but guaranteed. The creation of a launch facility in the region would tie Guiana, already a department of France, more firmly to France on both a social and economic level. During his March 1964 official visit to Guiana, General de Gaulle promised vaguely that 'We will create – you, here, and France with you – a great French work in Guiana.'[50] He implied that such a work would lead not only to material economic benefits for the population of Guiana but also to increased French interest in, and support for, the overseas department. Four years later, the launch site at Kourou, French Guiana, was inaugurated by the launch of a Véronique sounding rocket in April 1968. As the permanent launch facilities were not yet ready, the mobile launch unit was used, employed in Kourou the same way that it had been used in Antarctica and the Kerguelen Islands.[51] The still unfinished launch site would be baptised the Centre spatial guyanais (CSG).

From its initial colonisation in the seventeenth century to its status as an overseas department of France today, Guiana has a long and complicated imperial history. Largely covered by rainforest, the region is home to several groups of Indigenous peoples, including the Arawak, Carib, Teko and Kaliña. Historians mark a series of halting attempts at settler colonisation throughout the seventeenth and eighteenth centuries, including through the deportation of political prisoners and recalcitrant priests during the French Revolution.[52] These largely ill-fated attempts at settlement gave Guiana a reputation as an 'unhealthy' region, and population remained low even as settlers attempted to establish plantations for cotton, sugar, annatto and other secondary crops (indigo, cinnamon, pepper, cloves) with the labour of enslaved Africans. The French abolition of slavery in 1848 led to a new period in Guyanese history marked by uneasy economic and social relations between white settlers, mixed-race 'people of colour' and newly freed Black labourers, as well as Chinese and other Southeast Asian migrants, Maroons and their descendants, and Indigenous peoples.[53] The institution of penal transportation as a punishment for severe crimes and political dissent in 1852, and the ensuing establishment of a series of penal establishments, or *bagnes*, across Guiana, further complicated the colony's social and economic situation.[54] The region around Kourou was part of this constellation of penitentiaries and labour camps, with a penitentiary located in the city proper and infamous establishments for 'incorrigible' prisoners and political detainees located on the nearby Iles du Salut.[55] Transportation as a method of punishment officially ended in 1938, but Guiana's penal establishments were not dissolved until after the Second World War. Construction of the CSG at Kourou, then a city with fewer than 700 residents, was another episode in the long history of French attempts at centralised economic development of French Guiana.

Kourou lacked the spectacular visual isolation that had made Hammaguir so 'splendid' for Jacques Blamont, but that did not stop French officials from treating the area like another empty space – another Sahara or Antarctica. Workers from the CNES had the impression that they were building a launch site on empty terrain; Marius Le Fèvre recalled that 'the city of Kourou was nothing but an immense construction site'.[56] Yet the construction of the space centre required the clearance and expulsion of the village of Malmanoury, populated by Guyanese creoles and Saramaka maroons, who resented their forced move into tiny public housing apartments in the city of Kourou proper.[57] Local reactions to the creation of the CSG were mixed: the availability of electricity and running water came with higher costs of living and increased racial segregation and economic inequality in the region.[58] Staff at the CSG glossed over the role of the French state in displacing locals and changing their living conditions. Instead, they viewed their interactions with Kourou's populations through a racialised lens – not as astronauts on a strange planet, as in their 'lunar' encounters with the 'blue men' of the desert, but as settler colonists mourning the loss of an Eden that they had helped destroy. During his first trip to Guiana for the CNES, Marius Le Fèvre slipped back into the role of amateur ethnographer as he described 'a dreamland' populated by the (Black) Guyanese, who were 'radiant, kind, straightforward, knowing how to laugh, dance, and amuse themselves, full of humour'. Leaning into long-standing colonial stereotypes, he continued by lamenting that developing Kourou had caused the Guyanese 'to enter into our consumerist world'.[59] But by treating Kourou as a *terra nullius*, Le Fèvre and his compatriots avoided considering the role that they had played in bringing the 'consumerist world' to French Guiana, or the social and economic implications of the construction of the CSG.

In spite of ambitious visions for the CSG, sounding rockets in Kourou were launched by mobile launch units while construction was still underway. The first rocketry experiments in Guiana investigated solar radiation and ultraviolet astronomy, using the altitude reached by Véronique and

Eridan sounding rockets to obtain full-spectrum images of stellar radiation undiluted by passage through earth's atmosphere. The ambitious Project FAUST (Fusées astronomiques pour l'étude de l'ultraviolet stellaire, or Rockets for the Study of Ultraviolet Stellar Astronomy) of 1974 aimed to refine and economise ultraviolet astronomy. The project took advantage not only of Kourou's coastal location, which allowed film and experimental data to be recovered from the rocket's nose cones once they had parachuted into the ocean, but also of the wide range of visibility offered by the Guyanese skies, ideal for astronomical observation. While project managers envisioned around 30 launches, only four were carried out. Major budget cuts to CNES in 1974, and the reorientation of French spatial policy around European autonomy in terms of satellite launch power and telecommunications technology, led to the end of the sounding rocket programme and the restructuring of the rocketry division as the division of 'Systems and Scientific Projects'.[60] The CNES pivoted to focus on the development and testing of the larger Ariane rocket, designed to launch satellites into orbit. Meanwhile, members of the CNES rocketry teams moved on to other projects within French and European space programmes. The 'heroic period' of rocketry had ended, according to Marius Le Fèvre as he closed this episode in his memoirs, but it had left its mark through the creation and institutionalisation of the CNES, and the construction of a permanent base for rocket launches in Kourou.[61] Meanwhile, the long history of French colonialism, so integral to the rocketry programme, continues to make its legacy felt in French and European space science.

Since the end of the sounding rocket programme, the CSG has become one of the primary launch sites for orbital satellites, hosting Ariane, Vega and Soyuz rockets through CNES's partnership with the European Space Agency (ESA). The ESA website states, with no trace of irony, that 'Europe's Spaceport is situated in the north-east of South America', and goes on to highlight the spaceport's 'high levels of efficiency, safety and reliability' for satellite launches.[62] The CNES does more to publicly acknowledge Guiana's regional specificity, pointing out that 'while the CSG grants access to the grand infinity of space, it is also situated locally in a small, peripheral overseas territory, with which it maintains a strong relationship in matters of development'.[63] The presence of the CSG is not so simple for the Guyanese people, however, and the placement of 'Europe's Spaceport' has not gone uncontested. Protests erupted over further development of the CSG in 1994 and in 2005.[64] The largest protest movement thus far lasted from 16 March to 21 April 2017. The movement began with demonstrations in Kourou, but soon spread throughout Guiana as the collective Pou Lagwiyann Dekolé ('Launching Guiana') demanded that the metropolitan government address high crime rates, high unemployment, widespread economic inequality, the lack of clean drinking water and other infrastructure, and high rates of migration from neighbouring countries.[65] With its close ties to the French metropole as well as global satellite infrastructure, the CSG became a focal point for protesters. Strikes, protests and highway barricades led to the cancellation of a planned Ariane 5 launch and multiple delays in the CSG's operations while shutting down much of the rest of the country as well. The unrest prompted a visit from French Interior Minister Mathias Fecke and Overseas Minister Ericka Bareigts, and eventually led to the 'Guiana Accord', signed by Guyanese leaders and the national government on 21 April 2017. The accord promised an immediate €1 billion investment in local police forces, schools and infrastructure such as roads; €2 billion to be invested later in high-priority areas; and 400,000 ha of land to be ceded to Indigenous peoples of the region.[66] The CNES also got involved, allocating €10 million to develop local education and research, fund refurbishments and medical infrastructure in Kourou, and promote tourist sites such as the CNES-controlled Iles du Salut.[67] While Pou Lagwiyann Dekolé was not an outright independence movement, activists with the collective highlighted the colonial treatment of Guiana in comparison to other French departments. Two years after the movement and the government promises it prompted, few changes had been seen: the expansion of police and law enforcement infrastructure had not been matched by a similar expansion in access to education or medical care.[68] 'Europe's Spaceport' remains a local point of contention and a physical reminder of the colonial nature of France's space programme.

Conclusion

The French sounding rocket programme launched from Hammaguir in colonised Algeria and ended at Kourou in 'departmentalised' French Guiana, traversing French Antarctic territory in Terre Adélie and the Kerguelen Islands along the way. In the history of French rocketry, Antarctica is not an 'exceptional' zone. Instead, it is emblematic of the French colonial project around the globe. Regardless of whether or not these regions were inhabited, CNES and French state officials treated all launch sites as *terra nullius*: unclaimed, unpopulated and uncontested. Hammaguir was a flat plain 'offering nothing but sand and stones'; Terre Adélie presented an 'extraordinary silence' and an 'almost absolute calm'; Kourou was nothing but vast jungle and 'an immense construction site'.[69] For the scientists and technicians involved in the sounding rocket programme, political questions revolved around budgetary issues, institutionalisation and international collaboration – not the nature and the legal status of the territories from which they launched. The histories and cultures of each area were essentially irrelevant, making the desert of Hammaguir or the jungle of Kourou seem just as unpopulated as the tundra of the Kerguelen Islands or the rocky icescapes of Terre Adélie. The story of French sounding rockets became a story of scientific, institutional and geopolitical triumph. As Jacques Blamont argued, sounding rockets were 'the principal tool, unique [to France], for the nation's acquisition of one of the essential aspects of state power in the twenty-first century'.[70] Following Blamont and the other architects of French rocketry and space science, institutional historians have taken for granted the wide-ranging geography of the sounding rocket programme, and have focused instead on its national, European and global effects. But closer attention to the territory of these launches reveals how, even in a period of widespread decolonisation, the sounding rocket programme depended on and reinforced French sovereignty over colonised territory such as Algeria, Guiana, and France's Antarctic claims. The sounding rocket programme created the French space programme, but France's empire made the sounding rocket programme possible.

A terrestrial view of the French space programme brings to light the multiple ways imperial territory was mobilised to make space exploration possible. It also puts into the same frame of reference various imperial territories that are often studied separately – thus, analysis of the French sounding rocket programme brings together Algeria, Antarctica and French Guiana as sites of sounding rocket launches and experimentation. This approach has the added benefit of folding the history of Antarctica, long isolated as a story of scientific diplomacy or human triumph, back into the context of imperial expansion and decolonisation in the latter half of the twentieth century. It reveals how officials' concerns over Antarctic sovereignty animated the types of scientific research they chose to support, and how the spectacle of sounding rocket launches served as both symbol for and method of imperial rule. The sounding rocket programme is not the only aspect of the French space programme to take advantage of France's remaining empire. As French and European space programmes pivoted to prioritise European autonomy in telecommunications and launch capacities, ground-based satellite tracking stations were constructed in French colonial territories such as New Caledonia, Tahiti, French Guiana, the Kerguelen Islands and Terre Adélie. Satellite tracking networks continue to link French territories in the Antarctic and Southern Ocean to a vast network of ground stations in the wide-ranging remnants of Europe's transoceanic empires. Continued attention to these extraterrestrial geographies allows us to see and interrogate the vestiges of European empire that remain critical to French and European space science, satellite technology and polar geopolitics today.

Notes

1 See M. J . Peterson, 'The Use of Analogies in Developing Outer Space Law', *International Organization* 51:2 (1997), 245–74; Amel Kerrest, 'Outer Space as International Space: Lessons from Antarctica', in Paul Arthur Berkman, Michael A. Lang, David W. H. Walton and Oran R. Young (eds), *Science Diplomacy: Antarctica, Science, and the Governance of International Spaces* (Washington, DC: Smithsonian Institution Scholarly Press, 2011), pp. 133–42.

2 Günther Seibert, *The History of Sounding Rockets and Their Contribution to European Space Research* (Noordwijk: European Space Agency, 2006), p. 13.

3 See Dian Olson Belanger, *Deep Freeze: The United States, the International Geophysical Year, and the Origins of Antarctica's Age of Science* (Boulder: University Press of Colorado: 2010 [2006]); Naomi Oreskes and John Krige (eds), *Science and Technology in the Global Cold War* (Cambridge, MA: MIT Press, 2014); even Asif Siddiqi focuses on the USA and USSR in his call for a 'global history' of space exploration in Asif A. Siddiqi, 'Competing Technologies, National(ist) Narratives, and Universal Claims: Toward a Global History of Space Exploration', *Technology and Culture* 51:2 (2010), 425–43.

4 Walter A. McDougall, 'Space-Age Europe: Gaullism, Euro-Gaullism, and the American Dilemma', *Technology and Culture* 26:2 (1985), 179–203.

5 On French technological 'radiance' in response to loss of empire and national prestige, see McDougall, 'Space-Age Europe'; Gabrielle Hecht, *The Radiance of France: Nuclear Power and National Identity after World War II* (Cambridge, MA: MIT Press, 2009 [1998]). On 'internal colonisation', see Kristin Ross, *Fast Cars, Clean Bodies: Decolonization and the Reordering of French Culture* (Cambridge, MA: MIT Press, 1995), p. 7. McDougall also argues that De Gaulle 'liquidated imperial France' because he drained French resources and earned disapproval from the international community; 'Space-Age Europe', p. 181. Recent histories of French empire and decolonisation have demonstrated instead France's long-term efforts to cling to its overseas empire: see Todd Shepard, *The Invention of Decolonization: The Algerian War and the Remaking of France* (Ithaca, NY: Cornell University Press, 2008); Frederick Cooper, *Citizenship between Empire and Nation: Remaking France and French Africa, 1945–1960* (Princeton, NJ: Princeton University Press, 2014). It is worth noting that France maintains substantial overseas territories of varying legal statuses in spite of this supposed 'liquidation'.

6 Quoted by McDougall, 'Space-Age Europe', p. 186.

7 'Aeronomy' was an early term for the study of the upper atmosphere.

8 Marius Le Fèvre, *L'espace, du rêve à la réalité: Un grand bond pour l'Europe spatiale* (Paris: Editions Edite, 2010), p. 37. This and all future translations from French are mine.

9 Jacques Blamont, 'Les premières expériences d'aéronomie en France', in Brigitte Schürmann (ed.), *Actes de la première rencontre de l'IFHE sur l'essor des recherches spatiales en France: Des premières expériences scientifiques aux premiers satellites, October 24–25, 2000, ESA SP-472* (Noordwijk: European Space Agency, 2001), pp. 31–41 (p. 38).

10 'Hammaguir' is a contraction of 'Hamada du Guir' that quickly became the use-name for this region to its French occupiers.

11 See Dominique Kalifa, *Biribi: Les bagnes coloniaux de l'armée française* (Paris: Perrin, 2009).

12 Anne Charaudeau, 'Les réfugiés espagnols dans les camps d'internement en Afrique du Nord', *Hommes et migrations* 1158 (October 1992), 23–8 (p. 26), DOI: 10.3406/homig.1992.1894.

13 Alice Gorman, 'The Archaeology of Space Exploration', *The Sociological Review* 57:1 (May 2009), 132–45; Philippe Varnoteaux, '70 ans du CIEES', *Espace & Temps: Bulletin d'information de l'Institut français d'histoire de l'espace* 20 (June 2017), 3–13 (p. 10).

14 Blamont, 'Les premières expériences', p. 40.

15 Jacques Blamont, 'Préface', in Hervé Moulin (ed.), *Les débuts de la recherche spatiale française: Au temps des fusées-sondes* (Paris: Editions Edite, 2007), pp. 11–15 (p. 14).

16 Blamont, 'Préface', p. 14.

17 Le Fèvre had a long career in French space exploration. He would go on to become a mission chief of the mobile launch unit campaign, the director of operations at the Centre spatial guyanais (CSG), and director of ESA's European Space Research and Technology Centre (ESTEC) from 1985 to 1996.

18 Le Fèvre, *L'espace*, p. 39. For a discussion of the 'space age'/'Stone Age' metaphor, see Gorman, 'The Archaeology of Space Exploration', especially pp. 134–8.

19 Quoted in Gorman, 'The Archaeology of Space Exploration', p. 136.

20 See Jan Jansen, 'Politics of Remembrance, Colonialism and the Algerian War of Independence in France', in Małgorzata Pakier and Bo Stråth (eds), *A European Memory? Contested Histories and Politics of Remembrance* (New York: Berghahn Books, 2010), pp. 275–93.

21 Roxane Panchasi, ' "No Hiroshima in Africa": The Algerian War and the Question of French Nuclear Tests in the Sahara', *History of the Present* 9:1 (2019), 84–112 (p. 87).

22 Blamont, 'Préface', p. 15.

23 Panchasi, 'No Hiroshima in Africa', p. 91.

24 Varnoteaux, '70 ans du CIEES', *Espace & Temps: Bulletin d'information de l'Institut Français d'Histoire de l'Espace* 20 (June 2017), 7.

25 Marcel Gilli and Hervé Moulin, 'Le temps des Comités', in Moulin, *Les débuts de la recherche spatiale française*, pp. 45–68 (p. 54).

26 Varnoteaux, '70 ans du CIEES', p. 8.

27 The 'mobile launch units' broke down rocket launch infrastructure into several standard-sized, climate-controlled metal containers that could be transported by train, plane or ship. The only necessary infrastructure at the launch sites comprised two concrete platforms: one for setting up the launch ramp and its mobile shelter, the other for building a sheltered area in which to assemble the rockets.

28 Blamont, 'Préface', p. 15.

29 Observers at the time compared the two organisations; see Michel Alliot's report on 'La recherche scientifique dans le territoire des TAAF', 1976, Archives nationales Pierrefitte-sur-Seine (AN), 20010098/63.

30 Paul-Emile Victor's career would also make for an interesting study in the colonial roots of Antarctic exploration. A US Air Force engineer and pilot turned ethnographer, PEV spent years with various Inuit groups in Greenland, writing prolifically about their ways of life and working with French institutions such as the Musée de l'Homme to publish his work. He became interested in Antarctic exploration in the 1950s, spearheading the construction of Dumont d'Urville Base in 1959. His strong personality marked the early era of French Antarctic expansion from 1956 to 1976.

31 As recalled by Pierre Simon, 'Campagne de Terre Adélie 1966–1967: Le point de vue de l'Ingénieur', *Nos premières années*, http://nospremieresannees.fr/fusee_sonde_tout/fu09-campagne%20terre%20adelie/fu09d-texte_simonp/texte01.html (accessed 13 May 2021).

32 Le Fèvre, *L'espace*, p. 66.

33 See Peter Redfield, 'The Half-Life of Empire in Outer Space', *Social Studies of Science* 32:5 (2002), 791–825; Fraser Macdonald, 'Anti-*Astropolitik*: Outer Space and the Orbit of Geography', *Progress in Human Geography* 31:5 (2007), 592–615; Simon Naylor and James R. Ryan (eds), *New Spaces of Exploration: Geographies of Discovery in the Twentieth Century* (London: I.B. Tauris, 2010).

34 The United States, USSR and Argentina had previously launched rockets from the continent, and these rockets contained instrumentation to probe the upper atmosphere, rendering this French claim doubtful. However, the Dragon-type rockets launched in 1967 were the largest launched from the Antarctic continent to date.

35 Jean-Jacques Berthelier, Jean About, Jean-François Crifo, Jean-Claude Renou and Pierre Simon, 'Les campagnes "ionosphère"', in Moulin, *Les débuts de la recherche spatiale française*, pp. 259–69 (p. 266).

36 Simon, 'Campagne de Terre Adélie'.

37 Administrateur Supérieur des TAAF Pierre Rolland, note on 'Les activités scientifiques poursuivies dans le Territoire des TAAF', for the 8th SCAR conference, Paris 1964, AN 20070432/1.

38 'Note sur l'organisation du Territoire TAAF', 11 December 1962, AN 20160686/1.

39 Le Fèvre, *L'espace*, p. 120.

40 During ATS negotiations, French negotiators worked to keep the Kerguelen Islands and the Crozet archipelago out of Antarctic Treaty jurisdiction and to maintain full national sovereignty over both archipelagos. See Chavelli Sulikowski, 'The French Connection: The Role of France in the Antarctic Treaty System', in Anne-Marie Brady (ed.), *The Emerging Politics of Antarctica* (Abingdon: Routledge, 2012), pp. 163–90.

41 'La Recherche scientifique dans les TAAF', Direction des laboratoires scientifiques des TAAF, December 1969, AN 20160645/12.

42 For more detail, see Bernard Morlet, G. Charles, A. Hirtzman, and J. Lavergnat, 'Il y a 20 ans à Kerguelen: La campagne ARAKS octobre 1974/février 1975',

Terres australes et antarctiques françaises 64 (April–June 1975), 39–62; Robert Gendrin, 'The French–Soviet "Araks" Experiment', *Space Science Reviews* 15 (1974), 905–31.

43 Many of these publications can be found in NASA's Astrophysics Data System.
44 Jan-Claude Renou and Jean-Pierre Sanfourche, 'Les activités fusées-sondes du CNES', in Moulin, *Les débuts de la recherche spatiale française*, pp. 69–80 (p. 72).
45 See Arlène Ammar-Israël (ed.), *Les 50 ans de coopération spatiale, France–URSS/Russie: Genèse et évolutions 1966–2016* (Chantilly: Tessier & Ashpool, 2016).
46 Claude Salmon, 'Les lancements des fusées-sondes "Dragon" depuis la "Terre Adélie"', *Nos premières années*, http://nospremieresannees.fr/fusee_sonde_ tout/fu09-campagne%20terre%20adelie/fu09c-texte_salmon/texte03.html (accessed 13 May 2021).
47 Alliot, 'La recherche scientifique dans le territoire des TAAF'.
48 Philippe Varnoteaux, *L'aventure spatiale française: De 1945 à la naissance d'Ariane* (Paris: Nouveau Monde Editions, 2015), p. 239.
49 Quoted by Peter Redfield, *Space in the Tropics: From Convicts to Rockets in French Guiana* (Berkeley: University of California Press, 2000), p. 126.
50 Varnoteaux, *L'aventure spatiale française*, p. 239.
51 Le Fèvre, *L'espace*, p. 129.
52 See Miranda Spieler, *Empire and Underworld* (Cambridge, MA: Harvard University Press, 2012).
53 See Serge Mam Lam Fouck, *La Guyane française: Au temps de l'esclavage, de l'or et de la francisation (1802–1946)* (Petit-Bourg: Ibis Rouge Editions, 1999).
54 See Stephen Toth, *Beyond Papillon: The French Overseas Penal Colonies, 1854–1952* (Lincoln: University of Nebraska Press, 2006); Jean-Lucien Sanchez, *A perpétuité: Relégués au bagne de Guyane* (Paris: Vendémaire, 2013); Marine Coquet, 'Totalisation carcérale en terre coloniale: La *carcérali-sation* à Saint-Laurent-du-Maroni (XIXe–XXe siècles)', *Cultures & conflits* 90 (2013), 59–76.
55 These islands include 'Devil's Island' or 'Ile du Diable', where Alfred Dreyfus lived in solitary confinement from 1895 to 1899. Convict life in these penitentiaries and the other penal establishments around Guiana was made infamous by the descriptions of Albert Londres in his 1923 reportage *Au bagne*. Peter Redfield connects the history of Guiana's *bagnes* to the establishment of the CSG in *Space in the Tropics*. In terms of historical continuity between *bagne* and spaceport, it is interesting to note that Kourou's Hôtel des Roches was built over the old pénitencier des Roches, and that the CNES now owns the Iles du Salut – and evacuates them on launch days.
56 Le Fèvre, *L'espace*, p. 132.
57 Alice Gorman, 'La Terre et L'Espace: Rockets, Prisons, Protests, and Heritage in Australia and French Guiana', *Archaeologies: Journal of the World Archaeological Congress* 3:2 (2007), 153–68 (p. 161).

58 Redfield, *Space in the Tropics*, p. 133.
59 Le Fèvre, *L'espace*, p. 129.
60 Renou and Sanfourche, 'Les activités fusées-sondes', p. 76.
61 Le Fèvre, *L'espace*, p. 142.
62 European Space Agency, 'Enabling and Support: Europe's Spaceport', www. esa.int/Enabling_Support/Space_Transportation/Europe_s_Spaceport/Europe_s_ Spaceport2 (accessed 13 May 2021).
63 Centre national d'études spatiales, 'Kourou: Le Centre spatial guyanais, le port spatial européen', https://geoimage.cnes.fr/fr/geoimage/kourou-le-centre-spatial-guyanais-le-port-spatial-europeen (accessed 13 May 2021).
64 Redfield, 'The Half-Life of Empire'; Gorman, 'La Terre et L'Espace'.
65 According to *Newsweek*, the name of this collective was taken from a 1997 protest song by rapper Freaky Fan called 'La fusée décolle, mais la Guyane reste au sol' ('The Rocket Takes Off, but Guiana Stays on the Ground'). Katherine Hignett, 'French Guiana's Cutting-Edge Space Center Will Launch NASA's James Webb Space Telescope – but Locals Say They're Being Left Behind', *Newsweek*, 17 January 2019, www.newsweek.com/2019/01/25/fired-1292586.html (accessed 13 May 2021).
66 France, 'Accord de Guyane du 21 avril 2017: Protocole "Pou Lagwiyann dékolé"', *Journal officiel de la République française* 0103, 2 May 2017, www.legifrance.gouv.fr/jorf/id/JORFTEXT000034519630/ (accessed 13 May 2021).
67 Centre national d'études spatiales, 'CNES in Action. Education, Environment and Regional Development: CNES Steps into the Breach in French Guiana', *CNES Mag* 78 (November 2018), 21.
68 Clair Rivière, 'La fusée décolle, mais la Guyane reste au sol', *CQFD* 165, May 2018, http://cqfd-journal.org/La-fusee-decolle-mais-la-Guyane (accessed 13 May 2021).
69 Blamont, 'Préface', p. 14; Salmon, 'Les lancements de Fusées-sondes "Dragon"'; Le Fèvre, *L'espace*, p. 132.
70 Blamont, 'Préface', p. 15.

Bibliography

Ammar-Israël, Arlène (ed.). *Les 50 ans de coopération spatiale, France–URSS/ Russie: Genèse et évolutions 1966–2016*. Chantilly: Tessier & Ashpool, 2016.

Belanger, Dian Olson. *Deep Freeze: The United States, the International Geophysical Year, and the Origins of Antarctica's Age of Science*. Boulder: University Press of Colorado, 2010 [2006].

Berthelier, Jean-Jacques, Jean About, Jean-François Crifo, Jean-Claude Renou and Pierre Simon, 'Les campagnes "ionosphère"'. In *Les débuts de la recherche spatiale française: Au temps des fusées-sondes*, ed. Hervé Moulin, pp. 259–69. Paris: Editions Edite, 2007.

Blamont, Jacques. 'Préface'. In *Les débuts de la recherche spatiale française: Au temps des fusées-sondes*, ed. Hervé Moulin, pp. 11–15. Paris: Editions Edite, 2007.

Blamont, Jacques. 'Les premières expériences d'aéronomie en France'. In *Actes de la première rencontre de l'IFHE sur l'essor des recherches spatiales en France: Des premières expériences scientifiques aux premiers satellites, October 24–25, 2000*, ed. Brigitte Schürmann, pp. 31–41. ESA SP-472. Noordwijk: European Space Agency, 2001.

Centre national d'études spatiales (CNES). 'CNES in Action. Education, Environment and Regional Development: CNES Steps into the Breach in French Guiana', *CNES Mag* 78 (November 2018): 21.

Centre national d'études spatiales (CNES). 'Kourou: Le Centre spatial guyanais, le port spatial européen'. https://geoimage.cnes.fr/fr/geoimage/kourou-le-centre-spatial-guyanais-le-port-spatial-europeen. Accessed 13 May 2021.

Charaudeau, Anne. 'Les réfugiés espagnols dans les camps d'internement en Afrique du Nord'. *Hommes et migrations* 1158 (October 1992): 23–8. DOI: 10.3406/homig.1992.1894.

Cooper, Frederick. *Citizenship between Empire and Nation: Remaking France and French Africa, 1945–1960*. Princeton, NJ: Princeton University Press, 2014.

Coquet, Marine. 'Totalisation carcérale en terre coloniale: La *carcéralisation* à Saint-Laurent-du-Maroni (XIXe–XXe siècles)'. *Cultures & conflits* 90 (2013): 59–76.

European Space Agency. 'Enabling and Support: Europe's Spaceport'. www.esa.int/Enabling_Support/Space_Transportation/Europe_s_Spaceport/Europe_s_Spaceport2. Accessed 13 May 2021.

Fouck, Serge Mam Lam. *La Guyane française: Au temps de l'esclavage, de l'or et de la francisation (1802–1946)*. Petit-Bourg: Ibis Rouge Editions, 1999.

France. 'Accord de Guyane du 21 avril 2017: Protocole "Pou Lagwiyann dékolé"'. *Journal officiel de la République française* 0103, 2 May 2017. www.legifrance.gouv.fr/jorf/id/JORFTEXT000034519630/. Accessed 13 May 2021.

Gendrin, Robert. 'The French–Soviet "Araks" Experiment'. *Space Science Reviews* 15 (1974): 905–31.

Gilli, Marcel and Hervé Moulin. 'Le temps des Comités'. In *Les débuts de la recherche spatiale française: Au temps des fusées-sondes*, ed. Hervé Moulin, pp. 45–68. Paris: Editions Edite, 2007.

Gorman, Alice. 'The Archaeology of Space Exploration'. *The Sociological Review* 57, no. 1 (2009): 132–45.

Gorman, Alice. 'La Terre et L'Espace: Rockets, Prisons, Protests, and Heritage in Australia and French Guiana'. *Archaeologies: Journal of the World Archaeological Congress* 3, no. 2 (2007): 153–68.

Hecht, Gabrielle. *The Radiance of France: Nuclear Power and National Identity after World War II*. Cambridge, MA: MIT Press, 2009 [1998].

Hignett, Katherine. 'French Guiana's Cutting-Edge Space Center Will Launch NASA's James Webb Space Telescope – but Locals Say They're Being Left Behind'. *Newsweek*, 17 January 2019. www.newsweek.com/2019/01/25/fired-1292586.html. Accessed 13 May 2021.

Jansen, Jan. 'Politics of Remembrance, Colonialism and the Algerian War of Independence in France'. In *A European Memory? Contested Histories and Politics of Remembrance*, ed. Małgorzata Pakier and Bo Stråth, pp. 275–93. New York: Berghahn Books, 2010.

Kalifa, Dominique. *Biribi: Les bagnes coloniaux de l'armée française*. Paris: Perrin, 2009.

Kerrest, Amel. 'Outer Space as International Space: Lessons from Antarctica'. In *Science Diplomacy: Antarctica, Science, and the Governance of International*

Spaces, ed. Paul Arthur Berkman, Michael A. Lang, David W. H. Walton and Oran R. Young, pp. 133–42. Washington, DC: Smithsonian Institution Scholarly Press, 2011.

Le Fèvre, Marius. *L'espace, du rêve à la réalité: Un grand bond pour l'Europe spatiale*. Paris: Editions Edite, 2010.

Macdonald, Fraser. 'Anti-*Astropolitik*: Outer Space and the Orbit of Geography'. *Progress in Human Geography* 31, no. 5 (2007): 592–615.

McDougall, Walter A. 'Space-Age Europe: Gaullism, Euro-Gaullism, and the American Dilemma'. *Technology and Culture* 26, no. 2 (1985): 179–203.

Morlet, Bernard, G. Charles, A. Hirtzman and J. Lavergnat (eds). 'Il y a 20 ans à Kerguelen: La campagne ARAKS octobre 1974/février 1975'. *Terres australes et antarctiques françaises* 64 (April–June 1975): 39–62.

Naylor, Simon and James R. Ryan (eds). *New Spaces of Exploration: Geographies of Discovery in the Twentieth Century*. London: I.B. Tauris, 2010.

Oreskes, Naomi and John Krige (eds). *Science and Technology in the Global Cold War*. Cambridge, MA: MIT Press, 2014.

Panchasi, Roxanne. '"No Hiroshima in Africa": The Algerian War and the Question of French Nuclear Tests in the Sahara'. *History of the Present* 9, no. 1 (2019): 84–112.

Peterson, M. J. 'The Use of Analogies in Developing Outer Space Law'. *International Organization* 51, no. 2 (1997): 245–74.

Redfield, Peter. 'The Half-Life of Empire in Outer Space'. *Social Studies of Science* 32, no. 5 (2002): 791–825.

Redfield, Peter. *Space in the Tropics: From Convicts to Rockets in French Guiana*. Berkeley: University of California Press, 2000.

Renou, Jan-Claude and Jean-Pierre Sanfourche. 'Les activités fusées-sondes du CNES'. In *Les débuts de la recherche spatiale française: Au temps des fusées-sondes*, ed. Hervé Moulin, pp. 69–80. Paris: Editions Edite, 2007).

Rivière, Clair. 'La fusée décolle, mais la Guyane reste au sol'. *CQFD* 165, May 2018. http://cqfd-journal.org/La-fusee-decolle-mais-la-Guyane. Accessed 13 May 2021.

Ross, Kristin. *Fast Cars, Clean Bodies: Decolonization and the Reordering of French Culture*. Cambridge, MA: MIT Press, 1995.

Salmon, Claude. 'Les lancements des Fusées-sondes "Dragon" depuis la "Terre Adélie"'. *Nos premières années*. http://nospremieresannees.fr/fusee_sonde_tout/fu09-campagne%20terre%20adelie/fu09c-texte_salmon/texte03.html.

Sanchez, Jean-Lucien. *A perpétuité: Relégués au bagne de Guyane*. Paris: Vendémaire, 2013.

Seibert, Günther. *The History of Sounding Rockets and Their Contribution to European Space Research*. Noordwijk: European Space Agency, 2006.

Shepard, Todd. *The Invention of Decolonization: The Algerian War and the Remaking of France*. Ithaca, NY: Cornell University Press, 2008.

Siddiqi, Asif A. 'Competing Technologies, National(ist) Narratives, and Universal Claims: Toward a Global History of Space Exploration'. *Technology and Culture* 51, no. 2 (2010): 425–43.

Simon, Pierre. 'Campagne de Terre Adélie 1966–1967: Le point de vue de l'Ingénieur'. *Nos premières années*. http://nospremieresannees.fr/fusee_sonde_tout/fu09-campagne%20terre%20adelie/fu09d-texte_simonp/texte01.html. Accessed 13 May 2021.

Spieler, Miranda. *Empire and Underworld*. Cambridge, MA: Harvard University Press, 2012.

Sulikowski, Chavelli. 'The French Connection: The Role of France in the Antarctic Treaty System'. In *The Emerging Politics of Antarctica*, ed. Anne-Marie Brady, pp. 163–90. Abingdon: Routledge, 2012.

Toth, Stephen. *Beyond Papillon: The French Overseas Penal Colonies, 1854–1952*. Lincoln: University of Nebraska Press, 2006.

Varnoteaux, Philippe. '70 ans du CIEES'. *Espace & Temps: Bulletin d'information de l'Institut français d'histoire de l'espace* 20 (June 2017): 3–13.

Varnoteaux, Philippe. *L'aventure spatiale française: De 1945 à la naissance d'Ariane*. Paris: Nouveau Monde Editions, 2015.

3

Narratives of colonialism in Antarctica through the lens of Historic Sites and Monuments

Katarzyna Jarosz

Unlike on the other continents, human presence in Antarctica has a short history. Only definitively discovered by Europeans and North Americans in the early nineteenth century, its material culture reflects 200 years of exploration, exploitation, research and tourism in a place with no Indigenous population. Since 1899, when the first hut was built by Carsten Borchgrevink's British Antarctic Expedition, explorers, adventurers, researchers and tourists have left their traces in Antarctica: huts, shelters, cairns, plaques, masts, recycling bins, research stations and waste dumps, to list just a few examples. Antarctica is a region of important geopolitical significance – 'a battle of rival geopolitical imaginations' – and traces of human presence are not ideologically neutral but are often charged with ideological weight.[1]

This chapter will analyse how specific countries build their national and colonial narrative in Antarctica in order to justify territorial claims ideologically, based on cultural, moral or historical grounds. The issue of territorial claims has already received a great deal of analysis, and discussion about arguments that legitimate claims to occupy the territory of Antarctica go beyond the scope of this chapter. It does not seek to resolve historiographical disputes or to analyse justification for territorial claims, but focuses on the narratives that create these claims, and the strategies used to create such narratives.

Alejandra Mancilla observes, referring to the countries that have made territorial claims in Antarctica, that the reasons advanced to support territorial claims in Antarctica can be divided into two main groups. She writes: 'On the one hand, states use connection-based grounds that justify territorial claims on some morally relevant link between the state and the territory. On the other hand, there are official documents and geographical doctrines.'[2] Remarks and observations in this chapter will refer to non-claimant countries; therefore the *sine qua non* condition is that legal grounds cannot be taken into consideration but only claims of the first type: those based on moral rights as broadly understood.

A common element in colonialism is construction, which is undertaken with a set of tools often borrowed from a nationalist repertoire, but which find a fertile ground in colonialism. These play a key role in colonial narrative, which justifies the act of colonisation or/and confirms the coloniser's existence on a colonised territory. Political and state symbols, technology, flags, emblems, memorials, plaques, cairns, and funerary or religious objects play a central role, not only in the process of nation-building but also in that of colonising a territory. The meaning attributed to both artifacts and their context supports colonial narratives, and material culture is inextricably linked with the process of imposing colonial power. The idea of colonialism goes far beyond the idea of one civilisation conquering another. The materiality of colonialism is expressed in vernacular practices, weapons, and the physical arrangement of landscapes and settlements. Colonialism as a structure of dominance and control is a key determinant of technological choices, such as the development of railways, canals, quarries and mines, which become spatio-political instruments – i.e. tangible means of imposing entitlement to a specific land – and therefore these items played key roles as bearers of colonialism.

As an example, a recurring theme during the colonisation of Central Asia by the USSR was the use of technology as a core of the narrative, bringing modernisation and electricity to remote, backward areas. Colonial strategies are used not only to justify claims, but also to impose a specific 'stamp', confirming that a given territory belongs to the coloniser. Numerous tangible characteristics of the coloniser's culture are introduced, with the aim of expressing a right to the territory and establishing supremacy. These numerous acts and strategies, though considered characteristic of nationalism, go far beyond simple nation-building; in a specific and different context, they can be read as colonial, i.e. as a confirmation of a territorial claim. The act of hoisting the flag by Chinese scientists in Antarctica, or putting the Polish emblem on a memorial plaque on King George Island, differs from that of a citizen raising a flag in front of their own home to demonstrate a shared sense of national belonging. In the context of the former, it is a symbol of conquering new space and territory, of presence and control.

Monuments and statues are also part of the symbolic repository of colonialism. A common strategy used by colonisers in annexed territories was to erect monuments and statues. They became 'an insignia of colonial authority and a signifier of colonial desire and discipline'.[3]

Language is also a powerful instrument of colonialism; colonisers usually imposed their language onto the peoples they colonised. To give an example, after the collapse of the Soviet Union, renaming streets from Russian into local languages became a political instrument in the post-Soviet realm, as a symbolic break with the colonial past. In Antarctica, with no cultural imprint and no indigenous population, colonial practices may be introduced on a different level by giving toponyms derived from the coloniser's culture. Consequently, practices of imposing the coloniser's religion will consist not of enforcing new religious practices and eradicating the former ones, but rather of marking its presence with numerous religious symbols, such as churches, graveyards and crosses, or by introducing religious practices characteristic of a specific religious group.

The concepts of nationalism, imperialism and colonialism are often easy to confuse and are frequently used interchangeably.[4] This chapter takes a perhaps slightly simplistic but highly convenient way of understanding the word 'nationalism' as a principle holding that the political and national unit should be congruent, and 'imperialism' as the policy or idea of a country to influence other countries and to dominate them, while 'colonialism' will be understood as the systems and practices of setting up colonies and settlements in other territories. 'Colonisation' is defined here as the act of political, physical and intellectual occupation of space. In this approach, colonial practices are intertwined with imperial ideas and imperial domination, as they imply how the colonised were subjected not only to the exploitation of their resources, but also to the domination of epistemic, moral and symbolic resources in ways that reflected and reproduced empire.[5] The chapter will analyse whether, to what degree and in what way the strategies and techniques used by numerous creators of master narratives with regard to Historic Sites and Monuments (HSMs) of Antarctica can be considered colonial practices.

In order to achieve this, both primary and secondary sources were examined. Among the primary sources, the lists of HSMs approved by the Antarctic Treaty Consultative Meeting and compiled by the Antarctic Treaty Secretariat were consulted. Furthermore, numerous press articles from various eras, textbooks, popular publications, radio and television programmes, political speeches, and political resolutions were analysed regarding the history of particular HSMs or events related to them, in order to verify which narratives were built around a specific HSM. The *terminus a quo* for the research is the mid-1950s. As secondary sources, academic works were analysed that referred directly or indirectly to issues related to the history of Antarctic exploration, the politicisation and management of HSMs, and tourism in Antarctica.[6]

In order to demonstrate the full spectrum of these narratives, the material for the case studies is drawn from the list of 89 HSMs.[7] The issue of geopolitical significance of sites commemorating events, people or places before the International Geophysical Year (IGY) of the Antarctic Treaty has been subject to a large amount of analysis.[8] A detailed synthesis about how, whether and to what degree HSMs contribute to the process of creating

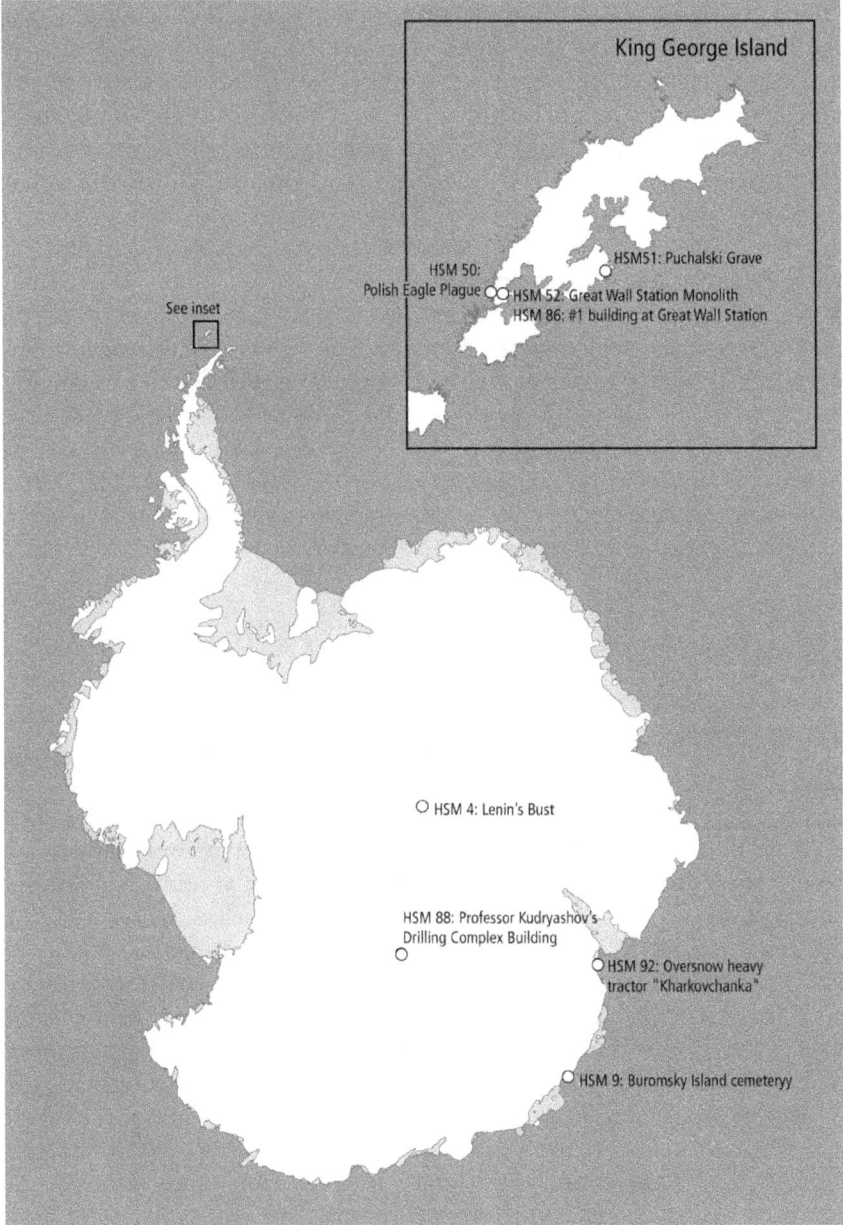

Map 3.1 Key locations mentioned in the chapter

colonial narratives regarding contemporary Antarctica is, however, currently lacking. It will be determined whether there is a universal set of strategies that might be considered supporting colonial narratives through the common denominator of HSMs, no matter which country is concerned. Examples illustrating specific strategies and processes will be drawn from HSMs commemorating people, events or places after the IGY. As areas that could have priority in the process of building narratives, the following were analysed: toponyms, technological achievements, historical markers and memory makers, and funerary landscapes.

These four paths of building narratives coexist and are interwoven – to give an example, technological achievements are built with the use of toponyms. The HSMs themselves will be examined, as well as their origin; the history of their creation; their primary and current function; their technical state; whether and to what degree they have been preserved, neglected; or destroyed; and their multidimensional contemporary meaning. The observations in this chapter are undoubtedly limited to specific HSMs that exist in a particular context, and that is the object of the analysis.

Background and brief presentation of the Historic Sites and Monuments of Antarctica

This chapter aims to analyse whether and to what degree HSMs can be used as instruments to build colonial narratives in Antarctica, as well as to identify the strategies and tools of building such narratives. In particular, it seeks to understand whether and to what degree HSMs can be considered as an instrument to introduce colonial practices. The idea of protecting historic sites was conceived for the first time in 1961. Nevertheless, it was as late as 1972, at the Seventh Antarctic Treaty Consultative Meeting, that the list of HSMs was created to protect these locations. Guidelines for HSM proposals were created in 1995 and, according to Annex V of the Environmental Protocol, they are protected areas. Any party can propose the designation of an HSM; there is no specific form or procedure for controlling them.

The first list of HSMs comprised 43 items (statues, huts, cairns, rock shelters, flag masts, crosses, memorial plaques, a meteorological observatory, a station, a metal monument-sledge and a heavy tractor). Since then, the list has been updated/amended, as some historical sites and monuments have been delisted while others have been registered.

As of 2021, the list comprises 89 HSMs, which form part of Antarctica's heritage. Each item is designated a number from HSM-1 to HSM-94. Some of the original HSMs have been delisted (e.g. HSM 58, a cairn with a memorial plaque erected at Whalers Bay, Deception Island, South Shetland Islands, to honour Captain Adolfus Amandus Andresen, an Antarctic pioneer who was the first to establish a whaling operation at Deception Island in 1906), and others have been merged, such as HSM-12 and HSM-13 (a cross and plaque at Cape Denison, George V Land, and a hut also at Cape Denison), which were removed from the Antarctic Treaty list and incorporated into HSM-77 (Cape Denison, Commonwealth Bay, George V Land, which includes Boat Harbour and the historic artifacts located within its waters).

Ricardo Roura has conducted a detailed analysis of Antarctic HSMs according to their features and functions, and his taxonomy will be the point of reference for the chapter.[9] A monument of recognised historical value can be proposed by any party for inclusion on the list; however, the procedures for accepting or rejecting the monument have already been described and analysed elsewhere, and go beyond the scope of this discussion.[10] The chapter aims to evaluate the role that HSMs play in the process of building colonial narratives, and whether and how HSMs contribute to the narrative that might justify territorial claims; it also aims to suggest what their place is in current writings on colonialism in the Antarctic region. For example, Rebecca Hingley has conducted analysis of the functions that heritage performs in Antarctica, and María Senatore, who observes that the topic of 'human–thing relationships' has sparked significant interest, argues, based on Adrian Howkins's observations, that 'the desire to possess, colonise, and appropriate space was fulfilled by things'.[11]

Intersections between colonial practices and *lieux de mémoire*

I will base my findings on the assumption that HSMs, as they are filled with meaning and have stories attached to them, are transformed from neutral sites into so-called *lieux de mémoire* (sites of memory), a concept developed by the French theorist Pierre Nora. A *lieu de mémoire* is any significant entity, whether material or non-material in nature, that, by dint of human will or the passing of time, has become a symbolic element of the memorial heritage of any community.[12] They are 'all significant units, of either material or ideal order, from which the will of men or the effect of time has created a symbolic element of the memorial patrimony of a community'.[13] This definition refers to places where collective memory condenses and is expressed. What distinguishes historical sites from *lieux de mémoire* is the fact that, in the former, history and memory interact and interplay; they are determined reciprocally. Without memory, a site is merely a historical site. Memory, unlike history, is not objective or firm or descriptive. It is volatile; it can be remembered and forgotten; it can be manipulated, created, or falsified; it can lie dormant and after a long period return to life. In other words, an old tale can be reinvented or new stories can be generated. *Lieux de mémoire* act as catalysts in the imposition of power, as well as the definition and endurance of identity.[14] In the colonial context, these are places where the memories of a nation might be constructed, contained and contested. They are containers of memory, a form of memorialisation. *Lieux de mémoire* need not refer merely to colonial practices. As an example, the Auschwitz concentration camp is a *lieu de mémoire* that lives in the collective memories of numerous communities, be it Jewish, German or Polish. In Antarctica the national memory that Nora refers to as homogenising local memories is, by definition, one that centres state possession of space, and so the site becomes a marker of that quest.

A key element and a priority of *lieux de mémoire* is the interpretation of the past. It is worth quoting Spencer Crew and James Sims here on the possibility of transparent and objective museology, as neither artifacts nor exhibitions are neutral: 'The problem with things is that they are dumb. They are not eloquent, as some thinkers in art museums claim. And if by some ventriloquism they seem to speak, they lie.'[15] *Lieux de mémoire* can be described as 'memory machines', creating stories through specific choices of exhibits, labels and captions. They authorise a master narrative – the official version of cultural identity – as imposed by policy-makers. The concept, elaborated by Nora with the aim of defining those *lieux de mémoire* which conceptualise France, can be applied to all societies. Here the concept will be extended to Antarctica and it will be established whether – and to what degree – HSMs, through acquired and invented meaning, can therefore act as *lieux de mémoire* with all their symbolic significance. It will also be established whether they can also act as an element in the process of imposing power and bolstering territorial claims.

Building colonial narratives

The role of toponyms in the process of symbolic colonisation

There is a deep connection between place, language and power. This subsection will focus on the relationship between colonialism and place names/ toponyms. In the literature on the subject, based mainly on case studies, renaming has been considered one of the key colonial practices.[16] Toponyms do not merely denote physical locations; in general they are a mirror of the perception of the world, of a given place, and 'possess a symbolic power that can inflame as well as claim'.[17] 'Naming becomes a primary colonising process because it appropriates, defines, captures the place in language', through which the colonisers use linguistic symbols, rich in connotative significance, and carrying ideological, social, historical or cultural meaning, with the aim of asserting power over the colonised territory.[18] On territories with no cultural imprint, in an originally neutral cultural environment such as that of Antarctica, using toponyms that have deep symbolic meaning in the source culture can be understood as an attempt to transplant cultural values from a specific country.[19] Not only are Antarctic geographical names elements of identification, orientation, location and navigation, thus providing an essential reference system for logistical operations and international scientific research, but they also reflect the history of the exploration of the continent.

A more detailed analysis of the Great Wall Station Monolith (HSM-52) can serve as a clear example how to build a colonial narrative based on toponyms. The Great Wall Station Monolith was erected to commemorate the establishment of the Great Wall Station (Chángchéng Zhàn), located at the southwestern tip of King George Island. The inscription on the monolith, engraved in Chinese, says 'The Great Wall Station, first Chinese Antarctic research expedition, 20 February 1985'. Not only is the Great Wall a globally recognised icon, but it is an object of patriotism, a symbol of China's self-definition. When, in September 1984, Deng Xiaoping launched a new economic policy, he did so with the words 'Let's love China and restore the Great Wall.' The Great Wall station thus locates the Chinese Antarctic programme within wider Chinese narratives: both the master narrative, as enforced by policy-makers, and the popular narrative, which started from the very beginning of its construction. Numerous press articles were published at the time that depicted the bravery of the 591 people who embarked on a historic voyage on the *Xianganghong 10* ocean-going expedition, and who in only four weeks built the station where 'for the first time, China placed the five-star red flag on the land of Antarctica'.[20] It is commonly accepted and known from history that the act of hoisting a flag goes far beyond a pure manifestation of nationalism and is symbolically considered an act of domination and colonialism.[21]

Much later, the 2018 resolution, adopted at the 18th National Congress of the Chinese Communist Party, refers to the station, putting it as one of the reasons for building a strong Chinese maritime empire.[22] The Great Wall is a symbol of China's unification, and in the Chinese national narrative it serves not to constrain the borders of China, but rather to expand it. A Chinese proverb says 'Both sides of the Great Wall are your hometowns.'[23] The Great Wall Station was also a departure point for other toponyms of great historic and cultural significance for China, deeply rooted in Chinese tradition. The Chinese toponyms of King George Island can be interpreted as an attempt to transfer the Chinese cultural landscape through a process of sinification.[24] Philippe Foret argues that the Great Wall Station is a place where Chinese cultural values regarding space have been transplanted outside the Chinese realm.[25] The very first task of the expedition was to give

Chinese names to the lake, bay and hills around the station, following the art of geomancy (*feng shui* (风水)). This created a metaphorical Chinese landscape in the Fildes Peninsula with topography and nomenclatures referring to Chinese culture.

Cutting-edge technology as an element of colonial practices

In the literature on colonialism, it has been observed that technological and scientific superiority is at the centre of the colonial narrative that justifies territorial claims, or proves rights to dominance at least in historical and moral terms.[26] 'Accessing and controlling environments', observed James Beattie, 'underpinned British imperialism'.[27] Beattie was referring to nineteenth-century British colonialism, though his statement can be easily applied to other practices of colonialism as well. Colonialism aimed to conquer not only peoples, but also environments. Technology is a tool that enables the outreach of environmental resources. Transport, weapons, medicines, wood-working machines and advanced technologies, as well as the professions, are just a few examples of the instruments of power wielded by colonialism, shaping its feasibility and determining to a large degree the successes of colonial projects. Technical infrastructure is a core element of colonialism. Soviet policy-makers considered science and technology an instrument whose goal was mastery over a new space.

Among the HSMs in the category of 'monuments presenting technological achievements', the Vostok Station Tractor (HSM-11) and the oversnow 'Kharkovchanka' heavy tractor that was used in Antarctica from 1959 to 2010 (HSM-92) – two heavy Soviet snow tractors – will be analysied in more detail, along with Professor Boris Kudryashov's Drilling Complex Building (HSM-88). Science and technology played a prominent role in Soviet self-identity. According to the official rhetoric, 'the construction of a new [communist] society [was] infeasible without the immediate involvement of science in the process'.[28] In 1924, Leon Trotsky wrote: 'Under socialism a man will become a Superhuman, changing courses of rivers, the heights of mountains and nature according to his needs and, after all, changing his own nature.'[29] Nowhere were tractors more enthusiastically appreciated than in the Soviet Union, and for ideological and practical reasons the tractor was assigned a key role in the development of socialism. Tractors were an instrument of Soviet propaganda – the tool of conquering and transforming land. The official ideology of the USSR was anti-colonial. The colonial essence of the Russian empire was recognised, but the Soviet Union, which arose after its fall, as proclaimed, did not bear any features of a colonial empire. Foreign Sovietologists, on the contrary, tried in every possible way to prove that the USSR was a colonial power. Mechanisation and industrialisation were supposed to transform life and permit humans to control and transform that territory.

In the Soviet state narrative related to the colonisation of Antarctica, technology occupies a significant place. A huge cruiser, a significant tool in colonial narrative, responds to the needs of empire and monumentalism and is proof of Soviet capabilities in the field of engineering and design. Monumentalism, so characteristic of Soviet buildings under Stalin, was not restricted purely to architecture. With bigger and better machine tools, hydropower stations and other forms of geological engineering, telemechanics and automation, the aim of monumental structures was much more than to be functional – they were also the encapsulation of colonialism. Their aim was to convey power; Charles Swithinbank, an American who spent a year working as a tractor driver at the Mirny station, mentions that Soviet equipment was always huge. 'A contemporary American motor sledge, as used in the Antarctic, weighs 300 kg', he wrote in 1966, 'the only motor vehicles in use on recent Soviet journeys weigh 25 and 35 tons; a contemporary Nansen sledge as used in the Antarctic weighs 40 kg. – the only Soviet sledge in use weighs seven tons'.[30] The huge, efficient sledge tractor was not only a perfect instrument to strengthen the pride of empire (or a former empire), but was also mainly a tool for conquering new territories, facilitating Soviet colonisation of new lands in the same way that Antarctica might be brought within the USSR's colonial orbit.

There is vast body of scholarship before and after the IGY, mainly by Russian authors, where the Soviets substantiated their claims to Antarctica, or where the Soviet attitude toward the acquisition of territorial sovereignty in Antarctica was analysed.[31] Popular culture further built the image of colonialisation of Antarctica by means of science and technology. Soviet (and later Russian) popular books, films, songs and even postage stamps often described the technological achievements of Soviet research in Antarctica and their role in the process of taming the forces of nature to subdue and replenish the earth. Numerous gigantic technological undertakings contributed to the sacralisation of Soviet policy and the dramaturgical self-portrayal of the Soviet system. An example is Professor Kudryashov's Drilling Complex Building. The building was constructed in the summer season of 1983–84. Under the leadership of Professor Boris Kudryashov, ancient mainland ice samples were obtained. Kudryashov, who from 1967 to 2002 was the leader of studies focused on developing the technique and equipment for ice drilling, was the embodiment of a geologist: one who was always at the vanguard of those who conquer and subjugate new territories. His achievements, first in the Soviet Union and later in Russia, were in 'scientific pioneering and priority in the world practice'.[32] The station is a natural continuation of colonial practices of subduing the earth and virgin lands; the conquest and colonisation of nature were among the key ideological frameworks and represented one of the pillars of Soviet ideological and colonial narratives, with earth sciences (such as geology and physical geography) taking a special place. One can observe that the colonisation of nature was a common refrain in Soviet narratives, with regard not only to the conquest and colonisation of Antarctica, but also to conquering and colonising Central Asia.[33] Under the tenure of Stalin, in the early 1950s, 50 percent of the total number of geologists all over the world were Soviet. In popular culture, geologists were romanticised and presented as brave figures because they knew how to exploit nature. A number of feature films, songs and adventure books depicted geologists as pioneers in the quest for new, undiscovered lands. Even in the 1980s, about 10 per cent of all press articles popularising science in the Soviet Union were about geology.

Historical markers and memory makers

The presence and political significance of monuments in Antarctica cannot be overlooked by scholars of colonial studies. They are a clear example of how material culture is weaponised in order to support colonial expansion. Monuments and memorial plaques represent a visual culture that was mobilised as a means to underline and justify supremacy throughout history, linked to a specific version of history; highlighting people and events; or, most importantly, giving a certain message about the past.

Not only do monuments, statues and memorials exist as common commemorative practices to memorialise events of special significance in society, but they also validate official top-down narratives across geographical and political contexts. A commemorative plaque is a brief verbal expression providing information about a person: who they were; the reason why they should be remembered; and also, in some cases, who 'we' are. Monuments and memorial plaques included in the list of HSMs commemorate members of expeditions, people who perished in Antarctica during their duties, the conquest of Antarctica by explorers, expedition visits, events related to research stations' activities and details of the stations' location. Monuments require commemorative vigilance, not only physical but also symbolic in their memory and maintenance.[34] The following examples will provide some insight into how specific HSMs are tools used to build specific colonial narratives.

An interesting example of a memorial plaque that has come to be woven into colonial narratives is a brass plaque (HSM-50) bearing the Polish Eagle; the national emblem of Poland, the dates 1975 and 1976; and, in Polish, English and Russian, 'In memory of the landing of members of the first Polish Antarctic marine research expedition on the vessels "Professor Siedlecki" and "Tazar" in February 1976.' The narrative built around the vessel *Professor Siedlecki*, a Polish fishery research vessel constructed to carry out research in the southern polar waters, is deeply ingrained in Polish popular identity. An object of admiration, commonly referred to in the Polish maritime press as a 'floating laboratory' and one of the most cutting-edge in the world at the time, was used for Antarctic oceanographic research from 1972 to 1992.[35] It was an object of pride, and in the Polish narrative the *Professor Siedlecki* is a symbolic conqueror of Antarctica. What is more, the narrative around the *Professor Siedlecki* went far beyond moral superiority and national pride and transformed into potential territorial claims. To illustrate this, two examples can be given.

A 1976 postcard from the *Professor Siedlecki* quotes a fragment from one of the oldest Polish songs, dating back to the turn of the twelfth century. It was sung by the warriors of Bolesław III the Wry-Mouthed when they conquered the Baltic strongholds:

> For our ancestors, salty and smelly fish were enough,
> *We come for fresh, splashing in the ocean!*
> *It was enough for our fathers, if they had strongholds,*
> *And we are not deterred by the storm or the roar of the waves.*
> *Our fathers hunted deer,*
> *And we catch treasures and monsters hidden in the ocean.*[36]

In Poland, the song has a deeply symbolic meaning. It speaks of conquering and colonising new lands and can be easily understood as a call to conquer Antarctica.

Another HSM that can serve as an example of strengthening colonial narratives is Lenin's Bust, together with a plaque in memory of the conquest of the Pole of Inaccessibility by Soviet Antarctic explorers, located at the Pole itself (HSM-4). The bust was delivered by a sledge-caterpillar train of the Third Soviet Antarctic Expedition, the first in the world to reach the Pole of Inaccessibility. Eighteen people, led by Evgeny Tolstikov, arrived at the Pole on 14 December 1958. Reaching that point – and beyond that, establishing a research centre there – was a matter of principle and national pride. The Pole of Inaccessibility was chosen specifically as a counter of sorts to the American South Pole Station, and not just any station, but one with a bust of Lenin on the roof. The Soviet polar explorers installed Lenin on a high pedestal made of two boxes so that he would not disappear from sight under the snow and would be seen from a distance. The bust faced in the direction of Moscow. Constructed during the Khrushchev era and maintained in the Brezhnev era at the peak of the Cold War, the monument remains a site glorifying first the Soviet, and later the Russian, nation. Now yellowing and covered with snow, this particular bust of Lenin raises a number of questions concerning relationships among monuments – historical memory, national identity in general and Russian-Soviet national identity.[37] During the Soviet period, statues were one way of anchoring a Soviet colonial presence; for example, among the hundreds of statues of Lenin the famous bust at Pyramiden in Svalbard can be highlighted. After the dissolution of the Soviet Union, the sculptures of Lenin and other figures were removed from their pedestals in formerly communist countries, where they had acted as symbols of occupation and/or colonisation.[38]

The bust of Lenin is a clear example of a co-opted glorified monument, strengthening the national narrative of a brave, infallible nation. In an article dedicated to the bust of Lenin, a leading Russian journal, *Аргументы и факты* (*Argumenty i fakty*), also highlighted the person of Leonid Rogozov, a member of the Soviet expedition to Antarctica in 1961–62.[39] He was a 26-year-old doctor who fell ill during a blizzard while at the Novolazarevskaya research station, but still managed to perform a successful appendectomy on himself. The article also recalls a song written by the Russian songwriter Vladimir Vysotsky that was dedicated to Rogozov's heroism. The last lines of the song are as follows:

> He's a hero! You can see it clearly.
> Nowhere else can they do it this way,
> Do we want the Antarctic and the Arctic?
> What about Albania and Poland![40]

The last line needs further clarification. It refers to the political situation from the late 1950s to the early 1960s between the two countries, which were not part of the USSR but were politically influenced by it as satellite countries and where Soviet military intervention had been considered. Albania had linked its fate with the USSR, benefiting enormously from Soviet economic assistance and cultural exchanges. However, at the 22nd Congress of the Communist Party of the Soviet Union in 1960, Khrushchev publicly attacked the Party of Labour of Albania for turning to China and becoming a political protectorate of Beijing. In Poland, the 1956 demonstrations of workers in Poznań against the communist government forced Moscow seriously tos consider the question of military intervention.

As an embodiment of the brave Soviet nation, Rogozov's achievement should have opened the door to claiming not only Antarctica but also other lands, in order to save them from the 'wrong' path.

Funeral landscapes as a marker of belonging

Among the researched material there are two cemeteries, three individual graves and eight crosses honouring the dead. These are more than places to catalogue the names of the dead or to dispose of unburnt bodies and cremated remains. As a physical place and a spiritual space, the cemetery fuses the physical, the emotional and the symbolic, allowing ideas and memories to survive. Physical spaces dedicated to memory and bereavement in funereal contexts are employed as a means of asserting and constructing cultural identity; with reference to Benedict Anderson, they are a key instrument in the construction of imagined communities.[41]

Cemeteries and graves are memorial landscapes, the ideological manifestation of belonging to a place. Funeral practices and funeral landscapes in many societies 'constitute a high point for the reaffirmation of belonging', of settling and occupying a place.[42] Graves demonstrate past and present occupations and engagements within the landscape; in the literature on the subject, it has been observed that there is a link between belonging and the materiality of graves and graveyards.[43] Graves, in addition to being geographical markers, are at the same time symbolic pivotal points of human attachments. The sense of belonging to the land or even becoming a part of the land is strengthened by death and by returning to the soil.

There is a set of formal and informal activities, performances, uses and behaviours, at the grave of Włodzimierz Puchalski, a Polish photographer, topped by an iron cross on a hill to the south of Arctowski station on King George Island (HSM-51); at a cemetery on Buromsky Island, near Mirny Observatory, where citizens of the Soviet Union (Russian Federation), Czechoslovakia, East Germany and Switzerland are buried (HSM-9); and also further afield at related sites. They reinforce the sense and narrative of belonging. Respectively, they signify and affirm the Polish and Soviet (later Russian) social and political presence in the Antarctic. This presence is constructed through this performativity and then reproduced by news stories in the media. A visit to the grave of Włodzimierz Puchalski is included in the schedule of numerous tourist trips made by Poles and others to Antarctica.[44] Through these performances the place becomes Polish. About 3,000 people visit the Arctowski station annually, and traditionally they go to Włodzimierz Puchalski's resting place to celebrate his memory and, according to Polish tradition, light a candle. Every year, on All Saints' Day (1 November), when Poles traditionally visit the graves of their relatives, scientists from the Arctowski station visit Puchalski's grave and light a candle for him. This tradition has been broadcast on television and radio.[45]

The Buromsky Cemetery (HSM-9), is the final resting place for 78 people, mainly Soviet and Russian citizens who perished while performing their duties at the Mirny station.[46] They also include a Swiss photographer – Bruno Zehnder – and citizens of Czechoslovakia and East Germany. The cemetery is still used and exists in the Russian narrative; funeral ceremonies still take place there, with an Orthodox priest and Orthodox rites. Not only are people who lost their lives in Antarctica laid to rest here, but it is also the site of the cremated remains of Pavel Kononovich Senko – a Soviet polar scientist, member and leader of numerous expeditions, and officer-in-charge of Mirny station on the ninth Soviet Antarctic Expedition – which were brought here and buried in accordance with his last wish.[47]

In a documentary film presenting people who are buried in the cemetery, a Russian Antarctic researcher from the Mirny station says 'When you turn back, you will see behind you a whole crowd of people; they are like an army, you can physically feel their presence.'[48] Religion plays an important role in funerary practices and works as an anchor of collective identity. Burials are performances where religion can be used as a tool to indicate an enduring presence in a specific place. The religious burials and practices at the Buromsky Cemetery and the lighting of a candle at Puchalski's grave are both activities that strengthen and reinforce the symbolic attachment to the place. As Peder Roberts observes, the sacrifice of human life to make a space belong to the nation is striking, quoting 'The Soldier' by Rupert Brooke: 'some corner of a foreign field / That is forever England'.[49] It also evokes a sense of conquest: that the space is controlled by means of religion, which of course also has a long history of being used in this way.

Conclusions and suggestions for future research

At HSMs, memory, power and nationhood, strengthened by colonial narrative, intersect. As Roman Khandozhko and Alejandra Mancilla suggest elsewhere in this volume, Antarctica is a place where colonialism existed, even if the actors did not recognise themselves as engaging in colonial practices. Through the variety of examples and case studies presented here, I have sought to highlight the usefulness of HSMs as a source for understanding the emergence and articulation of colonial narratives in Antarctica.

Through an analysis of HSMs, it can be observed that they are powerful instruments supporting colonial narratives, even in these postcolonial times. Colonial narratives rest on two main pillars – superiority and priority – demonstrated on different levels: religious, ideological and technological. Narratives around territorial claims are built using a number of tools and paraphernalia such as national symbols, including memorials, monuments, toponyms, funerary landscapes and rituals. Colonial narrative is built to a large degree on superiority over others. It transfers into a moral or ideological justification of territorial claims, expressed either explicitly or implicitly.

In this study, I have aimed to demonstrate how artifacts and history can be manipulated or instrumentalised and put to different political and partisan uses, leading to divergent historical interpretations and political goals. I am aware, given the number of HSMs, their heterogeneous history and nature, and their importance in both the history of Antarctica and its colonisation, that this chapter can only scratch the surface of the issue that Poland, the USSR and China are using colonial tactics and narratives, and are therefore engaging in colonialism in Antarctica. Further research is therefore needed. Following more extensive research, it may be possible to verify whether these observations are universal. It seems necessary to examine whether they also apply to other types of HSMs, and whether they can be applied on a larger scale. It is otherwise impossible to determine whether the narratives of the HSMs I have researched are local or paradigmatic.

Finally, it must be asked whether there is a distinction between claimant and non-claimant states in terms of creating HSMs. Out of 122 original proposal parties, as many as 99 (82 per cent), are from claimant countries, while only 23 (18 per cent) are from non-claimant countries. Very similar numbers can also be found in terms of parties undertaking the management of these sites: 74 per cent are from claimant countries compared to 26 per cent from non-claimant countries. These numbers clearly state that the role of HSMs is not purely to memorialise specific events, but is to strengthen the narrative regarding territorial claims. HSMs can obviously serve as tools to mark presence in a specific territory. This study has aimed to show that the idea of conquering the land and its emotional, colonialist power have been undertheorised in political geography. HSMs clearly comprise not only various forms of nationalism, but also a geohistorical, structural context and narrative elements embedded in the production and reproduction of the idea of colonialism. The ultimate purpose of the HSMs analysed here is far from mere landscape decoration or even tourist attractions. Their aim is to imprint history on the landscape, recruiting support for a particular version of history.

Notes

1 See, for example, Klaus J. Dodds, Alan D. Hemmings and Peder Roberts (eds), *Handbook on the Politics of Antarctica* (Cheltenham: Edward Elgar, 2017); Klaus J. Dodds, 'Antarctic Geopolitics', in Dodds *et al.*, *Handbook on the Politics of Antarctica* (Cheltenham: Edward Elgar Publishing, 2017), pp. 199–214 (p. 201).

2 Alejandra Mancilla, 'The Moral Limits of Territorial Claims in Antarctica', *Ethics & International Affairs* 32:3 (2018), 339–60 (p. 341).

3 Homi K. Bhabha, 'Signs Taken for Wonders: Questions of Ambivalence and Authority under a Tree outside Delhi, May 1817', *Critical Inquiry* 12:1 (1985), 144–65 (p. 144).

4 See, for example, Marcella Fultz, 'Bibliography of Books and Articles Published in English on Colonialism and Imperialism in 2009', *Journal of Colonialism*

and Colonial History 11:2 (2010), DOI: 10.1353/cch.2010.0007; Frederick Cooper, *Colonialism in Question: Theory, Knowledge, History* (Berkeley, CA: University of California Press, 2005); Vrajaindra Upadhyay, 'What Is Imperialism? Situating Imperialism in Relation to Capitalism and Colonialism', *SSRN Electronic Journal*, 30 July 2018, DOI: 10.2139/ssrn.3222573.

5 Walter D. Mignolo, 'Introduction', *Cultural Studies* 21:2–3 (2007), 155–67, DOI: 10.1080/09502380601162498.

6 See, for example, Andrés Zarankin and Melisa A. Salerno, 'Antarctic Archaeology', in Charles Orser, James Symonds, Pedro Paulo A. Funari, Andrés Zarankin and Susan Lawrence (eds), *The Routledge Handbook of Global Historical Archaeology* (London: Routledge, 2020), pp. 915–26, DOI: 10.4324/9781315202846-46; Elizabeth Leane, Tim Winter and Juan Francisco Salazar, 'Caught between Nationalism and Internationalism: Replicating Histories of Antarctica in Hobart', *International Journal of Heritage Studies* 22:3 (2016), 214–27, DOI: 10.1080/13527258.2015.1114010; Peder Roberts, Lize-Marié van der Watt and Adrian Howkins (eds), *Antarctica and the Humanities* (London: Palgrave Macmillan, 2016).

7 Secretariat of the Antarctic Treaty, 'Revised List of Historic Sites and Monuments Antarctic Treaty Database – Measure 23 (2021) – ATCM XLIII – CEP XXIII, Paris', www.ats.aq/devAS/Meetings/Measure/732 (accessed 12 January 2023).

8 See, for example, Ricardo Roura, 'Antarctic Cultural Heritage: Geopolitics and Management', in Dodds *et al.*, *Handbook on the Politics of Antarctica*, pp. 468–85; Bob Frame, Daniela Liggett, Kati Lindström, Ricardo M. Roura and Lize-Marié van der Watt, 'Tourism and Heritage in Antarctica: Exploring Cultural, Natural and Subliminal Experiences', *Polar Geography* 45:1 (2022), 37–57, DOI: 10.1080/1088937x.2021.1918787; Paul Chaplin, *The Historic Huts of the Ross Sea Region* (Christchurch: Antarctic Heritage Trust, 1999); David L. Harrowfield, *Icy Heritage: The Historic Sites of the Ross Sea Region, Antarctica* (Christchurch: Antarctic Heritage Trust, 1995).

9 Roura, 'Antarctic Cultural Heritage'.

10 See, for example, Roura, 'Antarctic Cultural Heritage'; Susan Barr, 'Twenty Years of Protection of Historic Values in Antarctica under the Madrid Protocol', *The Polar Journal* 8:2 (2018), 241–64, DOI: 10.1080/2154896X.2018.1541547.

11 Rebecca Hingley, 'Diverging Antarctic Heritage Discourses: The Geopolitical Ramifications of Non-State Actor Engagement with the "State-Sanctioned" Version of Antarctic Heritage', *The Geographical Journal* 189:1 (2021), 40–8, DOI: 10.1111/geoj.12383; María X. Senatore, 'Things in Antarctica: An Archaeological Perspective', *The Polar Journal* 10:2 (2020), 1–23 (p. 11), DOI: 10.1080/2154896x.2020.1799610.

12 Pierre Nora, 'Between Memory and History: *Les Lieux De Mémoire*', *Representations* 26 (1989), 7–24, DOI: 10.2307/2928520.

13 Pierre Nora, 'Comment écrire l'histoire de France', in Pierre Nora (ed.), *Les lieux de mémoire* (Paris: Gallimard, 1992), pp. 12–32.

14 Zeynap Çelik, 'France and Algeria: From Colonial Conflicts to Postcolonial Memories', *Historical Reflections/Réflexions historiques* 28:2 (2002), 143–62, DOI: 10.1080/09528829908576823.

15 Spencer R. Crew and James E. Sims, 'Locating Authenticity: Fragments of a Dialogue', in Ivan Karp and Stephen D. Lavine (eds), *Exhibiting Cultures: The Poetics and Politics of Museum Display* (Washington, DC: Smithsonian Institution Press, 1991), pp. 159–75 (p. 159).

16 See, for example, Klaus J. Dodds and Kathryn Yusoff, 'Settlement and Unsettlement in Aotearoa/New Zealand and Antarctica', *Polar Record* 41:217 (2005), 141–55; Liora Bigon, 'Names, Norms and Forms: French and Indigenous Toponyms in Early Colonial Dakar, Senegal', *Planning Perspectives* 23:4 (2008), 479–501, DOI: 10.1080/02665430802319021; Thomas Stolz and Ingo H. Warnke, 'When Places Change Their Names and When They Do Not. Selected Aspects of Colonial and Postcolonial Toponymy in Former French and Spanish Colonies in West Africa: The Cases of Saint Louis (Senegal) and the Western Sahara', *International Journal of the Sociology of Language* 2016:239 (2016), 29–56, DOI:10.1515/ijsl-2016-0004.

17 Mark Monmonier, *From Squaw Tit to Whorehouse Meadow: How Maps Name, Claim, and Inflame* (Chicago: University of Chicago Press, 2007), p. 121.

18 Bill Ashcroft, Gareth Girths and Helen Tiffin (eds), *The Post-Colonial Studies Reader* (London: Routledge, 2003), pp. 391–2.

19 Arseny Saparov, 'The Alteration of Place Names and the Construction of National Identity in Soviet Armenia', *Cahiers du Monde russe* 44:1 (2003), 179–98, DOI: 10.4000/monderusse.135.

20 'Zhōngguó Nánjí Chángchéng Zhàn Kao Cha Dian Jiu Xing Luo Cheng Dian Li', *Beijing Wan Bao*, 21 February 1985, p. 2.

21 Numerous examples can be recalled from history. According to legend, in 1219 the Danish flag fell from heaven during the Battle of Lyndanisse in Estonia, helping the Danish army to unexpected victory, and establishing a Danish dominion. In 1885, during the so-called Carolines Crisis between Germany and Spain over the sovereignty of the Caroline Islands and Palau, flags were hoisted on Yap and Palau to authorise these islands as a German colony.

22 National People's Congress of the People's Republic of China, '"关于发展海洋经济 加快建设海洋强国工作情况的报告." 关于发展海洋经济 加快建设海洋强国工作情况的报告_中国人大网', 24 December 2018, www.npc.gov.cn/npc/c12491/201812/83131907fb234bba96edd84b6cffd1f9.shtml (accessed 27 September 2021).

23 Originally '长城两边皆故乡' ('Chángchéng liǎngbiān jiē gùxiāng').

24 Neil Lindsay and Hong-Key Yoon, 'Toponyms on the Ice: The Symbolic and Iconographical Role of Antarctic Research Base Names', *Polar Record* 57, E22 (2021), 1–13, DOI: 10.1017/s003224742100022x.

25 Philippe Forêt, 'Mapping "Ancient" Chinese Antarctica', *Bulletin of the Museum of Far Eastern Antiquities (Östasiatika Museet)* 73 (2001), 193–215.

26 E.g. Ahuja Ravi, '"The Bridge-Builders": Some Notes on Railways, Pilgrimage and the British "Civilizing Mission" in Colonial India', in Harald Fischer-Tiné and Michael Mann (eds), *Colonialism as Civilizing Mission: Cultural Ideology in British India* (London: Anthem Press, 2004); James J. Beattie, 'Recent Themes in the Environmental History of the British Empire', *History Compass* 10:2 (2012), 129–39, DOI: 10.1111/j.1478-0542.2011.00824.x.

27 Beattie, 'Recent Themes in the Environmental History of the British Empire', p. 129.

28 Arno Köörna, *Science Serving the People* (Tallinn: Perioodika, 1986), p. 5.

29 Quoted in Alla Bolotova, 'Colonization of Nature in the Soviet Union: State Ideology, Public Discourse, and the Experience of Geologists', *Historical Social Research* 29:3 (2004), 104–23 (p. 110).

30 Charles Swithinbank, 'A Year with the Russians in Antarctica', *The Geographical Journal* 132:4 (1966), 463–74 (p. 473), DOI: 10.2307/1792525.

31 E.g. Peter A. Toma, 'Soviet Attitude towards the Acquisition of Territorial Sovereignty in the Antarctic', *American Journal of International Law* 50:3 (1956), 611–26, DOI: 10.2307/2195509; Bolesław A. Boczek, 'The Soviet Union and the Antarctic Regime', *American Journal of International Law* 78:4 (1984), 834–58, DOI: 10.2307/2202198; Erki Tammiksaar, 'The Russian Antarctic Expedition under the Command of Fabian Gottlieb von Bellingshausen and Its Reception in Russia and the World', *Polar Record* 52:5 (2016), 578–600, DOI: 10.1017/s0032247416000449.

32 Saint Petersburg Mining University Scientific Center, 'Remembering Boris Borisovich Kudryashov', https://ccarctic.com/en/boris-borisovich-kudryashov (accessed 26 September 2021).

33 Slava Gerovitch, ' "Why Are We Telling Lies?" The Creation of Soviet Space History Myths', *The Russian Review* 70:3 (2011), 460–84, DOI: 10.1111/j.1467-9434.2011.00624.x; Katarzyna Jarosz, 'National Narratives of "Occupation" in Historical Museums of the Post-Soviet Landscape', in Jeremy E. Taylor (ed.), *Visual Histories of Occupation: A Transcultural Dialogue* (London: Bloomsbury, 2021), pp. 229–46.

34 Nora, 'Between Memory and History', p. 7.

35 K. Stefański, 'Pływające Laboratorium Profesor Siedlecki', *Morze* 8 (2017), 79–87.

36 Author's translation from Polish.

37 For more about Soviet activities in Antarctica, see Roman Khandozhko's chapter in this volume.

38 The discussion as to whether the former republics were colonised or occupied is still open and goes far beyond the scope of this chapter. See, for example, Jarosz, 'National Narratives of "Occupation"'.

39 Dmitry Pisarenko, 'Куда смотрит Ленин? Интересные факты о российских станциях в Антарктиде', *Аргументы и факты*, 21 February 2021, pp. 2–4.

40 'Высоцкий Владимир (1963г) – ПЕСНЯ о …', YouTube, 25 January 2017. www.youtube.com/watch?v=T-28fdSmnuc. Accessed 20 January 2023. Translation by the author.

41 Benedict Anderson, *Imagined Communities: Reflections on the Origin and Spread of Nationalism* (London: Verso, 1991).

42 P. Geschiere, 'Funerals and Belonging: Different Patterns in South Cameroon', *African Studies Review* 48:2 (2005), 45–64, DOI: 10.1353/arw.2005.0059.

43 See, for example, Joost Fontein, 'Graves, Ruins, and Belonging: Towards an Anthropology of Proximity', *Journal of the Royal Anthropological Institute*

17:4 (2011), 706–27, DOI: 10.1111/j.1467-9655.2011.01715.x; Parker Shipton, *Mortgaging the Ancestors: Ideologies of Attachment in Africa* (New Haven, CT: Yale University Press, 2009).

44 See, for example, Marek Śliwka, 'Antarktyda – Wyprawa życia', https://wyprawy.pl/pl-PL/impresje-z-podrozy/antarktyda-wyprawa-zycia,4.html (accessed 2 October 2021).

45 'Na Antarktydzie uczcili pamięć polskiego przyrodnika', TVN24, 1 November 2010, https://tvn24.pl/polska/na-antarktydzie-uczcili-pamiec-polskiego-przyrodnika-ra150945–3591855 (accessed 17 October 2022).

46 As of 2020.

47 Olga Stefanova, personal communication.

48 Olga Stefanova (dir.), *Buromsky Island*, DVD (Lex Film, 2020).

49 Personal correspondence, January 2023.

Bibliography

Anderson, Benedict. *Imagined Communities: Reflections on the Origin and Spread of Nationalism*. London: Verso, 1991.

Ashcroft, Bill, Gareth Girths and Helen Tiffin (eds). *The Post-Colonial Studies Reader*. London: Routledge, 2003.

Barr, Susan. 'Twenty Years of Protection of Historic Values in Antarctica under the Madrid Protocol'. *The Polar Journal* 8, no. 2 (2018): 241–64. DOI: 10.1080/2154896X.2018.1541547.

Beattie, James J. 'Recent Themes in the Environmental History of the British Empire'. *History Compass* 10, no. 2 (2012): 129–39. DOI: 10.1111/j.1478-0542.2011.00824.x.

Beijing Wan Bao. 'Zhōngguó Nánjí Chángchéng Zhàn Kao Cha Dian Jiu Xing Luo Cheng Dian Li', *Beijing Wan Bao*, 21 February 1985, p. 2.

Bhabha, Homi K. 'Signs Taken for Wonders: Questions of Ambivalence and Authority under a Tree outside Delhi, May 1817'. *Critical Inquiry* 12, no. 1 (1985): 144–65.

Bigon, Liora. 'Names, Norms and Forms: French and Indigenous Toponyms in Early Colonial Dakar, Senegal'. *Planning Perspectives* 23, no. 4 (2008): 479–501. DOI: 10.1080/02665430802319021.

Boczek, Bolesław A. 'The Soviet Union and the Antarctic Regime'. *American Journal of International Law* 78, no. 4 (1984): 834–58. DOI: 10.2307/2202198.

Bolotova, Alla. 'Colonization of Nature in the Soviet Union: State Ideology, Public Discourse, and the Experience of Geologists'. *Historical Social Research* 29, no. 3 (2004): 104–23.

Çelik, Zeynep. 'France and Algeria: From Colonial Conflicts to Postcolonial Memories'. *Historical Reflections/Réflexions historiques* 28, no. 2 (2002): 143–62. DOI: 10.1080/09528829908576823.

Chaplin, Paul. *The Historic Huts of the Ross Sea Region*. Christchurch: Antarctic Heritage Trust, 1999.

Cooper, Frederick. *Colonialism in Question: Theory, Knowledge, History*. Berkeley, CA: University of California Press, 2005.

Crew, Spencer R. and James E. Sims. 'Locating Authenticity: Fragments of a Dialogue'. In *Exhibiting Cultures: The Poetics and Politics of Museum Display*, ed. Ivan Karp and Stephen D. Lavine, pp. 159–75. Washington, DC: Smithsonian Institution Press, 1991.

Dodds, Klaus J. 'Antarctic Geopolitics'. In *Handbook on the Politics of Antarctica*, ed. Klaus J. Dodds, Alan D. Hemmings and Peder Roberts, pp. 199–214. Cheltenham: Edward Elgar Publishing, 2017.

Dodds, Klaus J. and Kathryn Yusoff. 'Settlement and Unsettlement in Aotearoa/New Zealand and Antarctica'. *Polar Record* 41, no. 217 (2005): 141–55.

Dodds, Klaus J., Alan D. Hemmings and Peder Roberts (eds). *Handbook on the Politics of Antarctica*. Cheltenham: Edward Elgar Publishing, 2017.

Fontein, Joost. 'Graves, Ruins, and Belonging: Towards an Anthropology of Proximity'. *Journal of the Royal Anthropological Institute* 17, no. 4 (2011): 706–27. DOI: 10.1111/j.1467-9655.2011.01715.x.

Forêt, Philippe. 'Mapping "Ancient" Chinese Antarctica'. *Bulletin of the Museum of Far Eastern Antiquities (Östasiatika Museet)* 73 (2001): 193–215.

Frame, Bob, Daniela Liggett, Kati Lindström, Ricardo M. Roura and Lize-Marié van der Watt. 'Tourism and Heritage in Antarctica: Exploring Cultural, Natural and Subliminal Experiences'. *Polar Geography* 45, no. 1 (2022): 37–57. DOI: 10.1080/1088937x.2021.1918787.

Fultz, Marcella. 'Bibliography of Books and Articles Published in English on Colonialism and Imperialism in 2009'. *Journal of Colonialism and Colonial History* 11, no. 2 (2010). DOI: 10.1353/cch.2010.0007.

Gerovitch, Slava. '"Why Are We Telling Lies?" The Creation of Soviet Space History Myths'. *The Russian Review* 70, no. 3 (2011): 460–84. DOI: 10.1111/j.1467-9434.2011.00624.x.

Geschiere, Peter. 'Funerals and Belonging: Different Patterns in South Cameroon'. *African Studies Review* 48, no. 2 (2005): 45–64. DOI: 10.1353/arw.2005.0059.

Harrowfield, David L. *Icy Heritage: The Historic Sites of the Ross Sea Region, Antarctica*. Christchurch: Antarctic Heritage Trust, 1995.

Hingley, Rebecca. 'Diverging Antarctic Heritage Discourses: The Geopolitical Ramifications of Non-State Actor Engagement with the "State-Sanctioned" Version of Antarctic Heritage'. *The Geographical Journal* 189, no. 1 (2021): 40–8. DOI: 10.1111/geoj.12383.

Jarosz, Katarzyna. 'National Narratives of "Occupation" in Historical Museums of the Post-Soviet Landscape'. In *Visual Histories of Occupation: A Transcultural Dialogue*, ed. Jeremy E. Taylor, pp. 229–46. London: Bloomsbury, 2021.

Köörna, Arno. *Science Serving the People*. Tallinn: Perioodika, 1986.

Leane, Elizabeth, Tim Winter and Juan Francisco Salazar. 'Caught between Nationalism and Internationalism: Replicating Histories of Antarctica in Hobart'. *International Journal of Heritage Studies* 22, no. 3 (2016): 214–27. DOI: 10.1080/13527258.2015.1114010.

Lindsay, Neil and Hong-Key Yoon. 'Toponyms on the Ice: The Symbolic and Iconographical Role of Antarctic Research Base Names'. *Polar Record* 57, E22 (2021): 1–13. DOI: 10.1017/s003224742100022x.

Mancilla, Alejandra. 'The Moral Limits of Territorial Claims in Antarctica'. *Ethics & International Affairs* 32, no. 3 (2018): 339–60.

Mignolo, Walter D. 'Introduction'. *Cultural Studies* 21, nos 2–3 (2007): 155–67. DOI: 10.1080/09502380601162498.

Monmonier, Mark. *From Squaw Tit to Whorehouse Meadow: How Maps Name, Claim, and Inflame*. Chicago: University of Chicago Press, 2007.

National People's Congress of the People's Republic of China. '"关于发展海洋经济 加快建设海洋强国工作情况的报告." 关于发展海洋经济　加快建设海洋强国工作情况的报告_中国人大网', 24 December 2018. www.npc.gov.cn/npc/c12491/201812/83131907fb234bba96edd84b6cffd1f9.shtml. Accessed 27 September 2021.

Nora, Pierre. 'Between Memory and History: *Les Lieux De Mémoire*'. *Representations* 26 (1989): 7–24. DOI: 10.2307/2928520.

Nora, Pierre. 'Comment écrire l'histoire de France'. In *Les lieux de mémoire*, ed. Pierre Nora, pp. 12–32. Paris: Gallimard, 1992.

Pisarenko, Dmitry. 'Куда смотрит Ленин? Интересные факты о российских станциях в Антарктиде'. *Аргументы и факты*, 21 February 2021, pp. 2–4.

Ravi, Ahuja. '"The Bridge-Builders": Some Notes on Railways, Pilgrimage and the British "Civilizing Mission" in Colonial India'. In *Colonialism as Civilizing Mission: Cultural Ideology in British India*, ed. Harald Fischer-Tiné and Michael Mann, pp. 95–116. London: Anthem Press, 2004.

Roberts, Peder, Lize-Marié van der Watt and Adrian Howkins (eds). *Antarctica and the Humanities*. London: Palgrave Macmillan, 2016.

Roura, Ricardo. 'Antarctic Cultural Heritage: Geopolitics and Management'. In *Handbook on the Politics of Antarctica*, ed. Klaus J. Dodds, Alan D. Hemmings and Peder Roberts, pp. 468–85. Cheltenham: Edward Elgar Publishing, 2017.

Saint Petersburg Mining University Scientific Center, 'Remembering Boris Borisovich Kudryashov'. https://ccarctic.com/en/boris-borisovich-kudryashov. Accessed 26 September 2021.

Saparov, Arseny. 'The Alteration of Place Names and the Construction of National Identity in Soviet Armenia'. *Cahiers du Monde russe* 44, no. 1 (2003): 179–98. DOI: 10.4000/monderusse.135.

Secretariat of the Antarctic Treaty. 'Revised List of Historic Sites and Monuments Antarctic Treaty Database – Measure 23 (2021) – ATCM XLIII – CEP XXIII, Paris', www.ats.aq/devAS/Meetings/Measure/732. Accessed 12 January 2023.

Senatore, María X. 'Things in Antarctica: An Archaeological Perspective'. *The Polar Journal* 10, no. 2 (2020): 1–23. DOI: 10.1080/2154896x.2020.1799610.

Shipton, Parker. *Mortgaging the Ancestors: Ideologies of Attachment in Africa*. New Haven, CT: Yale University Press, 2009.

Śliwka, Marek. 'Antarktyda – Wyprawa Życia'. https://wyprawy.pl/pl-PL/impresje-z-podrozy/antarktyda-wyprawa-zycia,4.html. Accessed 2 October 2021.

Stefanova, Olga (dir.). *Buromsky Island*. DVD. Lex Film, 2020.

Stefański, Krzysztof. 'Pływające Laboratorium Profesor Siedlecki'. *Morze* 8 (2017): 79–87.

Stolz, Thomas and Ingo H. Warnke. 'When Places Change Their Names and when They Do Not. Selected Aspects of Colonial and Postcolonial Toponymy in Former French and Spanish Colonies in West Africa: The Cases of Saint Louis (Senegal) and the Western Sahara'. *International Journal of the Sociology of Language* 2016, no. 239 (2016): 29–56. DOI:10.1515/ijsl-2016-0004.

Swithinbank, Charles. 'A Year with the Russians in Antarctica'. *The Geographical Journal* 132, no. 4 (1966): 463–74. DOI: 10.2307/1792525.

Tammiksaar, Erki. 'The Russian Antarctic Expedition under the Command of Fabian Gottlieb von Bellingshausen and Its Reception in Russia and the World'. *Polar Record* 52, no. 5 (2016): 578–600. DOI: 10.1017/s0032247416000449.

Toma, Peter A. 'Soviet Attitude towards the Acquisition of Territorial Sovereignty in the Antarctic'. *American Journal of International Law* 50, no. 3 (1956): 611–26. DOI: 10.2307/2195509.

TVN24. 'Na Antarktydzie uczcili pamięć polskiego przyrodnika'. TVN24, 1 November 2010. https://tvn24.pl/polska/na-antarktydzie-uczcili-pamiec-polskiego-przyrodnika-ra150945-3591855. Accessed 17 October 2022.

Upadhyay, Vrajaindra. 'What Is Imperialism? Situating Imperialism in Relation to Capitalism and Colonialism'. *SSRN Electronic Journal*, 2018 (30 July). DOI: 10.2139/ssrn.3222573.

'Высоцкий Владимир (1963г) – ПЕСНЯ о …'. YouTube, 25 January 2017. www.youtube.com/watch?v=T-28fdSmnuc (accessed 20 January 2023).

Zarankin, Andrés and Melisa A. Salerno. 'Antarctic Archaeology'. In *The Routledge Handbook of Global Historical Archaeology*, ed. Charles Orser, James Symonds, Pedro Paulo A. Funari, Andrés Zarankin and Susan Lawrence, pp. 915–26. London: Routledge, 2020. DOI: 10.4324/9781315202846-46.

4

Argentina and Chile's Antarctic colonialism? A postcolonial critique to Eurocentric analysis

Ignacio Javier Cardone

The relationship between the Antarctic and colonialism presents academics with a fascinating case. The absence of Indigenous population questions the very applicability of the concept to the Antarctic. Nonetheless, a broader understanding of colonialism from a critical perspective leads us to approach the exploration of Antarctica as part of the wider global phenomenon of colonialism and the expansion of capitalism.[1] That changes our perspective on how to analyse and interpret the different nations' approaches to the white continent.

The main problem is presented by the fact that traditional approaches to Antarctic colonialism are imbued with western colonialist ideology that have considered certain colonial concepts, practices and relationships as natural, disregarding other approaches. The disregard with which Latin American involvement in Antarctica has been treated in the mainstream literature has been pointed out by Latin American authors, and recently by academics from Europe and the USA.[2] However, such an endeavour is far from being a straightforward and simple process and includes calling into question the very conceptual framework we use for analysing social reality.

Shirley Scott has pointed out the need to discriminate the distinct approach that different nations applied to their actions in the Antarctic.[3] Differentiating three waves of Antarctic imperialism, Scott calls to our attention the fact that the '[a]pplication of a post-colonial lens to the international political history of Antarctica facilitates identification of patterns of domination and resistance'.[4] That perspective is shared by Klaus J. Dodds and Christy Collis, but without differentiating the different forms of relationship with Antarctica, equating all claims to some form of colonialism.[5] Nicoletta Brazelli applies a similar interpretation, considering that all the Antarctic Treaty signatories were acting in a colonialist manner by deciding on behalf of humankind, but acknowledging the different perspectives opened up in southern nations by postcolonial approaches.[6]

The challenge, therefore, is to identify the diversity of approaches to Antarctica, including the need to overcome the view of South American nations as passive witnesses, avoiding the use of stereotypical Eurocentric frameworks and interpreting those practices on their own terms.[7] Scott's analysis certainly constitutes a first step in that direction by questioning and distinguishing the different principles of territorial expansion that ruled the different nations. Following that same path, I propose here to adopt an analysis of Argentina and Chile's actions in Antarctica, following a postcolonial analysis based on the international practice perspective.[8] Based on the idea of practices as relative stable patterns of socially meaningful actions, this perspective adds to the mere identification of external manifestations of doing (behaviour) and the intentional and intersubjective meaning (action) of the patterned character of practices.[9] It situates them in a field of struggle for recognition and significations both for actors and for practices themselves, and allows us to contest the naturalisation of meanings and structured situations typical of Eurocentric views, locating in the actors themselves the attribution of meanings and content to their actions. While in previous works I have analysed the building of an Antarctic identity in Argentina and Chile, my objective here is to provide an analysis of how Argentina and Chile's practices regarding Antarctica weigh against colonialist practices and how they fit within global dynamics.[10]

The international practice perspective provides a framework within which the actions of both countries can be interpreted in the wider scope of colonialist relations of domination and control, related to the legitimation of actors and practices and their encounter as a field in which power relations are expressed. I therefore analyse in what capacity Argentina and Chile were acknowledged by their Antarctic counterparts, and how their practices expressed a colonial relationship or a resistance to it.

The chapter consists of five parts. The first analyses the conceptual puzzle of defining colonialism, its link with imperialism, and the difference from nationalism and its hybrid character in postcolonial countries. The second considers the territorial dimension, how it relates to the phenomenon of colonialism, and how we can interpret Argentina and Chile's Antarctic involvement. The third part examines the approaches that Argentina and Chile have to Antarctic science, and how they differ from those of the European countries and the USA. The fourth looks into the economic exploitation of Antarctica, and how Argentina and Chile dealt with economic prospects and activities in the region. The final part presents the discussion and general conclusions.

The conceptual puzzle: Colonialism, imperialism and nationalism

Colonialism is a contested concept. It can be seen as a socio-economic practice, or as a complex device designed to establish political, cultural, social and economic domination of other peoples. The former, when taken in isolation, deprives the concept of its historical character and sociological significance, considering merely the settlement in new lands; maintaining a connection with a parent state; avoiding any reference to the encounter of peoples, conquest and domination.[11] Such a cleansed concept has the advantage of including practices across time and space, being applicable to any circumstances. However, it does not constitute an ideal type from a sociological perspective, lacking heuristic utility and turning the word into a sterile concept.[12]

On the other hand, from a sociological and historical viewpoint, colonialism can be interpreted as a set of practices through which territorial expansion aimed at economic exploitation is undertaken, imbued with a sense of superiority, irrespective of whether the targeted lands are inhabited or considered by other peoples as their domains. This requires that any people who could inhabit that territory or claim any bond with it be considered inferior, and that the incorporated territory be placed in a subordinated hierarchy that establishes a structural relationship of dependence. In other words, colonialism requires a distinction between homeland and colony and their respective populations, in which only the former is considered autonomous.

Historically, that expansion took the form of practices of exploration, conquest and domination, often conceived as a civilising quest over other peoples. It included a wide range of practices such as 'trade, settlement, plunder, negotiation, warfare, genocide, and enslavement', justified by an alleged superiority over the colonised.[13] While, analytically, colonialism and settler colonialism are distinct formations, it is important to highlight that both concepts located domination and control over other peoples at the centre, where the colonising force considered itself superior to the colonised.[14] This renders the idea of colonialism or settler colonialism without the colonised an empty concept, and calls one to look at the phenomenon of colonialism as an international practice in which representations of who are legitimate actors and which are legitimate practices are considered.[15]

Additionally, modern European colonialism added important changes to the social and economic structures of the colonies, establishing a circuit of capital, people and natural resources between the colonised and the colonising countries.[16] In this regard, it was a key factor in the expansion of European capitalism, and structured the geographically unequal distribution of wealth that persists today. Modern European colonialism projected

a system of political domination, social control and economic exploitation with global scope and expressed international practices that imposed
European ways as the universal expression of civilisation and modernity.[17]

This leads us to the concept of imperialism, which is different from colonialism but also closely related. While some authors identify them as parts
of the same phenomenon, I find it more appropriate to distinguish between
colonialism and imperialism.[18] While colonialism is the practice of political, social and economic oppression linked to the territorial control of the
land and the establishment of an asymmetrical and subordinated relationship, imperialism is a policy oriented to the political control outside the
homeland territory, aimed at ensuring a hegemonic position and advancing
interests beyond a state's national borders, irrespective of the relationship
established with the oppressed peoples. This could take the form of formal
empires or the more recent forms of neoimperialism, based on the deployment of military forces around the world and the use of non-military forms
of oppression.[19]

In this light, colonialism is usually implemented as a means to imperialism, but it is only one of the options available for the centre of power
to extend its political control. In other words, while colonialism is almost
unequivocally related to imperialism, the latter could adopt other forms,
including non-territorial methods of domination and control.

The form of colonialism adopted by modern European imperialism was
universalist, as it considered only European forms to be valid, modern and
civilised, and presumed that they needed to be imposed upon the colonised.
This facet of colonialism was expressed through the idea of common principles that ruled the relationships between 'civilised' nations, but which
excepted all other peoples and nations. In this regard, it is interesting to
note that European colonialism acknowledged a similar status for the other
European powers, while the rest of the world remained a place to be colonised and, therefore, civilised.

Such neglect of other cultures and social institutions translated into certain relationships with territory and with Indigenous populations. The idea
of a 'discovery' of the Americas, an already populated continent; the arbitrary division of the territory following colonialist interests; and the conception of the colonisation process as a 'conquest' are examples of the
territorial practices that disregarded any pre-existent right or socio-political
and territorial order. The subordinated relationship between the metropolis
and the colony reinforced that character and denied autonomy to the local
communities – either Indigenous or settlers – subjected to the political and
economic needs of the centre of political control.

In the cultural realm, the universalist character of modern European
colonialism was articulated by denying any value to Indigenous knowledge

and culture, making it invisible. However, this universalist character col-
lided with the colonialist relationship, based on the subordinated distinction
between the metropolis and the colony, the colonisers and the colonised.
The 'success' of the modernising project led to demands for autonomy and
an egalitarian status in the colonies – even when not necessarily between the
settlers' groups and Indigenous communities.[20] This resulted in nationalist
movements of independence that looked to refound the state under the idea
of the 'nation' in its modern, territorial form. In this process, they adopted
an anti-colonialist ethos, notwithstanding that they mirrored several characteristics of their former metropolis, and many times fostered the same
universalist discourse to advance effective territorial control.

The combination between local assertiveness; an anti-colonialist impe-
tus; and the adoption of forms, institutions and practices derived from the
former colonisers established what has been called the hybrid character
of postcolonial nations.[21] The territorial constitution of such nations followed the divisions established by the colonisation process and imported
many European social, political and administrative institutional forms.
Furthermore, the way in which many of those constituted nations treated
the Indigenous populations and their culture did not differ significantly from
colonialist ways, something that has been covered by settler colonialism
theory. However, the hybrid character differed from colonialist forms in
that it sought to abolish the typical colonialist relationships of subjugation,
being favourable to the implementation of federal and republican forms.
Furthermore, identities and culture typically amalgamated imported ideas
and customs with those inherited from the Indigenous populations, as well
as others that were developed by the 'criollos'. Such a process was not without violence, but it was the need to differentiate from the former metropolis,
adopting some local identity while remaining modern, that constituted the
hybrid character of these nation-state formations. As works on settler colonialism have highlighted, this process denied the Indigenous culture as such
by incorporating some of its traits into the national culture. However, it is
precisely this process, looking to incorporate individuals and territories into
the nation, that makes it different from colonialism.

The process of independence and the promotion of nationalism did not
therefore abolish the universalist claim of the modernist project, but foregrounded resistance to the differentiation characteristic of the colonial relationship. The nationalism that arose from the independence process was
not necessarily less racist, more humanitarian or respectful of Indigenous
cultures, but consisted of an expressive rearrangement of the political relationships of subordination and control among the different geographical
regions, and included the adaptation of the colonialist modernising project to domestic characteristics, interests and hybrid cultures. In particular,

nationalism differed from colonialism in that territoriality did not suppose a hierarchical relationship, at least formally. On the other hand, in the economic realm, the already established global relationships of dependency were not fundamentally altered – with the notable exception of the USA – relegating the new independent nations to a similarly subordinated economic position. And culturally, national identity was constructed through the amalgamation of modernist western values and traditional ones, underpinned by a strong anti-colonialist ethos.[22]

Thus, in the following, I argue that the approaches of Argentina and Chile to Antarctic territoriality, scientific research and economic activities resulting from their nationalism are distinct from the practices implemented by colonialist powers. While some of those practices have similar external manifestations, a more thorough analysis demonstrates that their determinants and expressions are distinct from colonial practices and should be interpreted accordingly. The hybrid character of Latin American nationalism certainly made it coincide with colonialist powers in references to sovereignty, national interests and the value of science, but also established a particular perspective that cannot be subsumed into a Eurocentric analysis.

Argentina and Chile's approaches to Antarctic territoriality

Territoriality is a basic constitutive element of the modern nation-state, in the sense that the definition of a nation's borders – the geographic space that it claims for itself – establishes the limits of its authority and sovereignty.[23] The territoriality linked to the colony is different from that aroused by the sense of the *fatherland* – or national territory – as the colonies are integrated as appendices to the nation in a subordinated role. In this regard, the colonialist territoriality is typically expansionist and linked to a push for conquest and domination, while territoriality linked to the idea of national territory is integrative and linked to a historical identity.

Other forms of spatiality and territoriality are possible, but these two hold special interest as they distinguish Argentina and Chile's territoriality from European colonialist practice. In Scott's words, 'Chile and Argentina perceived their territory in Antarctica as integral to their nation', distinguishing it from the colonialist territoriality that the European powers displayed in Antarctica.[24]

First, it is important to understand that Argentina and Chile's territoriality arose from struggles for independence and subsequent civil and regional wars. Following the independence process, the region was subject to struggles between forces of integration and division at the internal level, bordering disputes at the regional level, and resistance to colonialist practices from European powers – such as the British in the Islas Malvinas/Falkland Islands. The hybrid character of the nascent nations with its modernist project was expressed through efforts to control the greatest extension of land possible, mirroring the balance-of-power logic of European powers.[25] The extension of state control through its military and administrative presence was essential to extending the frontiers of primary production, thus fulfilling their inclusion within the circuits of global capitalism.

This advancement included the displacement, domination and decimation of Indigenous populations, paralleling European colonial practices. However, the way in which this territory was integrated into the national realm was fundamentally different.[26] This is to say not that such forms were more humane but that the territorial integration was substantially different and did not establish a colonial relationship. Behind those forces pushing for territorial control was an ideology that considered these territories part of the nation and a rightful inheritance from their Hispanic colonial past. In this process a national territorial conscience was constructed, usually accompanied by a sense of territorial loss.[27] Furthermore, these practices were a consequence of European imperialism, as they responded to demands for raw materials on the part of the centres of industrial production in Europe and were considered a way to secure territory and natural resources deemed necessary to ensure their security in the face of imperialist threats.[28]

During the 1800s, European powers and the USA participated in a series of incidents that Latin American countries regarded as direct attacks on their territorial integrity and sovereignty. Among them, the taking by force of the Malvinas /Falklands in 1833, and the invasion by Spain of the Chincha Islands in 1864, are exemplary.[29] Other conflicts, such as that over the intent to install a monarchy in Ecuador, and diplomatic strains resulting from abuses and challenges to the Latin American nations' jurisdiction over European citizens within their territory, cemented a sense of rejection of European colonial imperialism.[30]

The territoriality of Argentina and Chile interpreted their territory as extending as far as the South Pole, based on the idea of inheritance of the concession made by the papal bulls to Spain in 1493.[31] These inherited rights were coupled with the idea of proximity, geographical influence, contiguity, and the presence through economic activities undertaken by nationals and residents of both countries since the nineteenth century. From early on, the words and actions of Argentinians and Chileans expressed the idea of the Antarctic as juridically, naturally and historically bonded with their territories.

Early territorial interest in the region was articulated in the form of planned geographic and scientific expeditions, aid provided to other nations' explorers and the issue of regulations over activities to be undertaken in the southern regions. The idea of Antarctica as naturally bonded with the South American continent was manifest in the different expeditions proposed even before the Sixth International Geographical Congress's 1895 call to explore the Antarctic.[32] Such a bond was also manifest in the language of some European explorers such as Giacomo Bove and Otto Nordenskjöld, who tried to interest Argentina and Chile in the exploration of the region.[33]

The use of the southern ports by European expeditions raised the region's prominence in the awareness of the South American public and provided a loose sense of belonging through the provision of aid by means of products, services, meteorological information and a few notable rescues.[34] As part of the territorial imagination connecting South America with the southern regions, the idea of an American Antarctica started to arise as early as the late nineteenth century, becoming part of the public imagination of Argentina and Chile and acquiring a key role in the 1940s in the context of increasing tensions with the British.[35]

However, the nationalism applied to Antarctica limited their capacity to adopt a regional front.[36] In 1940, a US proposal to claim an Antarctic sector on behalf of all American republics was rejected, and Chile issued a decree defining the limits of its Antarctic sector, causing tensions with Argentina.[37] This demonstrated that American Antarctica was less a shared space than an idea that allowed opposition to the pretensions of extracontinental powers.[38] This notwithstanding, both countries reached some limited understanding in 1941, 1947 and 1948, and looked for the support of other Latin American countries in Pan American forums. They succeeded in including the American Antarctic sector within the region of the strategic defence of the InterAmerican Treaty of Reciprocal Assistance (TIAR, also known as the Rio Pact) in 1947. With time, both countries adopted the concept of South American Antarctica, which excluded the USA.[39]

Symbolic and cultural aspects also expressed a territoriality linked to nationalist practices that differed from colonialism. Argentina justified the 1904 acquisition of the Scottish explorer William Speirs Bruce's observatory on Laurie Island as a project 'related to the establishment of new magnetic and meteorological stations in the Southern Seas of the Republic'.[40] The flying of the Argentine flag at the station and the designation of a postmaster from such an early date symbolically connected the mainland with Antarctica, instead of constituting an episodic 'heroic' event. As the conflict over Antarctica was intensifying during the 1940s, Argentina and Chile looked to foster greater public awareness of Antarctica and promoted the inclusion of their respective Antarctic sectors on all maps of the national territory, a practice that continues today.[41] Nationalist movements in Argentina and Chile also promoted the inclusion of content related to Antarctica and their national rights within educational curricula. This was accompanied by public declarations and formal acts in the region with the usual expressions of national belonging, added to the installation of assistance to navigation and the establishment of communication structures, including permanent radio stations and post offices. Probably the most symbolic action was the establishment of families in Antarctica by Argentina in 1978 and by Chile in 1984, for periods of up to two years. Despite being commonly interpreted as colonialist practices, these settlements lacked the characteristics of the colonial relationship, being a manifestation of the presence of the state in what was considered a national territory, and not a proper colonialist practice, which would need to be aimed at economic extraction.[42]

Finally, the two South American nations approached the Antarctic territorially in the light of concerns about possible British imperialist actions. Considering the precedent of the Malvinas/Falklands and the presence of British interests in Patagonia at the beginning of the twentieth century, both nations feared a possible movement from the British, and looked for affirmative actions and to constitute a common front. The subsequent issue of Letters Patent by the British in 1908, establishing the Falkland Islands Dependencies, structured a confrontation between the approach of the two South American countries to Antarctica and the colonialist project of the British, which evolved up until the signing of the Antarctic Treaty.[43]

After this, a differential perception of the rights to the region was structured between the southern nations and the European powers. The latter built their positions on the basis of the Berlin Conference of 1884–85, which divided Africa among the European powers, while Argentina and Chile remained adamant regarding their privileged rights within, and their connection to, the region. European disregard of both countries' interests in communications, negotiations and analysis of the territorial situation in Antarctica prevented any thought of the South American states' being acknowledged as equals by Europe.[44] For Argentina and Chile, such negligence was another expression of colonial imperialism, expressed through pretensions to lands so distant from their homelands, which contrasted their own proximity and identity. This perception also expressed their resistance to the idea of the 'hero/conquistador', typical of the colonialist narrative, which was incarnated in the way the history of Antarctica was expressed in colonialist countries.[45]

At the same time, Argentina and Chile were resistant to the colonialist imprint that scientific activity in Antarctica took after the end of the first wave of international collaborative exploration during the first decade of the twentieth century, approaching Antarctic research in a very different manner.

Argentina and Chile's approaches to Antarctic research

Argentina and Chile's approaches to Antarctic research considered western science the highest expression of knowledge, overlooking the colonialist facet with which scientific enterprise is usually imbued. Thus, their original approach to scientific activities in Antarctica appealed to the western collaborative civilising spirit. Expressions of the universal value of science were common, and both countries offered unconditioned collaboration to foreign expeditions heading south just in exchange for public acknowledgement. However, their approach to Antarctic scientific research in projects of their own making was notably different.

In general, western science was permeated with important colonialist elements, presented as superior and represented in a triumphalist form that neglected their inheritance from other cultures and the participation of the local population and informants in the production of knowledge.[46] Moreover, western scientific practice itself presented a dynamic that resembled the colonialist circuit of peoples and resources, with a similar geographical asymmetry.

In Antarctica, this has been translated into neglecting the southern nations' collaboration in early Antarctic exploration, their being portrayed as little more than places of passage. Not only have their collaborations in other nations' scientific enterprises been ignored, but their own scientific activities have commonly been underestimated. Since early Antarctic exploration, doubts about methodological handling and scientific rigour were common in the European treatment of data and findings coming from Argentina and Chile, in a clear colonialist appreciation of those countries' scientific skills.[47]

But the most significant differential trait of the approaches of both countries to Antarctic science is the continuous character that their scientific effort acquired, in contrast with the event-based and temporal character of almost all colonialist exploratory endeavours. Antarctic expeditions by European powers were characterised by the colonialist practices of discovery and possession, with geographical surveying playing a central role because of the possibilities it opened for territorial claims. While science played a relevant part in many expeditions, geographical exploration ended up fuelling much Antarctic endeavour during the early twentieth century.

In contrast, Argentina and Chile devised their Antarctic plans as permanent projects, despite the failure of some to materialise and their having a very limited presence in the area up until the 1940s, with the notable exceptions of the Argentine Laurie Island and South Georgia stations. Plans for a series of meteorological stations were proposed by the Instituto Geográfico Argentino in the 1880s but insufficient resources were available. A similar project arose in 1905, intended to complement the recently built Laurie Island station with the planned South Georgia station and a third one on Wandel Island, but this last failed to be installed.[48] For its part, in Chile, the Minister of Foreign Affairs, Antonio Huneeus, also proposed an Antarctic expedition to install a permanent meteorological station in 1906, but the country was struck by a huge earthquake in Valparaíso, forcing it to concentrate its resources on the emergency and cancel all Antarctic plans.[49]

Although both countries eventually built their own Antarctic myths around some individuals and their feats – José María Sobral and Julián Irízar in Argentina and Luis Pardo Villalón in Chile – their actions in Antarctica were not inspired by a desire for fame and fortune as was the case with many European explorers. Most of the early European expeditions were private initiatives – except for the German expeditions – with some form of public funding, donations and financing through profits coming from books and other forms of publicity. This differed significantly from the official Argentinian expeditions since 1904, and from the actions taken in support of expeditions in distress. Those actions were oriented to exert a loose form of administration and assistance over the area, comparable in a sense with the British establishment of the Discovery Investigations, though these were in order to inform the creation of a regulatory framework that could ensure the sustainable exploitation of whales under British colonial authority.[50]

Such an approach was also present in cultural objects. As Pablo Fontana has argued, the 'heroic' – i.e. European and US – record of exploration was based on a linear account in which the expedition arrives, explores, overcomes some insurmountable difficulty and returns home.[51] On the other hand, the Argentine film about Laurie Island station, *Entre los hielos de las islas Orcadas* (*Within the Frozen Lands of the South Orkneys*), presented a circular story in which the beginning and the end connect, establishing a permanent cycle. This narrative not only expressed the permanent character of the Argentine presence, but also diluted the significance of the 'heroic' individual facet of exploration as a national commitment. While this cyclical character was also present in the scientific work undertaken through the Discovery Investigations at sea, it was not prevalent in the cultural imagination in the same way as the British involvement in the Antarctic.

Only in 1944, with the British Operation Tabarin, intended to undermine the Argentine position in the area, did European Antarctic science establish permanent land stations. By this time, any illusions held by Argentina and Chile about the cosmopolitan nature of the European scientific involvement in Antarctica had evaporated. Realising the political consequences of Europe's presence on the continent, both countries expressed their concerns over the political effects of scientific activities.[52]

The 1948 proposal by Chile for a status quo agreement regarding activities in Antarctica was aimed at promoting scientific international collaboration without compromising its national stake in the area.[53] It proposed a five-year moratorium during which activities would not be considered for the purposes of making claims, exchange of information would be facilitated, and taxes or other charges in the area would be exempted. The same view informed the Chilean resolve to include a resolution at the Antarctic Conferences of the Special Committee for the International Geophysical Year (IGY) that no scientific activity would alter the political status quo.[54] The provision ended up being incorporated into Article IV of the Antarctic Treaty, signed on 1 December 1959, constituting one of the political pillars of the agreement.[55]

After a first period of relative innocence regarding Antarctic science, therefore, Argentina and Chile started to be sceptical of its 'neutral' character. Despite being favourable, in general, to international collaboration in scientific research, this collaboration has been allowed as a consequence of the guarantees provided by the status quo agreement of the IGY and the Antarctic Treaty, and is still strongly tied to it. Such distrust was also motivated by their misgivings that research could inform economic exploitation and establish some form of hierarchy that might reproduce the economic colonialism of the past, described in the next section.

Argentina and Chile's approaches to Antarctic economic exploitation

The economic prospects of Antarctica have played a role in Argentina and Chile's relationship with it. However, internal conflicts, border disputes, lack of territorial control and scarcity of resources hindered any attempt systematically to develop, regulate and control economic activity in the region. At the beginning of the twentieth century, Chile and Argentina started to issue regulations extending to the southern parts of what they considered their territories.

For Argentina and Chile, the expansion of their administrative control and economic activities to the south was no more than a continuation of the movement of expansion of their economic frontiers that had been taking place since their integration into the global economy. Within this movement, effective presence and administration, economic interest and the affirmation of sovereignty were strongly linked. Distinct from typical colonialist economic practice, where political control and social violence are aimed mainly at extracting economic resources from the colonies, in the case of Latin America the expansion of economic activities in Antarctica had the advantage of fostering national presence with reduced costs, mainly aimed at developing those regions and reinforcing their territorial sovereignty.[56]

However, the development of a profitable commercial activity attracted other actors. The establishment of the first permanent whaling station in South Georgia, the port of Grytviken, in 1904, was followed by others, and motivated the first conflicts of jurisdiction. The Compañía Argentina de Pesca S.A. had been established with the assistance of the Argentine government, which exempted the company's products from import duties as the activities were coming from the national territory, while the British government in the Malvinas/Falklands claimed rights over those lands and demanded payment, using the presence of the warship *HMS Sappho* to guarantee the agreement with the company.[57] Instead of informing or negotiating with Argentina, the British government assumed a position that avoided controversy, considering its claims sufficient to establish a colonial relationship of subordination in South Georgia.

In contrast, the overlap between the ambitions of Argentina and Chile regarding the issue of permits evidenced the need to initiate negotiations, which – as we have seen – started in 1906 but reached no agreement. By this time, the British had come to see in Antarctica a possible source of resources to finance part of their colonial empire, resulting in the 1908 Letters Patent.[58] The whaling industry in Antarctica developed rapidly, associated with capital of diverse origin, but the British and Norwegians were dominant. Britain looked for a device that could allow it to control the colonial space and its main resource, the whales, creating the afore-mentioned Discovery Investigations programme.[59] What Adrian Howkins has described as the 'environmental authority', claimed by the British as a consequence of scientific data, was another expression of colonialism aimed at establishing a hierarchy that ensured the exploitation of resources in a profitable – and civilised – way.[60]

The decline of whaling after the Second World War saw no equivalent economic interest taking its place. The prospect of mineral resource exploitation was always present, but it did not go any further than public discourse aimed at attaining public attention and, potentially, government funding. If anything, the IGY served to confirm that Antarctica was at least a few generations away from profitable mineral exploitation.[61] Thus, the decline of whaling was also a decline of colonialist interest, opening the door for the political agreement that resulted in the Antarctic Treaty.

However, every time the issue of economic resources arose within the Antarctic regime, internal conflicts and external pressures surfaced. The dominant Argentine and Chilean position was to resist the new forms of economic domination and imperialism and resort to nationalism, being sceptical of the potential to establish a fair and equitable arrangement. This, added to their concerns over the potential environmental impacts of Antarctic economic activities across the American continent, led them to support a position favourable to environmental preservation. While the prospect of unforeseen mineral economic riches in Antarctica continues to be promoted to the public in both countries as a way to attract interest, that vision is linked not with colonialist practices but with images of national development, and is increasingly being replaced by the idea of environmental protection.

Conclusion

When considering Argentina and Chile's approach to Antarctica it is necessary to avoid being misled by Eurocentric analysis. Although the actions and attitudes of both South American countries were in some cases similar in form to those of the European colonialist powers and the USA, a number of significant differences call into question the use of categories that are descriptive and specific for the European case.

To begin with, it is necessary to highlight the hybrid character of Argentina and Chile, in the sense that they are products of a process of independence in which the European westernised element continued to be regarded as superior. It is no surprise that the civilising appeal of science and exploration was relevant in the attitudes of both South American countries to Antarctica. However, it is also important to acknowledge the aspect of resistance to colonial imperialism imprinted in their nationalism. This was especially reinforced in the case of Argentina, since the former colony had resisted two British invasions of Buenos Aires, and protested when the British took the Malvinas/Falklands in 1833.

As Scott has established, moreover, it is important to distinguish between the South American tradition inherited from Spain and the British imperialist tradition. Whether the former was considered a legacy that was attained through bloody struggles against the oppressor, the latter was the outcome of a colonialist philosophy instilled by a sense of superiority that justified the use of coercive force. South America did not consider British practices a basis for rights, especially as they were based on an imperialist and colonialist ethos that they had resisted. At the same time, they rejected the disregard with which European powers treated the involvement of both nations in Antarctica, and generally avoided being included in the dynamics of colonialist practices on which the European powers based their positions.

Furthermore, the European powers saw in Antarctica a place for imperial expansion and colonisation, if not in the sense of conquest and domination over people then at least in terms of territorial annexation and extraction of economic benefits. In this regard, they saw in Antarctica not part of their national territory, but a faraway land that could be incorporated into their systems of political and economic control. In contrast, both South American countries considered the Antarctic part of their national territory from the very beginning of their involvement, joining the two countries through imaginary, cultural and physical links.

The relationship of Argentina and Chile with Antarctica can therefore be understood to present a territoriality that is not colonialist in nature or in its practices. While such territoriality includes values and representations taken from western European culture, it also presents particularities that make it improper to subsume it into the categories and representations designed for the analysis of European colonialism. The way the Antarctic was thought about, imagined and perceived in Argentina and Chile did not correspond with the subordinated hierarchy typical of the colonialist relationship, nor with the self-image of superiority that characterised European colonialism.

In terms of the role that both Latin American countries gave to Antarctic science, it is also important to stress that scientific endeavour had a very different character in those countries compared with the mainly private, often commercially motivated and temporally limited features of the European involvement in the region at the beginning of the twentieth century. Seeing in science an expression of national commitment and a means to provide assistance and effective administration of the area, Argentina and Chile aimed for a continuous presence, despite the availability of resources and the internal political landscape limiting the potential to achieving this.

Once the colonising project of European-US science became evident to the two countries, their reluctance to accept Antarctic scientific involvement as politically neutral was mobilised in order to obtain guarantees that scientific activity would not impact political status. This struggle with the colonialist function of Antarctic science finally led to the IGY resolution that there must be no sovereignty outcomes from the event's activities, and helped to establish Article IV of the Antarctic Treaty, which constituted the basis for the political agreement that created the Antarctic regime.

Finally, while both nations saw in the Antarctic a region with economic potential, the way they approached commercial activities was mostly informed by their territorial and sovereignty concerns, rather than by any economic prospects. The regulation, tax burden and dependence typical of the colonialist relationship was what mediated the relationship between the European governments and economic activities in the Antarctic, while Argentina and Chile pursued neither a taxation policy, nor the establishment of a dependent relationship, but provided assistance and tax benefits to promote the consolidation of the nation's presence in the region.

The issues covered above implies not that Argentina and Chile's approaches to Antarctica are in any way better or ethically superior, but that they have distinctive characteristics that do not allow them to be interpreted within the framework of colonialism. Interpreting their action in Antarctica as colonialist is to force them to fit Eurocentric concepts that do not explain Argentina and Chile's realities, practices and place in the international system. What is needed, therefore, is to understand how those differences affect their perceptions of Antarctica, and how that impacts political attitudes.

As a final note, the present work suggests that Antarctic colonialism should be seen not as a relation between the colonialist nation and the Antarctic territory, but as a relationship in which asymmetries between different nations are expressed by practices that reflect one country's sense of superiority over the others. This results in universalist claims that disregard other agents' identity, significations or practices regarding Antarctica, denying them or subsuming within their own categories or representations – as with colonialism. Only by taking into consideration these aspects and the way in which they result in acts of resistance can a more thorough understanding of Antarctic practices and Antarctic colonialism be reached.

Notes

1 Klaus J. Dodds and Christy Collis distinguish Antarctic colonialism from other forms as being an 'un-evil' colonialism (see Klaus J. Dodds and Christy Collis, 'Post-Colonial Antarctica', in Klaus J. Dodds, Alan D. Hemmings and Peder Roberts (eds), *Handbook on the Politics of Antarctica* (Cheltenham: Edward Elgar Publishing, 2017), pp. 50–68 (p. 52)), but they do not consider the global scale of colonialism or distinguish different forms of appropriation and relationship with Antarctica that could be considered non-colonial.

2 For Latin American authors, see Jorge Berguño, 'El despertar de la conciencia antártica (1874–1914). Primera parte: Origen y desarrollo de la cooperación científica internacional', *Boletín Antártico Chileno* 17:2 (1998), 2–13; Jorge Berguño, 'The Intellectual Sources of the Antarctic Treaty', in Cornelia Lüdecke (ed.), *2nd SCAR Workshop on the History of Antarctic Research*, special issue of *Boletín Antártico Chileno* (Punta Arenas: Instituto Antártico Chileno, 2006), pp. 11–17; Ignacio Javier Cardone and Pablo Gabriel Fontana, 'Latin-American Contributions to the Creation of the Antarctic Regime', *The Polar Journal* 9:2 (2019), 300–23, DOI: 10.1080/2154896X.2019.1685174. For others, see Nicoletta Brazelli, 'Heroic and Post-Colonial Antarctic Narratives', in Dodds *et al.*, *Handbook on the Politics of Antarctica*, pp. 69–83; Dodds and Collis, 'Post-Colonial Antarctica'; Klaus J. Dodds, 'Post-Colonial Antarctica: An Emerging Engagement', *Polar Record* 42:1 (2006), 59–70, DOI: 10.1017/S0032247405004857; Shirley V. Scott, 'Ingenious and Innocuous? Article IV of the Antarctic Treaty as Imperialism', *Polar Journal* 1:1 (2011), 51–62, DOI: 10.1080/2154896X.2011.568787; Shirley V. Scott, 'Three Waves of Antarctic Imperialism', in Dodds *et al.*, *Handbook on the Politics of Antarctica*, pp. 37–49.

3 Scott, 'Three Waves of Antarctic Imperialism', p. 45.

4 Scott, 'Three Waves of Antarctic Imperialism', p. 45.

5 Dodds, 'Post-Colonial Antarctica'; Dodds and Collis, 'Post-Colonial Antarctica'.

6 Brazelli, 'Heroic and Post-Colonial Antarctic Narratives', pp. 75, 77.

7 Berguño, 'El despertar', p. 2.

8 Emanuel Adler and Vincent Pouliot (eds), *International Practices* (New York: Cambridge University Press, 2011); Theodore R. Schatzki, Karin Knorr Cetina and Eike von Savigny, *The Practice Turn in Contemporary Theory* (London: Routledge, 2001).

9 Adler and Pouliot, *International Practices*.

10 Ignacio Javier Cardone, 'Shaping an Antarctic Identity in Argentina and Chile', *Defence Strategic Communications* 8 (2020), 53–88, DOI: 10.30966/2018. RIGA.8.2.

11 Ania Loomba, *Colonialism/Postcolonialism*, 3rd edn (Abingdon: Routledge, 2015), pp. 19–20.

12 For the methodology of ideal types, see Max Weber, *Economy and Society: An Outline of Interpretive Sociology*, Vol. I (Berkeley: University of California Press, 2013), pp. 4–22.

13 Loomba, *Colonialism/Postcolonialism*, p. 20.

14 On the differentiation between colonialism and settler colonialism, see Lorenzo Veracini, 'Understanding Colonialism and Settler Colonialism as Distinct Formations', *Interventions* 16:5 (2014), 615–33, DOI: 10.1080/ 1369801X.2013.858983; Patrick Wolfe, 'Settler Colonialism and the Elimination of the Native', *Journal of Genocide Research* 8:4 (2006), 387–409, DOI: 10.1080/14623520601056240.

15 In this sense, I reject the idea, advanced by Adrian Howkins, of Antarctic settler colonialism as an ideal form, based on the fact that it has no Indigenous population (Adrian Howkins, 'Appropriating Space: Antarctic Imperialism and the Mentality of Settler Colonialism', in Tracey Banivanua Mar and Penelope Edmonds (eds), *Making Settler Colonial Space: Perspectives on Race, Place and Identity* (London: Palgrave Macmillan, 2010), p. 29–52), and Alejandra Mancilla's consideration that colonialism can be defined without the element of subjugation of one people to another, as argued elsewhere this volume. As I will explain later on, that implies not that there are no colonialist practices in Antarctica, but that the colonialist practices are not expressed over the Indigenous of Antarctica, and are instead a part of international colonialist practices that denied other actors and practices. Therefore, the subjugation and alleged superiority elements remain present.

16 Loomba, *Colonialism/Postcolonialism*, pp. 21–3. Loomba does not refer to the flow of capital. Nonetheless, I consider this essential to an understanding of modern colonialism.

17 Partha Chatterjee, *The Nation and Its Fragments: Colonial and Postcolonial Histories* (Princeton, NJ: Princeton University Press, 1993), Chapter 1.

18 Loomba, *Colonialism/Postcolonialism*, p. 25.

19 Even when it is usually backed up by military force. Non-military measures could include operations of internal destabilisation, economic sanctions, international naming and shaming, cultural imperialism etc.

20 This is what is highlighted by the literature on settler colonialism and is a key feature of the hybrid character described in the following.

21 Nestor Garcia Canclini, *Hybrid Cultures: Strategies for Entering and Leaving Modernity* (Minneapolis: University of Minnesota Press, 2005); Loomba, *Colonialism/Postcolonialism*; Robert J. C. Young, *Postcolonialism: A Very Short Introduction* (Oxford: Oxford University Press, 2003).

22 Canclini, *Hybrid Cultures*.

23 Anthony Giddens, *The Nation-State and Violence: Volume Two of a Contemporary Critique of Historical Materialism* (Cambridge: Polity Press, 1989), pp. 49–53; Robert D. Sack, 'Human Territoriality: A Theory', *Annals of the Association of American Geographers* 73:1 (1983), 55–74 (p. 55).

24 Scott, 'Three Waves of Antarctic Imperialism', p. 42.

25 See Robert N. Burr, *By Reason or Force: Chile and the Balancing of Power in South America, 1830–1905* (Berkeley: University of California Press, 1974).

26 While settler colonialism literature differentiates colonialism from settler colonialism and even questions the use of 'settler' as an appropriate term, I would add that the use of 'colonialism' could also be questioned, as it overlooks a really significant difference between the subordination status of individuals and that of territories.

27 Instead of the common idea of territorial expansion typical of colonialism.

28 To this it must added that many settlers in Patagonia were European immigrants and that the British dominated sheep farming.

29 The Argentinians were first evicted by force by US personnel from the Malvinas/Falklands in 1832, and then by the British in 1833 (Christian J. Maisch, 'The Falkland/Malvinas Islands Clash of 1831–32: US and British Diplomacy in the South Atlantic', *Diplomatic History* 24:2 (2000), 185–209). On the Guano War, see Edmundo A. Heredia, *El imperio del guano: América Latina ante la guerra de España en el Pacífico* (Córdoba: Alción Editora, 1998); Nicolás Terradas, 'Ordered Anarchy: The Origins and Evolution of a Society of States in South America, 1864–1939' (PhD thesis, Florida International University, 2018), Chapter 4.

30 On Ecuador, see Ralph W. Haskins, 'Juan José Flores and the Proposed Expedition against Ecuador, 1846–1847', *The Hispanic American Historical Review* 27:3 (1947), 467–95.

31 The papal bulls of 1493 conceded all lands, discovered or to be discovered, located 100 leagues west of the Azores or Cabo Verde Islands between the North and South Poles, to Spain. This would be superseded by the Tordesillas Treaty, signed by Spain and Portugal in 1494, which displaced this line to 370 leagues west of Cabo Verde.

32 See the assertions of Estanislao Zeballos and Francisco Seguí: Zeballos, cited in Giacomo Bove, *Expedición Austral Argentina* (Buenos Aires, 1883), p. V; Francisco Seguí, 'Las regiones polares', *Boletín del Instituto Geográfico Argentino* 18 (1897), 1–32 (p. 31).

33 See Bove, *Expedicion Austral Argentina*, p. x; Otto Nordenskjöld, J. Gunnar Andersson, C. A. Larsen and Carl Skottsberg, *Viaje al Polo Sur: Expedición sueca á bordo del 'Antártico'* (Barcelona: Casa Editorial Manucci, 1904), p. 41.

34 Argentina rescued Otto Nordenskjöld's expedition in 1903 and sent a relief operation to assist Jean-Baptiste Charcot's expedition in 1905, without finding it. The Chileans rescued Ernest Shackleton's *Endurance* party from Elephant Island in 1917.

35 In 1884, a Chilean geographer, Alejandro Huillard, officer of the Chilean Department of Limits, published a map in which the Antarctic region presented a continuation of the Andes mountain range, establishing a first direct physical link (Berguño, 'El Despertar'), followed in 1907 by the work of another Chilean geographer, Luis Riso Patrón, who theorised this continuity and named the region 'American Antarctica' (Luis Riso Patrón, 'La Antártida Americana', *Anales de la Universidad de Chile* 122 (1908), 243–65).

36 Negotiations between Argentina and Chile took place in 1941, coming to no agreement, but providing some common principles in the face of British pretensions. Chilean officials participated in the Argentine expeditions of 1941–42 and 1942–43, and there was a reciprocal presence of officials after the Chileans started their operation in Antarctica in 1947.

37 See Ignacio Javier Cardone, 'A Continent for Peace and Science: Antarctic Science and International Politics from the 6th International Geographical Congress to the Antarctic Treaty (1895–1959)' (PhD thesis, University of São Paulo/King's College London, 2019), pp. 204–16.

38 Adrian Howkins, 'Icy Relations: The Emergence of South American Antarctica during the Second World War', *Polar Record* 42:2 (2006), 153–65, DOI: 10.1017/S0032247406005274; Cardone, 'Shaping an Antarctic Identity', p. 69.

39 The use of South American instead of American was discussed in 1941, taken up by the Chilean Captain Enrique Madariaga Cordovez in his 1945 book *La Antártida Sudamericana* (Santiago de Chile: Editorial Nascimento, 1945), and adopted in 1947 and 1948 in the negotiations between Argentina and Chile.

40 'relativos al establecimiento de nuevas estaciones meteorológicas y magnéticas en los mares del Sur de la República'; 'Decree N/N', 2 January 1903, 'Boletín oficial de la República Argentina, 1904 XII (307)', p. 14396 (my translation). Publicly, the acquisition was presented as a transfer, although the Argentine government paid for the installations.

41 See Cardone, 'Shaping an Antarctic Identity', p. 72.

42 The relationship lacked the asymmetry and the purpose of economic extraction typical of colonial practice, as well as the permanent character and right to property or exploitation typical of the colonial settler. Alejandra Mancilla points out, correctly, that economic extraction has indeed been in Argentina and Chile's thinking on Antarctica (Alejandra Mancilla, 'South American Claims in Antarctica: Colonial, Malgré Tout', *The Polar Journal* 12:1 (2022), 22–41, DOI: 10.1080/2154896X.2022.2062558). However, the Argentine and Chilean settlements were not directed toward economic activities, as is the case with settler colonialism.

43 The Letters Patent claimed a huge sector of Antarctica and could be interpreted as including a big part of Patagonia. This possible interpretation was corrected with the Letters Patent of 1917.

44 This despite their being aware of the actions, interests and pretensions of both countries since at least 1906.

45 More on this in the following section.

46 See, for example, Marwa Elshakry, 'When Science Became Western: Historiographical Reflections', *Isis* 101:1 (2010), 98–109, DOI: 10.1086/652691; James Poskett, *Horizons: A Global Hisory of Science* (London: Viking, 2022).

47 Examples could be found in the judgement by the President of the Royal Geographical Society, Sir Clements Markham, of the Argentine magnetic observations on Staten Island as being of poor scientific value (despite the fact that the observatory was installed at Markham's own request for collaboration; see Sir Clements Markham, 'Plan of the Expedition, Dec. 1899, Joint Antarctic Committee 1898–99', London, Royal Geographical Society Archives, AA/1/5/4), and in the assessment of the Argentine and Chilean scientific credentials for the International Geographical Congress Antarctic programme. British and British installation of stations in the near vicinity of the Argentine Belgrano station were justified on these grounds; see Dian Olson Belanger, *Deep Freeze: The United States, the International Geophysical Year, and the Origins of Antarctica's Age of Science* (Boulder: University Press of Colorado, 2006), p. 36.

48 In 1906 weather conditions prevented the Argentines from installing the station in Wandel, and the sinking of their polar vessel *Austral* the next year made them abandon the project.

49 Antonio Huneeus Gana, *Antártida* (Santiago de Chile: Imprenta Chile, 1948).

50 Peder Roberts, *The European Antarctic: Science and Strategy in Scandinavia and the British Empire* (New York: Palgrave Macmillan, 2011), p. 27.

51 Paolo Gabriel Fontana, 'Between the Ice of the Orkney Islands: Filming the Beginnings of the Antarctic Overwintering Tradition', *The Polar Journal* 9:2 (2019), 340–57.

52 The Norwegian invitation to an exhibition of polar exploration, scheduled to be held in Bergen in 1940 but cancelled because of the war, had already alarmed the two countries and motivated the creation of their respective Antarctic Commissions.

53 Argentina was less worried about the possibility at this time, as it was much more active in the area.

54 Such provision was deemed unnecessary by the other parties until the USSR announced that they were joining the Antarctic programme of the IGY.

55 During negotiations some parts rejected the need to include such a provision, which motivated a strong rebuttal from Argentina and Chile.

56 Huneeus Gana, *Antártida*, p. 43.

57 The National Archives, Kew (TNA), Argentine Files 279-114449 (1906) (FO371/4). On the Compañía Argentina de Pesca S.A., see Ian B. Hart, *Pesca: The History of Compañía Argentina de Pesca Sociedad Anónima of*

Buenos Aires (Salcombe: Aidan Ellis Publishing, 2001). The author states that there is no evidence that the presence of naval troops exerted any form of coercion on the manager, Carl A. Larsen. However, he also presents the account of Larsen's daughter, which suggests otherwise (pp. 76–8).

58 In early 1906, because of the poor economic prospects of the Malvinas/Falklands, William Allardyce, British governor of the islands, suggested including the South Orkneys and South Shetlands as dependencies of the islands in order to expand their borders and rentability, fearing that Argentina and Chile would move first. See William Allardyce to the Earl of Elgin, 26 February 1906, file no. 275–277, TNA, Argentine Files 279-11449 (FO371/4).

59 Roberts, *The European Antarctic.*

60 Adrian Howkins, 'Frozen Empires: A History of the Antarctic Sovereignty Dispute between Britain, Argentina, and Chile, 1939–1959' (PhD thesis, University of Texas at Austin, 2008).

61 Walter Sullivan, *Assault on the Unknown: The International Geophysical Year* (London: Hodder & Stoughton, 1962), p. 336.

Bibliography

Adler, Emanuel and Vincent Pouliot (eds). *International Practices.* New York: Cambridge University Press, 2011.

Agnew, John A. 'The Territorial Trap: The Geographical Assumptions of International Relations Theory'. *Review of International Political Economy* 1, no. 1 (1994): 53–80. DOI: 10.1080/09692299408434268.

Belanger, Dian Olson. *Deep Freeze: The United States, the International Geophysical Year, and the Origins of Antarctica's Age of Science.* Boulder: University Press of Colorado, 2006.

Berguño, Jorge. 'El despertar de la conciencia antártica (1874–1914). Primera parte: Origen y desarrollo de la cooperación científica internacional'. *Boletín Antártico Chileno* 17, no. 2 (1998): 2–13.

Berguño, Jorge. 'The Intellectual Sources of the Antarctic Treaty'. In *2nd SCAR Workshop on the History of Antarctic Research*, ed. Cornelia Lüdecke, pp. 11–17. Special issue of *Boletín Antártico Chileno*. Punta Arenas: Instituto Antártico Chileno, 2006.

Bove, Giacomo. *Expedición Austral Argentina.* Buenos Aires, 1883.

Brazelli, Nicoletta. 'Heroic and Post-Colonial Antarctic Narratives'. In *Handbook on the Politics of Antarctica*, ed. Klaus J. Dodds, Alan D. Hemmings and Peder Roberts, pp. 69–83. Cheltenham: Edward Elgar Publishing, 2017.

Burr, Robert N. *By Reason or Force: Chile and the Balancing of Power in South America, 1830–1905.* Berkeley: University of California Press, 1974.

Canclini, Nestor Garcia. *Hybrid Cultures: Strategies for Entering and Leaving Modernity.* Minneapolis: University of Minnesota Press, 2005.

Cardone, Ignacio Javier. 'A Continent for Peace and Science: Antarctic Science and International Politics from the 6th International Geographical Congress to the Antarctic Treaty (1895–1959)'. PhD thesis. University of São Paulo/King's College London, 2019.

Cardone, Ignacio Javier. 'Shaping an Antarctic Identity in Argentina and Chile'. *Defence Strategic Communications* 8 (2020): 53–88. DOI: 10.30966/2018. RIGA.8.2.

Cardone, Ignacio Javier and Pablo Gabriel Fontana. 'Latin-American Contributions to the Creation of the Antarctic Regime'. *The Polar Journal* 9, no. 2 (2019): 300–23. DOI: 10.1080/2154896X.2019.1685174.

Chatterjee, Partha. *The Nation and Its Fragments: Colonial and Postcolonial Histories*. Princeton, NJ: Princeton University Press, 1993.

Cordovez Madariaga, Enrique. *La Antártida Sudamericana*. Santiago de Chile: Editorial Nascimento, 1945.

Dodds, Klaus J. 'Post-Colonial Antarctica: An Emerging Engagement'. *Polar Record* 42, no. 1 (2006): 59–70. 10.1017/S0032247405004857.

Dodds, Klaus J. and Christy Collis. 'Post-Colonial Antarctica'. In *Handbook on the Politics of Antarctica*, ed. Klaus J. Dodds, Alan D. Hemmings and Peder Roberts, pp. 50–68. Cheltenham: Edward Elgar Publishing, 2017.

Elshakry, Marwa. 'When Science Became Western: Historiographical Reflections'. *Isis* 101, no. 1 (2010): 98–109. DOI: 10.1086/652691.

Fontana, Pablo Gabriel. 'Between the Ice of the Orkney Islands: Filming the Beginnings of the Antarctic Overwintering Tradition'. *The Polar Journal* 9, no. 2 (2019): 340–57.

Giddens, Anthony. *The Nation-State and Violence: Volume Two of a Contemporary Critique of Historical Materialism*. Cambridge: Polity Press, 1989.

Hart, Ian B. *Pesca: The History of Compañía Argentina de Pesca Sociedad Anónima of Buenos Aires*. Salcombe: Aidan Ellis Publishing, 2001.

Haskins, Ralph W. 'Juan José Flores and the Proposed Expedition against Ecuador, 1846–1847'. *The Hispanic American Historical Review* 27, no. 3 (1947): 467–95.

Heredia, Edmundo A. *El imperio del guano: América Latina ante la guerra de España en el Pacífico*. Córdoba: Alción Editora, 1998.

Howkins, Adrian. 'Appropriating Space: Antarctic Imperialism and the Mentality of Settler Colonialism'. In *Making Settler Colonial Space: Perspectives on Race, Place and Identity*, ed. Tracey Banivanua Mar and Penelope Edmonds, pp. 29–52. London: Palgrave Macmillan, 2010.

Howkins, Adrian. 'Frozen Empires: A History of the Antarctic Sovereignty Dispute between Britain, Argentina, and Chile, 1939–1959'. PhD thesis. University of Texas at Austin, 2008.

Howkins, Adrian. 'Icy Relations: The Emergence of South American Antarctica during the Second World War'. *Polar Record* 42, no. 2 (2006): 153–65. DOI: https://doi.org/10.1017/S0032247406005274.

Huneeus Gana, Antonio. *Antártida*. Santiago de Chile: Imprenta Chile, 1948.

Loomba, Ania. *Colonialism/Postcolonialism*. 3rd edn. Abingdon: Routledge, 2015.

Maisch, Christian J. 'The Falkland/Malvinas Islands Clash of 1831–32: US and British Diplomacy in the South Atlantic'. *Diplomatic History* 24, no. 2 (2000): 185–209.

Mancilla, Alejandra. 'South American Claims in Antarctica: Colonial, Malgré Tout'. *The Polar Journal* 12, no. 1 (2022): 22–41. DOI: 10.1080/2154896X.2022.2062558.

Markham, Sir Clements, 'Plan of the Expedition, Dec. 1899, Joint Antarctic Committee 1898–99'. London, Royal Geographical Society Archives, AA/1/5/4.

Nordenskjöld, Otto, J. Gunnar Andersson, C. A. Larsen and Carl Skottsberg. *Viaje al Polo Sur: Expedición sueca á bordo del 'Antártico'*. Barcelona: Casa Editorial Manucci, 1904.

Poskett, James. *Horizons: A Global History of Science*. London: Viking, 2022.

Riso Patrón, Luis. 'La Antártida Americana'. *Anales de la Universidad de Chile* 122 (1908): 243–65.

Roberts, Peder. *The European Antarctic: Science and Strategy in Scandinavia and the British Empire*. New York: Palgrave Macmillan, 2011.

Sack, Robert D. 'Human Territoriality: A Theory'. *Annals of the Association of American Geographers* 73, no. 1 (1983): 55–74.

Schatzki, Theodore R., Karin Knorr Cetina and Eike von Savigny. *The Practice Turn in Contemporary Theory*. London: Routledge, 2001.

Scott, Shirley V. 'Ingenious and Innocuous? Article IV of the Antarctic Treaty as Imperialism'. *Polar Journal* 1, no. 1 (2011): 51–62. DOI: 10.1080/2154896X.2011.568787.

Scott, Shirley V. 'Three Waves of Antarctic Imperialism'. In *Handbook on the Politics of Antarctica*, ed. Klaus J. Dodds, Alan D. Hemmings and Peder Roberts, pp. 37–49. Cheltenham: Edward Elgar Publishing, 2017.

Seguí, Francisco. 'Las regiones polares'. *Boletín del Instituto Geográfico Argentino* 18 (1897): 1–32.

Sullivan, Walter. *Assault on the Unknown: The International Geophysical Year*. London: Hodder & Stoughton, 1962.

Terradas, Nicolás. 'Ordered Anarchy: The Origins and Evolution of a Society of States in South America, 1864–1939'. PhD thesis. Florida International University, 2018.

Veracini, Lorenzo. 'Understanding Colonialism and Settler Colonialism as Distinct Formations'. *Interventions* 16, no. 5 (2014): 615–33. DOI: 10.1080/1369801X.2013.858983.

Weber, Max. *Economy and Society: An Outline of Interpretive Sociology*, Vol. I. Berkeley: University of California Press, 2013.

Wolfe, Patrick. 'Settler Colonialism and the Elimination of the Native'. *Journal of Genocide Research* 8, no. 4 (2006): 387–409. DOI: 10.1080/14623520601056240.

Young, Robert J. C. *Postcolonialism: A Very Short Introduction*. Oxford: Oxford University Press, 2003.

5

South American claims in Antarctica: Colonial, *malgré tout*

Alejandra Mancilla

Chile has acquired Antarctica neither by treaty nor by conquest. It was given to it by nature, *uti possidetis*, polar possession and fishing. And it is ratified by Chile's honest and constant intention of full dominion.[1]

Not until the organisation of diverse international agreements among the powers interested in the Antarctic will Argentina recognise any claim over lands that history, geography, nature and law justify as being its exclusive property.[2]

Starting with Klaus Dodds's 2006 depiction of postcolonial Antarctica as 'an emerging engagement', the colonial and imperial underpinnings of Antarctic history have been well documented.[3] Dodds himself notes in his article that, even though there were no Indigenous peoples to be colonised in Antarctica, the continent serves as a point of departure for 'a critical evaluation of colonialism and associated practices such as mapping, surveying, and the subjugation of territory and non-human populations'.[4] For Dodds, moreover, the Antarctic Treaty 'rewarded' colonial occupation and annexation through its Article IV, which made it possible for the seven territorial claimants to retain their claims while opening the possibility that others (the USA and Soviet Union) could make their own claims in the future.[5] Adrian Howkins has suggested that Antarctica is a prime example of settler colonialism, epitomising 'the elitist, racist and exclusionary mentality of the settler colonial project ... brimming with potential economic wealth but also without the usual entanglements of empire' (i.e. the question of how to deal with the native populations).[6] Ben Maddison has pointed out how the usual understandings and procedures of colonial possession were 'unsettled' (although not halted) in Antarctica, where there were no natives – except penguins – to dispossess.[7] Shirley Scott has proposed reinterpreting Antarctic history as divided into three periods of imperialism: from Spain and Portugal's claims to the hypothetical *terra australis nondum cognita* in the fifteenth century, through the British acquisition of Antarctica as *terra nullius* from the end of the nineteenth century, to the US postwar *imperium* by science.[8] Sanjay Chaturvedi has argued that the process of penetration into the polar regions should be seen as part of a much larger one of colonialism and imperialism starting first in Europe and unfolding throughout the world, and Alan Hemmings has observed that 'the present Antarctic dispensation, including the treatment of territory, was arrived at prior to the existence of more than half of the world's present states, as a result of an imperial and colonial model now generally repudiated'.[9]

While most of the analyses so far have focused on the colonial and imperial actions of European powers (especially the United Kingdom), less has been written on the roles that Argentina and Chile specifically played as distinctly colonial actors in Antarctica during the first half of the twentieth century.[10] Dodds has suggested that, despite appealing to anti-colonial rhetoric to denounce the presence of the British in the Falkland Islands and the Antarctic Peninsula, Argentinian President Juan Domingo Perón nonetheless used colonial tactics to occupy the Argentine Antarctic Territory in the 1940s and 1950s.[11] Dodds and Christy Collis, furthermore, have questioned the 'naturalisation' of Antarctic territory by claimant states and have described Argentina and Chile's presence on the continent as a case of settler colonialism that had as a key component the creation of Antarctic communities.[12] The pioneering work of Jack Child could also be seen as pointing in this direction: without qualifying the positions of these countries as colonial, Child refers to Antarctica as a 'frozen *lebensraum*' that both Argentina and Chile considered key to furthering their geopolitical ambitions.[13]

Beyond these analyses, the position of the South American claimants has usually been identified as anti-colonial and anti-imperial, advancing their political interests as new republics and founding their claims (at least initially) not on discovery and annexation, but on 'natural' (i.e. geographical and geological) and historic rights. Moreover, while it is easy today to find literature taking a critical stance toward claimants from the 'north', the same cannot be said when it comes to the claimants from the 'south'.[14] With some exceptions (such as Carlos Escudé's critique of Argentina's expansionism toward the south), this omission is especially notorious if one looks at academic articles and books written in Spanish for mainly Latin American audiences.[15] There seems to be, thus, an unspoken premise that the claims of the 'north' were qualitatively different from the claims of the 'south' or, at least, different enough not to put them all together under the same postcolonial scrutiny.

In this chapter I contest that premise and suggest that the claims of Argentina and Chile should be examined more critically as distinctly colonial and colonising. By doing this, I aim to follow Dodds's call to pay 'a great deal more attention ... to the histories and geographies of "benign settlement"' – among which those of Argentina and Chile (as well as those of Australia and New Zealand) are exemplars.[16]

After reflecting on what made the claims of the northern powers colonial (while acknowledging their different trajectories), I turn to the arguments offered by the South American claimants and show how they stand in continuation, rather than in opposition, to the former. I then point to some implications and conclude.

Colonising Antarctica from the 'north'

Definitions of colonialism and imperialism vary from author to author. Sometimes they are kept separate, sometimes they overlap, and sometimes the former is subsumed under the latter. In this chapter, I propose an understanding of colonialism as a practice of domination through control over a territory, which customarily included the creation of settlements that kept their political allegiance to the colonising power.[17] It is worth noting that, contrary to a common understanding of colonialism, in this definition the existence of subjected people in the colonised territory is not a necessary condition.[18] Instead, what is necessary is the desire to conquer and appropriate land and natural resources.[19] I think this definition is useful because it helps us understand that the wrongs of colonialism are not limited to the unjust treatment of human beings, even though historically this has been its most obvious feature. Colonialism, I suggest, is also wrong as a specific attitude and logic of relating to land and the natural world, which – absent humans to be subjugated – comes out clearest in the Antarctic case. By imperialism, meanwhile, I understand the practice of states of extending their political power and dominion through means such as (but not exclusively) territorial appropriation.[20]

As said before, after Dodds's seminal 2006 article, it has become relatively uncontroversial that these definitions apply, intertwined, to the gradual appropriation of Antarctica from the second half of the nineteenth century to the 1930s. At least until the invention of factory ships by the Norwegians, economic control was required to exploit valuable marine resources, especially whale oil, which was key for industrial development at the time.[21] Political control, meanwhile, was required for securing present and future exploitation of these (and other, yet undiscovered) resources from potential competitors, as well as for strategically extending territory. As the Norwegian jurist Gustav Smedal put it:

A craving for acquisition of land in these parts of the world [i.e. the polar regions] has arisen. A State securing land gives its subjects a safe basis for their hunting industry. In that way such a State will also frequently be able to control hunting operations and render them dependent upon licences and dues collected by itself. The British policy in Antarctic waters gives the best illustration of this.[22]

The methods used by states to appropriate the land (or, rather, a combination of ice, rock and water) and claim it for themselves were also paradigmatically colonial. By discovering and annexing, mapping, and naming, the United Kingdom was the first unilaterally to claim territory all the way to the South Pole, using the sector principle, which had been recently proposed to divide claims to the Arctic. The original claim from 1908, however, was undertaken in such haste that a slice of Chilean and Argentinian Tierra del Fuego was included within it. It took nine years to correct it and reissue it, in 1917. As in other places around the globe, the British were above all concerned with regulating the extraction of the main economic resources – in this case, whales. They gave licences to hunters and established a Whale Ordinance in 1906, the observance of which was carried out by government officers appointed to some of the whaling stations during the summer season.[23]

The other 'northern' claimants followed a similar resource-territorial logic, although their presence on the continent had been even more tenuous than that of the British. From the discovery and further annexation of some islands and coastal spots, France projected its claims onto the Antarctic *Hinterland* (or, more accurately, *Hintereis*), all the way to the South Pole. Norway, which had been the most active whaling country alongside the UK and the USA, also based its claim upon its coastal presence, but was the only one to leave the southern limit toward the centre of Antarctica undefined.[24] New Zealand came into the picture by virtue of the Ross Dependency Boundaries and Government Order in Council 1923, which established that:

> that part of His Majesty's Dominions in the Antarctic seas which comprises all the islands and territories between the 160th degree of east longitude and the 150th degree of west longitude which are situated south of the 60th degree of south latitude shall be named the Ross Dependency and put in charge of the Governor-General and Commander-in-Chief of the Dominion of New Zealand.[25]

The Australian Antarctic Territory, finally, was 'accepted by the Commonwealth as a Territory under the authority of the Commonwealth.'[26]

It is telling that the Antarctic sectors claimed by the European powers plus Australia and New Zealand were and still are explicitly considered as part of their colonial dominions. For the United Kingdom, Antarctica was part of their Falkland Islands Dependencies until the early 1960s; for France, it belonged to its Overseas Territories;[27] for Norway, a special Act from 1930 amended in 1957 stipulated that Bouvet Island, Peter I Island and Dronning Maud Land were Norwegian Dependencies;[28] for Australia, it became one of seven External Territories;[29] and for New Zealand, as mentioned above, it was a dependency.

Colonising Antarctica from the 'south'

Shirley Scott has rejected the 'homogeneous claims interpretation' proposed by classic Antarctic anglophone historiography, which treats all claims to Antarctica as equivalent. In this reading, the UK appears as the pioneer, with the other countries, especially Chile and Argentina, as latecomers in the claiming game. Defending instead the uniqueness of South American claims, Scott affirms: 'Argentina and Chile had since independence believed that their territory extended as far south as the South Pole. They had not been involved in nineteenth century African colonialism and did not approach Antarctica with the assumed need to "claim" territory.'[30]

For Scott, the main issue for the two South American states was not to stake claims following the nineteenth-century colonial paradigm, but rather to agree on a boundary between their Antarctic territories – just as in Patagonia and Tierra del Fuego.[31] What she takes for granted, however, is a key, previous, question: how did they get those Antarctic territories in the first place (and, for that matter, not just them, but also their continental southern territories)?[32]

In this section, I examine the claims of Argentina and Chile over Antarctica and suggest that they are colonial, *malgré tout*. I point to four specific features where the colonial logic manifests itself. First, like their northern counterparts, both countries used the doctrines of continuity and contiguity, and the sector principle, to project their territories into the *Hintereis*. Second, they both uncritically invoked historic rights inherited from Spain, a colonial power par excellence. Third, they established military settlements to display and secure sovereignty over empty space. Fourth, despite their flowery appeals to unblemished nationalism to justify their claims, their motives for seeking control over Antarctica were economic and strategic like everyone else's and, in this sense, an example of resource colonialism.

Stretching effective occupation via continuity, contiguity and the sector principle

In 1940, the Argentinian Antarctic sector was delimited between meridians 25° and 74° west of Greenwich, and south of 60° south all the way to the pole. Argentina's main argument for claiming Antarctic territory was based on its effective, continued occupation of a meteorological station and postal office in the South Orkneys since 1904. This is indeed the oldest permanent settlement in the Antarctic and was transferred to the Argentinian government by Scottish expeditioner William Bruce.[33] In a book published in 1948, the Antarctic National Commission points out that 'this leaves no doubt that already 44 years ago these lands and seas were considered as part of our nation'.[34] Later, they add a quote from a member of the Bruce expedition, Rudmose Brown, who recalls in his memoirs that:

> when the *Scotia* returned to the islands in February 1904, with an Argentine staff to take over the meteorological observatory at Omond House under the auspices of the Argentine Government, the Argentine naval flag was hoisted on the cairn where formerly the Scottish Lion flew; and I presume the South Orkneys are looked upon as a possession of that power. The South Orkneys are certainly the only spot in the Antarctic regions that have been inhabited without a break for a period of over three years, and they bid to become a permanently inhabited meteorological observation-station of the Argentine Government; for that country has, for the present at least, agreed to keep a staff of six men there, to be relieved annually.[35]

The Commission emphasises that this is 'the opinion of a foreign expedition from a country that belongs to the United Kingdom, which forty years ago pointed to the Orkneys and Antarctic lands as indisputable Argentinian property'.[36] However, what they omit is perhaps the most telling sentence of the quote, which reflects Brown's critical attitude toward Argentina and his fear that this small possession in the Orkneys would perhaps be seen by 'ambitious Argentine expansionists' as 'the nucleus of an empire'.[37] Indeed, even if the rights of Argentina over the South Orkneys were undisputed, the question would remain as to how it is that, by the mere presence of a meteorological station on an island, one may acquire territorial rights over a whopping area of 1,461,597 km^2 beyond it, all the way into mostly uncharted and unknown space.[38]

The answer comes in the same book a few pages later: discussing the juridical rights of Argentina over its Antarctic sector, the Commission mentions both the sector principle applied in the Arctic, and the theses and doctrines of international law – in particular, continuity and contiguity:

> when a state has permanently occupied a territory, it acquires rights to occupy other lands surrounding it. This has been called the 'doctrine of continuity'. If a stretch of the coast were occupied, for example, the sovereignty of the state can be extended to the islands and lands close by, in which case the 'doctrine of contiguity' would be involved.[39]

While there is no attempt in the above text to question or reflect upon the use of these eminently colonial doctrines in Antarctica, the Chilean author and diplomat Oscar Pinochet de la Barra exerts himself to show how the rationale of applying the notions of polar effective occupation, continuity and contiguity, and the sector principle to Antarctica makes sense insofar as it secures state ownership and sovereignty. Pinochet relies on a few iconic international disputes and on the opinion of some international legal scholars who considered the question of what should count as effective occupation in the polar regions. His main point is that effective occupation should not be considered a static, rigid notion, but should adapt to the circumstances of the territory. His examples are the arbitrary awards in the Island of Palmas Case (1829), the Clipperton Islands Case (1931) and the Eastern Greenland Case (1933), in none of which a permanent settlement was required to prove effective occupation. Quoting the Russian legal scholar W. Lakhtine, Pinochet continues: 'the application of the rules for terrestrial territory to polar territory "must be recognized as absolutely irrational"'.[40] Consequently, some hunting regulations and the granting of fishing, commercial and industrial licences by the Chilean state in some sub-Antarctic islands and to the south of them are, for Pinochet, good enough signs of effective occupation. (It is interesting to note that the establishment of companies to secure states' rights in a cheaper and easier manner was one of the favourite methods used by imperial powers.)[41]

To explain how tenuous signs of occupation in a few specific spots can expand and end up covering the 1,250,000 km² claimed by Chile in 1940, the author invokes the sector principle.[42] He gives four reasons why its application makes sense in the Chilean case:

1. The presumption or belief that a country adjacent to an Antarctic territory has therein exercised, in permanent or almost permanent form, acts of dominion, with more frequency and political intention than [an]other that is non-adjacent.
2. The necessity for an adjacent country of possessing the Antarctic sector facing it, because of its national defense, the establishment of meteorological observatories for the development of its aviation, of its agriculture etc.
3. The possibility of exploiting its natural resources more properly.
4. The impossibility of delimiting rights over an immense, unoccupied, inaccessible continent, except by meridians that form a triangle with its vertex at the Pole – the occupation of certain accessible points along the coast being sufficient.[43]

Points 1 and 2 reveal a clear attempt to block 'saltwater' colonialist attempts in Antarctica, namely, long-distance attempts to control it by European powers, particularly the United Kingdom. Instead, these points favour what might be called Chile's 'adjacent' colonialism, naturalised in legal and geopolitical discourse and practice. As Robert L. Nelson points out, 'adjacent' colonialism is a surprisingly undertheorised topic, compared to the default, 'saltwater' version. While, in the 'saltwater' version, for something to count as colonialism the metropole and the periphery must be separated by an ocean (at least), 'adjacent' colonialism includes cases where a state extends its dominance over its neighbours – regardless of whether there is salt water between them or not.[44] What is remarkable is that, in strict theory, all claims to Antarctica are 'saltwater' claims. And yet Pinochet does not regard Chile's as falling into that category because of geographical, strategic and economic considerations. These considerations can only withhold scrutiny against the tacit assumptions made in points 3 and 4: namely, that more efficient exploiters have a better claim to territory than less efficient ones (and that those located closer to the resource will necessarily be more efficient exploiters), and that it is unthinkable to leave possessable territory unpossessed (*horror vacui* being a recurrent theme in the history of colonialism).[45] Furthermore, it is strange to claim that a country has rights over certain resources because it will be able to exploit them more properly, and then add that those resources are mostly inaccessible thus far. Finally, once again, the issue of delimitation comes to the fore: for, even if establishing meteorological stations is necessary for the country's aviation and agriculture, why is it that more than a shred of territory is needed to fulfil this purpose?

To sum up, by endorsing the doctrines of continuity, contiguity, and the sector principle, what Argentina and Chile effectively did was to condone essentially colonial methodologies developed to extend the areas of influence of colonial powers towards *Hinterländer*. This gave them almost no international recognition, but at the domestic level it helped further cement the view that their respective claims were legitimate.

At this point, supporters of the Argentinian and Chilean claims might object that this critique is unfair and anachronistic: for how could they have done otherwise if what they were seeking was to have their claims recognised by other states? While today it has become accepted that the genealogy of international law is inextricably linked to colonialism and imperialism, and that its rules were mostly written by the powerful, this was not the case 80 years ago. It was thus only by appealing to the rules shaped by their contenders that they had a chance to convince the rest of the world of the validity of their claims. In short, they had to speak the language of their opponents to be understood.

Indeed, following the dicta of international law was the only way to legitimise their claims vis-à-vis those of their counterparts. But what this shows, in my view, is that being a country on the southern side of the development equator is no impediment to behaving in a colonial manner. The procedures undertaken by these two new republics to expand their territories toward the south of the South American continent (and all the way to Polynesian Easter Island, in the case of Chile) were arguably as questionable as those used by European powers in their overseas colonies.[46] Because they met no indigenous populations, the case was easier to make, but the logic was the same.[47] Disregarding this fact and romanticising these claimants as engaging in a purer and nobler mission in Antarctica is thus unhelpful and distorting.

Embracing the colonial inheritance

As mentioned before, what Chile and Argentina call their historic rights over Antarctica were purportedly inherited from the time when they were Spanish colonies: respectively, the General Captaincy of Chile and the Viceroyalty of Río de la Plata. In fact, both countries start their Antarctic chronologies in the 1490s and nurture these chronologies with every shred of evidence to be found of Spanish ships nearing the area, such as Spanish shipwrecks indicating an early presence and, most importantly, Spanish official documents signalling that Antarctica was always considered part of its dominion in the Americas, even before it was discovered.[48] This follows the principle of *uti possidetis iuris*, by virtue of which the newly independent Latin American countries maintained the administrative borders established by Spain.

In the bull *Inter caetera* of 1493, Spanish Pope Alexander VI granted the monarchs of Castile and Aragon, Ferdinand and Isabella, rights over all lands discovered and to be discovered to the west of a meridian running 100 leagues west of the Azores and Cape Verde Islands. The following year, in the Treaty of Tordesillas, Portugal and Spain agreed on a new demarcation line running pole-to-pole 370 leagues west of the Cape Verde Islands. For the Chilean legal scholar José Berguño Barnes, the bull 'fully conformed to the public law of its time', while in the words of the Argentinian ambassador Pedro Radío, 'the Decree issued by the pope was universally recognised, in his role of supreme authority of Christendom'.[49] As for the treaty, Berguño states that it 'incorporated the bull as positive international law between the two kingdoms'.[50] In short, it was a legal act with universal juridical effects.

This is not, however, how the other European powers saw it at the time, or later. Although the Treaty of Tordesillas was generally respected by the two signing parties, neither Protestant nor Catholic powers ever acknowledged it.[51] The Dutch theorist Hugo Grotius explicitly questioned the legitimacy of the bull, arguing against the Portuguese monopoly over the trading routes in the East Indies.[52] And as the French legal scholar Paul Fauchille recalls: 'Catholic princes who had not been favoured with papal gifts were discontented. The King of France, Francis I, requested to be shown the will of Adam which deprived him of the right to acquire land in the New World.'[53]

With a detective eye, Pinochet de la Barra shows that in later centuries there were several treaties signed between Spain and the United Kingdom to distribute their possessions in the Americas: 'By means of the Treaty of Madrid dated the 18th day of July 1670 ... Spain recognised the English rights in America and the West Indies, but, only in those territories "that the said King of Great Britain and his subjects may have or possess at the present time. However, neither on account of this Treaty nor for any other reason, may or shall Great Britain ever claim anything else, nor raise any future demands (Art.7)."'[54] Another treaty between these two countries from 1713, the Treaty of Utrecht, confirmed again, according to Pinochet, the exclusive rights of the Spanish to the Southern Sea and to its American and Antarctic coast, although the rule was constantly violated by English vessels. The decisive treaty, for Pinochet, was the Nootka Sound Convention from 1790, which re-established the *status quo ante* and determined that:

> Neither the English may acquire any rights over the unoccupied regions (discovered or not), whether they be American, islands adjoining America or situated along the coasts bathed by the Southern Sea, or the Spanish improve their right of priority over them by establishing settlements ... A secret article established the only exception, providing that the agreement not to occupy said territories 'will not come into effect until the subjects of another power establish settlements in said places'.[55]

Putting aside whether the Bull and the subsequent Treaty were recognised by third parties, and putting aside also whether the British acknowledged Spanish sovereignty over the Southern Sea and the *terra australis nondum cognita*, what appears obvious is that both the bull and these treaties were essentially colonial devices created to allow for the appropriation of new territories by European powers on a scale and at a speed never seen before. By relying on *uti possidetis* to justify their Antarctic claims, what Argentina and Chile did was to condone Spanish colonisation and its methods. Furthermore, while one could argue that, pragmatically speaking, respecting the colonial borders over already inhabited areas in Latin America at the time of independence was a sensible path to follow, it is a stretch to extend *uti possidetis* to lands that were only speculation at the time. Here the principle would be not about maintaining the existing colonial borders, but rather about creating inchoate title over yet-to-be-discovered areas, purely based on Spain's *animus occupandi*. As the Chilean lawyer Antonio Huneeus Gana candidly admits: 'In the desert and hard-to-inhabit Antarctic lands, the will to master, well-founded and sincere, as it was Spain's, replaces the natural insufficiencies of apprehension and tenure. The former is right conscience, the latter is extremely difficult and arduous and even impossible, to the point that it gives way to force majeure.'[56]

What Huneeus does not explain is why the difficulty and near impossibility of apprehending Antarctic territory make *animus occupandi* good enough for justifying actual possession. Unless one stipulates – in colonial mode – that the earth is there for the north and the south to bring under our full dominion, it would be just as plausible to claim that territories that do not lend themselves to being occupied should be left beyond any state's jurisdiction.

To sum up, leaving aside the moral and legal problems of relying on a 500-year-old contract signed by two European kingdoms and never acknowledged by third parties, appealing to the Treaty of Tordesillas makes the South American claims colonial by inheritance.[57] Thus, while the treaties later signed between the UK and Spain may well serve as a reason to contest any privilege of the British over their southernmost 'dependencies', this comes at the cost of recognising that South American rights over Antarctica appeal to the same colonial logic – the inheritance of which these new republics were paradoxically trying to shake off as much as possible in other domains. One could again object that this criticism is unfair, as they were 'born' into that structure and had no other instruments available. If that is the case, however, a candid acknowledgement of this fact would be in order. For one thing, this acknowledgement might help to enrich the growing debate in both countries about the postindependence process of colonisation of the south. While this debate has so far remained limited to the continental territories, there is no reason why the incorporation of Antarctica into the Argentinian and Chilean maps should not be part of it.

Establishing military settlements

Into the 1940s, and in the face of the increased interest shown by the UK, it became clear to the South American claimants that their actual presence in Antarctica would be necessary to cement their freshly made formal claims. A Chilean author expressed it openly:

> If in 1906 the Foreign Affairs Ministry projected an expedition frustrated by the earthquake in Valparaíso, it is hard to understand why, from then until 1947, the navy did not send at least a ship to see a territory considered ours, what it looked like and what was going on there … It is good that our country is neither imperialist nor expansionist, but it is not so good to leave a part of its territory at the mercy of others.[58]

On the other side of the Andes, President Perón's Antarctic emissary, Hernán Pujato, emphasised 'the need for a permanent occupation of this part of Argentina's territory and wanted to bring women and children to the station

[Base San Martín, established in 1951] as a part of a plan for a genuine colonisation. He believed that Argentine children born in Antarctica would be "the greatest titles of our rights".'[59]

Although it took nearly three decades for Pujato's dream to become true (the first Antarctic Argentinian, Emilio Marcos Palma, was born in 1978 at Esperanza Base), in the 1940s and early 1950s the Argentinians and Chileans established military outposts across the territory to secure and display possession. In 1942, an Argentinian expedition visited Deception Island. They made an inventory of what was left in its deserted whaling facilities, erected a flagpole, hoisted their flag, and installed a plaque with details of the visit and a bronze tube with a document inside asserting Argentinian rights over the island.[60] They repeated the visit in 1943, with three invited Chilean officers on board – a display of South American unity against British advances. In 1947 and 1948, two new settlements were established: respectively, Destacamento Naval Melchior, and Destacamento Naval Decepción. In 1951, the military base General San Martín was built on the Antarctic Peninsula.[61]

In 1947, the first Chilean naval base (aptly named Sovereignty), was established on Greenwich Island, in the Southern Shetlands. One year later, the O'Higgins military base was built in Puerto Covadonga, to the north of the peninsula. This base was inaugurated by the first head of state ever to travel to Antarctica, Chilean President Gabriel González Videla.[62]

The reports coming from these incipient settlements reveal that these men thought of themselves as the avant-garde of the state in inhospitable territory that would eventually be tamed by human will. Lieutenant Hugo Schmidt Prado, who lived in Antarctica for a year as head of the O'Higgins military base, recalls in his memoirs how Professor Longerich, a scientist who came to visit during the summer expedition, 'took care of the nursery with Fueguian plants ... He would spread them through the plains thus initiating the biological and acclimatisation experiments of the Antarctic Department.'[63] Apart from the nursery, at O'Higgins there were sheep, hens and dogs (these last fed by around 250 seals a year, hunted by the military personnel).[64] There was a settler colonial impulse to domesticate Antarctica and convert it into something more familiar. If not exactly Lockean, their occupation was as agricultural as it could get, considering their location nearly 64° south.

Adrian Howkins, who has studied in detail the 'Antarctic problem' – namely, the conflict between the two South American claimants and the UK – presents these acts as an anti-colonial and anti-imperial response that was part of the 'wider anticolonial *zeitgeist*' of the time.[65] My suggestion, instead, is that Argentina and Chile were fighting the British insofar as they interfered with their own colonialist aims. This is why they did not question the deeper logic either of colonialism or of imperialism. As mentioned before, their own tactics to gain control over their continental territories were arguably as brutal as those used by 'saltwater' colonisers. In this regard, while disagreeing with E. W. Hunter Christie's overall diagnosis of the Antarctic problem, I think his interpretation of Argentina and Chile's goal in Antarctica is crude, but accurate. Latin American opinion, Christie says, is 'highly unfriendly to Britain over colonial questions, having a vested interest in abolishing British rule in her South American colonies ... The natural consequence of this interpretation was that the South American republics with British colonial possessions as their neighbours were determined to have their share of the spoil.'[66] In short: what they were after was not to question the 'spoil', but to demand a slice of it – just as Malaysia did when raising the Question of Antarctica in the United Nations, in the early 1980s.

The motives of resource colonialism

There has been no lack of lyricism when it comes to underscoring the purported Antarctic destiny of the South American claimants. In the 1940s, Pujato already 'believed that the continent offered quasi-mystical possibilities for the regeneration of the Argentine nation', while decades later, Argentinian ambassador Alberto Daverede waxed eloquent that:

> [Argentina] is a country with an Antarctic vocation. A vocation is something that has an origin, a genesis, that later becomes embodied in the individual and also in the people, and which necessarily leads to its externalisation ... A vocation recognises causes and has objectives. It imposes urgent needs and frustrates those who possess it and cannot manifest it.[67]

Perhaps the most glaring attempt to dress Antarctic interests in noble ideals comes from the controversial Chilean writer Miguel Serrano. Serrano was ambassador in India between 1953 and 1963, when India raised the possibility of internationalising Antarctica. In a memoir, he recalls addressing Prime Minister Jawaharlal Nehru about this issue, saying:

> 'India has again presented the Antarctic case in the United Nations, which means its internationalisation and, for Chile, the loss of its sacred rights in that mythical world region, logical and natural continuation of my long and narrow homeland. We are a very small country, Your Excellency, compared to the whole continent that is India. And a small country, to survive in this world, has only one thing to preserve: its honour and the dream of an ideal. If we lose that, we have lost everything and anyone can trample over us. Antarctica for Chile is its honour, its dream, Your Excellency! You understand. Withdraw

India's motion. Do it for Chile!' Serrano proceeds: [Nehru's] smile, which he first only insinuated, was open and beautiful: 'Ambassador, go in peace and inform your government that India will take into account Chile's honour and dream.'[68]

Without using the language of hegemons and subalterns, what Serrano is effectively telling Nehru is to back off not because he is wrong, but because his position would affect the interests of Chile – a subaltern country with which India (as another subaltern country) should show solidarity. And he is assuming that it is only by behaving in an expansionist manner that honour and ideals can be preserved.

Behind the veil of nationalist ideals, South American claimants were no different in regarding Antarctica as a treasure trove of resources. Salvador Reyes, one of the civilians invited to chronicle the Chilean 1954–55 campaign, is explicit about it: 'Chile must get ready to fulfil its mission during the "Pacific era", where dominion over its Antarctic Territory will be indispensable, because together with continental Chile that territory forms one geographic system of perfectly defined strategic and economic importance.'[69] On the other side of the Andes, prefacing the book *Argentinian Sovereignty in Antarctica* (from the National Antarctic Commission), President Perón refers to the 'major Antarctic issue, with the strategic and economic possibilities that it offers.'[70] Thus, even though the extraction of those resources lay in the faraway future, it was used to justify the colonising effort.[71]

Toward decolonisation

Although colonialism has been typically associated with the subjection of native peoples by foreign powers, its wrongs do not end there, but extend to a logic and attitude where land and nature (reduced to 'natural resources') are assumed to be up for grabs by (some) humans. Moreover, although colonialism has been routinely denounced in its 'saltwater' version, it is questionable whether colonial attitudes and procedures require an ocean to be triggered; 'adjacent' colonialism suggests just this.

In this chapter, I have advanced the idea that, just like their 'northern' counterparts, Argentina and Chile behaved in a colonial manner and utilised colonial procedures to justify their Antarctic claims. Consistent with resource colonialism, economic interests were important drivers of their claims, even when dressed up in an appeal to the mystical. Moreover, consistent with adjacent colonialism (or, to be more precise in this case, 'contiguous' colonialism), both countries emphasised their strategic needs when looking to the South Pole as a site for expansion.[72] A sustained emphasis on the nationalist and anti-imperialist character of South American claims to Antarctica has obscured, in my view, the fact that what they were fighting was an extra-continental power in order to prevent it from appropriating what they took to be their own grounds for appropriation. The colonial logic of appropriating and taking was itself never questioned, however. In sum, while in discourse they may have tried to separate their aims and motivations as much as possible from those of their common contender, the United Kingdom, in practice Argentina and Chile were engaged in the same game: to secure as much land (or rock, water and ice) and natural resources for themselves as possible.

An acknowledgment that their discourse regarding Antarctica was no less problematic than that used to incorporate huge swathes of continental land (via the displacement and systematic killing of people) into their respective states might be a welcome step forward both at the domestic and the international level. At the domestic level, Chileans and Argentinians are still taught from elementary school upwards that their respective countries own a slice of Antarctica, and they get feisty when the other makes claims that seem to threaten their own – something that has happened repeatedly apropos their respective claims to the continental shelf between South America and Antarctica.[73] As Carlos Escudé once noted:

> In the unlikely event that an Argentine government should ever acquire effective sovereignty rights over a part of this territory (and it is quite impossible for it to acquire the whole of it, if only because the overlap with Chile, whose claim is about as reasonable as Argentina's, makes a compromise inevitable), this achievement will not be perceived as a gain – which it certainly would be – but instead as a loss, and worse than that, by many, a sell-out.[74]

The same could be said of their neighbours, and this will remain the case for as long as they insist that they both have exclusive rights over overlapping territory. If, so far, the Chilean and Argentinian Antarctic territories have been presented as 'natural' continuations of both countries into the South Pole, it is high time to reckon that there is nothing 'natural' about them. *Pace* Serrano, their agenda has been less about honour and ideals and more about territorial expansion as the end goal. Leaving this agenda behind would take away one source of potential conflict and may even be the first step toward a stronger collaboration in Antarctic matters – and even beyond. As mentioned before, such an acknowledgement might also help us understand the histories of appropriation of the south of the continent and Antarctica as belonging to the same rather than different logics.[75]

At the international level, over 60 years after the Antarctic Treaty's entry came into force, an open recognition of the colonial spirit of these original claims could arguably trigger a new era for this international arrangement. As Alan Hemmings has suggested, since it is highly unlikely that territorial claims in Antarctica will ever be vindicated, it might be better 'to anticipate reality, and have some prospect of influencing the future, than to hold on to obsolete ideas and find oneself overtaken by events'.[76] In this spirit, Argentina and Chile could become pioneers among 'the original seven', shaking the Antarctic Treaty System after 30 years of relative immobility and stagnation, and giving it renewed force, by encouraging the other claimants to leave the language of sovereignty behind once and for all.[77]

Some might point out here that, examined from a *Realpolitik* perspective, what I am suggesting is naive: in a complex geopolitical scenario where western consultative parties fear an ambitious China and a revanchist Russia, and where Argentina and Chile are as adamant as any other claimant when it comes to vindicating their rights, what would be the incentives to make such a move? Granting that this is speculative, one answer could be that, confronted with the challenges of climate change and the depletion of marine life, states – maybe pushed by their own civil societies – may finally see the need to shift the focus from the hope of potential economic and political aggrandisement to more cooperation and environmental protection.

More generally, if the twentieth century marked the liberation of some colonial peoples, the twenty-first could mark global liberation from the colonial mindset and framework that made possible the appropriation and exploitation of most of the earth's land surface; its oceans and seabed; and, eventually, outer space. For this to happen, however, it will be necessary that those engaged in the game recognise themselves as players rather than victims.

Acknowledgements

I am grateful to Carsten-Andreas Schulz, Consuelo León, Peder Roberts and Julia Jabour for their comments on a previous draft, as well as to two anonymous reviewers from *The Polar Journal* (where this chapter was originally published) for thorough feedback. I also thank the audiences at the workshop 'Colonialism, Postcolonialism, and Antarctica', University of Oslo; the workshop in Latin American Political Theory, University of Florida; and the SCAR SC-HASS Biennial Conference; as well as Fabian Stenhaug, Oda Davanger and Yanko Martić for research assistance. I am also indebted to María Luisa Carvallo, Bernardita Zegers and Ed Shaw, who pointed me toward useful references.

This chapter originally appeared in *The Polar Journal* 12: 1 (2022): 22–41, and received funding from the European Research Council (ERC) under the European Union's Horizon 2020 research and innovation programme (grant agreement No 948964).

Notes

1 Antonio Huneeus Gana, *Antártida* (Santiago de Chile: Imprenta Chile, 1948), p. 7. This and all other translations from Spanish are mine.

2 Pedro Radío, *Soberanía argentina en la Antártida* (Valladolid: Seminario de Estudios Internacionales de Vázquez de Menchaca, Universidad de Valladolid, 1948), p. 40.

3 Klaus J. Dodds, 'Post-Colonial Antarctica: An Emerging Engagement', *Polar Record* 42:1 (2006), 59–70.

4 Dodds, 'Post-Colonial Antarctica', p. 61.

5 Dodds, 'Post-Colonial Antarctica', p. 63.

6 Adrian Howkins, 'Appropriating Space: Antarctic Imperialism and the Mentality of Settler Colonialism', in Tracey Banivanua Mar and Penelope Edmonds (eds), *Making Settler Colonial Space* (London: Palgrave Macmillan, 2010), pp. 29–52 (p. 31).

7 Ben Maddison, *Class and Colonialism in Antarctic Exploration, 1750–1920* (London: Pickering & Chatto, 2014), pp. 6, 52.

8 Shirley V. Scott, 'Three Waves of Antarctic Imperialism', in Klaus J. Dodds, Alan D. Hemmings and Peder Roberts (eds), *Handbook on the Politics of Antarctica* (Cheltenham: Edward Elgar Publishing, 2017), pp. 37–49.

9 Sanjay Chaturvedi, *The Polar Regions: A Political Geography* (Chichester: Wiley, 1993), p. 39; Alan D. Hemmings, 'Security beyond Claims', in Alan D. Hemmings, Donald R. Rothwell and Karen N. Scott (eds), *Antarctic Security in the Twenty-First Century: Legal and Policy Perspectives* (Abingdon: Routledge, 2012), pp. 70–96 (p. 77).

10 Klaus J. Dodds, *Pink Ice: Britain and the South Atlantic Empire* (London: I.B. Tauris, 2002).

11 Dodds, 'Post-Colonial Antarctica', p. 61.

12 Klaus J. Dodds and Christy Collis, 'Post-Colonial Antarctica', in Dodds *et al.*, *Handbook on the Politics of Antarctica*, pp. 50–68 (p. 56).

13 Jack Child, *Antarctica and South American Geopolitics: Frozen Lebensraum* (New York: Praeger, 1988).

14 Hereinafter, I take Australia and New Zealand as belonging in the group of 'northern claimants', insofar as both inherited their claims as former colonies of the United Kingdom.

15 Carlos Escudé, 'Argentine Territorial Nationalism', *Journal of Latin American Studies* 20:1 (1988), 139–65. One of the stated objectives of the Meeting of Latin American Antarctic Historians is 'to consolidate their own, characteristic vision of Latin American Antarctic history' – a vision (if I may add) that tends

to be more celebratory than critical. See Encuentro de historiadores antárticos latinoamericanos, 'Chile, 5–7 septiembre 2018: XVIII EHAL', www.antarkos. org.uy/EHAL/ (accessed 12 April 2021).

16 Dodds, 'Post-Colonial Antarctica', p. 61.

17 This definition is based on, but not identical to, that proposed by Margaret Kohn and Kavita Reddy, 'Colonialism', in Edward N. Zalta (ed.), *Stanford Encyclopedia of Philosophy*, fall 2017 edn, https://plato.stanford.edu/archives/ fall2017/entries/colonialism/ (accessed 14 February 2022).

18 Some definitions of colonialism that take the subjugation of one group of people over another as central can be found in Ronald J. Horvath, 'A Definition of Colonialism', *Current Anthropology* 13:1 (1972), 45–57; Dane Keith Kennedy, *Decolonization: A Very Short Introduction* (Oxford: Oxford University Press, 2016); L. Ypi, 'What's Wrong with Colonialism', *Philosophy & Public Affairs* 41:2 (2013), 158–91.

19 I thus follow closely the definition that Adrian Howkins uses for 'settler colonialism'; see Howkins, 'Appropriating Space', p. 48 n. 6.

20 I use the general definition from political science; see *Britannica*, s.v. 'imperialism', www.britannica.com/search?query=imperialism (accessed 6 June 2021).

21 Johan Nicolay Tønnessen and Arne Odd Johnsen, *The History of Modern Whaling* (London and Canberra: C. Hurst and Australian National University Press, 1982); Peder Roberts, *The European Antarctic: Science and Strategy in Scandinavia and the British Empire* (New York: Palgrave Macmillan, 2011).

22 Gustav Smedal, *Acquisition of Sovereignty over Polar Areas* (Oslo: Det kongelige departmentet for handel, sjøfart, industri, håndverk og fiskeri, 1931), p. 6.

23 International Court of Justice, 'Antarctica Cases (United Kingdom *v.* Argentina; United Kingdom *v.* Chile)', 1956, p. 16, www.icj-cij.org/public/files/case-related/27/027-19550504-APP-1-00-EN.pdf (accessed 14 February 2022).

24 This changed in 2015, when for the first time Norway seemed to enlarge its Antarctic sector to the South Pole; Ole Magnus Rapp, 'Norge utvider Dronning Maud Land helt frem til Sydpolen', *Aftenposten*, 19 September 2015, www. aftenposten.no/norge/Norge-utvider-Dronning-Maud-Land-helt-frem-til-Sydpolen-28019b.html (accessed 6 June 2021). In 1939, when Norway made its claim, it was more to prevent the Germans from doing it first than to secure commerce: at that stage there was no longer any need for land stations.

25 Ross Dependency Boundaries and Government Order in Council 1923, pp. 2–3, www.legislation.govt.nz/regulation/imperial/1923/0974/latest/ DLM1195.html (accessed 6 June 2021).

26 Australian Government, Australian Antarctic Territory Acceptance Act 1933, p. 1, www.legislation.gov.au/Details/C2004C00416 (accessed 14 February 2022).

27 France, 'Texte intégral de la Constitution du 4 octobre 1958 en vigueur', articles 72–3, www.conseil-constitutionnel.fr/le-bloc-de-constitutionnalite/texte-integral-de-la-constitution-du-4-octobre-1958-en-vigueur#:~:text=La%20 France%20est%20une%20R%C3%A9publique,Son%20organisation%20 est%20d%C3%A9centralis%C3%A9e (accessed 14 February 2022).

28 This means they are under Norwegian sovereignty, but are not formally considered part of the Kingdom of Norway. See Magnus Hovind Rognhaug, *Norway in the Antarctic* (Tromsø: Norsk Polarinstitutt, 2014), p. 23.

29 Australian Government, 'Australian Territories', www.regional.gov.au/territories/ (accessed 6 June 2021).

30 Shirley V. Scott, 'Ingenious and Innocuous? Article IV of the Antarctic Treaty as Imperialism', *The Polar Journal* 1:1 (2011), 51–62 (p. 55).

31 Scott, 'Ingenious and Innocuous?', p. 55.

32 See, for example, Klaus J. Dodds, 'Geography, Identity and the Creation of the Argentine State', *Bulletin of Latin American Research* 12:3 (1993), 311–31; Claudia Briones and Walter Delrio, 'La "Conquista del Desierto" desde perspectivas hegemónicas y subalternas', *Runa* 27 (2007), 23–48.

33 This transfer is generally referred to as a 'donation'. However, the building of Omond House and the instruments for meteorological observation were sold for 5,000 Argentinian pesos on one condition: 'that the sale be not made public but figure as a donation by Bruce to the [Argentinian] government in retribution for the aid received by the national navy on his trip to Buenos Aires' (Ricardo Capdevila and Santiago M. Comerci, *Historia antártica Argentina* (Buenos Aires: Dirección Nacional del Antártico, 1983), p. 62; it is ironic that the only condition on which the sale was made was not respected by the beneficiaries: what was supposed to be kept secret appeared publicly in Capdevila and Comerci's book, commissioned by the Dirección Nacional del Antártico).

34 Comisión Nacional del Antártico, *Soberanía argentina en la Antártida*, 2nd edn (Buenos Aires: Ministerio de Relaciones Exteriores y Culto, 1948), p. 36.

35 R. N. Rudmose Brown, Robert C. Mossman and J. H. Harvey Pirie, *The Voyage of the 'Scotia'* (Edinburgh: William Blackwood and Sons, 1906), p. 79.

36 Comisión Nacional del Antártico, *Soberanía argentina en la Antártida*, p. 53.

37 The sentence in full reads: 'I presume that the South Orkneys are looked upon as a possession of that power – the nucleus of an empire, perhaps, they may even seem to ambitious Argentine expansionists.' Brown *et al.*, *The Voyage of the 'Scotia'*, p. 79.

38 The Argentinian Antarctic Territory is slightly bigger than Peru.

39 Comisión Nacional del Antártico, *Soberanía argentina en la Antártida*, p. 65.

40 Oscar Pinochet de la Barra, *Chilean Sovereignty in Antarctica* (Santiago de Chile: Editorial del Pacífico, 1954), p. 32.

41 Martti Koskenniemi, *The Gentle Civilizer of Nations: The Rise and Fall of International Law 1870–1960* (Cambridge: Cambridge University Press, 2001), p. 175. Pinochet de la Barra mentions that in 1892 the Chilean government passed a resolution setting rules for the catching of fur seals and elephant seals in the southern regions. In 1902, the first concession was made to Pedro Pablo Benavides, who was authorised to catch fish and seals between Tierra del Fuego at the northern limit and with no limit to the south. In 1906, a concession to Enrique Fabry and Domingo de Toro Herrera was granted to exploit the animal and mineral wealth in 'the Shetland and the lands situated further to the south', on the condition that the grantees 'exercise the administrative acts that

the Government of Chile considers necessary to safeguard its interest in said regions'. Pinochet compares this last concession to the Tayler concession granted by Denmark over Eastern Greenland, which the International Court of Justice deemed sufficient to establish Danish sovereignty in that area between 1814 and 1915 (Pinochet de la Barra, *Chilean Sovereignty in Antarctica*, pp. 35–6).

42 In 1940, President Pedro Aguirre Cerda signed a decree establishing the Chilean Antarctic Territory from 53° to 90° west of Greenwich, all the way to the pole (Chilean and Argentinian territories thus overlap between 25° and 53° west of Greenwich). As Jack Child notes, the claim has no northern limit, an omission that 'can be interpreted as a deliberate emphasis of the idea of a seamless continuity between mainland and Antarctic Chile' (Child, *Antarctica and South American Geopolitics*, p. 117). Chile's Antarctic Territory is nearly the size of Peru.

43 Pinochet de la Barra, *Chilean Sovereignty in Antarctica*, pp. 46–7.

44 Robert L. Nelson, 'Introduction: Colonialism in Europe? The Case against Salt Water', in Robert L. Nelson (ed.), *Germans, Poland, and Colonial Expansion to the East* (New York: Palgrave Macmillan, 2009), pp. 1–9; Gunlög Fur, 'Colonialism and Swedish History: Unthinkable Connections?', in Magdalena Naum and Jonas M. Nordin (eds), *Scandinavian Colonialism and the Rise of Modernity: Small Time Agents in a Global Arena* (New York: Springer, 2013), pp. 17–36.

45 The Spanish version of point 3 is clearer than Pinochet's own translation: 'la posibilidad de explotar mejor sus riquezas' (Oscar Pinochet de la Barra, *La Antártica chilena*, 4th edn (Santiago de Chile: Editorial Andrés Bello, 1976), p. 74; literally, 'the possibility to better exploit its riches').

46 On how the Chilean and Argentinian states expanded their territories through systematic violence against the Indigenous inhabitants, see, among others, Jorge Iván Vergara and Héctor Mellado, 'La violencia política estatal contra el pueblo-nación mapuche durante la conquista tardía de la Araucanía y el proceso de radicación (Chile, 1850–1929)', *Diálogo andino* 55 (2018), 5–17; Miguel Alberto Bartolomé, 'Los pobladores del "desierto"', *Amérique latine histoire et mémoire* 10 (2005), 162–89; Carsten-Andreas Schulz, 'Territorial Sovereignty and the End of Inter-Cultural Diplomacy along the "Southern Frontier"', *European Journal of International Relations* 25:3 (2018), 878–903; Rolf Foerster, *Rapa Nui: El colonialismo republicano chileno cuestionado (1902–1905)* (Santiago de Chile: Catalonia, 2014).

47 Dodds, 'Post-Colonial Antarctica'.

48 Capdevila and Comerci, *Historia antártica Argentina*, pp. 98–117; Pinochet de la Barra, *La Antártica chilena*, pp. 47–74.

49 Jorge Berguño Barnes, 'Historia intelectual del Tratado Antártico', *Boletín Antártico Chileno* 19:1 (2000), 2–12 (p. 2); Radío, *Soberanía argentina en la Antártida*, p. 43.

50 Berguño Barnes, 'Historia intelectual del Tratado Antártico', p. 2.

51 But see the conflict over the Moluccas Islands between the Spanish and the Portuguese (C. H. M. Waldock, 'Disputed Sovereignty in the Falkland Islands Dependencies', *British Yearbook of International Law* 25 (1948), 311–53 (p. 322)).

52 'If they will use the division of Pope Alexander the Sixth, above all that is specially to be considered whether the Pope would only decide the controversies of Portugals and Spaniards, which surely he might do as a chosen arbitrator between them as the kings themselves had made certain covenants between them concerning that matter, and if it be so when the thing was done between others, it appertaineth not to the rest of the nations.' Hugo Grotius and William Welwod, *The Free Sea*, trans. Richard Hakluyt, ed. David Armitage (Indianapolis: Liberty Fund, 2004 [1609]), pp. 15–16.

53 Quoted in Smedal, *Acquisition of Sovereignty*, p. 14.

54 Pinochet de la Barra, *Chilean Sovereignty in Antarctica*, p. 20.

55 Pinochet de la Barra, *Chilean Sovereignty in Antarctica*, pp. 23–4.

56 Huneeus Gana, *Antártida*, p. 27.

57 For the moral limits of Antarctic claims based on historic rights, see Alejandra Mancilla, 'The Moral Limits of Territorial Claims in Antarctica', *Ethics & International Affairs* 32:3 (2018), 339–60.

58 Salvador Reyes, *El continente de los hombres solos* (Santiago: Ercilla, 1956), pp. 24–5.

59 Adrian Howkins, *Frozen Empires: An Environmental History of the Antarctic Peninsula* (Oxford: Oxford University Press, 2016), p. 119.

60 Comisión Nacional del Antártico, *Soberanía argentina en la Antártida*, p. 71.

61 Capdevila and Comerci, *Historia antártica Argentina*, pp. 109–10.

62 Capdevila and Comerci, *Historia antártica Argentina*, pp. 109–10.

63 Hugo Schmidt Prado (ed.), *¡Base O'Higgins sin novedad!*, 2nd edn (Santiago de Chile: Editorial La Noria, 1992 [1956]), pp. 38–9.

64 Reyes, *El continente de los hombres solos*, p. 92.

65 Howkins, *Frozen Empires*, p. 61.

66 Eric William Hunter Christie, *The Antarctic Problem* (London: George Allen & Unwin, 1951), p. 296.

67 Howkins, *Frozen Empires*, p. 115. Alberto L. Daverede, 'Política y actividades antárticas de la República Argentina', conference proceedings, *Aula de estudios antárticos* (1987), Madrid, p. 3.

68 Miguel Serrano, *Memorias de él y yo*, Vol. II (Santiago: Ediciones La Nueva Edad, 1997), p. 239.

69 Reyes, *El continente de los hombres solos*, p. 23.

70 Juan Domingo Perón, 'La Antártida argentina: Nota preliminar', in Comisión Nacional del Antártico, *Soberanía argentina en la Antártida*, pp. 9–11 (p. 10).

71 An analogy could be made with the 'Northern Vision' proposed in the 1950s by Canadian Prime Minister John Diefenbaker, when the northern hinterland was compared to the West of the nineteenth century: the place whose incorporation would make the country great. I thank Peder Roberts for pointing this out.

72 If and only if contiguity may be invoked for territories lying over 1,000 km apart and separated by an ocean.

73 See, for example, Ignacio Grimaldi, 'Chile y Argentina se disputan plataforma continental al sur de sus países', CNN Espanol, 2 September 2021, https://cnnespanol.cnn.com/2021/09/02/chile-argentina-plataforma-continental-orix-perspectivas-buenos-aires/ (accessed 14 February 2022).

74 Escudé, 'Argentine Territorial Nationalism', p. 160.

75 I leave out the question of whether this should also result in a greater Indigenous presence in the countries' respective Antarctic politics as a way of decolonising the continent. There are interesting parallels to be made here with the case of the Māori in New Zealand and their engagement with Antarctica (Priscilla M. Wehi, Vincent van Uitregt, Nigel J. Scott *et al.*, 'Transforming Antarctic Management and Policy with an Indigenous Māori Lens', *Nature Ecology & Evolution* 5 (2021), 1055–9), and how the state has, not unproblematically, 'brought' the Māori to Antarctica through the use of Māori names for places in the Ross Dependency (Klaus J. Dodds and Kathryn Yusoff, 'Settlement and Unsettlement in Aotearoa/ New Zealand and Antarctica', *Polar Record* 41:217 (2005), 141–55).

76 Hemmings, 'Security beyond Claims', p. 84.

77 Alejandra Mancilla, 'Decolonising Antarctica', in Alan D. Hemmings and Dawid Bunikowski (eds), *Philosophies of Polar Law* (Abingdon: Routledge, 2020), pp. 49–61.

Bibliography

Australian Government. Australian Antarctic Territory Acceptance Act 1933. www. legislation.gov.au/Details/C2004C00416. Accessed 14 February 2022.

Australian Government. 'Australian Territories'. www.regional.gov.au/territories/. Accessed 6 June 2021.

Barros Recabarren, Manuel. 'Presentación'. In *¡Base O'Higgins sin novedad!*, 2nd edn, ed. Hugo Schmidt Prado, pp. 13–14. Santiago de Chile: Editorial La Noria, 1992 [1956].

Bartolomé, Miguel Alberto. 'Los pobladores del "desierto"'. *Amérique latine histoire et mémoire* 10 (2005): 162–89.

Berguño Barnes, Jorge. 'Historia intelectual del Tratado Antártico'. *Boletín Antártico Chileno* 19, no. 1 (2000): 2–12.

Briones, Claudia and Walter Delrio. 'La "Conquista del Desierto" desde perspectivas hegemónicas y subalternas'. *Runa* 27 (2007): 23–48.

Britannica. www.britannica.com/. Accessed 6 June 2021.

Brown, R. N. Rudmose, Robert C. Mossman and J. H. Harvey Pirie. *The Voyage of the 'Scotia'*. Edinburgh: William Blackwood and Sons, 1906.

Capdevila, Ricardo and Santiago M. Comerci. *Historia antártica Argentina*. Buenos Aires: Dirección Nacional del Antártico, 1983.

Chaturvedi, Sanjay. *The Polar Regions: A Political Geography*. Chichester: Wiley, 1993.

Child, Jack. *Antarctica and South American Geopolitics: Frozen Lebensraum*. New York: Praeger, 1988.

Christie, Eric William Hunter. *The Antarctic Problem*. London: George Allen & Unwin, 1951.

Comisión Nacional del Antártico. *Soberanía argentina en la Antártida*. 2nd edn. Buenos Aires: Ministerio de Relaciones Exteriores y Culto, 1948.

Daverede, Alberto L. 'Política y actividades antárticas de la República Argentina'. Conference proceedings. *Aula de estudios antárticos* (1987), Madrid.

Dodds, Klaus J. 'Geography, Identity and the Creation of the Argentine State'. *Bulletin of Latin American Research* 12, no. 3 (1993): 311–31.

Dodds, Klaus J. *Pink Ice: Britain and the South Atlantic Empire*. London: I.B. Tauris, 2002.

Dodds, Klaus J. 'Post-Colonial Antarctica: An Emerging Engagement'. *Polar Record* 42, no. 1 (2006): 59–70.

Dodds, Klaus J. and Christy Collis. 'Post-Colonial Antarctica'. In *Handbook on the Politics of Antarctica*, ed. Klaus Dodds, Alan D. Hemmings and Peder Roberts, pp. 50–68. Cheltenham: Edward Elgar Publishing, 2017.

Dodds, Klaus J. and Kathryn Yusoff. 'Settlement and Unsettlement in Aotearoa/New Zealand and Antarctica'. *Polar Record* 41, no. 217 (2005): 141–55.

Encuentro de historiadores antárticos latinoamericanos. 'Chile, 5–7 septiembre 2018: XVIII EHAL'. www.antarkos.org.uy/EHAL/. Accessed 12 April 2021.

Escudé, Carlos. 'Argentine Territorial Nationalism'. *Journal of Latin American Studies* 20, no. 1 (1988): 139–65.

Foerster, Rolf. *Rapa Nui: El colonialismo republicano chileno cuestionado (1902–1905)*. Santiago de Chile: Catalonia, 2014.

France, 'Texte intégral de la Constitution du 4 octobre 1958 en vigueur'. www.conseil-constitutionnel.fr/le-bloc-de-constitutionnalite/texte-integral-de-la-constitution-du-4-octobre-1958-en-vigueur#:~:text=La%20France%20est%20une%20R%C3%A9publique,Son%20organisation%20est%20d%C3%A9centralis%C3%A9e. Accessed 14 February 2022.

Fur, Gunlög. 'Colonialism and Swedish History: Unthinkable Connections?'. In *Scandinavian Colonialism and the Rise of Modernity: Small Time Agents in a Global Arena*, ed. Magdalena Naum and Jonas M. Nordin, pp. 17–36. New York: Springer, 2013.

Grimaldi, Ignacio. 'Chile y Argentina se disputan plataforma continental al sur de sus países'. CNN Espanol, 2 September 2021. https://cnnespanol.cnn.com/2021/09/02/chile-argentina-plataforma-continental-orix-perspectivas-buenos-aires/. Accessed 14 February 2022.

Grotius, Hugo and William Welwod. *The Free Sea*, trans. Richard Hakluyt, ed. David Armitage. Indianapolis: Liberty Fund, 2004 [1609].

Hemmings, Alan D. 'Security beyond Claims'. In *Antarctic Security in the Twenty-First Century: Legal and Policy Perspectives*, ed. Alan D. Hemmings, Donald R. Rothwell and Karen N. Scott, pp. 70–96. Abingdon: Routledge, 2012.

Horvath, Ronald J. 'A Definition of Colonialism'. *Current Anthropology* 13, no. 1 (1972): 45–57.

Howkins, Adrian. 'Appropriating Space: Antarctic Imperialism and the Mentality of Settler Colonialism'. In *Making Settler Colonial Space*, ed. Tracey Banivanua Mar and Penelope Edmonds, pp. 29–52. London: Palgrave Macmillan, 2010.

Howkins, Adrian. *Frozen Empires: An Environmental History of the Antarctic Peninsula*. Oxford: Oxford University Press, 2016.

Huneeus Gana, Antonio. *Antártida*. Santiago de Chile: Imprenta Chile, 1948.

International Court of Justice. 'Antarctica Cases (United Kingdom *v.* Argentina; United Kingdom *v.* Chile)', 1956. www.icj-cij.org/public/files/case-related/27/027-19550504-APP-1-00-EN.pdf. Accessed 14 February 2022.

Kennedy, Dane Keith. *Decolonization: A Very Short Introduction*. Oxford: Oxford University Press, 2016.

Kohn, Margaret and Kavita Reddy. 'Colonialism'. In *Stanford Encyclopedia of Philosophy*. Fall 2017 edn, ed. Edward N. Zalta. https://plato.stanford.edu/archives/fall2017/entries/colonialism/. Accessed 14 February 2022.

Koskenniemi, Martti. *The Gentle Civilizer of Nations: The Rise and Fall of International Law 1870–1960.* Cambridge: Cambridge University Press, 2001.

Maddison, Ben. *Class and Colonialism in Antarctic Exploration, 1750–1920.* London: Pickering & Chatto, 2014.

Mancilla, Alejandra. 'Decolonising Antarctica'. In *Philosophies of Polar Law*, ed. Dawid Bunikowski and Alan D. Hemmings, pp. 49–61. Abingdon: Routledge, 2020.

Mancilla, Alejandra. 'The Moral Limits of Territorial Claims in Antarctica'. *Ethics & International Affairs* 32, no. 3 (2018): 339–60.

Nelson, Robert L. 'Introduction: Colonialism in Europe? The Case against Salt Water'. In *Germans, Poland, and Colonial Expansion to the East*, ed. Robert L. Nelson, pp. 1–9. New York: Palgrave Macmillan, 2009.

Perón, Juan Domingo. 'La Antártida argentina: Nota preliminar'. In Comisión Nacional del Antártico, *Soberanía argentina en la Antártida*, pp. 9–11. Buenos Aires: Ministerio de Relaciones Exteriores y Culto, 1948.

Pinochet de la Barra, Oscar. *La Antártica chilena.* 4th edn. Santiago de Chile: Editorial Andrés Bello, 1976.

Pinochet de la Barra, Oscar. *Chilean Sovereignty in Antarctica.* Santiago de Chile: Editorial del Pacífico, 1954.

Radío, Pedro. *Soberanía argentina en la Antártida.* Valladolid: Seminario de Estudios Internacionales de Vázquez de Menchaca, Universidad de Valladolid, 1948.

Rapp, Ole Magnus. 'Norge utvider Dronning Maud Land helt frem til Sydpolen'. *Aftenposten*, 19 September 2015. www.aftenposten.no/norge/Norge-utvider-Dronning-Maud-Land-helt-frem-til-Sydpolen-28019b.html. Accessed 6 June 2021.

Reyes, Salvador. *El continente de los hombres solos.* Santiago: Ercilla, 1956.

Roberts, Peder. *The European Antarctic: Science and Strategy in Scandinavia and the British Empire.* New York: Palgrave Macmillan, 2011.

Rognhaug, Magnus Hovind. *Norway in the Antarctic.* Tromsø: Norsk Polarinstitutt, 2014.

Ross Dependency Boundaries and Government Order in Council 1923. www.legislation.govt.nz/regulation/imperial/1923/0974/latest/DLM1195.html. Accessed 6 June 2021.

Schmidt Prado, Hugo (ed.). *¡Base O'Higgins sin novedad!.* 2nd edn. Santiago de Chile: Editorial La Noria, 1992 [1956].

Schulz, Carsten-Andreas. 'Territorial Sovereignty and the End of Inter-Cultural Diplomacy along the "Southern Frontier"'. *European Journal of International Relations* 25, no. 3 (2018): 878–903.

Scott, Shirley V. 'Ingenious and Innocuous? Article IV of the Antarctic Treaty as Imperialism'. *The Polar Journal* 1, no. 1 (2011): 51–62.

Scott, Shirley V. 'Three Waves of Antarctic Imperialism'. In *Handbook on the Politics of Antarctica*, ed. Klaus Dodds, Alan D. Hemmings and Peder Roberts, pp. 37–49. Cheltenham: Edward Elgar Publishing, 2017.

Serrano, Miguel. *Memorias de él y yo.* Vol. II. Santiago: Ediciones La Nueva Edad, 1997.

Smedal, Gustav. *Acquisition of Sovereignty over Polar Areas.* Oslo: Det kongelige departementet for handel, sjøfart, industri, håndverk og fiskeri, 1931.

Tønnessen, Johan Nicolay and Arne Odd Johnsen. *The History of Modern Whaling.* London and Canberra: C. Hurst and Australian National University Press, 1982.

Vergara, Jorge Iván and Héctor Mellado. 'La violencia política estatal contra el pueblo-nación mapuche durante la conquista tardía de la Araucanía y el proceso de radicación (Chile, 1850–1929)'. *Diálogo andino* 55 (2018): 5–17.

Waldock, C. H. M. 'Disputed Sovereignty in the Falkland Islands Dependencies'. *British Yearbook of International Law* 25 (1948): 311–53.

Wehi, Priscilla M., Vincent van Uitregt, Nigel J. Scott *et al.* 'Transforming Antarctic Management and Policy with an Indigenous Māori Lens'. *Nature Ecology & Evolution* 5 (2021): 1055–9.

Ypi, Lea. 'What's Wrong with Colonialism'. *Philosophy & Public Affairs* 41, no. 2 (2013): 158–91.

6

Colonialism without religion? Faith and politics in the history of Antarctica

Adrian Howkins

As Captain Scott's *Terra Nova* expedition set sail from the Welsh port of Cardiff toward Antarctica on 15 June 1910, hundreds of representatives of Protestant missionary organisations were gathering in Edinburgh for the first full day of the World Missionary Conference.[1] Lasting for nine days, this meeting of missionaries from across Europe and North America is widely regarded as the culmination of Christian efforts at global evangelism that accompanied the 'age of high imperialism' in the late nineteenth and early twentieth centuries.[2] While Scott's party were saying their fond farewells to family and friends in South Wales – some for the last time – delegates in the Scottish capital were listening to a report on 'carrying the Gospel to all the non-Christian world'.[3]

Upon first glance, the departure of the *Terra Nova* from Cardiff and the World Missionary Conference in Edinburgh might seem almost entirely disconnected events. Despite presumably constituting part of 'the non-Christian world', as the only unpopulated continent on the planet, Antarctica was not a major focus for the Edinburgh missionary conference. Although the Arctic was included in the report of the conference, there was no mention of Antarctica.[4] Protestant missionaries already faced more than enough challenges in their goal of converting the world to Christianity, without needing to consider the religious condition of Antarctica. On the other side, Scott's expedition drew ostensibly upon science rather than religion as a moral justification for its work.[5]

Rather than seeing the departure of the *Terra Nova* on the opening day of the Edinburgh Conference merely as a chronological coincidence, however, this chapter argues that the two events shared a similar worldview, in which religious faith, science and empire could not easily be disentangled. When Captain Scott and his companions stood at the South Pole on 17 January 1912, the ice they stood on was technically part of Britain's 1908 claim to the Falkland Islands Dependencies.[6] Building on a long tradition of 'spiritual conquest', the late nineteenth and early twentieth centuries witnessed a close, if not always harmonious, relationship between missionary endeavours and colonialism.[7] Religion and empire were linked by the concept of the 'White Man's Burden', by which the British saw themselves as divinely ordained to rule for the good of the world. Missionaries were often viewed as the advanced guard of imperial expansion, and for many people were the first point of contact with colonial powers.[8] In the pantheon of imperial adventurers, Captain Scott would not be far from the famous Scottish missionary to Africa David Livingstone.

While Captain Scott's *Terra Nova* expedition offers a particularly interesting example of the overlaps of faith, science and empire in the history of Antarctica, these overlaps were not confined to any single expedition, or any single country. A focused examination of the history of Antarctica demonstrates that religious faith has been embedded in many of the colonial enterprises that have taken place on the continent. Making this case relies on broad and somewhat permeable definitions of 'imperialism' and 'colonialism' as actions and activities connected to expansive projections of political power beyond established boundaries. Such an approach might lack the analytical precision of some of the other chapters in this volume, especially in the partial conflation of two terms that often have quite different meanings. But it reflects the often messy reality of the history of the continent, where imperialism and colonialism have frequently been used interchangeably. Around the time of Captain Scott's expedition, for example, Britain's Falkland Islands Dependencies were administered by the Colonial Office and were included in *The Oxford Survey of the British Empire* (1914), creating connections to both colonialism and imperialism.[9]

A focus on religion can, in turn, offer an interesting perspective from which to think about colonialism in Antarctica more generally. In some ways, of course, the religious experience of Antarctica was very different from much of the rest of the world. Most obviously, as it is a continent without an Indigenous population, it has not been possible – at least since the basic geographical facts of the continent were learned – to use religious conversion as a justification for imperial expansion, as was often the case, for example, in Spanish and Portuguese conquests in the Americas.[10] Similarly, in a place without permanent residents, religion has little value as a tool of social control. But religion has been a motivation for imperial interests on the continent, and this has had at least some impact on the outcome of expeditions. It has been a tool for putting forward sovereignty claims. And, perhaps most importantly, in relation to the idea of settler colonialism, it has played an important role in helping those living and working on the continent to feel at home in what are frequently quite unfamiliar surroundings.

This chapter begins with a discussion of the role of religion in British interests in Antarctica during the so-called 'heroic era' of exploration in the early twentieth century. While certainly not every member of the British expeditions of the heroic age would have considered himself religious, these efforts at geographical conquest were infused with the spirit of muscular Christianity that characterised much imperial expansion.[11] The second section considers the role of religion in Argentine and Chilean engagement with the continent. By challenging British sovereignty claims in the Antarctic Peninsula, much of this South American interest might be considered explicitly anti-imperial in its nature, but there are also elements of settler colonialism to these claims that Catholic nationalism helps to reveal through both legal arguments and domestication of the Antarctic environment. The third section turns attention to US diplomacy on the continent. There were certainly religious dimensions to the US experience in Antarctica, and it is possible to observe similar overlaps between religion and colonialism in the British and Latin American examples. Ultimately, however, the United States led the way in promoting the 1959 Antarctic Treaty as a way of governing Antarctica, in which science and not religion would be the main tool for perpetuating colonial interests.

It is not only in the Antarctic histories of Britain, Argentina and Chile, and the United States that important overlaps existed between religion and colonialism. The relative lack of overt religion in Roald Amundsen's successful expedition to the South Pole, for example, might make an interesting contrast to the British experience. More recently, the construction of orthodox chapels by Russia and Bulgaria might be seen as similar to the religious nationalism evident in Latin American settler colonialism on the continent. It would be interesting to examine the interactions of religion and politics in any country's activities on Antarctica. But a focus on examples from Britain, Argentina and Chile, and the United States allows a range of religious experiences to be examined across a broad chronological scope.

In addressing the overarching question of how thinking more directly about religion can help us to think in new ways about the history of Antarctic colonialism, the chapter makes two related arguments. The first is that religion has played a significant, if idiosyncratic, role in the history of Antarctic colonialism. Religion has been a motivation for imperial interests on the continent; a tool for putting forward sovereignty claims; and a form of domestication and a reminder of 'home' for those involved in the settler colonial enterprise of living in, working in, and claiming the continent. The second argument is that religion has proved much less effective than science in promoting the international approach to Antarctic politics, which has served to perpetuate imperial interests on the continent since the signing of the Antarctic Treaty in 1959.[12] Whereas science offers an accepted common activity, religion has the potential to be much more divisive.

Great Britain: Religion and empire

As a result of needing to attend to final expedition business, Captain Scott himself was not on board the *Terra Nova* as it left Wales in June 1910. He was probably far too busy to pay any attention to the World Missionary Conference taking place in Edinburgh. He was not really a religious person anyway. Francis Spufford speculates that Scott was probably a religious agnostic or even an atheist.[13] But Edwardian England remained a society saturated by religious influences. On Christmas Day 1910 Scott described the religious nature of the celebrations on board the *Terra Nova* as it sailed through the pack: 'the mess is gaily decorated with our various banners. There was full attendance at the Service this morning and a lusty singing of hymns.'[14] Even if personal belief was becoming less common, Christianity still enjoyed a tremendous cultural influence, and the religious rituals and ceremonies that reflected this cultural influence would, in turn, play an important role in domesticating unfamiliar territories such as Antarctica.

There is an ongoing debate about the motivations of the heroic era: some scholars argue that science was merely an excuse for exploration, while others suggest that important scientific research was conducted.[15] While popular histories tend to present the heroic age as politically neutral, most academic historians agree that there were strong connections to the politics of nationalism and imperialism, and associated ideas of race, gender and class.[16] The religious motivations for the heroic era have tended to receive less attention. But much like some of the leading explorers of the Arctic in the nineteenth century, such as James Clark Ross and John Franklin, at least some of the heroic era explorers – most notably Edward Wilson and Henry 'Birdie' Bowers – took with them a strong Christian faith.[17] In keeping with the spirit of the age, this Christian faith was not antithetical to the more commented-upon motivations for exploration (imperialism, nationalism, science), but rather was entangled with these other motivations. It was perfectly possible to explore Antarctica for the benefit of science, the pride of empire and the glory of God, without any sense of contradiction.

The life and death of Edward Wilson, one of Scott's chief scientists and his deputy leader, encapsulated the importance of religion to the history of the heroic era.[18] The son of a popular doctor, Wilson had grown up in Cheltenham and had attended the evangelical-influenced Cheltenham College. He was confirmed by the Bishop of Gloucester in March 1890, and religion would play an important role in his life.[19] Following in his father's footsteps he went to study medicine at Cambridge, where his education as an active and somewhat boisterous 'Christian Gentleman' continued. Alongside his medical studies and sporting activities (rowing, fencing, walking etc.), Wilson was keenly interested in botany and the natural world. Importantly, Wilson saw no contradiction between his religious faith and his scientific interests and, in fact, viewed science as a better way of understanding God's creation and, through creation, of understanding God. Among his heroes were both St Francis of Assisi and Charles Darwin, but unlike Darwin he came to see no contradictions between the theory of evolution by natural selection and Christian beliefs.[20] One of his friends from his early medical practice wrote that 'he sought and cared little for originality, but greatly and entirely for truth'.[21] While most scholars have focused on Wilson's scientific interests and his skills as an artist which accompanied these interests, it was his religious faith that served as a foundation for his passion for seeking to understand the natural world.

Wilson's quest for truth would take him on two expeditions to Antarctica with Captain Scott. Despite suffering from tuberculosis while completing his practical studies, his medical training, sporting interests and moral drive had made him an ideal candidate to be the expedition doctor on the *Discovery* expedition of 1901–04. He quickly became Scott's right-hand man. In Antarctica he kept up his daily practice of annotating the scriptures as part of his morning prayer, and he became known for his quiet religiosity. Every Sunday throughout the polar winter on the *Terra Nova* expedition, Wilson noted where they were in the Anglican liturgical calendar. His entry for Sunday 10 September 1911, for example, reads 'Thirteenth Sunday after Trinity. Church as usual. Horse exercising. Up the Ramp. Reading'.[22] This combination of science and religion is key to understanding Wilson's activities in Antarctica, which are hinted at by the one surviving poem that he wrote during the second expedition, titled 'The Barrier Silence':

> AND this was the thought that the Silence wrought
>   As it scorched and froze us through.
> Though secrets hidden are all forbidden
>   Till God means a man to know,
> We might be the men God meant should know
>   The heart of the Barrier snow,
>   In the heat of the sun, and the glow
>   And the glace from the glistening floe,
> As it scorched and froze us through and through
>   With the bite of the drifting snow.[23]

While Wilson may have lacked the literary talents of some of his companions, the idea conveyed by this poem that it was divine will that underlay the work of scientists struggling against the harsh environment to know 'the heart of the Barrier snow' neatly sums up his motivations for participation in the heroic age of Antarctic exploration.

Wilson was not alone in bringing a strong religious faith to Scott's *Terra Nova* expedition. As demonstrated in a study by Kellie Vernon, Henry 'Birdie' Bowers, an officer in the Royal Indian Marine Service, also had strong Christian beliefs.[24] Bowers's faith was much less conventional than Wilson's and he was influenced by the American Charles Taze Russel's millenarian Watch Tower movement. Following an extensive study of scripture, Taze Russel believed that the world would come to an end in a seven-year process between 1907 and 1915 and that Jesus Christ would return.[25] He challenged traditional Christian ideas of hell and the Trinity, and believed the Great Pyramids of Egypt held clues about humanity's relationship with God. While certainly not accepting all of Taze Russel's ideas uncritically, Bowers and his sister May expressed a strong interest in the Watch Tower movement. While Bowers was much less open about his religious faith than Wilson, Vernon suggests that his millenarian beliefs influenced his experiences during the expedition, as well as his motivations for being there.[26]

On 29 March 1912, on the return journey from the South Pole, both Wilson and Bowers died in a tent on 'the Barrier snow' in the middle of a blizzard, alongside Captain Scott. Shortly before dying himself, Scott wrote to Wilson's wife 'His [Wilson's] eyes have a comfortable blue look of hope, and his mind is peaceful with the satisfaction of his faith in regarding himself as part of the great scheme of the Almighty.'[27] More poignantly still, in his own dying letter to his 'old Dad and Mother' Wilson concluded 'However we have done all for the best believing in His guidance and we have both believed that whatever is, is His will, and in that faith I am prepared to meet Him and leave all you loved ones in His care till His own time is fulfilled.'[28] This sense of divine providence could explain some of the decisions taken that led to the tragic failure of Scott's expedition. Vernon suggests, for example, that Bowers's millenarian faith may help to explain why he did not attempt to make a final effort to get to the One Ton depot.[29] Equally importantly, a focus on religion in thinking about Antarctic history gives an insight into how at least some of the heroic age explorers understood Antarctica and what they were doing there. The line Wilson wrote in 'The Barrier Silence' that 'We might be the men God meant should know' encapsulates the mixture of religion, science, adventure and imperial pride that shaped the British imperial attitude toward Antarctica during the heroic era.

It was in the commemoration of the 'tragedy' of Captain Scott's polar party that religion really came into its own.[30] In Antarctica, the remaining members of the expedition constructed a memorial cross at the top of Observation Hill inscribed with words from Tennyson's *Ulysses*: 'To strive, to seek, to find, and not to yield'. Back in Britain, shortly after the news broke of the deaths of Scott, Wilson, Bowers, Captain Lawrence Oates and Petty Officer Edgar Evans, a commemorative service was held at St Paul's

Cathedral, described by a contemporary newspaper as 'the mother church, indeed, of the British Empire'.[31] The service included the lesson from 1 Corinthians 15:54–5 – 'Death has been swallowed up in victory. Where, O death, is your victory? Where, O Death, is your sting?'[32] In these ways, Christian theology played a central role in converting defeat and failure into a moral triumph. Seen through a religious lens, the deaths of Captain Scott and his companions could be interpreted as both a Christian sacrifice and a sacrifice for the greater good of the British empire. Memorials were constructed in local churches to commemorate the lives of the five explorers: St Mary's Church in Rhossili in South Wales, for example, contains a memorial to Evans, who was from the local area.

With the exception of the Japanese expedition of Nobu Shirase, all countries involved in the heroic era of Antarctica exploration could be labelled as 'Christian countries'. Religion was rarely overt, and there was significant variation in the way religious faith expressed itself in different expeditions. Roald Amundsen's successful expedition to the South Pole, for example, gave the distinct impression of being unashamedly secular and pragmatic in its approach (its lack of a higher purpose – whether religious or scientific – would provide cause for attacks by the defeated British polar establishment). Despite remaining largely in the background, however, Christian religious influences were inscribed onto the landscape of Antarctica during this period in place names (for example Cathedral Rocks) and the handful of memorial crosses that were left to commemorate the explorers who never made it home (for example Vince's Cross at Hut Point, from Scott's first expedition). As well as serving some sort of religious function, these references helped both to domesticate and lay claim to the continent, and the religious and political functions are difficult to untangle. Personal religious belief could have a strong impact on motivations for being in Antarctica, while broadly shared religious traditions could help to create common ground in the colonial enterprise of starting to occupy and settle the continent.

Latin America: Religion and anti-colonial nationalism

The decades following Scott's failure to be the first explorer to get to the South Pole were marked by a growing interest in the ownership of Antarctica. Britain had made a claim in 1908 to the Antarctic territory directly to the south of South America, which it labelled 'The Falkland Islands Dependencies'.[33] Over the next few decades this claim came to be bitterly contested by both Argentina and Chile.[34] While these two South American countries shared a common hostility toward British claims, they could not agree on the location of their respective borders in Antarctica any more than they could agree on the exact location of the border in southern Patagonia. This created a fascinating three-way sovereignty dispute in which Argentina and Chile were allied against Britain and British imperialism, but opposed to each other.

As Argentina and Chile sought more actively to assert their sovereignty over the Antarctic Peninsula in the 1930s and 1940s, these claims drew on a Roman Catholic heritage. Religious ideas and imagery infused Latin American representations of the far south. The Chilean intellectual Miguel Serrano, for example, would describe the crossing of the Drake Passage as 'purgatory'; the Chilean military officer Hugo Schmidt Prado would write how the 'game of lights' caused by the sunlight on the sea, icebergs and snow-covered mountains reminded him of his mother's 'beatific images'.[35] Latin American nationalism in Antarctica, especially that most strongly influenced by Catholicism, might be seen as having elements of both anticolonialism and colonialism. On the one hand, in making common cause against the British empire there were clear parallels with nationalist movements in places such as India and Egypt that were seeking to overthrow imperial rule. In Argentina, in particular, this was exacerbated by the sense that British economic influence constituted an 'informal empire' in the country.[36] On the other hand, there was often a pride and assertiveness to this nationalism in both Argentina and Chile, which meant that not infrequently it had imperialistic elements itself.[37] While intended to contribute to distinctive national visions of Antarctica opposed to British imperialism, the use of Roman Catholic symbolism in promoting these South American claims might also be seen as reinforcing the case for their colonial nature.

The legal basis for the Argentine and Chilean claim to Antarctica has a religious foundation, going back to the papal bull *Inter caetera* of 1493, issued by Pope Alexander VI, and the subsequent 1494 Treaty of Tordesillas.[38] These pronouncements divided the world from pole to pole, and created distinct Spanish and Portuguese spheres of influence. The link to papal authority gave an added religious dimension to these legal arguments, and the fact that it had been the pope who had arbitrated on the territorial divisions gave the resulting spheres a sense of divine authority. Despite the fact that the Antarctic continent remained unsighted until after the states that would become Argentina and Chile had each gained their independence in the early nineteenth century, both independent countries would later draw heavily on these early religiously infused legal pronouncements, which they claimed to have inherited through the legal concept of *uti possidetis*, in making their respective cases for Antarctic sovereignty.

The shared use by both Argentina and Chile of *Inter caetera* and the Treaty of Tordesillas highlighted a fundamental challenge faced by both countries. While they were distinctive, independent nations, Argentina and

Chile had in common many of the classic markers of national identity identified by scholars of nationalism: shared language, similar history, similar
culture and shared religion.[39] Separate Argentine and Chilean identities
needed to be developed from relatively small differences. In this context, the
importance of national territory and 'territorial integrity' came to play an
even more significant role.[40] Although interest in Antarctica would take a
while to develop owing to other more pressing priorities, the broadly similar
religious traditions of Argentina and Chile might be seen as contributing to
a heightened interest in Antarctic sovereignty in the twentieth century.

In that century's early decades, Argentina became the first of the two
South American countries to sustain an active presence in the Antarctic
Peninsula region when it took over the running of a meteorological station
on the South Orkney Islands. At this stage religion seems to have played a
minimal role in the history. There is little mention of religion, for example,
in José Manuel Moneta's classic account of living at the station, *Four Years
in the South Orkney Islands*.[41] At this time, the Argentine government
was doing relatively little to promote its sovereignty claims to Antarctica.
In what was perhaps an early example of the difficulties of combining
religion with internationalism, it also seems likely that the international
nature of the station – with many of the personnel being from northern
Europe, especially Scandinavia – contributed to the absence of any strong
religious presence.

But as Argentina began to intensify its claims to Antarctica in the late
1930s and 1940s, the use of religious rhetoric in support of these claims
also increased. This was in keeping with a brand of right-wing nationalism
that saw Catholicism as central to the Argentine national identity, as well
as creating connections to a broader pan-Hispanic nationalism.[42] On 20
February 1946, the first Catholic mass to be held in Antarctica took place
at the Stella Maris chapel at the Orcadas station, led by the Spanish Jesuit
Father Felipe Lérida.[43] An 8-metre cross was erected and the pope was con-
tacted by telegram. There was quite a bit of fanfare that an Argentine base
had been the site of the first mass on the continent, which drew on a long
tradition of religious rituals in the 'ceremonies of possession' used to make
claims to unknown lands.[44]

Four days after this mass took place, on 24 February 1946 a general election in Argentina saw Juan Domingo Perón win the presidency, inaugurating
a new phase of popular nationalism in Argentina. Building on the traditional
nationalist *irredenta* of the Islas Malvinas (known in English as the Falkland
Islands), Perón would be an active proponent of Argentine sovereignty in
the Antarctic Peninsula region during the years that followed his election.
His relations with the Catholic Church would frequently prove to be quite
fraught, and his brand of populist nationalism did not neatly correspond

to the more elite-driven Catholic nationalism.[45] But Perón was a consummate politician, and he was happy to take advantage of the overlap between Argentine nationalism and the Catholic faith wherever it suited his interests.[46]

At the same time as helping to make a legal case for sovereignty, the conduct of familiar religious rituals helped to domesticate Antarctica for the Argentines living and working in this unfamiliar landscape. As well as making Antarctica more Argentine, religion helped to make sense of the landscape, which is a goal of settler-colonial enterprises. Religious references appear frequently in much of the Argentine literature on Antarctica from this period, especially that written by naval officers, who continued to be influenced by Catholic nationalism.[47] For example, Emilio Díaz, a naval Captain who sailed 55,000 miles in Antarctic waters over the course of eight seasons, begins the published account of his experiences in the far south with an extended discussion of religious creationism in a chapter titled 'The Finger of God'.[48] In keeping with the biblical tradition of the wilderness, there was a strong moral dimension to many of these accounts, with Antarctica seen as an ideal testing ground for young Argentine men to prove their worth.[49]

Religion was no less prominent in Chile's nascent Antarctic programme, and it served similar purposes in helping to claim and domesticate the landscape. As part of his account of the 1947 Chilean expedition to Antarctica on board the *Angamos*, Eugenio Orrego Vicuña, professor of history at the University of Chile, recounts the raising of a large Christian cross at the O'Higgins military base on 19 March 1947.[50] 'The ceremony began with the Lord's Prayer, which was prayed together in unison. After the pronouncement of a short speech, Oliver Schneider read a chapter from the *Imitation of Christ*.' Summing up the occasion Orrego Vicuña noted:

> There was an inexpressible emotion that brought together the landscape and the ceremony; it was like a return to the days of early Christianity, when the sense of love overcame divisions, transcended class and annihilated prejudice. In that moment, before the altar of snow-covered mountains whose summits merged with the sky, in communion with a special sense of infinite solitude, those men far away from their homes, interests and appetites intuited, as in rare moments of their lives, that *something* that goes beyond *everything*.[51]

Orrego Vicuña's fusing of religion and landscape had a strongly nationalist dimension. He named the cross the 'Cross of Sovereignty', and later in his account he spoke of the need to 're-baptise' the places of the Antarctic Peninsula with Chilean names in order to promote Chilean ownership.[52] Not only was this a familiar ritual, but it was given particular potency by the Antarctic environment: fused with Catholic symbolism, Antarctica offered an ideal form of Chilean nationhood.

In March 1949, after spending a year as commander of the O'Higgins base, Captain Hugo Schmidt Prado gave an interview with *La Unión* newspaper of Valparaíso in which, with strong settler-colonial sentiments, he declared 'Antarctica appears to be a reserve that God has bequeathed to humanity; it is necessary to exploit it, both for our benefit and for the benefit of the whole world.'[53] He elaborated these ideas in the account of his time in Antarctica, *¡Base O'Higgins sin novedad!* (1956), in which he imbues Chilean interests in Antarctica with a distinctly spiritual dimension. For Schmidt Prado the sublime beauty of the Antarctic landscape helped to open him up to the reality of God. Below a line-drawing of a man standing in front of a cross in a blizzard, the caption reads 'Man in his distress takes account of the need to believe in God.'[54] This in turn created 'a sense of brotherhood' with land and air, things and beings.[55] More prosaically, in discussing what makes a good group of men (*sic*) for wintering in Antarctica, Schmidt Prado notes: 'They ought to be tolerant, sober and disposed to every kind of work and sacrifice. If possible, they ought to possess the same religion and belong to the same institution.'[56] Religion, Schmidt Prado recognised, could be both a source of togetherness and a source of division.

Following the signing of the Antarctic Treaty in 1959, in which both Argentina and Chile participated, religious activities at their stations did not disappear. There was, in fact, a resurgence of the connections between nationalism and Catholicism during periods of military dictatorship in both countries in the 1970s and 1980s. In video footage of Augusto Pinochet's visit to Antarctica in 1977, for example, the Chilean president and his wife are shown making the sign of the cross in front of a shrine to the Virgin Mary after singing the national anthem.[57] In 1978, the Argentine Esperanza station recorded the first marriage in Antarctica, the first baptism (following the first birth) and the first communion.[58] In response, Chile established the Villa Las Estrellas civilian settlement on King George Island in 1984, and made sure it had full religious provision for its inhabitants through the construction of a Catholic chapel.[59] The ongoing link between religion and sovereignty in the era of military dictatorships in Argentina and Chile helps to show something of the colonial nature of their respective interests in Antarctica. Nationalist claims – which had begun, at least in part, in opposition to British imperialism – had, by the 1970s and 1980s, developed a strong sense of colonialism of their own.[60]

United States: Religion, science and imperial continuity

In contrast to Britain, Argentina and Chile, all of which assert their ownership of a large part of Antarctica, the US position toward Antarctic sovereignty since the early twentieth century has been to reject all sovereignty claims while reserving its rights to claim any part of the continent.[61] This very different approach to Antarctic sovereignty is paralleled by a different approach to religion. Religion is certainly not absent from the US engagement with Antarctica, and in fact some of the most interesting expressions of religious faith on the continent have come from Americans. A broadly conceived view of American frontiers overseas as a continuation of a divinely inspired 'manifest destiny' might make some connection to religion as a motivation for US interest in Antarctica.[62] Similarly, there are examples of Americans using religion as part of the domestication involved in Antarctic settler colonialism. But rather than using religion to support sovereignty claims to Antarctica as Britain, Argentina and Chile have all to some extent done, it has been in the political interests of the United States – since at least the late 1950s – to promote Antarctica as a largely secular 'continent for peace and science'. While no less politically motivated than the attitudes toward religion of Britain, Argentina or Chile, the US approach to religion in Antarctica has led in a quite different direction.

As might be expected from a religiously pluralistic country such as the United States, there was a great diversity of religious experiences in Antarctica. Richard Byrd, for example, the first man to fly over the South Pole and probably the most famous American polar explorer, expressed some fascinating views about religion in his book *Alone*, an account of a winter spent on his own at a field camp known as Advanced Base on the Ross Ice Shelf.[63] As he found himself being slowly poisoned by the carbon monoxide of a faulty heating system, he felt a profound sense of connection with the world around him:

> For all my realism and scepticism there came over me, too powerfully to be denied, that exalted sense of identification – of oneness – with the outer world which is partly mystical but also certainty. I came to understand what Thoreau meant when he said, 'My body is all sentient.' There were moments when I felt more *alive* than at any other time in my life. Freed from materialistic distractions, my senses sharpened in new directions, and the random or commonplace affairs of the sky and the earth and the spirit, which ordinarily I would have ignored if I had noticed them at all, became exciting and portentous.[64]

These feelings intensified over time as his predicament became increasingly precarious, and by the 64th day at Advance Base (25 May) he was extending these feelings to the whole of the human race:

> The human race, my intuition tells me, is not outside the cosmic process and is not an accident. It is as much a part of the universe as the trees, the mountains, the aurora, and the stars. My reason approves this; and the findings of science, as I see them, point in the same direction. And, since man is a part of

the cosmos and subject to its laws, I see no reason to doubt that these same natural laws operate in the psychological as well as in the physical sphere and that their operation is manifest in the workings of the consciousness.[65]

'This whole concept', he noted, 'is summed up in the word harmony. For those who seek it, there is inexhaustible evidence of an all-pervading intelligence.' While he was not conventionally religious, Byrd's daughter would later describe him as 'a deeply spiritual man'.[66] The intensity of his experiences in Antarctica's extreme environment clearly played a role in shaping these views.

If American religious interests did have any coherence, this was provided by the chaplaincy provisions of the armed forces, especially the navy. During the US Operation Highjump expedition to Antarctica immediately after the Second World War, a Catholic Priest in the navy held the first full religious service actually on the continent.[67] During the construction of McMurdo station in 1956, volunteers constructed the Chapel of the Snows church (which was rebuilt in 1978 following a fire) . For the first 30 years of the station's existence, naval chaplains served the community in a similar way to their ministry to those on board a ship or at a military base. Following the transition to civilian contractors at McMurdo from the 1980s onward, Protestant pastors were recruited from across the United States to spend time at McMurdo (although interestingly until recently – 2015 – there was a tradition of Catholic priests coming from New Zealand).[68] These efforts can be seen as similar to British and Latin American efforts to use religion to help domesticate the continent in support of a settler-colonial agenda.

In general, however, the US Antarctic Programme has not emphasised religion as part of its reason for being in Antarctica, and religious faith has been overshadowed by science almost from the very beginning. Part of the reason for this may be the religious diversity of the United States, personified by the faith and spirituality of Richard Byrd, and the fact that there is no overarching 'national' religious denomination. But pragmatic diplomacy offers another explanation. Following the International Geophysical Year of 1957–58 it became US policy to promote an international treaty system for the continent, and the talks that led to the 1959 Antarctic Treaty took place in Washington, DC.[69] Of the original 12 signatories of the Antarctic Treaty, 10 could be described as Christian countries (and most of them had participated in some way in the heroic age of Antarctic exploration). Japan, once again, was an exception as a non-Christian country, as – at least nominally – was the Soviet Union, with its official ideology of atheist materialism. Despite the predominance of Christian countries among the original 12 signatories, however, the sort of doctrinal differences highlighted by the Catholic nationalism of Argentina and Chile meant that religion held out little possibility of serving as an international common language to unite countries in Antarctica. Instead, it would be science as an idea and scientific research as a practice that would become the glue that holds the Antarctic Treaty together, providing a shared activity and common language for all nations active on the continent.

Since the signing of the Antarctic Treaty in 1959 and its ratification in 1961, the number of consultative parties has more than doubled. Much of this growth took place in the 1980s during a period of intense speculation and diplomatic negotiation about the mineral resource potential of Antarctica. The growth in consultative parties has seen an expansion in the religious diversity of member states, especially with the accession of India (in 1983) and China (in 1985). The vast majority of countries involved in the Antarctic Treaty, however, remain at least nominally Christian, which reflects something of the imperial continuity that goes back at least as far as the heroic era of the early twentieth century. It is no surprise, perhaps, that the campaign that took place in the 1980s, to have responsibility for Antarctica handed over to the United Nations, was led by the majority Muslim state of Malaysia.[70] That this campaign was unsuccessful might be attributed to the members of the still largely nominally Christian 'Colonial Club', which Prime Minister Mahathir Mohamad accused of governing the continent, coming together to protect their shared interests.

Conclusion: Religion and the decolonisation of Antarctica

In thinking about the connections between religion and imperialism in the history of Antarctica, it is tempting to see Scott's *Terra Nova* expedition as something of a high point in the relationship between faith and politics. While religious faith was certainly not universal among the members of the expedition, an imperial-tinged Christianity formed an important part of the cultural background to the expedition, as epitomised by the World Missionary Conference that was taking place as the *Terra Nova* left Cardiff Bay. For Wilson and Bowers in particular, religious beliefs may help to explain at least some of their actions on the ill-fated journey to the South Pole. Religion came to the fore in the early memorialisation of the 'tragic' fate of the expedition as the British geographical and imperial establishment sought to mark an enduring claim to the continent and draw contrasts with what they perceived as the relative shallowness of Amundsen's successful Norwegian expedition.[71] An overarching sense of divine right to rule, summed by the concept of the White Man's Burden, both pervades and helps to explain the actions of Scott's *Terra Nova* expedition, and much of the heroic age of exploration more generally.

Although religion has not featured prominently in the writing of Antarctic history since the early twentieth century, the connections between religious faith and politics in Antarctica have not gone away. From the 1930s and 1940s, both Argentina and Chile have sought to incorporate a sense of Catholic nationalism into their respective sovereignty claims to the Antarctic Peninsula region. While these claims were anti-imperial in their intent to undermine the British claims to the Falkland Islands Dependencies, the underlying sense of religious destiny had parallels with the way the British had used religion early in the century, blurring the lines between nationalism and imperialism. As Alejandra Mancilla argues, despite the tendency for Argentines and Chileans to view their Antarctic claims as anti-imperial in nature, their expansive character also gives them an imperial dimension.[72] The role played by Catholic nationalism in making these claims helps to support this argument, as do the settler colonial associations with home created by religious ceremonies and religious buildings, thereby providing an important example of the connection between colonialism and religion in Antarctica.

The United States was the major driver of the move toward the limited internationalisation of the Antarctic continent brought about by the Antarctic Treaty of 1959. Within the wider context of the Cold War, the creation of an international treaty regime for Antarctica fitted neatly with US geopolitical objectives for the continent, allowing it to diffuse political tensions while retaining its reservation of rights. There were certainly elements of self-interest in this move, which can be seen as perpetuating imperial power on the continent.[73] Within the Antarctic Treaty System science and scientific research provide both common activities and a moral justification for the governing structure. In this broadly unified and functioning 'continent for science' there is little place for religious division. As a consequence, although religion has not disappeared from the history it has tended to be downplayed and ignored. The interests of powerful states in Antarctica are best served by emphasising science rather than religion. Arguably there is nowhere else in the world that is quite as reliant on the hegemony of a secular, scientific worldview to support its political system as contemporary Antarctica.

There is much more that could be written on the history of religion in general in Antarctica, and on the connections between religion and colonialism more specifically. The addition of other countries and other faiths to the analysis would probably complicate things further. In the context of the United Nations debates of the 1980s, for example, a study of Hinduism and Islam in Antarctica might reveal a more explicitly anti-colonial role for religion. As well as deepening our historical understanding in general terms, a greater emphasis on religion in the history of Antarctica has a role to play in offering an alternative to the monolithic idea of a 'continent for science'. In other parts of the world, science often played second fiddle to religion and commerce in European colonial enterprises; in Antarctica, these roles were reversed, with science being dominant from quite an early stage. A broader recognition that there are in fact multiple ways to understand and engage with the Antarctic continent, even if some of these other engagements themselves – including religion – have potentially problematic associations with colonialism, might help to unsettle the close connection of science and politics and shake the political status quo.

Notes

1 World Missionary Conference, *Report of Commission I: Carrying the Gospel to All the Non-Christian World. With Supplement: Presentation and Discussion of the Report in the Conference on 15th June 1910* (Edinburgh and London: Oliphant, Anderson and Ferrier, 1910).
2 Jeremy Morris (ed.), *The Oxford History of Anglicanism*, Vol. IV, *Global Western Anglicanism, c. 1910–Present* (Oxford: Oxford University Press, 2017).
3 World Missionary Conference, *Report of Commission I*.
4 World Missionary Conference, *Report of Commission I*.
5 Edward J. Larson, *An Empire of Ice: Scott, Shackleton, and the Heroic Age of Antarctic Science* (New Haven: Yale University Press, 2011).
6 Eric William Hunter Christie, *The Antarctic Problem: An Historical and Political Study* (London: Allen & Unwin, 1951).
7 There is an extensive literature on the connections between religion and empire. An important early work in the context of Spanish imperialism in the Americas is Robert Ricard, *Spiritual Conquest Mexico: An Essay on the Apostolate and the Evangelizing Methods of the Mendicant Orders in New Spain, 1523–1572* (Berkeley: University of California Press, 1992). An overview of the role of religion in the British empire is provided by Norman Etherington (ed.), *Missions and Empire: Illustrated Edition* (Oxford: Oxford University Press, 2005).
8 Ronald Edward Robinson and John Gallagher, *Africa and the Victorians* (New York: St Martin's Press, 1961); Jean Comaroff and John L. Comaroff, *Of Revelation and Revolution: Christianity, Colonialism, and Consciousness in South Africa* (Chicago: University of Chicago Press, 1991).
9 Andrew J. Herbertson and Osbert J. R. Howarth (eds), *The Oxford Survey of the British Empire*, Vol. IV (Oxford: Clarendon Press, 1914).
10 Ricard, *Spiritual Conquest Mexico*.
11 Etherington, *Missions and Empire*.
12 Shirley V. Scott, 'Ingenious and Innocuous? Article IV of the Antarctic Treaty as Imperialism', *Polar Journal* 1(1) (2011), 51–62.
13 Francis Spufford, *I May Be Some Time: Ice and the English Imagination* (London: Faber and Faber, 1996), p. 243.

14 Robert Falcon Scott and Max Jones, *Journals: Captain Scott's Last Expedition* (Oxford: Oxford University Press, 2005), p. 47.

15 For an important contribution to this debate, see Larson, *An Empire of Ice*.

16 Peder Roberts, Lize-Marié van der Watt and Adrian Howkins (eds), *Antarctica and the Humanities*, Palgrave Studies in the History of Science and Technology (London: Palgrave Macmillan, 2016).

17 For a discussion of nineteenth-century British exploration of the Arctic, see Fergus Fleming, *Barrow's Boys* (London: Granta Books, 1998). Studies of religion in British Antarctic exploration include George Seaver, *The Faith of Edward Wilson* (London: John Murray, 1948); Kellie Ann Vernon, 'Masculinity and Religion in the Life and Posthumous Representations of Antarctic Explorer H. R. Bowers, c. 1902–1939' (MPhil thesis, University of Manchester, 2014).

18 George Seaver, *Edward Wilson of the Antarctic: Naturalist and Friend* (London: John Murray, 1934 [1933]); George Seaver, *Edward Wilson: Nature Lover* (London: John Murray, 1937); Seaver, *The Faith of Edward Wilson*.

19 Isobel Williams, *With Scott in the Antarctic. Edward Wilson: Explorer, Naturalist, Artist* (Stroud: The History Press, 2009), p. 27.

20 Seaver, *The Faith of Edward Wilson*.

21 Seaver, *Edward Wilson: Nature Lover*, p. 41.

22 Edward Adrian Wilson, *Diary of the 'Terra Nova' Expedition to the Antarctic, 1910–12* (London: Littlehampton Book Services, 1972).

23 Wilson, *Diary of the 'Terra Nova' Expedition*, p. 177.

24 Vernon, *Masculinity and Religion*.

25 Vernon, *Masculinity and Religion*, p. 118.

26 Vernon, *Masculinity and Religion*, p. 138.

27 Seaver, *The Faith of Edward Wilson*, p. 48.

28 Wilson, *Diary of the 'Terra Nova' Expedition*, p. 247.

29 Vernon, *Masculinity and Religion*, p. 138.

30 Spufford, *I May Be Some Time*; Max Jones, *The Last Great Quest: Captain Scott's Antarctic Sacrifice* (Oxford: Oxford University Press, 2003).

31 Jones, *The Last Great Quest*, p. 132.

32 Jones, *The Last Great Quest*, p. 132.

33 Adrian Howkins, *Frozen Empires: An Environmental History of the Antarctic Peninsula* (New York: Oxford University Press, 2017).

34 Pablo Fontana, *La pugna antártica, el conflicto por el sexto continente: 1939–1959* (Buenos Aires: Guazuvira Ediciones, 2014).

35 Miguel Serrano, *La Antártica y otros mitos* (Santiago de Chile: Titania, 1948), p. 96; Hugo Schmidt Prado, *¡Base O'Higgins sin novedad!*, 2nd edn (Santiago de Chile: Editorial La Noria, 1992 [1956]).

36 Ronald Robinson and Jack Gallagher, 'The Imperialism of Free Trade', *The Economic History Review* 6 (1953), 1–15.

37 Howkins, *Frozen Empires*; see also Alejandra Mancilla's contribution to this volume.

38 Schmidt Prado, *¡Base O'Higgins sin novedad!*, p. 147; Juan Carlos Puig, *La Antártida argentina ante el derecho* (Buenos Aires: R. Depalma, 1960).

39 Benedict Anderson, *Imagined Communities: Reflections on the Origin and Spread of Nationalism* (London: Verso, 1983).

40 Carlos Escudé, *Patología del nacionalismo: El caso argentino* (Buenos Aires: Instituto Torcuato di Tella, 1987).

41 Jose Manuel Moneta, *Four Antarctic Years in the South Orkney Islands: An Annotated Translation of 'Cuatro años en las Orcadas del Sur'* (London: Bernard Quaritch, 2017).

42 Nicolas Shumway, *The Invention of Argentina* (Berkeley: University of California Press, 1991).

43 Gianni Varetto, 'Stella Maris Chapel, at Orcadas Base', 31 October 2019, WAP: World Antarctic Programme, www.waponline.it/stella-maris-chapel-at-orcadas-base-wap-arg-15/ (accessed 20 June 2020).

44 Patricia Seed, *Ceremonies of Possession in Europe's Conquest of the New World, 1492–1640* (New York: Cambridge University Press, 1995).

45 Hugo Gambini, *Historia del Peronismo* (Buenos Aires: Editorial Planeta, 1999).

46 Howkins, *Frozen Empires*.

47 Sandra McGee Deutsch and Ronald H. Dolkart, *The Argentine Right: Its History and Intellectual Origins, 1910 to the Present* (Wilmington, DE: SR Books, 1993).

48 Emilio L. Díaz, *Relatos antárticos* (Buenos Aires: Editorial Losada, 1958), pp. 15–20.

49 Díaz, *Relatos Antárticos*.

50 Eugenio Orrego Vicuña, *Terra australis* (Santiago de Chile: Zig-zag, 1948). All translations are my own.

51 Orrego Vicuña, *Terra australis*, p. 126.

52 Orrego Vicuña, *Terra australis*, pp. 126, 196.

53 Consuelo León Wöppke, *Antártica: Testimonios periodísticos 1947–1957* (Valparaíso: Puntángeles, 2003), pp. 151–2.

54 Schmidt Prado, *¡Base O'Higgins sin novedad!*, p. 70.

55 Schmidt Prado, *¡Base O'Higgins sin novedad!*, p. 69.

56 Schmidt Prado, *¡Base O'Higgins sin novedad!*, p. 173.

57 YouTube, 'Pinochet Visit to Antarctica & Singing the National Anthem of Chile', YouTube, www.youtube.com/watch?app=desktop&v=SKf1JTBvj68 (accessed 9 March 2024).

58 Wikipedia, 'Religion in Antarctica', https://en.wikipedia.org/w/index.php?title=Religion_in_Antarctica&oldid=964795888 (accessed 27 June 2020).

59 Wikipedia, 'Religion in Antarctica'.

60 See Mancilla, chapter in this volume.

61 Christopher C. Joyner, *Eagle over the Ice: The U.S. in the Antarctic* (Hanover, NH: University Press of New England, 1997).

62 Adrian Howkins, 'The Significance of the Frontier in Antarctic History: How the US West Has Shaped the Geopolitics of the Far South', *The Polar Journal* 3:1 (2013), 1–22, DOI: 10.1080/2154896x.2013.768417.

63 Richard E. Byrd, *Alone: The Classic Polar Adventure* (Washington, DC: Island Press, 2013 [1938]).

64 Byrd, *Alone*, p. 120.

65 Byrd, *Alone*, p. 161.
66 Lisle Abbott Rose, *Explorer: The Life of Richard E. Byrd* (Columbia: University of Missouri Press, 2008), p. 149.
67 Wikipedia, 'Religion in Antarctica'.
68 Anna Jones, 'The Last Catholic Priest in the Antarctic', BBC News, 29 July 2015, www.bbc.co.uk/news/world-asia-33647390 (accessed 9 March 2024).
69 Klaus J. Dodds, 'Reflecting on the 60th Anniversary of the Antarctic Treaty', *Polar Record* 55:5 (2019), 311–16, DOI: 10.1017/S0032247419000536.
70 Howkins, *Frozen Empires*.
71 Jones, *The Last Great Quest*.
72 Mancilla, this volume.
73 Scott, 'Ingenious and Innocuous?'; Howkins, *Frozen Empires*.

Bibliography

Anderson, Benedict. *Imagined Communities: Reflections on the Origin and Spread of Nationalism*. London: Verso, 1983.
Byrd, Richard E. *Alone: The Classic Polar Adventure*. Washington, DC: Island Press, 2013 [1938].
Christie, Eric William Hunter. *The Antarctic Problem: An Historical and Political Study*. London: Allen & Unwin, 1951.
Comaroff, Jean and John L. Comaroff. *Of Revelation and Revolution: Christianity, Colonialism, and Consciousness in South Africa*. Chicago: University of Chicago Press, 1991.
Deutsch, Sandra McGee and Ronald H. Dolkart. *The Argentine Right: Its History and Intellectual Origins, 1910 to the Present*. Wilmington, DE: SR Books, 1993.
Díaz, Emilio L. *Relatos antárticos*. Buenos Aires: Editorial Losada, 1958.
Dodds, Klaus J. 'Reflecting on the 60th Anniversary of the Antarctic Treaty'. *Polar Record* 55, no. 5 (2019): 311–16. DOI: 10.1017/S0032247419000536.
Escudé, Carlos. *Patología del nacionalismo: El caso argentino*. Buenos Aires: Instituto Torcuato di Tella, 1987.
Etherington, Norman (ed.). *Missions and Empire: Illustrated Edition*. Oxford: Oxford University Press, 2005.
Fleming, Fergus. *Barrow's Boys*. London: Granta Books, 1998.
Fontana, Pablo. *La pugna antártica, el conflicto por el sexto continente: 1939–1959*. Vol. II. Buenos Aires: Guazuvira Ediciones, 2014.
Gambini, Hugo. *Historia del Peronismo*. Buenos Aires: Editorial Planeta, 1999.
Herbertson, Andrew J. and Osbert J. R. Howarth (eds). *The Oxford Survey of the British Empire*. Vol. IV. Oxford: Clarendon Press, 1914.
Howkins, Adrian. *Frozen Empires: An Environmental History of the Antarctic Peninsula*. New York: Oxford University Press, 2017.
Howkins, Adrian. 'The Significance of the Frontier in Antarctic History: How the US West Has Shaped the Geopolitics of the Far South'. *The Polar Journal* 3, no. 1 (2013): 1–22. DOI: 10.1080/2154896x.2013.768417.
Jones, Anna. 'The Last Catholic Priest in the Antarctic'. BBC News, 29 July 2015. www.bbc.co.uk/news/world-asia-33647390. Accessed 9 March 2024.
Jones, Max. *The Last Great Quest: Captain Scott's Antarctic Sacrifice*. Oxford: Oxford University Press, 2003.

Joyner, Christopher C. *Eagle over the Ice: The U.S. in the Antarctic*. Hanover, NH: University Press of New England, 1997.

Larson, Edward J. *An Empire of Ice: Scott, Shackleton, and the Heroic Age of Antarctic Science*. New Haven: Yale University Press, 2011.

León Wöppke, Consuelo. *Antártica: Testimonios periodísticos 1947–1957*. Valparaíso: Puntángeles, 2003.

Moneta, Jose Manuel. *Four Antarctic Years in the South Orkney Islands: An Annotated Translation of 'Cuatro años en las Orcadas del Sur'*. London: Bernard Quaritch, 2017.

Morris, Jeremy (ed.). *The Oxford History of Anglicanism*, Vol. IV, *Global Western Anglicanism, c. 1910–Present*. Oxford: Oxford University Press, 2017.

Orrego Vicuña, Eugenio. *Terra australis*. Santiago de Chile: Zig-zag, 1948.

Puig, Juan Carlos. *La Antártida argentina ante el derecho*. Buenos Aires: R. Depalma, 1960.

Ricard, Robert. *Spiritual Conquest Mexico: An Essay on the Apostolate and the Evangelizing Methods of the Mendicant Orders in New Spain, 1523–1572*. Berkeley: University of California Press, 1992.

Roberts, Peder, Lize-Marié van der Watt and Adrian Howkins (eds). *Antarctica and the Humanities*. Palgrave Studies in the History of Science and Technology. London: Palgrave Macmillan, 2016.

Robinson, Ronald Edward and John Gallagher. *Africa and the Victorians*. New York: St Martin's Press, 1961.

Robinson, Ronald and Jack Gallagher. 'The Imperialism of Free Trade'. *The Economic History Review* 6 (1953): 1–15.

Rose, Lisle Abbott. *Explorer: The Life of Richard E. Byrd*. Columbia: University of Missouri Press, 2008.

Schmidt Prado, Hugo (ed.). *¡Base O'Higgins sin novedad!* 2nd edn. Santiago de Chile: Editorial La Noria, 1992 [1956].

Scott, Robert Falcon and Max Jones. *Journals: Captain Scott's Last Expedition*. Oxford: Oxford University Press, 2005.

Scott, Shirley V. 'Ingenious and Innocuous? Article IV of the Antarctic Treaty as Imperialism'. *Polar Journal* 1, no. 1 (2011): 51–62.

Seaver, George. *Edward Wilson: Nature Lover*. London: John Murray, 1937.

Seaver, George. *Edward Wilson of the Antarctic: Naturalist and Friend*. London: John Murray, 1934 [1933].

Seaver, George. *The Faith of Edward Wilson*. London: John Murray, 1948.

Seed, Patricia. *Ceremonies of Possession in Europe's Conquest of the New World, 1492–1640*. New York: Cambridge University Press, 1995.

Serrano, Miguel. *La Antártica y otros mitos*. Santiago de Chile: Titania, 1948.

Shumway, Nicolas. *The Invention of Argentina*. Berkeley: University of California Press, 1991.

Spufford, Francis. *I May Be Some Time: Ice and the English Imagination*. London: Faber and Faber, 1996.

Varetto, Gianni. 'Stella Maris Chapel, at Orcadas Base', 31 October 2019. WAP: World Antarctic Progamme. www.waponline.it/stella-maris-chapel-at-orcadas-base-wap-arg-15/. Accessed 20 June 2020.

Vernon, Kellie Ann. 'Masculinity and Religion in the Life and Posthumous Representations of Antarctic Explorer H. R. Bowers, c. 1902–1939'. MPhil thesis. University of Manchester, 2014.

Wikipedia. 'Religion in Antarctica'. https://en.wikipedia.org/w/index.php?title=Religion_in_Antarctica&oldid=964795888. Accessed 27 June 2020.

Williams, Isobel. *With Scott in the Antarctic. Edward Wilson: Explorer, Naturalist, Artist.* Stroud: The History Press, 2009.

Wilson, Edward Adrian. *Diary of the 'Terra Nova' Expedition to the Antarctic, 1910–12.* London: Littlehampton Book Services, 1972.

World Missionary Conference. *Report of Commission I: Carrying the Gospel to All the Non-Christian World. With Supplement: Presentation and Discussion of the Report in the Conference on 15th June 1910.* Edinburgh and London: Oliphant, Anderson and Ferrier, 1910.

YouTube. 'Pinochet Visit to Antarctica & Singing the National Anthem of Chile'. YouTube, www.youtube.com/watch?app=desktop&v=SKf1JTBvj68 (accessed 9 March 2024).

7

The colonial and extracolonial bordering of Antarctica

Germana Nicklin

Colonisation is commonly associated with resource exploitation, disruption and destruction of Indigenous communities, and paternalism.[1] Areas of Antarctica were claimed by seven states prior to 1959 but it was never colonised in this common understanding of the word. Rather, conquering the ice continent was as much a type of imperialism.[2] The 1959 Antarctic Treaty stemmed the expansion of claims, setting them aside for collective governance that focused on peace, science and, later, environmental protection. However, the seven claims have also created an undercurrent of territorial tension within the collective of the 54 signatory states.[3] One way this has been managed is effectively to avoid reference to territory, and thus borders, in the operation of the Antarctic Treaty System (ATS). Borders do exist, however, and affect practices in Antarctica in unseen ways.[4]

This chapter uses a postcolonial geographical lens to examine the relationship between colonialism and borders within the ATS, creating a new understanding of the presence and effects of borders in the politically borderless Antarctic. Sovereign borders are territorial in nature, and as such are strongly associated with conquest and colonisation.[5] At the time of western expansion across the globe, colonisation involved the heroic endeavour of exploring and discovering new lands, and civilising the people who lived there, or, as Allan Greer succinctly put it, 'the imposition of power from abroad over peoples and spaces'.[6] A term that encapsulates the essence of colonisation is 'new frontiers'. A frontier was more active than a border and less precise. It represented an opening up, a moving band of civilising forces sweeping the new land.[7] The frontier process inevitably ended in the settling of colonial borders – of delineating and establishing power over conquered spaces.

Using postcolonial analysis is a unique entry point into problems that other perspectives lack in examining colonial and postcolonial aspects of Antarctic territoriality. This enquiry situates the bordering of Antarctica within Tariq Jazeel's 2019 postcolonial examination of the geographical elements of space, identity and knowledge.[8] The analysis reveals a paradox: the bordering nature of ATS rules is shown to contain lingering colonial effects that divide decision-makers, and yet the ways the rules are performed by those going to Antarctica point to a strong connection with Antarctica. Antarctic Gateways are where this paradox is most observable.

To see how these elements play out, I drew on responses from a survey, taken from a project on developing further knowledge about Antarctic borders, some of which will be found in what follows. The survey involved in-depth interviews with 10 people in a range of roles – scientists, students, artists, tourists, one official – from Europe, New Zealand, the United Kingdom and the United States.[9] Some interviewees had travelled to Antarctica multiple times in more than one capacity. The aim of the survey was to obtain empirical evidence of everyday borders in Antarctica. As such, I asked questions about people's experiences of borders when accessing and working on Antarctica, as well as their relationship with Antarctica. As much as possible, I gave space for people to define borders in their own way, to see what influenced their thinking, and to help build a picture of the Antarctic border landscape. They revealed how very bordered their experiences were, by Antarctic rules but also by the continent itself.

The subsequent analysis demonstrates that borderlessness does not excise colonial sensibilities in Antarctic governance. Instead, ATS bordering processes are underpinned by the colonial origins of the original signatories and maintained by a modern type of colonial bordering that gatekeeps access to decision-making. But these bordering processes also result in the performance of the collective goals of the ATS. The chapter concludes by arguing for the new term, *extracolonialism*. This term aims to keep the colonial aspects of the ATS in view, while at the same time providing a new space for the development of a broader and more inclusive Antarctic society. This type of society would see humans partnering with nature rather than conquering it, and borders as a positive force for collective action.

Colonisation and Antarctica: From frontiers to borders

Up to 1959, the states involved in exploring and laying claims to Antarctica seemed to be on the path to colonising the continent. The conquest of Antarctica was of the physical space and place. The absence of an Indigenous people against whom violence would normally have been directed did not detract from the other colonising elements. Rather, the presence to be conquered and the violence to be encountered was the physical geography, not a resident people. These encounters of struggle and death have become legendary, the expeditions in the early twentieth century emphasising the 'heroic' (and very male) nature of this conquest.[10] This heroic age of exploration celebrated man's conquering of geographical space and the opening up of the Antarctic frontier – the very basis of colonisation.[11]

Once conquered, states' next colonising move was to make territorial claims across Antarctica. By 1956, the borders of these claims were represented on maps of Antarctica as seven wedges, three of which were overlapping.[12] Such cartographical representations of the conquering of space are a tool of colonisation.[13] Demonstrating human possession of these bordered spaces was intermittent and only at the outer border of the continent, initially in the form of expeditions, but more permanently through the building of stations.[14] This colonisation was further enacted through mechanisms such as claimant states' domestic legislation that defined the physical space of the claim, and state narratives and actions that built cultural meaning around the possession (see, for example, Alejandra Mancilla's chapter in this volume).

The process of colonisation varies somewhat from the norm at this point, with frontiers never becoming settled borders in international law.[15] The Antarctic Treaty of 1959 paused the colonial process, although it did not remove the colonial sensibility.[16] That sensibility exists within the text of the Antarctic Treaty through its objectification of Antarctica as conquered and controlled territory, albeit collectively. For example, the text begins 'Recognising that it is in the interest of all mankind that Antarctica shall continue for ever to be used exclusively for peaceful purposes and shall not become the scene or object of international discord'.[17] Despite expressing liberal aspirations, this introduction assumes human power over the continent through the language 'used' and 'object'. A physical expression of colonial sensibility is the United States station at the South Pole, which is juxtaposed with the Ceremonial Pole bearing the flags of the 12 original signatories, telling a tale of colonial territoriality while purporting to represent collective Antarctic governance.[18] Furthermore, Article IV of the Antarctic Treaty maintains the existence of the seven claimant states, with Russia and the USA having an obliquely stated right to make future claims.[19]

Thus, the Antarctic Treaty created two coexisting sets of colonial bordering. The first is the continuance of the pre-1959 colonial claims. While officially unable to be enacted, their existence exerts influence on Antarctic actors. For example, claimant states tend to place their stations in their 'own' territory. Along with symbols of sovereignty such as flags and place names, these claimants, particularly those in contested areas, continue to push their case. Even though Argentina and Chile argue that they are not colonising, but rather rightfully in possession of their claimant areas, these two states' establishment of human settlements on the Antarctic Peninsula (1978) and South Shetland Islands (1983) are still acts of staking out their territory.[20] The overlapping nature of these territorial spaces also belies the 'rightful possession' argument.

The second set of colonial bordering occurred post 1959, in the bordering of the ATS. The bar for decision-making rights is high, requiring a substantive science presence on the continent.[21] Global South countries spearheaded by Malaysia have found that bar difficult to exceed, as recorded in a United Nations report in 1984 and over the 20 years following.[22] While the ATS has become more accessible in other ways, the bar to achieving voting rights remains, with less than a third of Antarctic Treaty Consultative Meeting (ATCM) states from the Global South, and almost complete exclusion of least developed countries.[23] This is a different sort of colonial possession, exercising power over entry.

In addition to these bordering challenges, the new instrument of the Antarctic Treaty resulted in the formation of a type of collective governance that eradicated not only the language but the sensibility of territorial borders from Antarctica. The consequences are that 'border' appears to have become a forbidden word, not to be spoken – an Antarctic version of bad luck invoked by actors speaking the name of Shakespeare's play *Macbeth*. I experienced this at a New Zealand Antarctic conference, where I presented a paper on Antarctic borders, and could almost hear a gasp of horror in the room. Thus, there is a dissonance between the permitted language of the (colonial) claims and the excising of the language of borders.

Postcolonial geography as an analytical lens

Geography critically examines human interactions with spaces, particularly power relations over spaces, both physical and imaginary. As such, geography and colonialism are intimately connected. Postcolonial geography provides a set of analytical framings to enquire into human interactions with Antarctica from both a colonial and a postcolonial perspective.[24]

Jazeel argues that geography can break open the subjugating effects of colonial and imperial expansions across the globe, by thinking in ways different from the norm.[25] One area of subjugation is that of human interactions with nature. Jazeel traces colonial attitudes to nature that continue today in the western scientific method. He argues that enlightenment ideas of humans as separate from nature served colonising states well. Nature was objectified as something to be tamed and contained. When looking at Antarctica, evidence of such objectification of nature can be subtle. For example, the 1991 Protocol on Environmental Protection to the Antarctic Treaty (Environmental Protocol) appears to foreground the environment.[26] However, its base document is the Antarctic Treaty, which, as illustrated above, is human-centred. Thus, the Environmental Protocol, while aimed at protecting the environment, in a broader sense assumes the right of humans to be there – to possess the continent, albeit carefully.

Postcolonial thinking addresses multiple and often contradictory ways and scales of looking at a situation: enquiry that requires 'border-crossing', which can include interactions between humans and non-humans.[27] Such border-crossing is particularly relevant to the Antarctic, where the continent and its flora and fauna have such a profound effect on humans.[28] Antarctica could be said to be protecting itself through its coat of ice and snow and its encirclement of ice floes. Of particular relevance, then, are postcolonial geographic approaches, which give more agency to and invite multiple readings and imaginings of nature. They not only recontextualise nature and the environment, but also textualise it, rendering landscapes visible through different types of representation.

Jazeel focuses his postcolonial enquiry on three elements of geography – space, identity/hybridity and knowledge.[29] He refers to 'imaginative geography' as creating meaning from the imagining of spaces and stabilising that meaning through discursive practices.[30] Identity/hybridity focuses on the coexistence of multiple cultural identities and on articulating their differences. Finally, the lens of postcolonial knowledge, Jazeel argues, is not only to debate but also to transcend the colonial legacies of controlling the production of and access to knowledge.[31]

Further light on postcolonial geography is shed by insights from Indigenous worldviews wherein the nature of Indigenous people's relations with their environment is local and reciprocal.[32] Vanessa Watts characterises society as the interactions between different worlds – the animal, mineral and plant worlds; the spirit world; the female world – underlining the interconnectedness of humans and non-humans. She differentiates this type of society from the West, where non-humans are essentially employed in the service of human society.[33] Using this framing, Antarctica can be seen as a society in which the environment is interacting with multiple human and non-human worlds. This multiplicity of interactions is rendered invisible in human-centred schemes – such as the ATS – that could be characterised as colonial.

Kanngieser and Todd's exploration of environment as kin spans place, listening and practice – categories that connect strongly with Jazeer's space, identity and knowledge. The imaginary and real spaces of Antarctica are complex relationships of non-humans and humans. To those humans with a specific relationship with Antarctica, such as those who have visited or done research in Antarctica, it is kin. Knowledge of Antarctica as kin comes from practices that derive from listening to the environment. To see and 'hear' that place, humans gain awareness by placing themselves in the society that is Antarctica, thus identifying with it.

Border analysis adds to this postcolonial enquiry. Spaces imply borders and vice versa. In postcolonial enquiry, borders are dynamic and complex social spaces that include but also encompass much more than state territoriality and power.[34] From this viewpoint, borders are assemblages of human and non-human actors; they are processes and performances that are part of the global circulation of goods and human flows of mobilities; they are experienced by and have effects on humans and non-humans.[35] For Antarctica, the tight control over its borders is a particular type of colonial possession, for these borders are about the collective control of the whole Antarctic continent.[36]

Antarctic spaces

This section examines the bordering mechanisms that stabilise the Antarctic imaginary and affect the relationships between Antarctica and humans. It highlights a varied, border landscape that is grounded in colonialism but also contains something else. Antarctic border practices are for the collective good of the ATS. The rules and practices in the member states that provide access to Antarctica derive from the Antarctic Treaty and its governance mechanisms, the ATCM and the Commission for the Conservation of Antarctic Marine Living Resources (CCAMLR). While these access points are managed by sovereign states, the overriding presence is Antarctica as a bordered and bordering space in which the continent itself is an actor and the bordering is between it and humans rather than between states.[37]

The continent itself is an actor in the Antarctic imaginary not just through human translations of its wonders, but also in causing human activities to be defined. Much has been written about Antarctica as an imaginary space.[38] Its remoteness, its icy vastness have inspired explorers and artists alike. This perspective moves attention from the broad expanse of Antarctica as a whole to the particular effects of the continent on humans – important because, as Alessandro Antonello warns, ignoring the particular is dangerous.[39] The relevant particulars in Antarctica are the ATS policy rules and guidelines that border human movement on Antarctica. They are designed to keep people safe and to some extent protect the environment, but they also stabilise human 'possession' of the continent. For example, Antarctic Specially Managed Areas and Antarctic Specially Protected Areas can be characterised as bordered spaces, both geographically and from conditions applying to human activities in these spaces.[40]

The context for these particulars is Antarctica as a political space. The ATCM and CCAMLR are the two main governance bodies that set the rules and guidelines for human activities on the continent. The documents that record these rules and guidelines are 'immutable mobiles'.[41] Immutable mobiles are physical representations of meaning that can be passed on from one person to another.[42] Their power is in helping to spread knowledge and ideas beyond their originating point. This is particularly relevant in the Antarctic context where there is no permanent human Antarctic society as such. Rather, the Antarctic documents define human spaces. As Jessica O'Reilly states, '[t]hese [biogeographical] documents are the materials that form the border'.[43] In the Antarctic, each member state translates the Antarctic documents into their own laws and practices, resulting in multiple sites and multiple interpretations. For example, the rules for moving scientific samples from Antarctica to New Zealand will differ from those for moving samples from Antarctica to the USA.[44]

These multiple sites and interpretations of human activity create multiple Antarctic spaces that are separated by distance, time and culture, and also coexist as part of the same space bordered by the ATS. The experiences of interviewees demonstrated that the dispersed nature of Antarctic spaces and the relationship between time and culture become more tangible the closer one gets to the continent itself. Getting to Antarctica is dispersed, involving different continents and time zones. The primary pathways to Antarctica pass through the five states closest to Antarctica: South Africa, Australia, New Zealand, Chile and Argentina. Facilities for getting to Antarctica are based at a particular city within those states – Capetown, Hobart, Christchurch, Punta Arenas and Ushuaia respectively – and the states that use these facilities often have formal agreements with the host state.[45] Each pathway will have slightly different approaches to Antarctic access, based on each government's priorities and what facilities they offer. For example, Hobart offers seaport and airport facilities, and a dedicated Antarctic and cruise terminal, with further investment planned; the Argentinian government has plans to develop Ushuaia into a logistics centre; Capetown has begun promoting itself as a tourism departure point.[46]

As bordering spaces, these pathways, known informally as gateways, are nodes through which power and identity are projected in multiple ways. Through these nodes, gateway states are able to exert their influence and power into Antarctic spaces.[47] The terminology 'Gateway' with a capital 'G' is being used increasingly; for example, Christchurch has used the phrase 'Gateway to Antarctica' as a marketing strategy, highlighting the confluence of local, state and Antarctic interests; researchers have focused research on the Gateway Cities, and the term has even been used in ATCM papers.[48] The term 'Gateway' creates the idea of border towns and, more controversially because of the territorial connotations, border states for Antarctica. Given that all five Gateway states were colonies – of Britain for South African, New Zealand and Australian Gateways, and of Spain for Chilean and Argentinian Gateways – these territorial connotations carry the legacy of colonisation. It is not surprising, then, that in the ATCM, the term 'Gateway' is not officially used. The potential influence of Gateway spaces is implicit in this avoidance and one that the ATCM has not yet addressed.[49]

Nevertheless, this avoidance misses the point that Gateway Cities are transition spaces, bridging colonial and Antarctic spaces. In border studies, transitions are liminal spaces between one border and another.[50] Gateway Cities are where travellers prepare to move from a specifically sovereign space to the unfamiliar wild space of Antarctica. This transition is cultural: from non-Antarctic to Antarctic sensibilities and practices, from implicitly colonial to explicitly collective space. Gateway Cities that promote themselves as such therefore create a connection between their communities and Antarctica, bridging the state space and the collective Antarctic space.[51] There is also cooperation between these cities, and although this cooperation has not yielded any collective action, the potential for more tangible collectivity exists. The colonial legacy arguably constrains this potential for an explicitly collective Antarctic space across Gateway Cities.

Passing through a liminal space can involve ritualistic processes.[52] The ritualistic nature of transitioning through the Christchurch Gateway, for example, involves getting kitted up in Antarctic gear. Interviewees marked this as the point when going to the continent became real for them, especially as it was summer outside. Arriving in Antarctica completed the transition: 'Arriving at Scott Base is another [border], almost feels like crossing into another world' (Student 3). These transition spaces are important for enabling adjustment and preparation for moving from the familiar to the unfamiliar.

Once on the continent, humans experience borders through enacting ATS rules. For example, at McMurdo and Scott bases, footpaths are marked by flags and poles. The effect of these man-made borders on this interviewee contrasts with the physically unbordered landscape:

> It's almost like you're fenced in at McMurdo in a way – like you can only go to these certain areas and you can't go anywhere else … so it is like vast vastness that you can see forever, and it seems endless and there's so much freedom, but also there's not. There's like an invisible fence. (logistics person)

A further expression of this juxtaposition of bordered space and unbordered vastness is evident in the work of photographer Anne Noble. She captures the 'piss pole' flags in her book *The Last Road*.[53] The photographs show the incongruity of yellow piss at the base of these flagpoles amidst a vast and wild whiteness. The flags also mark the presence of humans, much like the US flag on the moon. Unlike that flag, these yellow flags are stateless. Noble's photographs highlight that the enactment of ATS rules contains human impacts on the continent – the enacting of collective control.

Identity/hybridity in Antarctica

Identity is a socially constructed concept redolent of borders and bordered spaces that divide and separate different groups into us and other, inside and outside.[54] Colonial powers othered the races they conquered, representing them as separate from and less advanced than the colonists. Postcolonial identity looks beyond these power relations that differentiate the colonisers from the colonised. It recognises that people can have multiple, border-spanning identities.

The ATS created a particular identity for Antarctica as a space unowned by any state, but this identity is not as simple as it sounds. It has been created by humans for humans and is enacted through the Antarctic Treaty. That treaty has created three key narratives that drive Antarctic human interactions on the continent today: of Antarctica as a place of peace, of science and as an environment to be protected. A particular tension within these narratives lies between the collective interests they represent and the continued colonial sensibilities noted earlier. The avoidance of the mention of borders resulting from these tensions indicates an awareness of the potentially destabilising effect of anything relating to state territory on the continent and, implicitly, the colonising effect of territoriality. This avoidance suggests a sensitivity to the power of language. These two aspects – the avoidance and the sensitivity – signal a deliberate attempt to create a new political identity for Antarctica that transcends, or at the very least dampens, colonial interests. However, because it is based on avoidance, that identity is lopsided, creating problems for governance.

One of these problems is that the above narratives present Antarctica as a place for all humanity, but in reality, the Antarctic Treaty rules create a nesting of us and other – the us being the signatories; the inner us being the decision-making consultative parties; and the other being everyone else, including the United Nations. This is an identity for Antarctica that is totally political, and that privileges those states with the resources to establish science programmes on the continent. Arguably this identity has not escaped its colonial origins, as Yelena Yermakova also argues in this volume.[55] And while it includes humans working *for* Antarctica in terms of protecting its environment from exploitation, the extent of that protection is questionable, given the extensive human activity on the continent and in its surrounding ocean.[56]

The enacting of the Antarctic Treaty in formal meetings is complex, therefore. These meetings involve working on behalf of Antarctica along-side the multiple territorial and sovereign interests of the inner and outer us. In these meetings, then, representation flows back and forth across invisible borders. O'Reilly hints at fluidity in her observation that 'formal, state-level concerns flourish alongside the usually slow-moving process of achieving complete consensus in Antarctic Treaty consultative meetings'.[57]

Examples of particular interest are the almost annual disputes at ATCM and CCAMLR meetings between Argentina and Britain about the sover-eignty of the Malvinas/Falkland Islands, or the performances of obstruction in negotiations; examples of collective agreement are the Ross Sea Marine Protected Area and Antarctic Specially Protected Areas.[58] The dual nature of Gateway spaces discussed earlier also involves border-crossing between identities, but the colonial identity is subjugated within the ATS.

Antarctica's identity is more than the ATS, though. Those who travel to the continent experience Antarctica as transformative: 'it just puts your whole life in perspective ... that was a big almost cognitive dissonance in my mind; the whole time I was there I was thinking "Oh my gosh, this place is so pristine and here I am – am I worthy to be here?"' (Student 3). Figure 7.1 shows an Antarctic scientist still connected with Antarctica when back home. In these examples, Antarctica is not an object. It is an exchange, a relationship. This relationship endures beyond these people's presence on the continent, as expressed in the Tweet in Figure 7.1 and by this inter-viewee: 'It is somewhere that, once I was there, I can't get it out of my mind ... it's that kind of place that pulls you in and then you always want to try to figure out how to get back' (logistics person). That relationship places these people in the same space as Antarctica, in which Antarctica's presence is deeply felt.

These examples show that humans identify with Antarctica in different ways and that Antarctica presents itself differently to different groups. To ATCM and CCAMLR, Antarctica is variously a place and an object; to those who organise people to go to Antarctica, it is a process; to those who travel to Antarctica, it is an experience and a personal relationship. Some people transition through more than one of these Antarcticas.

There is, as previously noted, a recognition in postcolonial border litera-ture of liminality – of transitional spaces that occur between the us/other duality.[59] Liminality also creates possibility. Gateway spaces exemplify this liminality, both spatially and in identity terms. Gateway transitions are from colonial to collective identities. Those collective identities could encompass Watt's multispecies society, but currently don't within the ATS.

Dr Hanne Nielsen
@WideWhiteStage   ...

"It may not be as Instagram-worthy as a porthole onto
a frozen vista, but it's a reminder that the little slice of
#Antarctica lodged deep within all of us can also
manifest back home" - my piece on "Delivering the
Polar Product" is now up on @envhistnow
envhistnow.com/2021/02/04/del...

5:44 PM · Feb 25, 2021 · Twitter Web App

Figure 7.1 Tweet showing pictures of sheets on a clothes line alongside pictures of Antarctica. Reproduced by kind permission of Hanne Nielsen.

Knowledge in Antarctica

The production and dissemination of knowledge in Antarctica are mediated by a range of gatekeepers, highlighting its bordered nature. Henk van Houtum references Janus, the Roman god of doorways and transitions, as a useful representation of this aspect of borders.[60] Gatekeepers control movement from one space to another. This section focuses on the modernist gatekeeping bias of science in Antarctica that prioritises natural science over social sciences and humanities.

The ATS is the ultimate gatekeeper through its requirement to achieve decision-making status in Article IX.2. Key to this requirement is having 'substantial scientific research activity' on the continent. This limits membership to those states that can afford such an endeavour. The limited number of Global South members is one effect of this gatekeeping.

A subtler type of gatekeeping is represented by the types of Antarctic science that get prioritised and thus funded. The Scientific Community of Antarctic Research, the pre-eminent Antarctic science body, only recently included humanities and social science as a standing committee.[61] Funding bodies within states have taken their lead from the science community as well as adding their own state priorities to funding, exacerbating this bias. For example, Aotearoa New Zealand Antarctic Research Directions and Priorities 2021–30 gives limited attention to humanities or social sciences, or to the value that they contribute to Antarctic knowledge.[62] This is an instance of structural gatekeeping that effectively excludes some researchers and research groups, emanating from the science community itself. An emphasis on science, technology, engineering and mathematics (STEM) school subjects by many states contributes to the bias.[63] This bias raises the question of the global framing of science. Suman Seth articulates starkly that the scientific method is inextricably connected with the European colonial expansions of the seventeenth and eighteenth centuries: 'The history of almost all modern science, it has become clear, must be understood as "science in a colonial context".'[64] While the language of science might be considered to be global, its colonial origins have shaped the form of that language.

A flow-on effect of science gatekeeping can be seen in the choices about which Antarctic science gets to influence government policies. O'Reilly provides an instructive window into the bordering of biosecurity science as it makes its way into Antarctic policy – the filtering of knowledge, the limiting of scope, the power relations in the choice of spokespeople and the role of texts in achieving consensus at ATCM meetings.[65] She notes the 'heavily ritualised, mediated conversations' at meetings of scientific experts, the rituals providing a clue to their bordering.[66] More detailed research like this on other areas of Antarctic governance would enrich understanding of the bordered nature of Antarctic science.

An area important in the context of colonialism is that of Indigenous knowledge of Antarctica. This knowledge is bordered by the ubiquitous references to Antarctica's being without an Indigenous population.[67] New Zealand provides an example for other states in addressing this absence by incorporating *mātauranga Māori* (Māori knowledge) into the domain of Antarctic research. An enacted example of that relationship is the commissioning of a *whakairo*, a wooden carving, to surround the doorway into Scott Base. The designs on this carving tell an intricate story of the two-way interaction between humans and Antarctica, marking a transition point into a space where 'all of humanity is working together'.[68] The partnership between Māori and Antarctica in New Zealand is evidence of a postcolonial awareness that Indigenous knowledge adds something unique and transformational to western research via insights into 'true collective management and conservation of Antarctica'.[69] Part of that change has come from the findings of western science validating centuries of Māori observations and knowledge of the natural environment. For example, Captain James Cook certifiably crossed the Antarctic Circle, whereas the Indigenous stories that long preceded him were treated as myth.[70] Thus, while the doorway for *mātauranga Māori* is in place, the door is only partly open and the postcolonialists are still in control of who passes through. Even so, through that partly open door can be seen potential for a broader and more inclusive approach to collective action with Antarctica as an active participant.[71] Understanding the borders and barriers affecting the production of knowledge about Antarctica is therefore important for looking beyond coloniality and for not being unwittingly captured by colonial sensibilities.

More-than-colonial borders in Antarctica

The examination of spaces, hybridity of identity, and knowledge through the lens of borders and bordering has highlighted several key points. First, the analysis highlights that Antarctic Gateways are points at which collective Antarctic and state interests intersect. While the Antarctic Treaty involved freezing colonial ambitions, the Gateway states do exercise power over their Gateway spaces, as evidenced by the agreements between states who want to use a specific Gateway and the relevant Gateway state. Colonial ambitions are also still evident in the national stories attached to the respective Gateways. These stories call on historical national connections with Antarctica; in the case of New Zealand, they reflect an emerging postcolonial awareness. As previously noted, four of the five Gateways are situated in claimant states, and all five are original signatory states. In the example of the Christchurch Gateway, the duality, and the colonial legacies of these histories, are not immediately obvious to foreigners who use the Gateway but are obvious to New Zealand nationals. Collective Antarctic processes therefore coexist with colonial interests.

Second, Antarctic knowledge is bordered by national Antarctic science programmes. These programmes determine what is perceived to be valuable and, thus, who can access the continent to conduct research. This bordering of national interests is a projection of power over space that is not of itself colonial. Nevertheless, the dynamics of Antarctic science are derived from colonial framings that control definitions of what is and is not science and how it contributes to policy. The presence of Indigenous knowledge in Antarctic science is fragile still, but will be strengthened by global developments in the validity of Indigenous knowledge rather than any developments in Antarctic science per se.

Third, and most significantly, the Antarctic continent is not only a bordered space but is specifically a collectively bordered space. That space involves a much more diverse range of actors now than in the past, in that many more states are involved in science programmes on the continent than in the early days of the Antarctic Treaty. This collectivity operates in multiple spaces within the ATS. Antarctica also occupies a physical and an imaginary space that is transitioned into and out of. It is like moving to a different country, taking on a new identity for a time and then returning home, even for those not actually visiting the continent.

Extracoloniality as an expression of collectively bordered space

The effects of collective rules for those involved in getting to Antarctica point to a sensibility that has colonial roots, but which has the additional element of humans acting alongside one another to achieve the Antarctic Treaty objectives of peace, science and environmental protection, and potentially even more than that. These mechanisms that border access to and movement around the continent have been collectively designed by member states. The rules are the same for all consultative parties. The importance of the collective aspect is that it came out of the colonial sensibility that created the Antarctic Treaty, but it is not fully colonial or national in nature. Thus, while enacted through state institutions, the access and movement processes are Antarctic rather than state border processes. The state is clearly present in this landscape, both as a contributing creator and as an enactor of Antarctic rules and guidelines, with the collective aims set out in the Antarctic Treaty as the unifying force.

But something unexpected has also emerged from this unifying force – the power of the collective in the performance of the rules. People enacting Antarctic rules take on the collective interest for Antarctica. In other words, action for the collective interest is an outcome of the Antarctic rules. The colonial order that resulted in the ATS controls access to collective decision-making. But the scope of action for collective interests (collective-action) includes everything from policy development and decision-making to activities on the continent, to public education and participation dispersed across the globe. And the borders of collective-action could be expanded to include non-human actors. This expansion would enable action for Antarctica as 'society', in the sense of human–non-human interconnectedness described by Vanessa Watt.[72] In other words, this performative power could be harnessed for greater collective benefit, including that of the Antarctic environment. In short, the collective aspects of the ATS have the potential to deliver more than they currently do.

A term that attempts to capture this 'more' is *extracolonial*, which I have coined to mean colonial structures that generate collective-action, with the *extra-* taking the meaning of in addition to what is usual or expected.[73] Such a term is useful because it incorporates both the legacies of the colonial past and the power of collective-action. This approach has the potential to address the aforementioned lopsidedness by enabling 'borders' to become a tool of action, rather than a colonial legacy to be avoided. In this, extracolonialism is different from the oft-used term for Antarctic governance – exceptionalism – which sets Antarctica apart from other international systems.[74] Rather, extracolonialism has a different function. It keeps the colonial origins and design of Antarctic governance visible, while harnessing the power of the *something else* of its collectivity.

While the terminology 'extracolonial' may be debated, I argue that the distinction between the collective rule making, with all its colonial undercurrents, and the actions taken for the benefit of the collective interest is valuable: especially so, if the action aspect incorporates the expanded view of Antarctic society. Use of a term such as extracolonialism could also provide a space to create more connections between states working for Antarctica; it may even provide a platform to examine exclusionary practices.[75] Extracolonialism thus provides a sense of hope and vision that there are other ways of doing things, even within a state-dominated system founded in colonialism. The term could even be time-limited, functioning as a milestone on the way to a decolonised Antarctic future. It is a differently bordered space than either colonialism or postcolonialism.[76]

But something will need to change for this to occur. At present, there is neither the will, nor any particular driver from within the ATS, to reborder the collective and open up to different ways of operating. The growing calls for the reform of the ATS point to a stasis that even postcolonial thinking has not yet broken through.[77] A large part of the challenge is the gatekeeping effect of membership. The original signatories occupy a colonial space that they are not likely to want to relinquish, regardless of the text of the ATS.

Conclusion

This chapter set out to explore colonialism in Antarctica through postcolonial geographical analysis with a border lens. This lens has shown the existence but non-discussion of Antarctic borders as analogous to the existence but lack of recognition of colonial practices in the ATS. It has also revealed that something different is happening at borders, most observably at the

Antarctic Gateways. Antarctic borders, as discussed in this chapter, are spaces of paradox – where colonial influences and interests coexist alongside the enacting of the collective, which potentially benefits both humans and Antarctica. The use of the term 'extracolonial', rather than that of the usual term 'exceptionalism', is an attempt to open up this paradox. Then, if extracolonialism is part of the answer to continued peace, science and environmental protection in Antarctica, and understanding which borders constrain and which borders assist its enactment, will be critical for the future. This understanding suggests a need for further examination in this underresearched area. A starting place could be collective-action. More focus on collective-action could strengthen Antarctic governance for the long term.

As a final note, Antarctica is a space where the colonial past and the extracolonial present both collide and connect. Student 2, on playing the violin in the Discovery Hut, spoke to the Antarctic ancestors thus: 'I played three Yiddish tunes in the Discovery Hut and thought "These old ghosts have never heard these tunes before. It'll jolly them up a bit."'

This connection would be well recognised by Māori, whose knowledge of Antarctica is not bound by western concepts of time and space. Extracoloniality requires more of us to inhabit this space.

Notes

1 Robin L. Anderson, *Colonization as Exploitation in the Amazon Rain Forest, 1758–1911* (Gainesville: University Press of Florida, 1999); Marc Ferro, *Colonization: A Global History* (New York: Routledge, 1997).

2 Shirley V. Scott, 'Three Waves of Antarctic Imperialism', in Klaus J. Dodds, Alan D. Hemmings and Peder Roberts (eds), *Handbook on the Politics of Antarctica* (Cheltenham: Edward Elgar Publishing, 2017), pp. 37–49.

3 Alan D. Hemmings, 'Beyond Claims: Towards a Non-Territorial Antarctic Security Prism for Australia and New Zealand', *New Zealand Yearbook of International Law* 6 (2008), 77–91, DOI: https://doi.org/10.3316/informit.883501946327170.

4 Germana Nicklin, 'Turning Attention to the Layered and Dispersed Access Management System of the Antarctic Treaty System', *The Polar Journal* 9:2 (2019), 424–44, DOI: 10.1080/2154896X.2019.1685170; Germana Nicklin, 'The Implied Border Mechanisms of Antarctica: Arguing the Case for an Antarctic Borderscape', *Borderlands* 19:1 (2020): 27–62, DOI: 10.21307/borderlands-2020-003.

5 James Anderson and Liam O'Dowd, 'Borders, Border Regions and Territoriality: Contradictory Meanings, Changing Significance', *Regional Studies* 33:7 (1999), 593–604, DOI: 10.1080/00343409950078648.

6 Ferro, *Colonization*; Allan Greer, 'Settler Colonialism and Beyond', *Journal of the Canadian Historical Association/Revue de la Société historique du Canada* 30:1 (2019), 61–86 (p. 63), DOI: 10.7202/1070631ar.

7 Ainslie Thomas Embree and Mark Juergensmeyer, *Frontiers into Borders: Defining South Asian States, 1757–1857* (Oxford: Oxford University Press, 2020); William Walters, 'The Frontiers of the European Union: A Geostrategic Perspective', *Geopolitics* 9 (2004), 674–98, DOI: 10.1080/14650040490478738.

8 Tariq Jazeel, *Postcolonialism* (Abingdon: Routledge, 2019).

9 Ethics approval Massey University HEC: Southern A Application SOA 20/02.

10 George Finkel, *Antarctica: The Heroic Age* (Sydney: Collins, 1976); Elena Glasberg, *Antarctica as Cultural Critique: The Gendered Politics of Scientific Exploration and Climate Change* (London: Palgrave Macmillan, 2012); Edward J. Larson, *An Empire of Ice: Scott, Shackleton, and the Heroic Age of Antarctic Science* (New Haven: Yale University Press, 2011).

11 Jazeel, *Postcolonialism*, p. 97.

12 Central Intelligence Agency (CIA), 'Antarctic Exploration and Claims: As of 1 February 1956', Polar Geospatial Center, 2017, https://maps.apps.pgc.umn.edu/id/966 (accessed 10 March 2024).

13 Francis P. Hutchinson, 'Mapping and Imagined Futures: Beyond Colonising Cartography', *Journal of Futures Studies* 9:4 (2005), 1–14.

14 Christy Collis and Quentin Stevens, 'Cold Colonies: Antarctic Spatialities at Mawson and McMurdo Stations', *Cultural Geographies* 14:2 (2007), 234–54, DOI: 10.1177/1474474007075356; Klaus J. Dodds, Alan D. Hemmings and Peder Roberts (eds), *Handbook on the Politics of Antarctica* (Cheltenham: Edward Elgar Publishing, 2017); Peder Roberts, Lize-Marié van der Watt and Adrian Howkins (eds), *Antarctica and the Humanities* (London: Palgrave Macmillan, 2016).

15 It is important to note that for the claimant states, their borders are settled, as evidenced by state maps and legislation.

16 Scott, 'Three Waves of Antarctic Imperialism'; Klaus J. Dodds and Christy Collis, 'Post-Colonial Antarctica', in Dodds, Hemmings and Roberts, *Handbook on the Politics of Antarctica*, pp. 50–68.

17 Governments of Argentina, Australia, Belgium, Chile, French Republic, Japan *et al.*, 'The Antarctic Treaty', Secretariat of the Antarctic Treaty, 1959, https://documents.ats.aq/ats/treaty_original.pdf (accessed 10 March 2024).

18 Elizabeth Leane and Julia Jabour, 'Performing Sovereignty over an Ice Continent', in Carolyn Philpott, Elizabeth Leane and Matt Delbridge (eds), *Performing Ice* (Cham: Springer, 2020), pp. 171–93.

19 Government of Argentina *et al.*, 'The Antarctic Treaty'.

20 Doaa Abdel-Motaal, 'Averting the Battle for Antarctica', *Yale Journal of International Affairs* 12:1 (2017), 1–12; Nelson Llanos, 'Housewives at the End of the World: Chilean Women Living in Antarctica, 1984–1986', *The Polar Journal* 9:2 (2019), 358–70, DOI: 10.1080/2154896X.2019.1685175.

21 Discussed in more detail under the subsection 'Knowledge', pp. 000–000.

22 Peter J. Beck, 'The United Nations' Study on Antarctica, 1984', *Polar Record* 22:140 (1985), 499–504, DOI: 10.1017/S0032247400005945; Peter J. Beck, 'The United Nations and Antarctica, 2005: The End of the "Question of Antarctica"?', *Polar Record* 42:3 (2006), 217–27.

23 Alan D. Hemmings, 'The Functional Exclusion of Least Developed Countries from the Antarctic Regime', *The Polar Journal* 12:1 (2022), 88–107, DOI: 10.1080/2154896X.2022.2058223. Hemmings highlights that some least developed countries are signatories to some of the Antarctic instruments but that none are full decision-making members.

24 Jazeel, *Postcolonialism*.

25 Jazeel, *Postcolonialism*.

26 Antarctic Treaty Consultative Meeting (ATCM), 'The Protocol on Environmental Protection to the Antarctic Treaty', Secretariat of the Antarctic Treaty, 1991, https://documents.ats.aq/cep/handbook/Protocol_e.pdf (accessed 10 March 2024).

27 Dipesh Chakrabarty, 'Postcolonial Studies and the Challenge of Climate Change', *New Literary History* 43:1 (2012), 1–18 (p. 5).

28 Falk Huettmann (ed.), *Protection of the Three Poles* (Tokyo: Springer, 2012).

29 Jazeel, *Postcolonialism*.

30 Jazeel, *Postcolonialism*, p. 9.

31 Jazeel, *Postcolonialism*.

32 Anja Kanngieser and Zoe Todd, '3. From Environmental Case Study to Environmental Kin Study', *History & Theory* 59:3 (2020), 385–93, DOI: 10.1111/hith.12166; Ramya Nair, Dhee, Omkar Patil *et al.*, 'Sharing Spaces and Entanglements with Big Cats: The Warli and Their Waghoba in Maharashtra, India', *Frontiers in Conservation Science* 2 (2021), DOI: 10.3389/fcosc.2021.683356; Natalie Stoeckl, Diane Jarvis, Silva Larson, Anna Larson, Daniel Grainger and Ewamian Aboriginal Corporation, 'Australian Indigenous Insights into Ecosystem Services: Beyond Services towards Connectedness – People, Place and Time', *Ecosystem Services* 50 (2021), 101341, DOI: 10.1016/j.ecoser.2021.101341.

33 Vanessa Watts, 'Indigenous Place-Thought and Agency amongst Humans and Non Humans (First Woman and Sky Woman Go on a European World Tour!)', *Decolonization: Indigeneity, Education & Society* 2:1 (2013).

34 Corey Johnson, Reece Jones, Anssi Paasi *et al.*, 'Interventions on Rethinking "the Border" in Border Studies', *Political Geography* 30:2 (2011), 61–9, DOI: 10.1016/j.polgeo.2011.01.002; David Newman, 'Borders and Bordering: Towards an Interdisciplinary Dialogue', *European Journal of Social Theory* 9:2 (2006), 171–86, DOI: 10.1177/1368431006063331.

35 Tugba Basaran, Didier Bigo, Emmanuel-Pierre Guittet and Rob B. J. Walker (eds), *International Political Sociology: Transversal Lines* (Abingdon: Routledge, 2016); Germana Nicklin, 'Trans-Tasman Border Stories: Actor–Network Theory and Policy Narrative in Action' (PhD thesis, Victoria University of Wellington, 2015), http://researcharchive.vuw.ac.nz/handle/10063/4704?show=full (accessed 10 March 2024); Mark B. Salter (ed.),

Making Things International 1: Circuits and Motion (Minneapolis: University of Minnesota Press, 2015).

36 Nicklin, 'Turning Attention'; Nicklin, 'The Implied Border Mechanisms'.

37 Nicklin, 'The Implied Border Mechanisms'.

38 Elena Glasberg, 'Antarctica in Fiction: Imaginative Narratives of the Far South', *The Polar Journal* 4:1 (2014), 227–9, DOI: 10.1080/2154896X.2014.913916; Hanne E. F. Nielsen, 'Identifying with Antarctica in the Ecocultural Imaginary', in Tema Milstein and José Castro-Sotomayor (eds), *Routledge Handbook of Ecocultural Identity* (London: Routledge, 2020), pp. 225–39; Jessica O'Reilly, *The Technocratic Antarctic: An Ethnography of Scientific Expertise and Environmental Governance*, Expertise: Cultures and Technologies of Knowledge (Ithaca, NY: Cornell University Press, 2017); Juan Francisco Salazar and Elias Barticevic, 'Digital Storytelling Antarctica', *Critical Arts* 29:5 (2015), 576–90, DOI: 10.1080/02560046.2015.1125087; Kathryn Yusoff, 'Visualizing Antarctica as a Place in Time: From the Geological Sublime to "Real Time"', *Space and Culture* 8:4 (2005), 381–98.

39 Alessandro Antonello, 'Finding Place in Antarctica', in Roberts *et al.*, *Antarctica and the Humanities*, pp. 181–204 (p. 187).

40 Secretariat of the Antarctic Treaty, 'Area Protection and Management/Historic Sites and Monuments', 2023, www.ats.aq/e/protected.html (accessed 10 March 2024).

41 Bruno Latour, *Science in Action* (Cambridge, MA: Harvard University Press, 1987), p. 227.

42 These days they are all online, but they are a proxy for physical documents, in that they can be printed out.

43 O'Reilly, *The Technocratic Antarctic*, p. 100.

44 O'Reilly, *The Technocratic Antarctic*.

45 New Zealand has agreements or formal statements of cooperation with the USA (New Zealand Treaties Online, 'Exchange of Notes between the Government of New Zealand and the Government of the United States of America Regarding the Provision of Facilities in New Zealand for United States Antarctic Expeditions', www.treaties.mfat.govt.nz/search/details/t/3164/10 (accessed 15 March 2024)), Italy (New Zealand Ministry of Foreign Affairs and Trade, 'Exchnage of Letters Comprising an Agreement between New Zealand and the Republic of Italy Concerning Antarctic Co-operation', 8 April 1987, https://natlib. govt.nz/records/21814149?search%5Bi%5D%5Bcreator%5D=Italy.&search %5Bi%5D%5Bis_catalog_record%5D=true&search%5Bi%5D%5Bsubject %5D=Antarctica+--+Research+--+New+Zealand&search%5Bpath%5 D=items (accessed 15 March 2024)), the Republic of Korea (New Zealand Treaties Online, 'Agreement between the Government of New Zealand and the Government of the Republic of Korea on Antarctic Cooperation', www. treaties.mfat.govt.nz/search/details/t/3758/c_1 (accessed 10 March 2024)) and China (New Zealand Government, 'NZ/China Joint Statement of Antarctic Cooperation', Beehive.govt.nz, 22 January 1999, www.beehive.govt.nz/release/ nzchina-joint-statement-antarctic-cooperation (accessed 10 March 2024)).

Australia has an agreement with China (Australian Antarctic Programme, 'Australia and China Strengthen Antarctic Ties', Australian Government, 18 November 2014, www.antarctica.gov.au/news/2014/australia-and-china-strengthen-antarctic-ties/ (accessed 10 March 2024)).

46 Tasmanian Government, 'Infrastructure', Antarctic Tasmania, www.antarctic.tas.gov.au/about/infrastructure (accessed 13 February 2024); Heiner Kubny, 'Argentina Plans Antarctic Logistics Center in Ushuaia', *Polar Journal*, 27 July 2021, https://polarjournal.ch/en/2021/07/27/argentina-plans-antarctic-logistics-center-in-ushuaia/ (accessed 13 February 2023); Adrienne Bredeveldt, 'Mayor Puts Cape Town on the Map as a Gateway Destination to Antarctica', *CapeTown ETC*, 7 February 2023, www.capetownetc.com/cape-town/mayor-puts-cape-town-on-the-map-as-a-gateway-destination-to-antarctica/ (accessed 13 February 2023).

47 Elizabeth Leane, Chloe Lucas, Katie Marx, Doita Datta, Hanne Nielsen and Juan Francisco Salazar, 'From Gateway to Custodian City: Understanding Urban Residents' Sense of Connectedness to Antarctica', *Geographical Research* 59:4 (2021), 522–36, DOI: 10.1111/1745-5871.12490.

48 ChristchurchNZ, 'Christchurch: The Gateway to Antarctica', ChristchurchNZ, 2023, www.christchurchnz.com/christchurch-the-gateway-to-antarctica/ (accessed 13 September 2023); Leane *et al.*, 'From Gateway to Custodian City'; Argentine Republic, 'Gateways to Antarctica: Facilitation of Access to Antarctica for Purposes of Scientific and Technical Activities in the Framework of the Antarctic Treaty', information paper ATCM XLI (Buenos Aires: Antarctic Treaty Consultative Meeting, 2018), www.ats.aq/devAS/Meetings/Documents/85 (accessed 10 March 2024).

49 Klaus J. Dodds, ' "Awkward Antarctic Nationalism": Bodies, Ice Cores and Gateways in and beyond Australian Antarctic Territory/East Antarctica', *Polar Record* 53:1 (2017), 16–30; Nicklin, 'Turning Attention'.

50 Elia Zureik and Mark B. Salter (eds), *Global Surveillance and Policing: Borders, Security, Identity* (Portland, OR: Willan Publishing, 2005).

51 Leane *et al.*, 'From Gateway to Custodian City'.

52 Zureik and Salter, *Global Surveillance and Policing*.

53 Anne Noble, *The Last Road* (Christchurch, NZ: Clouds, 2014).

54 Newman, 'Borders and Bordering'.

55 Dodds and Collis, 'Post-Colonial Antarctica'.

56 Kevin A. Hughes, Peter Convey and John Turner, 'Developing Resilience to Climate Change Impacts in Antarctica: An Evaluation of Antarctic Treaty System Protected Area Policy', *Environmental Science & Policy* 124 (2021), 12–22, DOI: https://doi.org/10.1016/j.envsci.2021.05.023.

57 O'Reilly, *The Technocratic Antarctic*, p. 118.

58 Leane and Jabour, 'Performing Sovereignty'; O'Reilly, *The Technocratic Antarctic*. This agreement was also deeply mediated by sovereign interests, particularly those of China and Russia.

59 Mark B. Salter, 'Theory of the /: The Suture and Critical Border Studies', *Geopolitics* 17:4 (2012), 734–55, DOI: 10.1080/14650045.2012.660580;

Janet Wilson and Daria Tunca, 'Postcolonial Thresholds: Gateways and Borders', *Journal of Postcolonial Writing* 51:1 (2015), 1–6, DOI: 10.1080/ 17449855.2014.988434; Zureik and Salter (eds), *Global Surveillance and Policing*.

60 Henk van Houtum, Oliver Thomas Kramsch and Wolfgang Zierhofer, 'Prologue', in Henk van Houtum, Oliver Thomas Kramsch and Wolfgang Zierhofer (eds), *B/Ordering Space*, Border Regions Series (Aldershot: Ashgate, 2005), pp. 1–13, https://henkvanhoutum.nl/wp-content/uploads/2013/05/ borderingspace.pdf (accessed 10 March 2024).

61 Kees Bastmeijer, 'Humanities and Social Sciences and the Polar Regions', *The Polar Journal* 8:2 (2018), 227–9, DOI: 10.1080/2154896X.2018.1542860; Roberts *et al.*, *Antarctica and the Humanities*.

62 New Zealand Government, *Aotearoa New Zealand Antarctic Research Directions and Priorities 2021–30*, www.mfat.govt.nz/assets/Environment/ Antarctica-and-the-Southern-Ocean/Aotearoa-New-Zealand-Antarctic- Research-Directions-and-Priorities-2021-2030.pdf (accessed 20 March 2024). The New Zealand Humanities and Social Science Antarctic community submit- ted a proposal for a new focus area addressing this gap, but it was declined.

63 Brigid Freeman, Simon Marginson and Russell Tytler, 'An International View of STEM Education', in Alpaslan Sahin and Margaret J. Mohr-Schroeder (eds), *STEM Education 2.0* (Leiden: Brill Sense, 2019), pp. 350–63.

64 Suman Seth, 'Putting Knowledge in Its Place: Science, Colonialism, and the Postcolonial', *Postcolonial Studies* 12:4 (2009), 373–88.

65 O'Reilly, *The Technocratic Antarctic*.

66 O'Reilly, *The Technocratic Antarctic*, pp. 103–4.

67 Christy Collis, 'Territories beyond Possession? Antarctica and Outer Space', *The Polar Journal* 7:2 (2017), 287–302, DOI: 10.1080/2154896X.2017.1373912; Dodds *et al.*, *Handbook on the Politics of Antarctica*; Ursula Rack, 'Exploring and Mapping the Antarctic', in Mark Nuttall, Torben R. Christensen and Martin J. Siegert (eds), *The Routledge Handbook of the Polar Regions* (Abingdon: Routledge, 2018), pp. 34–44; Ricardo Roura, 'Antarctic Cultural Heritage: Geopolitics and Management', in Dodds *et al.*, *Handbook on the Politics of Antarctica*, pp. 468–85.

68 Vanessa Wells (dir.), *Te Whakairo: The Carvings Carry the Stories of the World*, documentary (Elanti Media, 2020), available at *Māori and Antarctica*, https:// maoriantarctica.org/te-whakairo/ (accessed 12 September 2023).

69 Abstract in Priscilla M. Wehi, Vincent van Uitregt, Nigel J. Scott *et al.*, 'Transforming Antarctic Management and Policy with an Indigenous Māori Lens', *Nature Ecology & Evolution* 5 (2021), 1055–9, DOI: 10.1038/ s41559-021-01466-4.

70 O'Reilly, *The Technocratic Antarctic*, p. 18.

71 This idea is supported in Leane *et al.*, 'From Gateway to Custodian City'.

72 Watts, 'Indigenous Place-Thought'.

73 As defined by Etymonline.com, s.v. 'extra-', www.etymonline.com/word/extra- (accessed 13 September 2023).

74 Daniela Porta Sampaio, 'The Antarctic Exception: Sovereignty and the Antarctic Treaty Governance' (PhD thesis, Universidade de São Paulo, 2017).

75 An initiative to create a Declaration for the Rights of Antarctica has begun that picks up the need for Antarctica to have a voice: Antarctica Rights, 'Declaration for the Rights of Antarctica', www.antarcticarights.org/ (accessed 13 September 2023).

76 The European Union has created a supranational infrastructure that enacts its collectivism. Antarctic collectivism is much looser by comparison.

77 Anne-Marie Brady, 'Diplomatic Chill: Politics Trumps Science in Antarctic Treaty System', *World Politics Review*, 19 March 2013, www.worldpolitics review.com/articles/12802/diplomatic-chill-politics-trumps-science-in-antarctic-treaty-system (accessed 10 March 2024); Wygene Chong, 'Thawing the Ice: A Contemporary Solution to Antarctic Sovereignty', *Polar Record* 53:4 (2017), 436–47, DOI: 10.1017/S0032247417000389; Alan D. Hemmings, 'The Hollowing of Antarctic Governance', in Prem Shankar Goel, Rasik Ravindra and Sulagna Chattopadhyay (eds), *Science and Geopolitics of the White World* (Cham: Springer, 2018), pp. 17–31; Nicklin, 'Turning Attention'; Yelena Yermakova, 'Legitimacy of the Antarctic Treaty System: Is It Time for a Reform?', *The Polar Journal* 11:2 (2021), 342–59, DOI: 10.1080/2154896X.2021.1977048.

Bibliography

Abdel-Motaal, Doaa. 'Averting the Battle for Antarctica'. *Yale Journal of International Affairs* 12, no. 1 (2017): 1–12.

Anderson, James and Liam O'Dowd. 'Borders, Border Regions and Territoriality: Contradictory Meanings, Changing Significance'. *Regional Studies* 33, no. 7 (1999): 593–604. DOI: 10.1080/00343409950078648.

Anderson, Robin L. *Colonization as Exploitation in the Amazon Rain Forest, 1758–1911*. Gainesville: University Press of Florida, 1999.

Antarctic Treaty Consultative Meeting [ATCM]. 'The Protocol on Environmental Protection to the Antarctic Treaty'. Secretariat of the Antarctic Treaty, 1991. https://documents.ats.aq/cep/handbook/Protocol_e.pdf. Accessed 10 March 2024.

Antarctica Rights. 'Declaration for the Rights of Antarctica'. www.antarcticarights. org/. Accessed 13 September 2023.

Antonello, Alessandro. 'Finding Place in Antarctica'. In *Antarctica and the Humanities*, ed. Peder Roberts, Lize-Marié van der Watt and Adrian Howkins, pp. 181–204. London: Palgrave Macmillan, 2016.

Argentine Republic. 'Gateways to Antarctica: Facilitation of Access to Antarctica for Purposes of Scientific and Technical Activities in the Framework of the Antarctic Treaty'. Information paper ATCM XLI. Buenos Aires: Antarctic Treaty Consultative Meeting, 2018. www.ats.aq/devAS/Meetings/Documents/85. Accessed 10 March 2024.

Australian Antarctic Programme. 'Australia and China Strengthen Antarctic Ties'. Australian Government, 18 November 2014. www.antarctica.gov.au/news/2014/australia-and-china-strengthen-antarctic-ties/. Accessed 10 March 2024.

Basaran, Tugba, Didier Bigo, Emmanuel-Pierre Guittet and Rob B. J. Walker (eds). *International Political Sociology: Transversal Lines*. Abingdon: Routledge, 2016.

Bastmeijer, Kees. 'Humanities and Social Sciences and the Polar Regions'. *The Polar Journal* 8, no. 2 (2018): 227–9. DOI: 10.1080/2154896X.2018.1542860.

Beck, Peter J. 'The United Nations and Antarctica, 2005: The End of the "Question of Antarctica"?'. *Polar Record* 42, no. 3 (2006): 217–27.

Beck, Peter J. 'The United Nations' Study on Antarctica, 1984'. *Polar Record* 22, no. 140 (1985): 499–504. DOI: 10.1017/S0032247400005945.

Brady, Anne-Marie. 'Diplomatic Chill: Politics Trumps Science in Antarctic Treaty System'. *World Politics Review*, 19 March 2013. www.worldpoliticsreview.com/articles/12802/diplomatic-chill-politics-trumps-science-in-antarctic-treaty-system. Accessed 10 March 2024.

Bredeveldt, Adrienne. 'Mayor Puts Cape Town on the Map as a Gateway Destination to Antarctica', *Cape Town ETC*, 7 February 2023. www.capetownetc.com/cape-town/mayor-puts-cape-town-on-the-map-as-a-gateway-destination-to-antarctica/. Accessed 13 February 2023.

Central Intelligence Agency [CIA]. 'Antarctic Exploration and Claims: As of 1 February 1956'. Polar Geospatial Center, 2017. https://maps.apps.pgc.umn.edu/id/966. Accessed 10 March 2024.

Chakrabarty, Dipesh. 'Postcolonial Studies and the Challenge of Climate Change'. *New Literary History* 43, no. 1 (2012): 1–18.

Chong, Wygene. 'Thawing the Ice: A Contemporary Solution to Antarctic Sovereignty'. *Polar Record* 53, no. 4 (2017): 436–47. DOI: 10.1017/S0032247417000389.

ChristchurchNZ. 'Christchurch: The Gateway to Antarctica'. ChristchurchNZ, 2023. www.christchurchnz.com/christchurch-the-gateway-to-antarctica/. Accessed 10 March 2024.

Collis, Christy. 'Territories beyond Possession? Antarctica and Outer Space'. *The Polar Journal* 7, no. 2 (2017): 287–302. DOI: 10.1080/2154896X.2017.1373912.

Collis, Christy and Quentin Stevens. 'Cold Colonies: Antarctic Spatialities at Mawson and McMurdo Stations'. *Cultural Geographies* 14, no. 2 (2007): 234–54. DOI: 10.1177/1474474007075356.

Dodds, Klaus J. ' "Awkward Antarctic Nationalism": Bodies, Ice Cores and Gateways in and beyond Australian Antarctic Territory/East Antarctica'. *Polar Record* 53, no. 1 (2017): 16–30.

Dodds, Klaus J. and Christy Collis. 'Post-Colonial Antarctica'. In *Handbook on the Politics of Antarctica*, ed. Klaus J. Dodds, Alan D. Hemmings and Peder Roberts, pp. 50–68. Cheltenham: Edward Elgar Publishing, 2017.

Dodds, Klaus J., Alan D. Hemmings and Peder Roberts (eds). *Handbook on the Politics of Antarctica*. Cheltenham: Edward Elgar Publishing, 2017.

Embree, Ainslie Thomas and Mark Juergensmeyer. *Frontiers into Borders: Defining South Asian States, 1757–1857*. Oxford: Oxford University Press, 2020.

Etymonline.com. www.etymonline.com/. Accessed 13 September 2023.

Ferro, Marc. *Colonization: A Global History*. New York: Routledge, 1997.

Finkel, George. *Antarctica: The Heroic Age*. Sydney: Collins, 1976.

Freeman, Brigid, Simon Marginson and Russell Tytler. 'An International View of STEM Education'. In *STEM Education 2.0*, ed. Alpaslan Sahin and Margaret J. Mohr-Schroeder, pp. 350–63. Leiden: Brill Sense, 2019.

Glasberg, Elena. *Antarctica as Cultural Critique: The Gendered Politics of Scientific Exploration and Climate Change*. London: Palgrave Macmillan, 2012.

Glasberg, Elena. 'Antarctica in Fiction: Imaginative Narratives of the Far South'. *The Polar Journal* 4, no. 1 (2014): 227–9. DOI: 10.1080/2154896X.2014.913916.

Governments of Argentina, Australia, Belgium, Chile, French Republic, Japan *et al.* 'The Antarctic Treaty'. Secretariat of the Antarctic Treaty, 1959. https://documents. ats.aq/ats/treaty_original.pdf. Accessed 10 March 2024.

Greer, Allan. 'Settler Colonialism and Beyond'. *Journal of the Canadian Historical Association/Revue de la Société historique du Canada* 30, no. 1 (2019): 61–86. DOI: 10.7202/1070631ar.

Hemmings, Alan D. 'Beyond Claims: Towards a Non-Territorial Antarctic Security Prism for Australia and New Zealand'. *New Zealand Yearbook of International Law* 6 (2008): 77–91. DOI: https://doi.org/10.3316/informit.883501946327170.

Hemmings, Alan D. 'The Functional Exclusion of Least Developed Countries from the Antarctic Regime'. *The Polar Journal* 12, no. 1 (2022): 88–107. DOI: 10.1080/2154896X.2022.2058223.

Hemmings, Alan D. 'The Hollowing of Antarctic Governance'. In *Science and Geopolitics of the White World*, ed. Prem Shankar Goel, Rasik Ravindra and Sulagna Chattopadhyay, pp. 17–31. Cham: Springer, 2018.

Huettmann, Falk (ed.). *Protection of the Three Poles*. Tokyo: Springer, 2012.

Hughes, Kevin A., Peter Convey and John Turner. 'Developing Resilience to Climate Change Impacts in Antarctica: An Evaluation of Antarctic Treaty System Protected Area Policy'. *Environmental Science & Policy* 124 (2021): 12–22. DOI: 10.1016/j.envsci.2021.05.023.

Hutchinson, Francis P. 'Mapping and Imagined Futures: Beyond Colonising Cartography'. *Journal of Futures Studies* 9, no. 4 (2005): 1–14.

Jazeel, Tariq. *Postcolonialism*. London: Routledge, 2019.

Johnson, Corey, Reece Jones, Anssi Paasi *et al.* 'Interventions on Rethinking "the Border" in Border Studies'. *Political Geography* 30, no. 2 (2011): 61–9. DOI: 10.1016/j.polgeo.2011.01.002.

Kanngieser, Anja and Zoe Todd. '3. From Environmental Case Study to Environmental Kin Study'. *History & Theory* 59, no. 3 (2020): 385–93. DOI: 10.1111/hith.12166.

Kubny, Heiner. 'Argentina Plans Antarctic Logistics Center in Ushuaia'. *PolarJournal*, 27 July 2021. https://polarjournal.ch/en/2021/07/27/argentina-plans-antarctic-logistics-center-in-ushuaia/. Accessed 13 February 2023.

Larson, Edward J. *An Empire of Ice: Scott, Shackleton, and the Heroic Age of Antarctic Science*. New Haven: Yale University Press, 2011.

Latour, Bruno. *Science in Action*. Cambridge, MA: Harvard University Press, 1987.

Leane, Elizabeth and Julia Jabour. 'Performing Sovereignty over an Ice Continent'. In *Performing Ice*, ed. Carolyn Philpott, Elizabeth Leane and Matt Delbridge, pp. 171–93. Cham: Springer, 2020.

Leane, Elizabeth, Chloe Lucas, Katie Marx, Doita Datta, Hanne Nielsen and Juan Francisco Salazar. 'From Gateway to Custodian City: Understanding Urban Residents' Sense of Connectedness to Antarctica'. *Geographical Research* 59, no. 4 (2021): 522–36. DOI: 10.1111/1745-5871.12490.

Llanos, Nelson. 'Housewives at the End of the World: Chilean Women Living in Antarctica, 1984–1986'. *The Polar Journal* 9, no. 2 (J2019): 358–70. DOI: 10.1080/2154896X.2019.1685175.

New Zealand Government. *Aotearoa New Zealand Antarctic Research Directions and Priorities 2021–30*. www.mfat.govt.nz/assets/Environment/Antarctica-and-the-Southern-Ocean/Aotearoa-New-Zealand-Antarctic-Research-Directions-and-Priorities-2021-2030.pdf. Accessed 20 March 2024.

New Zealand Government. 'NZ/China Joint Statement of Antarctic Cooperation'. Beehive.govt.nz, 22 January 1999. www.beehive.govt.nz/release/nzchina-joint-statement-antarctic-cooperation. Accessed 10 March 2024,

New Zealand Government and United States Government. 'Memorandum of Understanding'. New Zealand Government and United States Government, 1958.

New Zealand Ministry for Culture and Heritage Te Manatu Taonga. 'Antarctic Claims and Stations'. Story: Antarctica and New Zealand. Te Ara Encyclopedia of New Zealand. Ministry for Culture and Heritage Te Manatu Taonga, 2012. https://teara.govt.nz/en/map/37196/antarctic-claims-and-stations. Accessed 10 March 2024.

New Zealand Ministry of Foreign Affairs and Trade. 'Exchange of Letters Comprising an Agreement between New Zealand and the Republic of Italy Concerning Antarctic Co-operation', 8 April 1987. https://natlib.govt.nz/records/21814149?search%5Bi%5D%5Bcreator%5D=Italy.&search%5Bi%5D%5Bis_catalog_record%5D=true&search%5Bi%5D%5Bsubject%5D=Antarctica+--+Research+--+New+Zealand&search%5Bpath%5D=items. Accessed 15 March 2024.

New Zealand Treaties Online. 'Agreement between the Government of New Zealand and the Government of the Republic of Korea on Antarctic Cooperation'. www.treaties.mfat.govt.nz/search/details/t/3758/c_1. Accessed 10 March 2024.

New Zealand Treaties Online. 'Exchange of Notes between the Government of New Zealand and the Government of the United States of America Regarding the Provision of Facilities in New Zealand for United States Antarctic Expeditions'. www.treaties.mfat.govt.nz/search/details/t/3164/10. Accessed 15 March 2024.

Newman, David. 'Borders and Bordering: Towards an Interdisciplinary Dialogue'. *European Journal of Social Theory* 9, no. 2 (2006): 171–86. DOI: 10.1177/1368431006063331.

Nicklin, Germana. 'The Implied Border Mechanisms of Antarctica: Arguing the Case for an Antarctic Borderscape'. *Borderlands* 19, no. 1 (2020): 27–62. DOI: 10.21307/borderlands-2020-003.

Nicklin, Germana. 'Trans-Tasman Border Stories: Actor–Network Theory and Policy Narrative in Action'. PhD thesis. Victoria University of Wellington, 2015. http://researcharchive.vuw.ac.nz/handle/10063/4704?show=full. Accessed 10 March 2024.

Nicklin, Germana. 'Turning Attention to the Layered and Dispersed Access Management System of the Antarctic Treaty System'. *The Polar Journal* 9, no. 2 (2019): 424–44. DOI: 10.1080/2154896X.2019.1685170.

Nielsen, Hanne E. F. 'Identifying with Antarctica in the Ecocultural Imaginary'. In *Routledge Handbook of Ecocultural Identity*, ed. Tema Milstein and José Castro-Sotomayor, pp. 225–39. New York: Routledge, 2020.

Noble, Anne. *The Last Road*. Christchurch, NZ: Clouds, 2014.

O'Reilly, Jessica. *The Technocratic Antarctic: An Ethnography of Scientific Expertise and Environmental Governance*. Expertise: Cultures and Technologies of Knowledge. Ithaca, NY: Cornell University Press, 2017.

Rack, Ursula. 'Exploring and Mapping the Antarctic'. In *The Routledge Handbook of the Polar Regions*, ed. Mark Nuttall, Torben R. Christensen and Martin J. Siegert, pp. 34–44. Abingdon: Routledge, 2018.

Ramya Nair, Dhee, Omkar Patil, Nikit Surve, Anish Andheria, John D. C. Linnell and Vidya Athreya. 'Sharing Spaces and Entanglements with Big Cats: The Warli and Their Waghoba in Maharashtra, India'. *Frontiers in Conservation Science* 2 (2021). DOI: 10.3389/fcosc.2021.683356.

Roberts, Peder, Lize-Marié van der Watt and Adrian Howkins (eds). *Antarctica and the Humanities*. London: Palgrave Macmillan, 2016.

Roura, Ricardo. 'Antarctic Cultural Heritage: Geopolitics and Management'. In *Handbook on the Politics of Antarctica*, ed. Klaus J. Dodds, Alan D. Hemmings and Peder Roberts, pp. 468–85. Cheltenham: Edward Elgar Publishing, 2017.

Salazar, Juan Francisco and Elias Barticevic. 'Digital Storytelling Antarctica'. *Critical Arts* 29, no. 5 (2015): 576–90. DOI: 10.1080/02560046.2015.1125087.

Salter, Mark B. (ed.). *Making Things International 1: Circuits and Motion*. Minneapolis: University of Minnesota Press, 2015.

Salter, Mark B. 'Theory of the /: The Suture and Critical Border Studies'. *Geopolitics* 17, no. 4 (2012): 734–55. DOI: 10.1080/14650045.2012.660580.

Sampaio, Daniela Portella. 'The Antarctic Exception: Sovereignty and the Antarctic Treaty Governance'. PhD thesis. Universidade de São Paulo, 2017.

Scott, Shirley V. 'Three Waves of Antarctic Imperialism'. In *Handbook on the Politics of Antarctica*, ed. Klaus J. Dodds, Alan D. Hemmings and Peder Roberts, pp. 37–49. Cheltenham: Edward Elgar Publishing, 2017.

Secretariat of the Antarctic Treaty. 'Area Protection and Management/Historic Sites and Monuments', 2023. www.ats.aq/e/protected.html. Accessed 10 March 2024.

Seth, Suman. 'Putting Knowledge in Its Place: Science, Colonialism, and the Postcolonial'. *Postcolonial Studies* 12, no. 4 (2009): 373–88.

Stoeckl, Natalie, Diane Jarvis, Silva Larson, Anna Larson, Daniel Grainger and Ewamian Aboriginal Corporation. 'Australian Indigenous Insights into Ecosystem Services: Beyond Services towards Connectedness – People, Place and Time'. *Ecosystem Services* 50 (2021): 101341. DOI: 10.1016/j.ecoser.2021.101341.

Tasmanian Government. 'Infrastructure'. Antarctic Tasmania. www.antarctic.tas. gov.au/about/infrastructure. Accessed 13 February 2023.

Van Houtum, Henk, Olivier Thomas Kramsch and Wolfgang Zierhofer. 'Prologue'. In *B/Ordering Space*, ed. Henk van Houtum, Olivier Thomas Kramsch and Wolfgang Zierhofer, pp. 1–13. Border Regions Series. Aldershot: Ashgate, 2005. https://henkvanhoutum.nl/wp-content/uploads/2013/05/borderingspace.pdf. Accessed 10 March 2024.

Walters, William. 'The Frontiers of the European Union: A Geostrategic Perspective'. *Geopolitics* 9 (2004): 674–98. DOI: 10.1080/14650040490478738.

Watts, Vanessa. 'Indigenous Place-Thought and Agency amongst Humans and Non Humans (First Woman and Sky Woman Go on a European World Tour!)'. *Decolonization: Indigeneity, Education & Society* 2, no. 1 (2013).

Wehi, Priscilla M., Vincent van Uitregt, Nigel J. Scott *et al.* 'Transforming Antarctic Management and Policy with an Indigenous Māori Lens'. *Nature Ecology & Evolution* 5 (2021): 1055–9. DOI: 10.1038/s41559-021-01466-4.

Wells, Vanessa (dir.). *Te Whakairo: The Carvings Carry the Stories of the World*. Documentary. Elanti Media, 2020. Available at *Māori and Antarctica*. https://maoriantarctica.org/te-whakairo/. Accessed 12 September 2023.

Wilson, Janet and Daria Tunca. 'Postcolonial Thresholds: Gateways and Borders'. *Journal of Postcolonial Writing* 51, no. 1 (2015): 1–6. DOI: 10.1080/17449855.2014.988434.

Yermakova, Yelena. 'Legitimacy of the Antarctic Treaty System: Is It Time for a Reform?'. *The Polar Journal* 11, no. 2 (2021): 342–59. DOI: 10.1080/2154896X.2021.1977048.

Yusoff, Kathryn. 'Visualizing Antarctica as a Place in Time: From the Geological Sublime to "Real Time"'. *Space and Culture* 8, no. 4 (2005): 381–98.

Zureik, Elia and Mark B. Salter (eds). *Global Surveillance and Policing: Borders, Security, Identity*. Portland, OR: Willan Publishing, 2005.

8

Nineteenth-century connections between capitalism and colonialism in Antarctica: The case of sealing in the South Shetlands

María Jimena Cruz, Melisa A. Salerno and Andrés Zarankin

In recent decades, a growing body of work has begun to consider colonialism not as a homogeneous process, but as a diverse and complex one. Researchers adopting a postcolonial perspective have understood that instead of ticking all the boxes on a universal checklist of colonial features (including attempts to control a given territory through the establishment of settlements and cultural domination of native populations, among others), it would be relevant to critically discuss the singularities that colonial social practices and relationships may have acquired in different contexts.[1]

Following this trend, scholars have begun to debate whether or not it is appropriate to speak of colonialism in Antarctica.[2] There is a growing consensus that although Antarctica is different from other colonial settings, it has not been able to escape colonial dynamics, either at specific moments in the past or in the present. However, it is worth noting that scholars have generally failed to consider economic exploitation as a significant factor in colonialism in the region. As a result, the capitalist logic of colonialism has tended to be downplayed.

This does not necessarily mean that capitalism has not played a particular role in Antarctica. In the second half of the twentieth century, the region was defined as a territory for peace, science and environmental protection. Although the economic relevance of the region has declined, it remains present in subtle, covert or latent ways (tourism activities and investments in scientific research and bases are just two of many examples). Considering capitalism in discussions of colonialism is not trivial, as capitalism and colonialism were – and still are – closely related processes in the construction of the modern world.[3]

Some periods of Antarctic history show a stronger influence of capitalism than others. This was the case in the nineteenth century, when sealing vessels representing the interests of capitalist companies sailed to Antarctica to supply world markets with skins and oil.[4] The sealing era thus offers an opportunity to deepen the discussion of the early links between capitalism and colonialism in the southern continent. Paradoxically, while debates on colonialism have focused on later periods of Antarctic history, leaving the sealing era behind, studies of the sealing era have explored its capitalist nature, largely ignoring potential colonial dynamics.

This chapter offers a reflection on colonialism and Antarctic sealing, considering how sealing may have shaped (or been shaped by) specific colonial dynamics. In particular, we discuss how colonialism and capitalism may have been complementary and indeed mutually reinforcing. By bringing colonialism into sealing, we offer an alternative understanding of an industry that has been approached primarily from a capitalist perspective. Drawing on insights from postcolonial studies, we also discuss the presence of specific colonial practices and relations that animated the industry.

We begin with an overview of the history of Antarctica, looking at the interactions that people have had with the territory over time. This is important in determining whether capitalist or colonial dynamics acquired greater relevance at different moments, leading scholars to approach different periods through the lens of capitalism or colonialism alone. Later, we present some tools for discussing colonialism and capitalism in the region, exploring how they may have worked together in the sealing era. Research from the 'Landscapes in White' project, to which the three authors belong, contributes to the analysis.

Approaching Antarctic history

Antarctica has distinctive features that make it unique, and these have been emphasised over time by discourses that portray the region as an absolute 'otherness'.[5] Human interactions with the southern continent have a relatively short history, given that the widely accepted and clearly documented version of its discovery dates only from the early nineteenth century.[6] Since colonialism is usually thought of as being exercised over inhabited regions, characterised by the establishment of settlements and cultural domination, it is understandable that a place with no Indigenous or permanent population is not immediately associated with colonial dynamics. However, as mentioned above, we agree with the argument that colonialism – like capitalism – was present in Antarctica as a historical process.[7]

Although human interactions with Antarctica are relatively 'new', they are not lacking in complexity or heterogeneity. In the eighteenth century, a number of expeditions (including the voyages of James Cook) attempted to find the postulated *Terra Australis Incognita*.[8] Knowledge of the world's oceans, both as geographical spaces and as routes for travel and trade, was important to Britain at that time. In February 1819, William Smith – the English captain of a merchant vessel sailing from Buenos Aires to Valparaíso – sighted the South Shetland Islands (the closest Antarctic archipelago to South America) when he deviated from his intended route. News about the abundance of animal resources spread quickly, attracting sealers to the region.[9]

Although the number of sealing vessels operating in Antarctica fluctuated over time, sealers were the dominant human presence in the region for over a century. Eighteenth-century voyages in search of the southern continent were explicitly described as exploratory, although it was clear that geographical findings could also be relevant in economic and colonial terms. The prospect of exploitation was the reason why sealers sailed to the 'end of the world' to take skins and oil to sell on to various markets. However, there is no doubt that sealers also contributed to the early exploration of the territory.[10]

Whaling in Antarctica can probably be seen as as an extension of the sealing industry in that it focused on the exploitation of animal resources. The activity gained strength in the late nineteenth and early twentieth centuries, when whaling benefited from naval and technological changes. The activity was initially based on factory ships, and later became shore-based. Whaling stations were established in the South Shetlands and the South Orkneys, including production areas and workers' facilities, which were abandoned when the companies ceased operations. Like the sealers, some whalers engaged in geographical exploration, both for prestige and for profit.[11]

In 1895, the Sixth International Geographical Congress called for a concerted effort to explore Antarctica as the largest undiscovered place on earth.[12] At the time, information about the Antarctic mainland was limited to very small areas along the coast.[13] The ongoing construction of the territory as *terra incognita*, at a time of fierce competition for territory among the European powers (the 'Scramble for Africa' was still ongoing), made the southern continent a desirable destination for explorers and adventurers. Within a few years, the so-called 'heroic age' of Antarctic exploration had begun, during which several parties (mostly from Europe) visited the region between the late nineteenth and the early twentieth centuries with the aim of expanding the frontiers of geographical knowledge.

The term 'heroic age' has become popular because it emphasises the difficulties faced by expedition leaders and their parties (including Ernest Shackleton, Robert Scott etc.) in exploring Antarctica at a time when the continent was almost completely unknown. This period plays a significant part in dominant discourses of the southern continent, to the extent that it is usually presented as the founding period of Antarctic history.[14] The heroic age combines attractive features for both researchers and the public, such as nationalism, individualism, romanticism, survival in difficult circumstances, and even heroism in suffering and death. The economic aspects behind exploration are rarely considered in these narratives.[15] Capitalism is sidelined, and the sealers are thus marginalised from the mainstream of Antarctic history.

The achievements of heroic age explorers, supported by nationalist discourses, increased the interest of several countries in Antarctica. The region then became the focus of sovereignty claims based on first sightings, landings and national presence in the territory (particularly during the Second World War and the Cold War).[16] Sovereignty claims could be linked to visions of prosperous commercial activity or settlement.[17] The Antarctic Treaty of 1959 agreed to freeze sovereignty claims and set aside the continent as a space for peace and science. The Protocol on Environmental Protection to the Antarctic Treaty was signed in 1991, adding a special emphasis on conservation.[18] Nevertheless, the protocol came against a background of pessimism about whether Antarctica's minerals were economically valuable – and claims by countries such as Malaysia that if they were, then a system that excluded most of the world's countries echoed colonialism.[19]

Focusing on the material structures of human presence in Antarctica can reveal more about the purposes of their inhabitants. Heroic age huts were bases of operations for explorers and scientific facilities, but presence at these sites was generally short-lived. It was not until the mid-twentieth century that various nations considered establishing permanent stations to support territorial claims and research activities. Under the Antarctic Treaty System (ATS), science became the main way for nations to be in Antarctica.[20] Today, there are more than 70 permanent stations in Antarctica, some of which resemble 'large frontier towns'.[21] They have both summer and winter populations, including scientists and support staff.

This overview shows how human interactions with Antarctica appear to have shifted from an explicit interest in exploiting natural resources to an overt concern with exploration and science.[22] While at first glance the logics of economy/exploitation and knowledge/exploration appear to be mutually exclusive, a closer looks reveals something different. Both logics are always present in Antarctic history, although at certain moments one tends to take precedence over the other. Following Edward LiPuma's ideas, they are more an expression of dualism than a real dichotomy, with historical discourses often denying the role played by the term left in the background.[23]

Research on colonialism has focused on the period when the logic of knowledge/exploration came to the fore (from the heroic age to the present). It was during this period that some of the features that have traditionally defined colonialism in other world contexts became more or less tangible in

Antarctica (including territorial claims, the establishment of scientific bases etc.), transforming the region into an instance of the globally recognisable colonial project.[24] The period of the ATS is considered particularly interesting because it implies the materialisation of the geopolitical interests and strategies of the signatory countries, and the reproduction of imperialist relations among them.

From a postcolonial perspective, researchers have critically challenged the seemingly 'neutral', 'cooperative' and 'science-only' image of Antarctica by discussing, among other things, the nature of scientific research in the region, decision-making processes, the current status of territorial claims, and heritage conservation policies.[25] Although the ideals of the ATS may suggest otherwise, Antarctica is a place where asymmetric power relations are present, albeit expressed differently than in other contexts.[26]

Territorial claims and the establishment of settlements (bases) were not prominent features of the period when the logic of economy/exploitation became dominant. This is probably one of the reasons why scholars approaching colonialism in Antarctica have not focused on the sealing era. However, as noted above, the sealing era – a period that does not necessarily represent the ideals of science, international cooperation and conservation emphasised by the ATS – has traditionally not received the same attention from scholars as later moments in Antarctic history.[27] In one way or another, the sealing era ended up being approached through the lens of capitalism alone.[28]

The analysis of capitalism and colonialism in Antarctica is thus split, as if they were mutually exclusive processes responding to different moments in time. This has ultimately contributed to the construction of a new dichotomy, closely related to the economy/exploitation vs. exploration/science dichotomy described above (or to the construction of a kind of historical progression from exploitation to exploration of the region). A probable exception to the dominant approaches to the sealing era is the work of Ben Maddison.[29] His analysis of the period ranging from 1819 to 1943 sees global capitalism and colonialism as the historical framework that enabled the expansion of sealers across the South Seas, facilitating – among other things – maritime routes for trade, colonial outposts to supplement crews and a general willingness to explore.

Research on sealing and capitalism has followed different but related lines of enquiry. Some work has emphasised the economic contribution of Antarctic sealing to the global economy, defining the duration of sealing cycles, the types and quantities of resources taken, and the relationships between local production and the demands of world markets.[30] Other studies have approached the presence of sealers in the South Shetland Islands as a result of the expansion of capitalism into new territories. The 'passive' role of Antarctica in this process is debated, as the region is presented as relevant to the development of the very system that seeks to control it.[31]

Some work has also discussed whether the principles of capitalism that governed the contexts in which sealing companies were based might have had a relevant impact on sealers' lives in Antarctica. With this in mind, researchers (mainly archaeologists) have looked at how sealers actually worked and survived in the region, assessing a range of practices (sheltering, clothing, food etc.). Discussions have included the relationship and tensions between the provision and degree of control over workers by companies, and the ability of sealers to rely on their own resources in a difficult living and working scenario. Among other things, these works have stimulated reflection on the creation of 'intimate economies' and the experience of everyday life in Antarctica.[32]

In the following section, we critically examine the relationship between capitalism and colonialism in the Antarctic sealing era, drawing on the work of the 'Landscapes in White' project. This research project, coordinated by Andrés Zarankin and based at the University of Minas Gerais (Brazil), brings together researchers (mostly, but not all, archaeologists) from different countries to study the role of sealing in the incorporation of Antarctica into the modern capitalist world.[33] Asking questions about colonialism could help us reflect from an alternative perspective on issues we have addressed or are currently addressing, such as the invisibility of sealers in dominant narratives of Antarctic history, or the diverse composition of sealing gangs.[34] Moreover, it could shed light on more general questions arising from the specific study of the Antarctic sealing industry.

Conceptualising colonialism, capitalism and their connections

While there are many ways to define colonialism, the term is characterised by the expansion of a country into a given territory for the purpose of economic exploitation, usually involving the establishment of colonies and cultural domination.[35] From our perspective, western colonialism in the modern world implies an attempt to incorporate colonial territories into a global system of political, social and/or economic control. This form of colonialism depends on a particular understanding of what is perceived as the 'other' – be it territory, natural resources or people – underpinned by dominant discourses in which western characteristics, practices and ideas are defined as expressions of civilisation or moral superiority at the expense of the 'other', thus producing asymmetries in power dynamics.[36] Extractivism and the subjugation of different groups, among other thingss, are some of the expressions of a long history of colonial encounters.

In the case of Antarctica, the absence of an Indigenous population, the location of the territory and its extreme environmental conditions have fostered somewhat different approaches to colonialism than those most commonly assessed in other regions of the world.[37] Researchers working from a postcolonial perspective have argued that there is no reason to assume that the region was not shaped by colonial practices simply because the relationships at issue were not between the region and a particular nation that sought to incorporate it as part of its territory.[38] Instead, colonial practices and relations need to be understood as multidimensional and multidirectional phenomena, within the framework of a particular attitude toward the 'other' described above.[39]

Since colonialism is neither spatially nor temporally homogeneous, an assessment of its diversity is required. From a postcolonial perspective, the focus should not be on the relationship between two different societies or territories, where one is simply dominant over a passive other, but on the new practices and connections that have developed as a result of a complex process that has integrated several points of the planet into a single logic – each of which has some kind of influence on the other (without denying the impact of power imbalances). According to this, colonialism is a reality that has manifested in different places, not only those traditionally labelled as 'colonial' but also in other contexts, such as Antarctica. These are some of the ideas that guide our analysis of the sealing era.

In addition to providing working definitions for colonialism and capitalism, it is worth emphasising that both historical processes were (and are) mutually constituted.[40] Both were (and are) associated with the formation of the modern world – defined by Chris Gosden as capitalism emerging along with the possibilities for colonialism.[41] Therefore, the study of capitalism and colonialism as isolated processes should at least be problematised, while recognising that the formation of the modern world is also intimately linked to other historical processes such as nationalism, ethnocentrism and imperialism.[42] At this point, it is worth mentioning that although colonialism and imperialism are usually related processes, and some researchers do not find a strict distinction between them, we believe that colonialism is associated with practical and concrete relations of domination (of a territory, people or resources) through political, social and economic control.[43] On the other hand, we believe that imperialism is defined by the specific policies emanating from a nation-state and aimed at gaining control over a territory.[44] While some authors state that colonialism is one of the strategies used by imperialism to achieve its goals, we also consider that colonialist practices can take place beyond the scope of imperialist policies.

Archaeology has much to offer to the discussion of the multiple connections between colonialism and capitalism, as these are not only abstract ideas but are materially active processes in the construction of people's lives.[45] Furthermore, archaeology has a particular potential to democratise the past. While documents are often produced by people in positions of power, everybody can leave a material footprint (especially in the form of waste). In this way, the archaeological record opens up the possibility of telling alternative stories to the dominant narratives.[46]

Published sources such as Antarctic sealing journals are scarce, while unpublished documents such as logbooks pose challenges to researchers (including the biases that affect the representation of different subjects). In this context, the remains of sealing camps provide important evidence of sealers' presence. However, as all archaeology in Antarctica is historical archaeology (covering a period when writing was available), approaches to the sealing era inevitably involve the combined use of archaeological and historical evidence. Within the 'Landscapes in White' project, logbooks and crew lists, among other documents, are currently being approached from new perspectives, including their dialogue with material remains (following the methodological suggestions of Patricia Galloway and Mary Beaudry).[47]

Both capitalism and colonialism are traditional subjects of research in historical archaeology.[48] While scholars initially sought to identify universal features defining the development of modern society in different world contexts, in the last two decades more and more researchers have insisted on the need to discuss how western capitalism and colonialism might have been either accepted, rejected or transformed in particular settings.[49] Moreover, archaeologists adopting a postcolonial stance have insisted on the need to deconstruct narratives of western dominance.[50]

Approaching capitalism (and colonialism) in the Antarctic sealing industry

Antarctic sealing was clearly linked to capitalism. Here, we briefly describe the markets and products of sealing, the expansionary dynamics of the industry, and the characteristics of the companies and their social actors.[51] Commercial sealing intensified in the eighteenth century as seal skins (mainly from fur seals) and the oil tried out from seal blubber (mainly from elephant seals) were increasingly seen as alternatives to sea otter skins and whale oil, respectively.[52] Sealing thus became a global industry that responded to supply–demand and cost–benefit logics.

Seal skins were first sold in Canton (China), and later in New York and London, while oil was more widely demanded. Fur seal skins could be used as pelts to make coats and hats. The fur could also be shaved and felted, with felted fur used to make hats, and shaved skins used to make shoes and gloves, among other things. Elephant seal oil was mainly used for lighting and lubricating machinery.[53]

Sealing was a highly extractive industry that brought animal colonies to the brink of local extinction. Sealers were constantly looking for new hunting grounds. Sealing cycles responded to resource availability and market demand. By the end of the eighteenth century, sealers were already operating in Patagonia, Tierra del Fuego and the Malvinas/Falkland Islands.[54] They soon reached the South Shetland Islands. The first sealing cycle in the archipelago (1819–28) involved more than 120 vessels, and at least 300,000 seal skins were taken. Subsequent cycles (1830–50 and 1870–90) failed to match these figures, as the seal colonies never fully recover.[55]

Most of the sealing companies operating in Antarctica were of British or United States origin. Like any capitalist enterprise, the sealing industry involved a distinction between capital and labour. Company owners provided the initial capital for the voyages (vessels, equipment and advance payments for workers). Sealing crews signed contracts setting out the characteristics of the voyage and the money they would receive in exchange for their labour. Sealers were paid in specific 'lays' or 'shares' of the final proceeds of the voyage, depending on their rank. Crews were organised hierarchically, and included the captain, officers, a number of workers to perform specific tasks (cooper, carpenter, cook etc.), and the able seamen and 'green hands' (or inexperienced men).[56]

While the links between sealing and capitalism seem clear, we consider some other dynamics that may have shaped (and been shaped by) social practices and relationships, not only between sealers and the Antarctic territory, but also between the people involved in the Antarctic sealing industry themselves. Colonial dynamics are therefore brought into focus by assessing whether some of the features often considered relevant to the definition of colonialism were also present in early Antarctic sealing: in particular, the representation of nation-state interests, the characteristics of the sealing population and power relations, and the establishment of a presence in the territory. We take a critical approach to the peculiarities of Antarctica and nineteenth-century sealing, recognising that colonial practices and relations can take complex and varied forms.

Representation of nation-state interests

Works on colonialism often evaluate the direct involvement of nation-states to gain control over territories. However, it is often argued that Antarctic sealing was carried out by private companies with no direct state involvement. In this context, the only influence that nation-states appear to have had on Antarctic sealing was through general impositions on the maritime industry. Sealers were nonetheless part of a society in which nation-states played a significant role in economic and geopolitical affairs. Examining the possible links between Antarctic sealing and national interests is therefore an interesting and important way of discussing the possibility of early colonialism (or at least an early attempt at colonialism) in Antarctica. In the following section, we refer mainly to the case of the United States, as the 'Landscapes in White' project focuses on the analysis of US documents.

News of the discovery of the South Shetlands attracted the attention of government authorities as well as sealing entrepreneurs. When Jeremy Robinson (US State Department agent in Valparaíso) heard about the newly discovered islands in November 1819, he sent a letter to the Secretary of State describing William Smith's sighting. Among other things, he suggested that the United States should send a vessel to explore and discover the 'new sources of wealth', since the British intended to sail to the archipelago.[57] Robinson was not mistaken: the British eventually sent Edward Bransfield of the Royal Navy on an exploratory voyage in January and February 1820, charting the northern part of the archipelago.[58]

The owners of the sealing companies also sought to involve nation-states in the exploration and exploitation of the region. James Byers, a prominent sealing merchant from New York, asked the US government to send the navy to protect American sealers from the British, and suggested the establishment of a settlement on the South Shetlands as a site from which US authority could be projected over nearby territory.[59] He also stressed the importance of surveying and naming the islands, and offered to help get US representatives to Antarctica. Although Byers's letters reached James Monroe, he received no support. Almost a decade afterwards, in 1828, Jeremiah Reynolds, a lecturer and explorer, addressed Congress to persuade national representatives to explore the South Pole. Although Reynolds succeeded in getting the government interested and the project was approved, Andrew Jackson was elected president of the United States while the expedition was being organised, and he cancelled it. Nevertheless, Reynolds was able to continue with his idea by attracting private financial support, particularly from sealing companies. Thus, in 1829, a commercial and geographical expedition was carried out without any significant results in terms of discovering new land.[60]

American sealers also brought Antarctica to the public eye. By making the southern continent real to American citizens, the sealers helped to make it a subject that the state could seek to know and control. The discovery of the South Shetlands, as well as accounts of American sealers arriving shortly after the British, were reported in newspapers, demonstrating an interest in the territory and its resources.[61] The sealers were aware of the interest that could be generated by revealing the features of the continent. During their voyage to the South Shetlands in 1820–21, B. Astor, a member of the crew of the *Jane Maria*, and MacKay of the *Sarah* collected rock specimens for the American Museum of National History.[62] A few years later, Reynolds's expedition included the naturalist James Eights, the first American scientist to enter Antarctica to make observations.[63] These observations were subsequently published in seven papers in a variety of journals, including the *Boston Journal of Natural History* and the *American Journal of Agriculture and Science*. The overall effect was to link knowledge of the earth's far south with its exploitation and, potentially, its control.

Sealing has often been characterised as a secretive business in which geographical knowledge was kept confidential and competitors were denied access to new hunting grounds.[64] Nevertheless, sealers contributed to the production and dissemination of geographic knowledge about Antarctica, and thus established a dialogue with information produced by national explorers (especially in the British case).[65] Exploration was clearly necessary for sealers to locate resources and make decisions about sailing and sealing. In this process, sealers described the South Shetlands in their accounts, assigned place names to geographical features and sometimes produced their own charts of the South Shetlands – such as the one elaborated by British sealer George Powell in 1821.[66] As will be seen below, the attribution of place names was important not only for the identification of places but also for the symbolic establishment of a presence in a particular area. The use of a place name was thus linked to the presence of an industry that exploited the territory in question.

These examples show that in addition to the British, who claimed South Georgia as early as 1775, US sealers also sought to know and control the territory as part of their activities. Why did this not lead to declarations of US sovereignty or formal political control? Political circumstances probably prevented this. The first sealing cycle in the archipelago took place at a time when the United States was preoccupied with its internal affairs, having recently ended the War of 1812.[67] The owners of the American sealing companies wanted to involve their government in the exploration of the region: they knew that a national presence was important to secure resources, but also to enhance national prestige on the world stage. Although they received no concrete help from their government, the American sealers succeeded in bringing Antarctica into the national imagination, while the sealing operations represented a kind of national presence in the territory.

Population and power relationships

Colonialism sometimes takes place in inhabited territories, creating coloniser/colonised relationships where power dynamics come into play. Although Antarctica was an uninhabited place, more than 180 sealing vessels sailed to the South Shetlands in the nineteenth century. Given that sealing crews averaged 20 men, more than 3,500 sealers may have visited the region during this period (although some may have visited the archipelago more than once).[68] The sealers brought with them specific social dynamics, including some of a colonial nature (involving an imbalance of power between westerners and those perceived as 'others' because of their place of origin – including colonial enclaves or other peripheral regions – and especially because of racist ideologies). Dominant narratives have emphasised the role of white men in Antarctic history, although more recent approaches –mainly from a postcolonial perspective – have begun to discuss the participation of some other groups, particularly since the heroic age of exploration.[69] Questions remain about the specific composition of sealing crews visiting Antarctica, as the literature often ignores their potential diversity.[70]

The 'Landscapes in White' project has analysed the crew lists of sealing vessels sailing from New London to the South Shetlands in the second half of the nineteenth century.[71] Although Americans made up the majority of the crews, a significant number of sealers came from Portuguese and British colonial enclaves, such as the Cape Verde Islands and Tristan da Cunha (a fact also noted by Anthony Dickinson and Maddison).[72] Following the racialising categories of 'complexion' provided by historical documents, the identities of the crews were varied. While people described as 'light or fair' made up the majority, Black men were the largest minority group – including people born not only in African colonies but also in the United States. These initial findings for the Antarctic sealing grounds appear to be consistent with anecdotal evidence of the cosmopolitan character of the sealing and whaling industries in general.[73]

Under US law, sealers – like all sailors – had to be hired as wage labourers. Most of the men who made up sealing crews were recruited in the ports of departure. In the nineteenth century, American society was undergoing significant demographic and socio-political changes, and the recruited workers represented a mixture of the new working class that was beginning to emerge in the cities as a product of industrialisation, and minority groups still tied to the social dynamics of the previous colonial order (an order deeply rooted in the subjugation of Native Americans and the enslavement of Africans). In this context, the sealing industry was a source of income not only for the working class, but also – where state legislations allowed it – for people with fewer opportunities, such as recently freed African Americans.[74] Despite this, they were often paid less than white men for the same work and had difficulty in gaining promotion to higher ranks. There were clear ethnic/racial inequalities.

Men were also recruited outside American ports, sometimes in a poorly regulated way. While sealing crews were often completed in various ports of call, such as the Azores, there is evidence that captains sometimes recruited Indigenous people more informally in places such as the coasts of Patagonia. Men recruited in various ports of call were generally included on crew lists, although they were sometimes paid less than those recruited in the United States (especially in the case of people of African descent).[75] Meanwhile, Indigenous people were not even mentioned in official documents, and there are serious doubts about how they were actually recruited and paid (as some may have been forced labour). Researcher Rubén Stehberg has attempted to provide archaeological evidence of the presence of these invisible groups in nineteenth-century sealing camps in Antarctica.[76]

The sealing industry clearly responded to capitalist interests in trying to get the most out of workers at the lowest possible cost. Because the 'lay' system meant that the owners of sealing companies were not obliged to pay the workers fixed amounts of money, it was common for the men to be paid less than expected at the end of the voyages, and even to go into debt buying 'slops' (products such as tobacco, clothing etc. kept on board for sale to the crew). Many sealers had no choice but to go on another sealing voyage to survive and pay off their debts.[77] Crews were heavily dependent on the good will of sealing company owners and captains (who acted as company representatives outside their home ports). They were also often exploited in ways that were more akin to indentured servitude than capitalist wage labour. The scenario was clearly worse for those recruited in irregular circumstances.

In addition to the textual record, the 'Landscapes in White' project is currently exploring alternative ways of making minority groups visible through the analysis of archaeological evidence, considering the potential of archaeology to tell richer and more diverse stories of the past. Nevertheless, study of the remains of sealing camps in the South Shetlands has already shed light on the poor material conditions in which sealers lived and worked. With little food to last more than a few days on the islands, the men had to rely on themselves to find shelter (either by occupying caves, living under their upturned boats or building small structures from local materials), food (including sea birds, seals and elephant seals) and clothing (by either repairing their own clothing or quickly making new items).[78]

Sealing was a capitalist industry closely linked to colonial dynamics, which implied a particular way of understanding and dealing with the 'other'. Sealing crews visiting Antarctica were the product of a labour market in which maritime legislation was just beginning to recognise workers' rights. The production of crew lists was an attempt to account for the whereabouts of the people who made up the crews when the vessels returned home, just as shipping articles served as a declaration of the lays, and the destination and duration of the voyages. Despite this, there were still major gaps in protecting workers from abuse, and companies found other ways to increase their profits. A social order still shaped by a colonial view of difference allowed shipowners and captains to find cheaper labour in home ports, as well as in some other places where state control was weak or non-existent. Sealing crews brought a complex set of colonial relationships with them to Antarctica. Colonial ideologies and practices were manifested in the social relations on board. How they were enacted in the Antarctic territory is a subject for further study.

Establishing a presence in Antarctic territory

Colonialism is usually associated with the establishment of colonies to control territories. Owing to both the extreme environmental conditions and the extractive nature of the industry, Antarctic sealing did not involve long-term settlements. In the absence of policies and local authorities to regulate exploitation or favour one nation's operations over another, the first sealing vessels to reach productive beaches had the right to exploit them.[79] Sealing gangs established camps of varying duration, depending on the amount of resources available at each site and the activities carried out there. Sealing camps could not last longer than the summer season. However, the limited duration of these occupations did not necessarily mean that the sealers were not interested in establishing control over the territory – control that could be considered colonial in the sense of the assertion of authority by a group with privileged knowledge of the area. It was therefore important to establish a presence in the South Shetlands, whether by exploring the region, naming geographical features or deploying gangs on the beaches.

When the sealers first arrived in the archipelago, the South Shetlands were *terra incognita*. They knew nothing about the geography of the islands, the location of animal colonies etc. Exploration was necessary, as vessels that gathered more information had a clear advantage over their rivals. Understanding and knowing the landscape made it possible to dominate the region. This included building settlements and exploiting seals, but also forming alliances with other sealers, not only to join forces and exploit resources, but also to exchange important information, such as the location of animal colonies or places to harbour in a competitive scenario.[80] Meanwhile, the sealers named various geographical features, including islands, harbours, beaches etc. As the region was a blank slate, it was important to make it recognisable and knowable. Giving place names effectively marked the territory, while leaving evidence of one's presence in the region.

Place names often described geographical features (for example Deception Island, Rugged Island) or referred to animal resources (for example Elephant Point, Seals Rocks). But sealers also named some places after vessels, captains or towns, linking them to their history, background or nationality. For example, Hersilia Cove on Rugged Island was named by Captain Sheffield after his vessel, the brig *Hersilia* from Stonington, USA, which used the cove as an anchorage in the summer of 1819–20. Meanwhile, Yankee Harbour on Greenwich Island was the mooring site of Captain Fanning's fleet from Stonington in 1820–21.[81] Competition for control of a space and the people working in it, as well as its resources, could also be expressed through contested naming: the British called Yankee Harbour Hospital Cove.[82]

Exploration was both part of and a prerequisite for sealing strategies. The distribution of gangs across the South Shetlands depended not only on the identification of animal colonies, but also on the ability of sealers to establish some form of control over hunting grounds. In the early stages of the first sealing cycle, the distribution of gangs was more geographically restricted than in later periods. The abundance of resources meant that there was no need for sealing vessels to exploit animals throughout the archipelago. Furthermore, the existence of other fleets and gangs that dominated specific areas in a highly competitive scenario reinforced this spatial focus.[83] The distribution of gangs over a given area made it possible to secure and control productive beaches: authority required presence in addition to a name on a map. The formation of alliances between sealing vessels could be almost analogous to alliances between states, in that they allowed mutual recognition of control over particular spaces.

The gangs established campsites that marked the beaches where sealers exercised their right of exploitation until there were no more animals left to kill. Archaeological work by the 'Landscapes in White' project has identified and studied the remains of more than 30 sealing camps on Byers Peninsula and Elephant Point on Livingston Island.[84] Most of these sites date from the early nineteenth century, a time when abundant game and the need to secure some areas for continued use justified the establishment of camps for several weeks or more than a month. The project also identified concentrations of archaeological sites in several specific areas. While these camps could have been established by different vessels during different hunting seasons, the possibility remains that they were established by gangs from the same vessel or fleet to increase their control over specific areas. Further research, including a deeper dialogue between historical and archaeological evidence, may provide more answers to this question.

These examples show that sealers gained control of territory and resources in the South Shetland Islands via a range of strategies involving the assertion of authority through presence and knowledge. While this presence did not require the establishment of long-term settlements, it clearly met the sealers' objectives of controlling and exploiting resources. The imposition of place names created a symbolic control that continues to this day – as do the remains of their camps. In addition, the territorial occupation of sealing involved a dynamic relationship with the landscape, its resources and the presence of competitors through the strategic distribution of gangs on the beaches. The term colonialism can be useful in capturing some of the dynamics of these processes through its focus on human control over territory and resources, including the exclusion or forcible marginalisation of some groups, and its focus on structural power relations within groups. Although campsites were ephemeral occupations, the material remains of these sites still represent the most abundant type of archaeological site in all of Antarctica.

Conclusions

If colonialism exists in any form in Antarctica, then its first stages – or at least, its first attempts – must be sought in the sealing era, a period that witnessed the first significant human interactions with the region. Colonialism is a complex process that takes different forms over time. In cases where western expansion took place over inhabited territories, some scholars have used the expression 'cultural contact' to describe the initial – sporadic and fleeting – interactions between westerners and native people, leaving the term 'colonialism' for later periods, characterised by more enduring relationships. Notwithstanding this distinction, recent work has commented on the artificiality of such segmentations, as they tend to produce a biased picture of history in which colonialism is only approached in full swing, preventing researchers from understanding how initial moments may have been relevant to later decisions, or from discussing the continuities and ruptures between colonial stages (for example, considering the different understandings and treatments of colonial 'others').[85] Omitting the sealing era from the history of Antarctic colonialism could also raise a critical voice.

Conceptual definitions have traditionally indicated that colonialism involves the control of a given territory for the purpose of, among other things, exploiting its resources. In the case of Antarctica, the economic aspects of colonialism have not always been considered, as intensive exploitation of marine mammals took place in the early stages of the continent's history. For those moments, researchers have focused on the capitalist dimension of sealing operations, implicitly assuming that colonialism was not present because of the lack of a sustained national presence and more-or-less permanent settlements. From our point of view, colonialism understands the 'otherness' of the regions where western expansion occurred as if it was simply destined to serve its interests. Extractivism responds to this idea, and although it has been suggested that colonialism needs to ensure its continuity through a regulated exploitation of resources, it is also true that this is not always the case (especially in ultra-peripheral and uninhabited contexts, within the framework of early capitalism).

The subjugation of what is defined as the 'other' (be it a given territory, natural resources or people) is inevitably linked to an ethnocentric view in which there is no possible identification with what is perceived as different. On the contrary, the 'other' is understood simply as an object to be dominated. Nevertheless, and in silence, the 'other', defined as an alien reality, inevitably represents the 'constitutive outside' (*sensu* Judith Butler) that facilitates the formation of the dominant centre.[86] In this sense, peripheral or ultra-peripheral territories were essential to the existence of the core regions. For example, the resources extracted from Antarctica eventually fed the commercial markets of distant regions, providing the raw materials necessary for an ongoing process of industrialisation and urbanisation. Although not everyone was aware of it, the candles that people lit, the oil that they used to lubricate machines and the furs that they used for clothing sometimes came from this most remote region of the world. Moreover, the capitals that the Antarctic sealing industry eventually produced became available for the development of other capitalist and colonial projects around the world.

As discussed above, neither economy/exploitation and knowledge/exploration, nor capitalism and colonialism, should be seen as mutually exclusive concepts in Antarctic history. On the contrary, both capitalism and colonialism have played an important role in the incorporation of Antarctica into the modern world. From this perspective, capitalism may have laid the foundations for the development of colonialism in the region, and vice versa. If we reflect on this point for a moment, the territorial claims that are currently latent within the ATS, and which are expected eventually to be based on the sustained presence of national states over the territory, still have the exploitation of natural resources as a potential future goal. The manifestations of colonialism most commonly associated with Antarctica are not necessarily divorced from economic dynamics.

As a global process, colonialism has been closely linked to western expansion into inhabited and uninhabited territories. The exclusion of Antarctica from this process simply deepens the exoticisation of the region, while reducing the possibilities for dialogue with other contexts. From a critical standpoint, as suggested by postcolonial approaches, it is possible to understand the singularities of Antarctica while discussing its connections with the wider world.

The establishment of colonies is probably one of the most widely accepted criteria for defining the exercise of colonialism in a given context. It is true that Antarctic sealing involved not colonial settlements, but rather the establishment of summer camps that were rarely reoccupied. Nevertheless, it is probably time to discuss the rigidity of the temporal criterion for defining the existence of a colony, while assessing the existence of different practices for gaining control over a territory. Perhaps, in the early stages of some colonial processes, the establishment of colonies was not considered a priority. Perhaps the presence of colonies was not a prerequisite for achieving the expected goals. Perhaps there were factors that prevented the establishment of such places, including extreme environmental conditions and geographical isolation as in the case of Antarctica, as well as material and technical limitations to deal with them effectively.

Antarctic sealing involved different practices from those traditionally used in some other colonial contexts. Nation-states showed an early interest in Antarctica, but for a variety of reasons this was not sufficient to establish a permanent presence in the region. However, sealers – as representatives of sealing companies from different nations – contributed to the geographical knowledge of the South Shetlands and, consciously or not, acted as a vanguard for their own countries, contributing to their economies and expansionist interests.[87]

Sealers established their presence in Antarctica through different actions. They assigned place names to geographical features and developed specific strategies to occupy hunting grounds in a competitive scenario. Although some works define the establishment of a colonial presence in terms of long-term strategies, we argue that it may be relevant to discuss whether colonial projects can effectively present different temporal expectations. In the case of extractivist exploitation, short-term occupations may be sufficient to take over resources. After all, no colonial system is guaranteed a permanent existence independent of the intentions of those who maintain it.

Finally, the fact that Antarctica was uninhabited at the time of its discovery does not mean that social relations among sealers visiting the region were unaffected by colonial dynamics. Sealing companies relied on a capitalist labour market, but also on the opportunities offered by a colonial world to recruit men. As a result, the presence of minority groups in Antarctica should not be underestimated, and it may be asked whether this reflects the decision to exclude Antarctica from historical processes that are clearly evident in other world contexts. Efforts to make these people visible are key to deconstructing the dominant history of the territory – a history that is often presented as exclusively white, without nuances.

Antarctica is a fascinating place to explore the particularities of colonialism in extreme world contexts and its links to capitalist extractivism, particularly in the sealing era. Although the analysis presented in this chapter is preliminary, we believe we have outlined ideas that could help deconstruct normative models of colonialism in the region. Historical archaeology, as a discipline with the potential to challenge dominant narratives and shed light on the lives of invisible people, could play an important role in this process.

Notes

1 Sarah Croucher and Lindsay Weiss, 'The Archaeology of Capitalism in Colonial Contexts: An Introduction. Provincializing Historical Archaeology', in Sarah Croucher and Lindsay Weiss (eds), *The Archaeology of Capitalism in Colonial Contexts: Postcolonial Historical Archaeologies* (New York: Springer, 2011), pp. 9–13; Klaus J. Dodds, 'Post-Colonial Antarctica: An Emerging Engagement', *Polar Record* 42:1 (2006), 59–70 (p. 61).

2 See, for example, Nicoletta Brazelli, 'Heroic and Post-Colonial Antarctic Narratives', in Klaus J. Dodds, Alan D. Hemmings and Peder Roberts (eds), *Handbook on the Politics of Antarctica* (Cheltenham: Edward Elgar Publishing, 2017), pp. 69–83; Dodds, 'Post-Colonial Antarctica', p. 59; Klaus J. Dodds and Christy Collis, 'Post-Colonial Antarctica', in Dodds *et al.*, *Handbook on the Politics of Antarctica*, pp. 50–68; Adrian Howkins, 'Appropriating Space: Antarctic Imperialism and the Mentality of Settler Colonialism', in Tracey Banivanua Mar and Penelope Edmonds (eds), *Making Settler Colonial Space* (London: Palgrave Macmillan, 2010), pp. 29–52; Ben Maddison, *Class and Colonialism in Antarctic Exploration, 1750–1920* (London: Pickering and Chatto, 2014); Ignacio J. Cardone in this volume; Alejandra Mancilla, 'Decolonising Antarctica', in Dawid Bunikowski and Alan D. Hemmings (eds), *Philosophies of Polar Law* (Abingdon: Routledge, 2020), pp. 49–61; Alejandra Mancilla, 'South American Claims in Antarctica: Colonial, *Malgré Tout*', *The Polar Journal* 12:1 (2022), 22–41, DOI: 10.1080/2154896X.2022.2062558; Luís Guilherme Resende de Assis, 'A proa pressentida: Táticas oceanográficas para atravessar a duração e avistar baleias no Estreito de Gerlache, Península Antártica' (PhD thesis, Universidade Federal de Santa Catarina, 2019).

3 Stephen A. Mrozowski, 'Imagining an Archaeology of the Future: Capitalism and Colonialism Past and Present', *International Journal of Historical Archaeology* 18 (2014), 340–60 (p. 341), DOI: 10.1007/s10761-014-0261-6; Charles Orser, *A Historical Archaeology of the Modern World* (New York: Plenum Press, 1996).

4 Briton Cooper Busch, *The War against the Seals: A History of the North American Seal Fishery* (Kingston: McGill-Queen's University Press, 1985), pp. 22–5; Andrés Zarankin and María Ximena Senatore, *Historias de un pasado en blanco: Arqueología histórica antártica* (Belo Horizonte: Argumentum, 2007), pp. 20–5.

5 Elizabeth Leane, *Antarctica in Fiction: Imaginative Narratives of the Far South* (Cambridge: Cambridge University Press, 2012), pp. 15–16; Andrés Zarankin and Melisa A. Salerno, ' "So Far, So Close": Approaching Experience

in the Study of the Encounter between Sealers and the South Shetland Islands (Antarctica, Nineteenth Century)', in Peder Roberts, Lize-Marié van der Watt and Adrian Howkins (eds), *Antarctica and the Humanities* (London: Palgrave Macmillan, 2016), pp. 79–103 (p. 80).

6 Andrés Zarankin, Michael Pearson and Melisa A. Salerno, *Antarctic Archaeology* (London: Routledge, 2023). New research is currently suggesting the possibility that Māori groups could have known and visited the continent in the early seventh century. See Priscilla M. Wehi, Nigel J. Scott, Jacinta Beckwith *et al.*, 'A Short Scan of Māori Journeys to Antarctica', *Journal of the Royal Society of New Zealand*, 52:5 (2021), 587–98 (p. 590).

7 Brazelli, 'Heroic and Post-Colonial Antarctic Narratives'; Dodds, 'Post-Colonial Antarctica'; Dodds and Collis, 'Post-Colonial Antarctica'; Howkins, 'Appropriating Space'; Maddison, *Class and Colonialism*; Mancilla, 'Decolonising Antarctica'; Mancilla, 'South American Claims'; Resende de Assis, 'A proa pressentida'.

8 Edwin S. Balch, *Antarctica* (Philadelphia, PA: Press of Allen, Lane & Scott, 1902), p. 68.

9 Kenneth. J. Bertrand, *Americans in Antarctica, 1775–1948* (Burlington, VT: Lane Press, 1971), p. 32; Edouard A. Stackpole, *The Voyage of the Huron and the Huntress: The American Sealers and the Discovery of the Continent of Antarctica* (Mystic: Marine Historical Association, 1955), p. 7; Busch, *The War against the Seals*, p. 23.

10 As an example of this we can mention Captain John Davis from the *Huron*. During the 1820 sealing season, as the South Shetlands were still mainly unknown, he sent shallops to explore the different islands.

11 Peder Roberts, 'The Union of Hunting and Research', in Peder Roberts (ed.), *The European Antarctic: Science and Strategy in Scandinavia and the British Empire* (New York: Palgrave Macmillan, 2011), pp. 53–76.

12 Hugh Robert Mill (ed.), *Report of the Sixth International Geographical Congress* (London: John Murray, 1896), pp. 163–7.

13 Pedro Alonso, Ignacio Partarrieu Garcia and Arturo Scheidegger, 'Antarctica: Dead Reckoning', *ARQ* 83 (2013), 16–25 (p. 16).

14 Zarankin *et al.*, *Antarctic Archaeology*, p. 19.

15 Peder Roberts, 'The Politics of Early Occupation', in Dodds *et al.*, *Handbook on the Politics of Antarctica*, pp. 318–32.

16 Elena Glasberg, *Antarctica as Cultural Critique: The Gendered Politics of Scientific Exploration and Climate Change* (New York: Palgrave Macmillan, 2012), p. 5.

17 Brigid Hains, *The Ice and the Inland: Mawson, Flynn and the Myth of the Frontier* (Victoria: Melbourne University Press, 2002).

18 Dodds, 'Post-Colonial Antarctica', p. 59; Zarankin *et al.*, *Antarctic Archaeology*, pp. 2–3.

19 Andrew Jackson, *Who Saved Antarctica? The Heroic Era of Antarctic Diplomacy* (Cham: Palgrave Macmillan, 2021).

20 Resende de Assis, 'A proa pressentida', p. 24.

21 Council of Managers of National Antarctic Programs (COMNAP), *Antarctic Station Catalogue* (New Zealand: COMNAP, 2017); Zarankin *et al.*, *Antarctic Archaeology*, p. 1.

22 Andrés Zarankin and Melisa A. Salerno, 'Antarctic Archaeology: Discussing the History of the Southernmost End of the World', in James Symonds and Vesa-Pekka Herva (eds), *The Oxford Handbook of Historical Archaeology* (Oxford: Oxford University Press, 2017), p. 2, https://academic.oup.com/edited-volume/34744/chapter-abstract/296571813?redirectedFrom=fulltext (accessed 11 March 2024); Andrés Zarankin and María Ximena Senatore, 'Archaeology in Antarctica: Nineteenth-Century Capitalism Expansion Strategies', *International Journal of Historical Archaeology* 9:1 (2005), 43–56.

23 Edward LiPuma, *Encompassing Others: The Magic of Modernity in Melanesia* (Ann Arbor: University of Michigan Press, 2002).

24 Dodds, 'Post-Colonial Antarctica', p. 60; Mancilla, 'Decolonising Antarctica'; Resende de Assis, 'A proa pressentida', p. 24.

25 Cardone in this volume; Dodds, 'Post-Colonial Antarctica', p. 61; Mancilla, 'Decolonising Antarctica', pp. 49–61; Mancilla, 'South American Claims in Antarctica', pp. 22–41; Brazelli, 'Heroic and Post-Colonial Antarctic Narratives'.

26 Ignacio Javier Cardone in this volume; Mancilla, 'Decolonising Antarctica'.

27 Michael Pearson and Melisa A. Salerno, 'Stateless Heritage: The Sealing Sites of the South Shetland Islands, Antarctica', in Barry L. Stiefel and Shelley-Anne Peleg (eds), *Yearbook of Transnational History*, Vol. VI (London: Fairleigh Dickinson University Press, 2023), pp. 195–222.

28 See, for example, Bjorn L. Basberg and Robert. K. Headland, *The 19th Century Antarctic Sealing Industry: Source, Data and Economic Significance* (Bergen: Institutt for Samfunnøkonomi, 2008), pp. 1–3; Melisa A. Salerno, Jimena Cruz and Andrés Zarankin, 'The First Antarctic Laborers', in Adrian Howkins and Peder Roberts (eds), *The Cambridge History of the Polar Regions* (Cambridge: Cambridge University Press, 2023), pp. 407–29; María Ximena Senatore and Andrés Zarankin, 'Arqueología histórica y expansión capitalista: Prácticas cotidianas y grupos operarios en Peninsula Byers, Isla Livingston de las Shetland del Sur', in Andrés Zarankin and Felix Acuto (eds), *Sed non satiata: Teoria social en la arqueología latinoamericana contemporánea* (Buenos Aires: Ediciones del Tridente, 1999), pp. 171–88 (pp. 174–5); Andrés Zarankin and Melisa A. Salerno, 'The "Wild" Continent? Some Discussions on the Anthropocene in Antarctica', *Journal of Contemporary Archaeology* 1:1 (2014), 114–18 (pp. 116–17); Zarankin and Senatore, *Historias de un pasado en blanco*, pp. 40–2.

29 Maddison, *Class and Colonialism*, pp. 9–123.

30 Basberg and Headland, *The 19th Century Antarctic Sealing Industry*; Busch, *The War against the Seals*.

31 Zarankin and Salerno, 'The "Wild" Continent?', p. 115.

32 Melisa A. Salerno, María Jimena Cruz and Andrés Zarankin, 'Inside or outside Capitalism? Sealers' Lives, Food, and Clothing onboard Sealing Vessels

and on Antarctic Hunting Grounds', in James Nyman, Kevin Fogle and Mary Beaudry (eds), *Historical Archaeology of Shadow and Intimate Economies* (Gainesville: University Press of Florida, 2019), pp. 171–3; Melisa A. Salerno, 'Persona y cuerpo-vestido en la modernidad: Un enfoque arqueológico' (PhD thesis, Universidad de Buenos Aires, 2011); Melisa A. Salerno and Andrés Zarankin, 'En busca de las experiencias perdidas: Arqueología del encuentro entre los loberos y las Islas Shetland del Sur (Antártida, Siglo XIX)', *Vestígios: Revista Latino-Americana de Arqueologia Histórica* 8:1 (2014), 131–57 (p. 133); Zarankin and Salerno, 'So Far, So Close'.

33 Senatore and Zarankin, 'Arqueología histórica y expansión capitalista', p. 172; Zarankin and Senatore, 'Archaeology in Antarctica', pp. 46–8; Zarankin and Senatore, *Historias de un pasado en blanco*, pp. 43–7; Andrés Zarankin, Sarah Hissa, Melisa A. Salerno *et al.*, 'Paisagens em branco: Arqueologia e antropologia antárticas – avanços e desafios', *Vestígios: Revista Latino-Americana de Arqueologia Histórica*, 5:2 (2011), 9–51 (pp. 14–15).

34 Andrés Zarankin, Melisa A. Salerno and Adrian Howkins, 'From the Antarctic to New England: Remembrance of Sealing and Sealers', in Robert K. Headland (ed.), *Historical Antarctic Sealing Industry: Proceedings of an International Conference in Cambridge* (Cambridge: Scott Polar Research Institute, 2018), pp. 107–8; Andrés Zarankin and María Ximena Senatore, 'Storytelling, Big Fish y arqueologia: Repensando o caso da Antartida', in Walter F. Morales and Flavia Moi (eds), *Tempos ancestrais* (São Paulo: Annablume, 2013), pp. 281–301 (p. 288); Melisa A. Salerno, María Jimena Cruz, Romina Rigone and Andrés Zarankin, 'Making Visible the Invisible: Discussing Heterogeneity among Sealing Groups on the South Shetland Islands', presentation at the SCAR SC-HASS Biennial Conference, Kobe, 18–19 November 2021.

35 Cardone in this volume; Gil. J. Stein, 'Colonies without Colonialism: A Trade Diaspora Model of Fourth Millennium B.C. Mesopotamian Enclaves in Anatolia', in C. L. Lyons and J. K. Papadopoulos (eds), *The Archaeology of Colonialism* (Los Angeles: Getty Research Institute, 2002), pp. 26–64 (p. 30).

36 Jane Burbank and Frederick Cooper, *Empires in World History: Power and the Politics of Difference* (Princeton, NJ: Princeton University Press, 2010), pp. 149–84; Cardone in this volume; Croucher and Weiss, 'The Archaeology of Capitalism', pp. 5–6; Howkins, 'Appropriating Space', p. 32; Orser, *A Historical Archaeology*, pp. 57–66.

37 Cardone in this volume; Dodds, 'Post-Colonial Antarctica', p. 61; Mancilla, 'South American Claims'.

38 Cardone in this volume; Howkins, 'Appropriating Space', p. 32.

39 See, for example, Croucher and Weiss, 'The Archaeology of Capitalism', p. 10; Susan Lawrence, *Archaeologies of the British: Explorations of Identity in Great Britain and Its Colonies, 1600–1945* (Abingdon: Routledge, 2003).

40 Croucher and Weiss, 'The Archaeology of Capitalism', p. 10; Virginia Dellino-Musgrave, *Maritime Archaeology and Social Relations: British Action in the Southern Hemisphere* (New York: Springer, 2006), p. 72.

41 Pedro P. Funari, Siân Jones and Martin Hall, 'Introduction: Archaeology in History', in Pedro P. Funari, Martin Hall and Siân Jones (eds), *Historical*

Archaeology: Back from the Edge (London: Routledge, 1999), pp. 1–20 (p. 7); Matthew Johnson, *An Archaeology of Capitalism* (Oxford: Blackwell, 1996); Mark Leone, 'Setting Some Terms for Historical Archaeologies of Capitalism', in Mark Leone and Parker B. Potter Jr (eds), *Historical Archaeologies of Capitalism* (New York: Kluwer Academic/Plenum Publishers, 1999), pp. 3–20; Orser, *A Historical Archaeology*; Chris Gosden, *Archaeology and Colonialism: Cultural Contact from 5000 BC to the Present* (Cambridge: Cambridge University Press, 2004), p. 4.

42 Croucher and Weiss, 'The Archaeology of Capitalism', p. 13.

43 Cardone in this volume; Mancilla, 'Decolonising Antarctica', p. 52.

44 Cardone in this volume.

45 Dellino-Musgrave, *Maritime Archaeology and Social Relations*, p. 71; Christopher Matthews, 'Context and Interpretation: An Archaeology of Cultural Production', *International Journal of Historical Archaeology* 3 (1999), 261–82 (p. 263).

46 Zarankin and Senatore, *Historias de un pasado en blanco*, p. 37.

47 Mary Beaudry, 'Above Vulgar Economy: The Intersection of Historical Archaeology and Microhistory in Writing Archaeological Biographies of Two New England Merchants', in James F. Brooks, Christopher DeCorse and John Walton (eds), *Small Worlds: Method, Meaning and Narratives in Microhistory* (Santa Fe, NM: School for Advanced Research Press, 2008), pp. 173–98 (p. 176); Patricia Galloway, 'Material Culture and Text: Exploring the Spaces within and Between', in Martin Hall and Stephen W. Silliman (eds), *Historical Archaeology* (Malden, MA: Blackwell, 2006), pp. 42–64.

48 Croucher and Weiss, 'The Archaeology of Capitalism', pp. 10–13; Johnson, *An Archaeology of Capitalism*; Leone, 'Setting Some Terms'; Tania Andrade Lima, 'O papel da arqueologia historica no mundo civilizado', in Andrés Zarankin and María Ximena Senatore (eds), *Arqueologia da sociedade moderna na America do Sul: Cultura material, discursos y práticas* (Buenos Aires: Ediciones del Tridente, 2002), pp. 117–27; Orser, *A Historical Archaeology*, pp. 57–81; Stephen W. Silliman, 'Colonialism in Historical Archaeology: A Review of Issues and Perspectives', in Charles E. Orser, Andrés Zarankin, Pedro P. Funari, Susan Lawrence and James Symonds (eds), *The Routledge Handbook of Global Historical Archaeology* (Abingdon: Routledge, 2020), pp. 41–60 (p. 53).

49 Andrade Lima, 'O papel da arqueologia historica'; Orser, *A Historical Archaeology*, pp. 57–81.

50 Croucher and Weiss, 'The Archaeology of Capitalism', pp. 9–15.

51 See, for instance, Salerno *et al.*, 'Inside or outside Capitalism?'.

52 Busch, *The War against the Seals*. This process involved rendering oil from pieces of blubber using huge iron pots; Ian W. G. Smith, *The New Zealand Sealing Industry: History, Archaeology and Heritage Management* (Wellington: Department of Conservation, 2002), p. 21.

53 Robert Burton, 'From Shoes to Shawls: Utilization of "South Seas" Fur Seal Pelts in Late 18th and Early 19th Century England', in Headland, *Historical Antarctic Sealing Industry*, pp. 87–93 (pp. 89–90); Zarankin *et al.*, *Antarctic Archaeology*, pp. 11–12.

54 Sergio Caviglia, *Malvinas: Soberanía, memoria y justicia*, Vol. II, *Balleneros, loberos, misioneros, S. XVIII–XIX* (Rawson: Ministerio de Educación de la Provincia de Chubut, 2015), p. 18; Marcelo Mayorga, 'Actividad lobera temprana en la Patagonia Oriental: Caza de mamíferos marinos', *RIVAR* 4:11 (2017), 31–51 (p. 34); Melisa A. Salerno, Romina Rigone and Andrés Zarankin, 'Explorando bitácoras: Aproximaciones al accionar de loberos y balleneros en Tierra del Fuego durante el siglo XIX', presentation at VII Congreso Nacional de Arqueología Histórica, Rosario, 22–6 October 2018.

55 Robert K. Headland, *A Chronology of Antarctic Exploration: A Synopsis of Events and Activities from the Earliest Times until the International Polar Years, 2007–09* (London: Quaritch, 2009), pp. 59–62; Michael Pearson, 'Charting the Sealing Islands of the Southern Ocean', *Journal of the Australian and New Zealand Map Society* 80 (2016), 33–56 (p. 52).

56 Salerno *et al.*, 'Inside or outside capitalism?', p. 161; Salerno *et al.*, 'The First Antarctic Laborers', p. 414; Rubén L. Stehberg, *Arqueología histórica antártica: Aborígenes sudamericanos en los mares subantárticos en el siglo XIX* (Santiago: Centro de Investigaciones Diego Barros Arana, 2003), p. 24.

57 Bertrand, *Americans in Antarctica*, p. 34.

58 Bertrand, *Americans in Antarctica*, p. 70.

59 Bertrand, *Americans in Antarctica*, pp. 34–5.

60 Bertrand, *Americans in Antarctica*, pp. 147–8.

61 Thomas A. Stevens, *The First American Sealers in the Antarctic, 1812–1819 and the First Voyage of the Brig 'Hersilia' of Stonington, Connecticut, 1819–1820* (Deep River, CT: US Department of State, 1954), pp. 4–13.

62 Headland, *A Chronology of Antarctic Exploration*, p. 130.

63 Bertrand, *Americans in Antarctica*, p. 148.

64 Pearson, 'Charting the Sealing Islands', p. 54.

65 Pearson, 'Charting the Sealing Islands', p. 53.

66 Rupert T. Gould, 'The Charting of the South Shetlands, 1819–28', *Mariner's Mirror* 27:3 (1941), 206–42 (p. 229).

67 Pearson and Salerno, 'Stateless Heritage'.

68 Salerno *et al.*, 'The First Antarctic Laborers', p. 410.

69 Maddison, *Class and Colonialism*, p. 102; Morgan Seag, *There Was No 'First Woman': The Historical Politics of Gender, Science, and Exploration in Twentieth-Century US Antarctic Fieldwork* (PhD thesis, University of Cambridge, 2021); Zarankin *et al.*, 'From the Antarctic to New England', pp. 113–15; Zarankin and Senatore, *Historias de un pasado en blanco*, p. 37.

70 For an important exception on the potential presence of Indigenous persons in Antarctic sealing camps, see Stehberg, *Arqueología histórica antártica*.

71 Salerno *et al.*, 'Making Visible the Invisible'.

72 Anthony B. Dickinson, 'A History of Sealing in the Falkland Islands and Dependencies, 1764–1972' (PhD thesis, University of Cambridge, 1987), p. 118; Maddison, *Class and Colonialism*, p. 76.

73 Jeffrey W. Bolster, *Black Jacks: African American Seamen in the Age of Sail* (Cambridge, MA: Harvard University Press, 1997); Martha Putney, *Black*

Sailors: *Afro-American Merchant Seamen and Whalemen prior to the Civil War* (New York: Greenwood Press, 1987).

74 Putney, *Black Sailors*, pp. 98–100.

75 Briton Cooper Busch, 'Cape Verdeans in the American Whaling and Sealing Industry', *The American Neptune* 45:2 (1985), 103–16 (p. 110).

76 Stehberg, *Arqueología histórica antártica*; Rubén L. Stehberg and Víctor Lucero, 'Arqueología histórica de la Isla Desolación: Evidencias de coexistencia entre cazadores de lobo de origen europeo y aborígenes del extremo sur americano, en la segunda década del siglo pasado', *Serie científica del Instituto Antártico Chileno* 45 (1985), 67–88.

77 Salerno *et al.*, 'Inside or outside Capitalism?', p. 162; Salerno *et al.*, 'The First Antarctic Laborers', p. 414.

78 María Jimena Cruz, 'Memórias de um mundo congelado: A indústria lobeira e as experiências antárticas no século XIX' (PhD thesis, Universidade Federal de Minas Gerais, 2019); Salerno, 'Persona y cuerpo-vestido en la modernidad'; Salerno *et al.*, 'Inside or outside Capitalism?'; Zarankin and Senatore, *Historias de un pasado en blanco.*

79 Stackpole, *The Voyage of the Huron and the Huntress*, p. 9; Stehberg, *Arqueología histórica antártica*, p. 46.

80 Melisa A. Salerno and María Jimena Cruz, 'Between Words and Oceans: Logbooks and the Antarctic Sealing Industry', presentation, SCAR SC-HASS Conference, 'Antarctic Connections at the End of the World: Understanding the Past and Shaping the Future', Ushuaia, 3–5 April 2019; Melisa A. Salerno and María Jimena Cruz, 'Logbooks and Antarctic Sealing: Approaching Early- and Late-19th-Century Exploitation Strategies and their Archaeological Footprint', *Polar Record* 59 (2023), 1–18.

81 Secretariat SCAR, 'Composite Gazetteer of Antarctica, Scientific Committee on Antarctic Research: GCMD Metadata', 2014, http://gcmd.nasa.gov/records/SCAR_Gazetteer.html (accessed 15 May 2022).

82 Secretariat SCAR, 'Composite Gazetteer of Antarctica'.

83 Salerno and Cruz, 'Between Words and Oceans'; Salerno and Cruz, 'Logbooks and Antarctic Sealing'.

84 Zarankin *et al.*, *Antarctic Archaeology*, p. 113.

85 Stephen W. Silliman, 'Culture Contact or Colonialism? Challenges in the Archaeology of Native North America', *American Antiquity* 70:1 (2005), 55–74.

86 Judith Butler, *Bodies that Matter: On the Discursive Limits of 'Sex'* (New York: Routledge, 1993).

87 Marcelo Mayorga, *Pieles, tabaco y quillangos: Relaciones entre loberos angloestadounidenses y aborígenes australes en la Patagonia (1780–1850)* (Santiago: Ediciones de la Subdirección de Investigación, 2020).

Bibliography

Alonso, Pedro, Ignacio Partarrieu Garcia and Arturo Scheidegger. 'Antarctica: Dead Reckoning'. *ARQ* 83 (2013): 16–25.

Andrade Lima, Tania. 'O papel da arqueologia historica no mundo civilizado'. In *Arqueologia da sociedade moderna na América do Sul: Cultura material, discursos y práticas*, ed. Andrés Zarankin and María Ximena Senatore, pp. 117–27. Buenos Aires: Ediciones del Tridente, 2002.

Balch, Edwin S. *Antarctica*. Philadelphia, PA: Press of Allen, Lane & Scott, 1902.

Basberg, Bjorn L. and Robert K. Headland. *The 19th Century Antarctic Sealing Industry: Source, Data and Economic Significance*. Bergen: Institutt for Samfunnsøkonomi, 2008.

Beaudry, Mary. 'Above Vulgar Economy: The Intersection of Historical Archaeology and Microhistory in Writing Archaeological Biographies of Two New England Merchants'. In *Small Worlds: Method, Meaning and Narratives in Microhistory*, ed. James F. Brooks, Christopher DeCorse and John Walton, pp. 173–98. Santa Fe, NM: School for Advanced Research Press, 2008.

Bertrand, Kenneth. J. *Americans in Antarctica, 1775–1948*. Burlington, VT: Lane Press, 1971.

Bolster, W. Jeffrey. *Black Jacks: African American Seamen in the Age of Sail*. Cambridge, MA: Harvard University Press, 1997.

Brazelli, Nicoletta. 'Heroic and Post-Colonial Antarctic Narratives'. In *Handbook on the Politics of Antarctica*, ed. Klaus J. Dodds, Alan D. Hemmings and Peder Roberts, pp. 69–83. Cheltenham: Edward Elgar Publishing, 2017.

Burbank, Jane and Frederick Cooper. *Empires in World History: Power and the Politics of Difference*. Princeton, NJ: Princeton University Press, 2010.

Burton, Robert. 'From Shoes to Shawls: Utilization of "South Seas" Fur Seal Pelts in Late 18th and Early 19th Century England'. In *Historical Antarctic Sealing Industry: Proceedings of an International Conference in Cambridge*, ed. Robert K. Headland, pp. 87–93. Cambridge: Scott Polar Research Institute, 2018.

Busch, Briton Cooper. *The War against the Seals: A History of the North American Seal Fishery*. Kingston: McGill-Queen's University Press, 1985.

Busch, Briton Cooper. 'Cape Verdeans in the American Whaling and Sealing Industry'. *The American Neptune 45*, no. 2 (1985): 103–16.

Butler, Judith. *Bodies that Matter: On the Discursive Limits of 'Sex'*. New York: Routledge, 1993.

Caviglia, Sergio. *Malvinas: Soberanía, memoria y justicia*. Vol. II. *Balleneros, loberos, misioneros, S. XVIII–XIX*. Rawson: Ministerio de Educación de la Provincia de Chubut, 2015.

Council of Managers of National Antarctic Programs [COMNAP]. *Antarctic Station Catalogue*. New Zealand: COMNAP, 2017.

Croucher, Sarah and Lindsay Weiss. 'The Archaeology of Capitalism in Colonial Contexts: An Introduction. Provincializing Historical Archaeology'. In *The Archaeology of Capitalism in Colonial Contexts: Postcolonial Historical Archaeologies*, ed. Sarah Croucher and Lindsay Weiss, pp. 1–37. New York: Springer, 2011.

Cruz, María Jimena. 'Memórias de um mundo congelado: A indústria lobeira e as experiências antárticas no século XIX'. PhD thesis. Universidade Federal de Minas Gerais, 2019.

Dellino-Musgrave, Virginia. *Maritime Archaeology and Social Relations: British Action in the Southern Hemisphere*. New York: Springer, 2006.

Dickinson, Anthony B. 'A History of Sealing in the Falkland Islands and Dependencies, 1764–1972'. PhD thesis. University of Cambridge, 1987.

Dodds, Klaus J. 'Post-Colonial Antarctica: An Emerging Engagement'. *Polar Record* 42, no. 1 (2006): 59–70.

Dodds, Klaus J. and Christy Collis. 'Post-Colonial Antarctica'. In *Handbook on the Politics of Antarctica*, ed. Klaus J. Dodds, Alan D. Hemmings and Peder Roberts, pp. 50–68. Cheltenham: Edward Elgar Publishing, 2017.

Funari, Pedro P., Siân Jones and Martin Hall. 'Introduction: Archaeology in History'. In *Historical Archaeology: Back from the Edge*, ed. Pedro P. Funari, Martin Hall and Siân Jones, pp. 1–20. London: Routledge, 1999.

Galloway, Patricia. 'Material Culture and Text: Exploring the Spaces within and Between'. In *Historical Archaeology*, ed. Martin Hall and Stephen W. Silliman, pp. 42–64. Malden, MA: Blackwell, 2006.

Glasberg, Elena. *Antarctica as Cultural Critique: The Gendered Politics of Scientific Exploration and Climate Change*. New York: Palgrave Macmillan, 2012.

Gosden, Chris. *Archaeology and Colonialism: Cultural Contact from 5000 BC to the Present*. Cambridge: Cambridge University Press, 2004.

Gould, Rupert T. 'The Charting of the South Shetlands, 1819–28'. *Mariner's Mirror* 27, no. 3 (1941): 206–42.

Hains, Brigid. *The Ice and the Inland: Mawson, Flynn and the Myth of the Frontier*. Victoria: Melbourne University Press, 2002.

Headland, Robert K. *A Chronology of Antarctic Exploration: A Synopsis of Events and Activities from the Earliest Times until the International Polar Years, 2007–09*. London: Quaritch, 2009.

Howkins, Adrian. 'Appropriating Space: Antarctic Imperialism and the Mentality of Settler Colonialism'. In *Making Settler Colonial Space*, ed. Tracey Banivanua Mar and Penelope Edmonds, pp. 29–52. London: Palgrave Macmillan, 2010.

Jackson, Andrew. *Who Saved Antarctica? The Heroic Era of Antarctic Diplomacy*. Cham: Palgrave Macmillan, 2021.

Johnson, Matthew. *An Archaeology of Capitalism*. Oxford: Blackwell, 1996.

Lawrence, Susan (ed.). *Archaeologies of the British: Explorations of Identity in Great Britain and Its Colonies, 1600–1945*. Abingdon: Routledge, 2003.

Leane, Elizabeth. *Antarctica in Fiction: Imaginative Narratives of the Far South*. Cambridge: Cambridge University Press, 2012.

Leone, Mark. 'Setting Some Terms for Historical Archaeologies of Capitalism'. In *Historical Archaeologies of Capitalism*, ed. Mark Leone and Parker B. Potter Jr, pp. 3–20. New York: Kluwer Academic/Plenum Publishers, 1999.

LiPuma, Edward. *Encompassing Others: The Magic of Modernity in Melanesia*. Ann Arbor: University of Michigan Press, 2002.

Maddison, Ben. *Class and Colonialism in Antarctic Exploration, 1750–1920*. London: Pickering and Chatto, 2014.

Mancilla, Alejandra. 'Decolonising Antarctica'. In *Philosophies of Polar Law*, ed. Dawid Bunikowski and Alan D. Hemmings, pp. 49–61. Abingddon: Routledge, 2020.

Mancilla, Alejandra. 'South American Claims in Antarctica: Colonial, *Malgré Tout*'. *The Polar Journal* 12, no. 1 (2022): 22–41. DOI: 10.1080/2154896X.2022.2062558.

Matthews, Christopher. 'Context and Interpretation: An Archaeology of Cultural Production'. *International Journal of Historical Archaeology* 3 (1999): 261–82.

Mayorga, Marcelo. 'Actividad lobera temprana en la Patagonia Oriental: Caza de mamíferos marinos'. *RIVAR* 4, no. 11 (2017): 31–51.

Mayorga, Marcelo. *Pieles, tabaco y quillangos: Relaciones entre loberos angloesta-dounidenses y aborígenes australes en la Patagonia (1780–1850)*. Santiago: Ediciones de la Subdirección de Investigación, 2020.

Mill, Hugh Robert (ed.). *Report of the Sixth International Geographical Congress*. London: John Murray, 1896.

Mrozowski, Stephen A. 'Imagining an Archaeology of the Future: Capitalism and Colonialism Past and Present'. *International Journal of Historical Archaeology* 18 (2014): 340–60. DOI: 10.1007/s10761-014-0261-6.

Orser, Charles. *A Historical Archaeology of the Modern World*. New York: Plenum Press, 1996.

Pearson, Michael. 'Charting the Sealing Islands of the Southern Ocean'. *Journal of the Australian and New Zealand Map Society* 80 (2016): 33–56.

Pearson, Michael and Melisa A. Salerno. 'Stateless Heritage: The Sealing Sites of the South Shetland Islands, Antarctica'. In *Yearbook of Transnational History*, Vol. VI, ed. Barry L. Stiefel and Shelley-Anne Peleg, pp. 195–222. London: Fairleigh Dickinson University Press, 2023.

Putney, Martha. *Black Sailors: Afro-American Merchant Seamen and Whalemen prior to the Civil War*. New York: Greenwood Press, 1987.

Resende de Assis, Luís Guilherme. 'A proa pressentida: Táticas oceanográficas para atravessar a duração e avistar baleias no Estreito de Gerlache, Península Antártica'. PhD thesis. Universidade Federal de Santa Catarina, 2019.

Roberts, Peder. 'The Politics of Early Occupation'. In *Handbook on the Politics of Antarctica*, ed. Klaus J. Dodds, Alan D. Hemmings and Peder Roberts, pp. 318–32. Cheltenham: Edward Elgar Publishing, 2017.

Roberts, Peder. 'The Union of Hunting and Research'. In *The European Antarctic Science and Strategy in Scandinavia and the British Empire*, ed. Peder Roberts, pp. 53–76. New York: Palgrave Macmillan, 2011.

Rowlands, Michael J. 'The Archaeology of Colonialism: In Social Transformations'. In *Archaeology: Global and Local Perspectives*, ed. Kristian Kristiansen and Michael J. Rowlands, pp. 327–33. London: Routledge, 1998.

Salerno, Melisa A. 'Persona y cuerpo-vestido en la modernidad: Un enfoque arque-ológico'. PhD thesis. Universidad de Buenos Aires, 2011.

Salerno, Melisa A. and María Jimena Cruz. 'Between Words and Oceans: Logbooks and the Antarctic Sealing Industry'. Presentation at the SCAR SC-HASS Biennal Conference, 'Antarctic Connections at the End of the World: Understanding the Past and Shaping the Future', Ushuaia, 3–5 April 2019.

Salerno, Melisa A. and María Jimena Cruz. 'Logbooks and Antarctic Sealing: Approaching Early- and Late-19th-Century Exploitation Strategies and their Archaeological Footprint'. *Polar Record* 59 (2023): 1–18.

Salerno, Melisa A. and Andrés Zarankin. 'En busca de las experiencias perdi-das: Arqueología del encuentro entre los loberos y las Islas Shetland del Sur (Antártida, siglo XIX)'. *Vestigios: Revista Latino-Americana de Arqueologia Histórica* 8, no. 1 (2014): 131–57.

Salerno, Melisa A., María Jimena Cruz, Romina Rigone and Andrés Zarankin. 'Making Visible the Invisible: Discussing Heterogeneity among Sealing Groups on the South Shetland Islands'. Presentation at the SCAR SC-HASS Biennial Conference, Kobe, 18–19 November 2021.

Salerno, Melisa A., María Jimena Cruz and Andrés Zarankin. 'The First Antarctic Laborers'. In *The Cambridge History of the Polar Regions*, ed.

Adrian Howkins and Peder Roberts, pp. 407–29. Cambridge: Cambridge University Press, 2023.

Salerno, Melisa A., María Jimena Cruz and Andrés Zarankin. 'Inside or outside Capitalism? Sealers' Lives, Food, and Clothing onboard Sealing Vessels and on Antarctic Hunting Grounds'. In *Historical Archaeology of Shadow and Intimate Economies*, ed. James Nyman, Kevin Fogle and Mary Beaudry, pp. 158–77. Gainesville: University Press of Florida, 2019.

Salerno, Melisa A., Romina Rigone and Andrés Zarankin. 'Explorando bitácoras: Aproximaciones al accionar de loberos y balleneros en Tierra del Fuego durante el siglo XIX'. Presentation at VII Congreso Nacional de Arqueología Histórica, Rosario, 22–6 October 2018.

Seag, Morgan. *There Was No 'First Woman': The Historical Politics of Gender, Science, and Exploration in Twentieth-Century US Antarctic Fieldwork*. PhD thesis. University of Cambridge, 2021.

Secretariat SCAR. 'Composite Gazetteer of Antarctica, Scientific Committee on Antarctic Research: GCMD Metadata', 2014. http://gcmd.nasa.gov/records/SCAR_Gazetteer.html. Accessed 15 May 2022.

Senatore, María Ximena and Andrés Zarankin. 'Arqueología histórica y expansión capitalista: Prácticas cotidianas y grupos operarios en Peninsula Byers, Isla Livingston de las Shatland del Sur'. In *Sed non satiata: Teoria social en la arqueología latinoamericana contemporánea*, ed. Andrés Zarankin and Felix Acuto, pp. 171–88. Buenos Aires: Ediciones del Tridente, 1999.

Silliman, Stephen W. 'Colonialism in Historical Archaeology: A Review of Issues and Perspectives'. In *The Routledge Handbook of Global Historical Archaeology*, ed. Charles E. Orser, Andrés Zarankin, Pedro P. Funari, Susan Lawrence and James Symonds, pp. 41–60. Abingdon: Routledge, 2020.

Silliman, Stephen W. 'Culture Contact or Colonialism? Challenges in the Archaeology of Native North America'. *American Antiquity* 70, no. 1 (2005): 55–74.

Smith, Ian W. G. *The New Zealand Sealing Industry: History, Archaeology and Heritage Management*. Wellington: Department of Conservation, 2002.

Stackpole, Edouard A. *The Voyage of the Huron and the Huntress: The American Sealers and the Discovery of the Continent of Antarctica*. Mystic: Marine Historical Association, 1955.

Stehberg, Rubén L. *Arqueología histórica antártica: Aborígenes sudamericanos en los mares subantárticos en el siglo XIX*. Santiago: Centro de Investigaciones Diego Barros Arana, 2003.

Stehberg, Rubén L. and Víctor Lucero. 'Arqueología histórica de la Isla Desolación: Evidencias de coexistencia entre cazadores de lobo de origen europeo y aborígenes del extremo sur americano, en la segunda década del siglo pasado'. *Serie científica del Instituto Antártico Chileno* 45 (1985): 67–88.

Stein, Gil J. 'Colonies without Colonialism: A Trade Diaspora Model of Fourth Millennium B.C. Mesopotamian Enclaves in Anatolia'. In *The Archaeology of Colonialism*, ed. C. L. Lyons and J. K. Papadopoulos, pp. 26–64. Los Angeles: Getty Research Institute, 2002.

Stevens, Thomas A. *The First American Sealers in the Antarctic, 1812–1819 and the First Voyage of the Brig 'Hersilia' of Stonington, Connecticut, 1819–1820*. Deep River, CT: US Department of State, 1954.

Wehi, Priscilla M., Nigel J. Scott, Jacinta Beckwith *et al.* 'A Short Scan of Māori Journeys to Antarctica'. *Journal of the Royal Society of New Zealand* 52, no. 5 (2021): 587–98.

Zarankin, Andrés and Melisa A. Salerno. 'Antarctic Archaeology: Discussing the History of the Southernmost End of the World'. In *The Oxford Handbook of Historical Archaeology*, ed. James Symonds and Vesa-Pekka Herva. Oxford: Oxford University Press, 2017. https://academic.oup.com/edited-volume/34744/chapter-abstract/296571813?redirectedFrom=fulltext. Accessed 11 March 2024.

Zarankin, Andrés and Melisa A. Salerno. ' "So Far, So Close": Approaching Experience in the Study of the Encounter between Sealers and the South Shetland Islands (Antarctica, Nineteenth Century)'. In *Antarctica and the Humanities*, ed. Peder Roberts, Lize-Marié van der Watt and Adrian Howkins, pp. 79–103. London: Palgrave Macmillan, 2016.

Zarankin, Andrés and Melisa A. Salerno. 'The "Wild" Continent? Some Discussions on the Anthropocene in Antarctica'. *Journal of Contemporary Archaeology* 1, no. 1 (2014): 114–18.

Zarankin, Andrés and María Ximena Senatore. 'Archaeology in Antarctica: Nineteenth-Century Capitalism Expansion Strategies'. *International Journal of Historical Archaeology* 9, no. 1 (2005): 43–56.

Zarankin, Andrés and María Ximena Senatore. *Historias de un pasado en blanco: Arqueología histórica antártica*. Belo Horizonte: Argumentum, 2007.

Zarankin, Andrés and María Ximena Senatore. 'Storytelling, Big Fish y arqueologia: Repensando o caso da Antartida'. In *Tempos ancestrais*, ed. Walter F. Morales and Flavia Moi, pp. 281–301. São Paulo: Annablume, 2013.

Zarankin, Andrés, Sarah Hissa, Melisa A. Salerno *et al.* 'Paisagens em branco: Arqueologia e antropologia antárticas – avanços e desafios.' *Vestígios: Revista Latino-Americana de Arqueología Histórica* 5, no. 2 (2011): 9–51.

Zarankin, Andrés, Michael Pearson and Melisa A. Salerno. *Antarctic Archaeology*. London: Routledge, 2023.

Zarankin, Andrés, Melisa A. Salerno and Adrian Howkins. 'From the Antarctic to New England: Remembrance of Sealing and Sealers'. In *Historical Antarctic Sealing Industry: Proceedings of an International Conference in Cambridge*, ed. Robert K. Headland, pp. 107–19. Cambridge: Scott Polar Research Institute, 2018.

9

Animals, colonialism and Antarctica

Peder Roberts and Kati Lindström

Managing people and managing animals have often gone hand in hand within colonial regimes. Caribou in Canada, tigers in India and other examples all speak to a concern for exercising authority over people by exercising authority over animals.[1] The disruption by colonial invaders of existing relationships between animals and Indigenous peoples may fairly be considered part of the wider colonial project of restructuring power relations in the image of the coloniser. Indeed, human–animal relationships could help actually to produce colonialism.[2] But can this dynamic be produced without a subject human population?

There are two possible positive answers to this question. The first is to argue that in the absence of human subjects, animals could be mobilised as ersatz subjects over which humans could exercise dominion. While we suggest that the evidence for this is questionable, the recurring tendency of humans to present charismatic Antarctic fauna – i.e. penguins – as Antarctica's inhabitants might still reveal something about how the thought processes employed by those humans were shaped by colonialism. This leads to the second argument, which takes as its premise the observation that Antarctica has been explored, settled and studied within the context of colonialism. Does this necessarily mean that the treatment of its animals can be considered 'colonial' in a meaningful sense? If the conquest of the Antarctic environment has been described in colonial terms (in the discussion around the Question of Antarctica in the United Nations, for example), does that automatically mean that colonialism is at play?

We begin by discussing imperialism, colonialism and Antarctica as related to animals. This includes discussion of the role of capitalism, which is often (rightly) regarded as allied to colonialism, but which we do not believe is itself necessarily an indicator of colonialism. Following this we offer some concrete examples and question whether these human–animal relations can be characterised either as colonial or as acts of colonialism. This involves reflection on whether the absence of Indigenous human presence in Antarctica created special conditions for rethinking colonial encounters, in addition to the status of Antarctic fauna as both inhabitants and resources. This final aspect became particularly salient in the 1980s when Greenpeace dressed its activists as penguins in order to advance arguments for a World Park and the abandonment of the Convention on the Regulation of Antarctic Mineral Resource Activities (CRAMRA). We conclude by reflecting on some of the larger consequences of these questions, in particular the relationship between capitalism and colonialism and the potential risks of broadening the explanatory category of colonialism to include Antarctica.

Colonialism, animals and Antarctica

The concept of treating exotic (to Europeans) animals unethically is often considered part of a colonial mindset. This is particularly true in the Arctic, where the gaze of the disinterested wildlife biologist has been characterised as part of a colonial structure, the knowledge that underpins the biologist's certainty being a branch of the same tree that legitimised colonial ways of regulating both animals and peoples.[3] Important distinctions exist also between the places that animals hold in Indigenous cultures and in the extractive logic of capitalism that defined how states and companies viewed Arctic fauna (particularly those rich in oil or with fine pelts). The argument might be taken further by locating the roots of extractive harvesting of animals in colonialism. The same drive to subjugate people and reorder social and economic relationships to the benefit of the coloniser informed attitudes toward animals – an argument also recapitulated in the Arctic, where the relations between Indigenous peoples and the animals on which they rely can often stand in contrast to the relationships between commercial hunters and their quarry.

We follow in broad terms the argument that the nineteenth-century discovery of Antarctica, and the exploitation of its fur seals and elephant seals, took place in the context of the global capitalist system.[4] Ben Maddison argues that Antarctic explorers such as James Clark Ross depended on the infrastructures of colonial empire both to justify their work (such as magnetic mapping) and to facilitate it (such as ports).[5] Animals could even become indices of how fit a country was to exercise power in Antarctica. Norwegian whaling entrepreneurs increasingly moved their operations to the high seas in the late 1920s, prompting accusations from Britain that by taking their operations out of territorial waters – and hence out of British control – the Norwegians were disavowing rational, cautious management in favour of atavistic slaughter.[6] The context was clearly imperial: Britain sought to extend its authority over the Antarctic continent and its seas, and argued that it was more fit than Norway to hold such authority by reference to its supposedly superior management of whales.

The reduction of the fur seals to economic units – pelts inconveniently attached to living beings – was fully in the spirit of capitalism. But we question whether whalers or sealers were always agents of colonialism, rather than capitalism. Whalers and sealers often kept their finds to themselves as privileged commercial information. Even into the twentieth century – when Antarctic territorial claims came into vogue – whalers could be headaches for states as well as assets, given that their goals did not always align (notably when the Norwegian government refrained from annexing Antarctic territory during the 1930s for fear of disturbing its bilateral relationship with Britain).[7] The islands that composed part of the habitats of the seals were relevant to the first sealers only inasmuch as it was there that the seals were found. The goal was not dispossession of territory, but rather the accumulation of capital through the extraction of resources. Even when Britain declared sovereignty over the islands and adjacent seas in which Antarctic whaling was booming in the early twentieth century, the aim was not to subjugate Indigenous residents, but rather to ensure that the wheels of capitalist extraction continued to roll efficiently.

Many species of seals and whales were hunted to a fraction of their former numbers, while thousands of seals and penguins were killed as food for both humans and their dogs. But whales and seals could never be civilised into a mimicry of colonising humans.[8] The structural power relations being configured were less between humans and whales and more between one group of humans and another, each of which sought to gain value from whales. Britain sought to control the whales because it wanted to position itself as superior to Norway, to ensure that the revenue from whaling did not end up in Norwegian or (perhaps even worse) German pockets. When biologist Sidney Harmer criticised his Norwegian counterpart Johan Hjort for being on the side of the whaler rather than the whale, his argument was less about granting autonomy to the whales over their lives in any meaningful sense and more about not killing the goose that laid the golden eggs (another metaphor that he used).[9] Certainly the situation reflected the structural power dynamic between Britain and Norway. Whether colonialism is the most appropriate or useful term is the more vexing question, in our view, given that the wider relationship between Britain and Norway in the early twentieth century has generally been described as one of a small state to a large state – moderated by additional factors such as multinational capital – but never of a colony to a colonial master.[10]

Could animals ever step in as the subjects of colonialism within such a structure? The 'unbridgeable gap between ruler and ruled' within colonialism described by Jürgen Osterhammel depends upon the reification of human cultural difference as fundamental.[11] Even his metaphor of a colonial society expanding beyond its original habitat does not imply that those for whom the habitat was natural could be other than human.[12] Frederick Cooper has stressed the importance of citizenship, and the practices that institutionalise structural inequality and discrimination. The attainment of equality becomes a matter of negotiation, which in turn is predicated upon political agency.[13] Can this be applied to animals?

The relationship between humans and Antarctic animals was long one of resource management and, in more recent years, of trusteeship – both of which could be achieved through science. This last point about trusteeship opens up another conceptualisation of a colonial relationship, given the use of that term to legitimise the rule of one group over another (notably under the auspices of the League of Nations).[14] But trusteeship under the mandate system was presumed to be a tutelary stage on the path to self-determination – a destination that seals and penguins can never reach.[15] Even theorists such as Sue Donaldson and Will Kymlicka, who have advocated for political rights for animals, regard non-domesticated animal communities as sovereign, and hence properly outside any process of integration within a shared human–animal political community.[16] The state of trusteeship implied by the instruments of the Antarctic Treaty System (ATS), notably the 1991 Protocol on Environmental Protection, must therefore be permanent rather than transient.

Might Antarctica be defined as a space in which colonialism has taken place – and not just a space in which actors with colonial mindsets have acted – if the sovereignty of those animal communities has been infringed? This is problematic, not least because despite their central goal of extending a human category (political rights such as citizenship and sovereignty) to animals, Donaldson and Kymlicka consider human sovereignty different from animal sovereignty, and the colonisation (their term) of animal communities by humans as fundamentally different from that of Indigenous by non-Indigenous peoples.[17] On the continent itself the rights of animal communities to be free from human interference remains contingent, overridden when humans decide that other activities (from the construction of infrastructure to the conduct of biological research) take priority.

Antarctica has seen relationships between humans and animals in which the animals are either mobilised as substitutes for subaltern humans or play other roles that may be identified with those of the colonial subject. Such a relationship might be discerned in ceremonies of possession, which enacted claims to authority over territory, but also over the newly subject people.[18] Maddison argues that the absence of a human population unsettled the colonial gaze when Europeans came to Antarctica because possession required dispossession. As evidence he points to the French officer Dubouzet on the D'Urville expedition (1839–40), who could at the same time assert that the French claim to Adélie Land had been 'a wholly pacific conquest' and describe penguins as being 'brutally dispossessed of the island, to which they were the sole inhabitants', with some of the birds being taken back to France.[19] Maddison similarly notes James Clark Ross's claim to authority over the appropriately named Possession Island without resistance from the penguins.[20] Mobilising animals as dispossessed inhabitants points to a need on the part of the explorer to exercise dominion over new territory through dominion over those encountered. Such ceremonies articulated the concerns of the newcomer even if they went entirely over the heads of those being colonised. The tradition of anthropomorphising penguins is a long one, as Stephen Martin has noted.[21] This makes perfect sense: groping for signs of the familiar, explorers may be forgiven for placing penguins into such a category.[22]

The dispossession of penguins thus enabled the theatrical performance of possession to achieve greater force. But the key word here is performance. Michael Robinson has contrasted the 'imperial theatre' of the Arctic with the more concrete imperialism associated with the exercise of power over territory, and we see merit in extending his analysis to Antarctica.[23] The emblematic example of a human–penguin encounter is the famous photograph of a member of the 1902–04 Scottish National Antarctic Expedition playing the bagpipes to a penguin (cover image to this book). The image raises a smile precisely because the penguin is *not* capable of being part of a reciprocal cultural encounter (unless it were to express its displeasure by pecking the piper, perhaps?) If Ross and D'Urville performed drama, the Scottish piper performed comedy, but they were both acts of theatre – the penguins props rather than actors. More commonly the penguins were regarded as irrelevant to questions of possession or negotiation – animals in their habitats rather than people in their homelands.

By far the longer tradition in Antarctica, as Martin notes, is to regard penguins as resources for science, sustenance and amusement. Douglas Mawson imagined the Antarctic south of Australia as a space filled with sanatoria and fox farms – which could draw upon local fauna for food. Brigid Hains has focused on the imperial dimension of Mawson's vision and drawn an intriguing parallel with the missionary John Flynn's vision of the Australian inland.[24] But ideologies of care premised upon the coloniser's superior authority could flourish in outback Australia in a way that they never could in Antarctica: the presence of native fauna could not be compared to the presence of Indigenous people. The structural racism that naturalised the inferior social and economic positions of Indigenous Australians did not preclude their being targets for either labour or religious conversion – members of a potential flock, similar to the Inuit. Such an option was clearly not applicable to the penguins.

Power through animals?

If they could not function as colonial subjects, we nevertheless recognise that the status of Antarctica as empty of people enhanced the value of animals as vehicles whereby power could be articulated through control. This could take the form of conservation, either over Antarctic spaces – such as Norway's banning fur seal harvesting near Bouvet Island in 1928 – or over other individuals and collectives, such as Britain's seeking to limit whaling on the high seas within the overall context of asserting its claim to superior moral authority.[25] Alternatively, using animals to claim authority over a territory could take the form of whaling and sealing from fixed stations, over which the declared sovereign power could exercise authority through inspections, regulations and other forms of policing activity. The common thread between both approaches was that it was less about the animals and more about the people who profited either from the harvesting itself or from the authority that its regulation evidenced.

Ultimately, then, through the first half of the twentieth century Antarctic animals continued to be viewed primarily as resources. Here it may be argued that the very act of placing animals in the category of resources is itself indicative of a colonial relationship, and that different ways of relating humans to animals outside such mental frameworks may be posited instead. To treat penguins as commodities to be slaughtered and studied was itself indicative of a colonialist mindset. We have sympathy with this view, but counter it in three interlinked ways, all of which acknowledge that extractive violence directed at Antarctic animals could be (and was) connected with colonialism without necessarily placing that violence in the same category as colonial violence against either people or animals elsewhere in the world.

First, we stress the importance of distinguishing between acts that recall colonialism and acts that constitute colonialism, because eliding the categories of the human and the non-human in this context risks evacuating colonialism of an essential meaning. Constructed hierarchies between different groups of humans underpinned colonialism and legitimised the violence (physical and otherwise) that was inherent within it. Scholars such as Rohan Deb Roy and Jonathan Saha have argued for a 'nonhuman empire' or 'interspecies empire' in which animals can be regarded as agents rather than simply incidental subjects.[26] While recognising the power of this approach in spaces such as British India, we see a difference between the co-constitution of human and animal subjects under colonialism and a scenario in which animals alone are the subjects. Echoes of violent dispossession might be discerned in the treatment of penguins, and their incorporation within schemes of extractive production of knowledge and capital, without necessarily equating the penguins with the human victims of colonialism.

The second is to return to our earlier point about the need to differentiate between capitalism and colonialism, and to keep in mind the importance to the latter of a subjugated Indigenous population. The extractive logic of capitalism that reduced whales to floating oil barrels could reinforce the extractive logic of colonialism without dictating that all forms of resource extraction constituted acts of colonialism. Had the Congo Free State been devoid of people we suspect that even the most violent and atavistic slaughter of its animals would not have attracted the label of colonialism: it was the brutal treatment of the people, and their violent subordination to King Leopold's economic goals, that defined this horrific episode.[27] Moreover, as the brutal history of Soviet whaling demonstrated, the logic of the command economy was no less disposed to violence against Antarctic animals – just as the Soviet state was no less disposed toward colonialism within its own eastern territorial borders, or over its satellites immediately to the west.[28]

The third concerns the absence of a human population for whom the acts of violence against animals enforced subjugation. There was no Antarctic population with pre-existing cultures that related differently to animals, like the Inuit in the Arctic. Nor were there local populations for whom the harvesting of seals, penguins or whales produced disadvantage through the withdrawal of either the resource itself or access to the territory in which that resource was located, as Indians were denied access to forests under British rule.[29] The class of actors recognised as disadvantaged by the Norwegian dominance of whaling comprised not whales, but other countries that felt they ought to get the same whales through the same methods for the same ends. There was no dispute that the whale was a floating oil barrel; the only question was who should get access to it. Consequently, arguments for the colonial character of power over such extractive activity work at the broader level of restricting access to others who might wish to partake, rather than a group whose pre-existing patterns of usage were terminated.

None of these points legitimises violence against Antarctic animals. That violence is real, from the decimation of fur seals and whales to the killing of large numbers of penguins and seals to feed humans and their dogs. We feel it is entirely possible to condemn this violence, to locate its roots in the logic of extractive accumulation and to note that many of those who participated did so within the context of European imperialism. Our objection is rather that violence and dispossession of humans under colonialism are sufficiently different from violence and dispossession of penguins for the term colonialism potentially to be inappropriate. A more interesting question, in our view, is whether the overarching structures of colonialism sufficiently informed human actions in Antarctica to justify a view of the continent as inflected by colonialism – to the point where it too might be considered in need of decolonisation.

Can Antarctic animals be decolonised?

The dual status of Indigenous peoples as counterparts in a cultural encounter and resources to be studied, moved and removed is well established. As mentioned above, we are unconvinced that the first part holds for Antarctic animals (or indeed for animals in general), at least within the worldviews that have been associated with European colonialism. Are there alternative constructions of the human–animal relationship that are unburdened by colonialism, and which could be relevant to Antarctica?

Many cultures have relationships with animals that are premised on cosmic affinity and mutuality in a relational space that foreclose the possibility of animals being regarded exclusively as resources. Nobu Shirase's Japanese expedition (1910–12) and several Indigenous members of other historic Antarctic expeditions came from non-western cultures, but their stay in Antarctica was nevertheless firmly embedded in the western colonial or imperial discourse. Unni Aas Sandholm has described the participation of Sami men Per Savio and Ole Must on his 1898–1900 Antarctic expedition, noting that Carsten Borchgrevink referred to the two men at one point as 'children of nature' (*naturbørn*) who he believed had developed an instinctive ability to find seals.[30] This strikes us as a classic case of othering in the sense articulated by Edward Said.[31] How Savio and Must related to the seals they encountered was not foregrounded. They were represented instead through Borchgrevink's exoticised contrast of reason with instinct, the western with the non-western, which could only ever locate the two men within a subordinate position as effective providers of seal meat to an expedition with goals he had defined as greater.

Priscilla Wehi and her colleagues have recently argued for the relevance of Māori perspectives to Antarctic environmental management, in particular a relational view of human–non-human relations that recasts animals as kin rather than simply resources.[32] This is a valuable correction to the Eurocentric assumptions that underpin Antarctic governance. But should this knowledge be accorded privileged status? While there is evidence for Māori visitation of sub-Antarctic regions, the relationship of Inuit, Sami, Dene and others to their Arctic homelands is much more direct and enduring than the relationship of the Māori to Antarctica. Wehi *et al.* make the stronger argument that the colonial nature of Aotearoa/New Zealand warrants redress in the form of including Māori perspectives, as part of the more general work of decolonising the state. This is a sound argument but one not specific to Antarctica, as its premise remains that the Aotearoa/New Zealand voice within Antarctic decision-making ought to represent the bicultural state, rather than asserting a privileged Indigenous relationship between Māori and Antarctica (and its fauna). We agree entirely with the authors in identifying 'western liberal bias' in Antarctic governance without describing it as 'colonial'.

Wehi *et al.* make another important point, albeit implicitly, that the animals of Antarctica are the subjects of a western gaze often emanating from settler colonial states, and that it is the responsibility of those doing the gazing to alter their own perspectives. Animals do not assert or negotiate such status themselves. In the past, Argentinians and Chileans attempted to grow trees on the Antarctic peninsula, and Richard Byrd brought dairy cows on his 1933–35 United States expedition to West Antarctica.[33] Like the history of pigsties and chicken coops on Svalbard, domestic animals were involuntary embodiments of a colonial imaginary.[34]

The ordering gaze can have restorative as well as extractive ambitions. It is widely accepted that the introduction of new species to the sub-Antarctic with humans has been highly regrettable, which has only strengthened a sense that animals in Antarctica proper ought to be carefully controlled. Perhaps the most telling case concerns the reindeer of South Georgia, introduced to provide familiarity and sport to the Norwegian managers of whaling stations on the island in the early twentieth century.[35] There is a cruel irony in their having settled and thrived, only to be exterminated between 2013 and 2014, when Britain decided to slaughter them all (over 2,500 animals) in the name of restoring a previous environment, a move that might also be read as an attempt to cleanse the national conscience by reversing the actions of their own predecessors. Zoologist Martin Collins, at the time fisheries director for the government of South Georgia, was quoted as saying 'I'm delighted that we'll be able to turn back the clock and return the place to what it used to be.'[36] Collins was obviously referring to the ecological state that prevailed before British rule. Yet we find ourselves thinking about animals and colonialism more generally. It proved much easier for Britain to erase the stain of earlier actions that took place on its watch, but which are now deemed wrong, when the corrective action involved slaughtering reindeer rather than reckoning with the legacies of structural discrimination against subjugated peoples. From this follows the question of justice. Postcolonialism is fundamentally a political as well as a scholarly project because it delineates and addresses the enduring violence of colonialism and, if not erasing the legacy of colonialism, then at least charting the contours of its ongoing presence. Recognising injustice is a prerequisite for attempting its remediation. Could the reindeer of South Georgia have been respected as animals with a right not to be exterminated in the name of management?

The ATS contains instruments that regulate human interactions with animals, most notably as a result of including the 1991 Protocol on Environmental Protection (widely known as the Madrid Protocol). Does the

Protocol, with its rigorous policing of who and what belongs (and does not belong) in Antarctica, constitute a form of restitution for past wrongs inflicted on Antarctic animals by guaranteeing their freedom from human intrusion in the future? We are sceptical because the Protocol places humans in an exempted category of animals that are permitted to be present in Antarctica despite not being indigenous to it. Humans have determined that the animals of Antarctica should be left alone, rather than the animals voicing that concern themselves, and it is humans who do the policing. (We might also note that exemptions remain for scientific study – which would most definitely not be acceptable for sovereign human communities.)[37] While arguments against killing Antarctic whales for oil or destroying penguin rookeries for research infrastructure are relatively uncontroversial, the animals have no capacity to voice alternative positions, including – more controversially – that they might sometimes enjoy human company.[38] In this regard we sympathise with Donaldson and Kymlicka's argument that considering wild animals as sovereign communities can force a rethink of the ethical foundations of their management 'through a process akin to decolonisation'.[39]

We might also consider the circumstances leading up to the Protocol's creation, in which a particular environmental group – Greenpeace – mobilised penguins as the charismatic representatives of Antarctica to contest the ongoing negotiations for a minerals regime. By examining the use of animals in a struggle that aligned (at least in part) with concerns that Antarctica's governance system was a vestige of imperialism, we ask whether the penguins were mobilised as actors in a struggle for their own decolonisation – and what this might reveal more broadly.

Greenpeace, penguins and the World Park

The environmental non-governmental organisation (NGO) Greenpeace was founded in 1971 in British Columbia, Canada, with an initial focus on stopping US nuclear tests at Amchitka in Alaska.[40] The organisation's name signalled a link between environmentalism and anti-militarisation that fitted its opposition to nuclear testing. But Greenpeace was not necessarily an anti-colonial organisation. Its campaign against French nuclear testing in the South Pacific during the 1980s aligned opposition to environmental destruction with anti-colonialism, focusing on French Polynesia. On the other hand, its opposition to the Canadian seal hunt was decried as colonial itself, an attempt by Europeans to impose their values on Indigenous communities that depended economically upon sealing.[41] This was the context in which Greenpeace began its campaign against CRAMRA and for an alternative that it described as the World Park.

Mineral resource extraction first surfaced at the 1970 Antarctic Treaty meeting in Tokyo, when the issue was tabled by New Zealand. The consultative parties were initially hesitant, as mineral extraction was deemed likely to destabilise the system by raising the issue of who constituted 'relevant authorities', but also because of the perceived imbalance between the consultative parties from the Global North and its members from the Global South (Argentina and Chile). Already, at this early stage, Japanese diplomats worried that developing countries might rise against the Antarctic Treaty (and its consultative parties) if the new minerals regime did not include a broader spectrum of the world's states. Closed but troubled negotiations continued through the 1970s. The group of consultative parties was increasing – Poland attained the status in 1977 – but slowly, and neither observers nor non-consultative parties were allowed to join the Special Antarctic Treaty Consultative Meetings (SATCMs) on minerals. As the mineral negotiations picked up speed after 1980, this unsurprisingly caused outrage among the countries left out. For NGOs such as Greenpeace or the Antarctica and Southern Ocean Coalition, the only options available to influence the negotiations were media campaigns, public protests and lobbying activity.

Malaysia and Antigua and Barbuda placed the 'Question of Antarctica' on the agenda of the United Nations General Assembly in 1983. Earlier that year, Malaysian president Mahathir Mohamad had addressed the Seventh Conference of the Heads of State or Government of the Non-Aligned Countries in New Delhi. After criticising interventions – from Vietnam in Kampuchea (later Cambodia) to the USSR in Afghanistan and South Africa in Namibia – he demanded that 'Antarctica, the last undeveloped continent on earth, should be regarded as a common heritage of mankind and not just the exclusive preserve of a few nations that have access to it.' Antarctica 'can, and must, pave the way for genuine international co-operation for the exploitation of its resources to ensure that the benefits would be equitably shared among all nations of the world'.[42] While the exact objections shifted as the situation developed and the CRAMRA negotiations advanced, the tone of the 'Question of Antarctica' discussion at the United Nations and outside was decidedly anti-colonial.[43] The ATS was criticised for its lack of transparency, accountability and democracy, and environmental protection of the continent was demanded beside equitable sharing of its resources. The UN General Assembly of 1985 strongly condemned the inclusion of the racist apartheid regime of South Africa at the Antarctic Treaty table, connecting the mineral resources and environmental protection agenda strongly to an anti-colonial discourse.

Greenpeace articulated its opposition to the ATS both through actions in Antarctica itself and through actions in the states from which Antarctic programmes were sent. The World Park that Greenpeace promoted was, as the name suggests, an alternative to the national park – an institution that has often been linked to colonial power structures, but which in this case could be cleanly presented as an alternative to both extractive industry and the governance of an international space by a select group of states.[44] Their repertoire included lobbying dinners with the delegates attending ATCMs, effective occupation and obstructions, as well as spectacular pranks such as delivering several tons of snow to the doorstep of the European Commission, and serious scientific environmental monitoring work, including scientific expeditions and a base in Antarctica. Their media presence and capacity to generate flashy news was impressive – including the use of penguins, which were ubiquitous in Greenpeace's Antarctic campaign, even if other species (whales) could sometimes figure, particularly in the context of Greenpeace's campaign against Japanese whaling. On the occasion of the important Antarctic Treaty meetings concerning minerals, the newsletter *ECO*, a joint publication of several environmental NGOs, was packed with images of penguins. At times they were depicted as graceful and tender animals, at times in cheeky cartoons making political claims or soliciting a chuckle with witty juxtapositions, and at times as suffering innocents.[45] Each set of representations showed the penguins as custodians for the environment, performing the role that Elizabeth Leane and Stephanie Pfennigwerth have described as 'synecdoches for pristine nature'.[46]

Outside Antarctica, Greenpeace frequently dressed its activists in penguin costumes. This included protests at negotiating sessions for what became CRAMRA, in addition to occasional direct actions in infrastructure related to Antarctic expeditions. As CRAMRA was about to fall apart, 200 penguin-clad activists delivered 2 million signatures in support of making Antarctica into a World Park to ATCM delegates in Bonn.[47] On the occasion of declaring Antarctica a World Park, Greenpeace transformed its headquarters in five world countries into Antarctic embassies. Human penguins arrived at the 'embassy' in Sweden in a limousine, conveniently performing the high-end snobbishness of white explorers in tuxedos while standing up for the oppressed and unprivileged.

Greenpeace also used penguin-costumed protesters in actions against the planned French airstrip at Adélie Land during the 1980s (see Figure 9.1). Controversial from the start, the airstrip would significantly interfere with penguin rookeries, a cost that French planners considered worthwhile given the logistical benefits.[48] Disruption to penguins from infrastructure was not a new phenomenon, but the sensibilities of the late 1980s were different from those of the 1950s. Greenpeace took direct action at the site of the airstrip in addition to staging protests in Europe. The airstrip was ultimately built

Figure 9.1 Greenpeace action calling for a World Park in Antarctica, London, 1 January 1989. Copyright Hawkes/Greenpeace.

despite these objections, only to be damaged substantially in a storm just after its completion in 1994 – at which point France gave up and abandoned the project.

The destruction of the penguin rookeries was an ideal subject for opposition because it positioned the French as aggressors committing violence against the rightful inhabitants of Antarctica. Yet the penguins could not speak for themselves or exert other forms of agency to disrupt the plans of the French. This is where Greenpeace stepped in and claimed to speak on behalf of Antarctica and its fauna, with the penguins mobilised as the charismatic representatives of the oppressed and the threatened. The actions of France may be considered both as manifestations of the state's long (and ongoing) history of colonialism and of the more general attitude of ATS signatory states to the territory over which they exercised authority. To blast the homes of penguins in order to construct an airstrip was an act of violence that rested easily with the mindset of a state that as recently as 1985 had bombed the Greenpeace ship *Rainbow Warrior* in Auckland Harbour to prevent its campaigning against French nuclear testing in the South Pacific, killing a photographer and attracting worldwide condemnation.[49] To mobilise penguins to speak against French designs in Antarctica was therefore to trade on their status as victims of a state with colonial baggage and imperial designs, the Indigenous inhabitants of the space France wished to change to their detriment.

The French choices, first to advocate for CRAMRA and then to construct the airstrip, both rested on the assumption that penguins lacked agency to resist. In mobilising resistance in the name of the penguins Greenpeace presumed to speak and to act for them. This again resonated with the longer tradition of Greenpeace's direct action on behalf of the environment, notably its anti-whaling campaigns, which resisted an extractive conception of whales as resources independent of any consideration of their right to live undisturbed. This position aligned with critiques of extractive capitalism, but not necessarily with a decolonising mindset, as Greenpeace centred the rights of whales independently of alternative relations with humans that could deny their status simply as resources while accepting their place as objects of hunting. To speak on behalf of the whales, as in Greenpeace's earlier claims to speak on behalf of Arctic seals, was to assert a privileged right to tell the world what those animals actually wanted – an assertion labelled as colonial in the case of Arctic seals.

Did this also apply to Antarctic penguins? The absence of Indigenous Antarctic communities, for whom the penguins could constitute part of a worldview premised on relationality rather than binary distinctions between the human and the non-human, was important, because it cleared the path for the dominant conception of Antarctic fauna as picturesque resources. To destroy a penguin rookery was not an act to be undertaken wantonly. But it could be justified, either to avoid starvation on the part of the humans (or their dogs) or to make space for infrastructure.

The actions of Greenpeace went further in that they mobilised penguins not as actors with their own voices to be heard and respected – a position that non-Indigenous defenders of the rights of Indigenous peoples have in recent years been at pains to take – but rather as actors in a play that Greenpeace directed.[50] Greenpeace was aware of the colonial dimension to the discussion around Antarctica and engaged the image of penguins, the ultimate symbol of Antarctica, skilfully in this discourse. When Greenpeace activists dressed as penguins they could claim to be acting on behalf of penguins – and as defenders of their rights – but they could not escape their own positionality, and the conventions that defined how a penguin should perform within this human (indeed western) play.

Malaysia and other states contested the club-like nature of the Treaty and its status as a hangover from the days of European imperialism. Yet their argument was not that Antarctica should be left to the penguins, but rather that the category of states who should have access to the resources (and intrude on the penguins) should be expanded. Greenpeace, on the other hand, was glad that for once they could advocate for environmental protection without entering into potential conflicts with Indigenous peoples, and considered environmental protection a universal value with priority over colonialism-related inequalities between human groups.[51] To give a concrete example, in Greenpeace's view a developing country's desire for access to marine protein could not be privileged over the capacity of the ecosystem.[52] Greenpeace's 1983 campaign strategy even foresaw 'educating' the non-Antarctic Treaty nations 'on the long term benefits to the world community of protecting the region'.[53] Surely if the Group of 77 had decided unanimously to mine Antarctica, this would have been an unobjectionable decision from the point of view of creating a new postcolonial world order. This is exactly the position that was taken, for example, by Japan, whose negotiating strategies for ATCM consistently described Antarctica as a 'common heritage of mankind' and a resource for fuelling and feeding the poor nations of the world in the future.[54] Ironically, Japan's position found no support from Greenpeace, who considered them the 'worst offenders', thus proving that the Antarctic environmental protection campaign remained by and large defined by the European, tacitly colonial view of nature as requiring management through the rational science of privileged states.

Does conflating Indigenous lands with penguin rookeries risk equating homelands to habitats? In the case of humans the objection is obvious, reducing Indigenous cultures to responses to environmental pressures. But we think it may also be problematic if the habitats of animals are characterised as homelands. Certain animals have attachments to specific places within the overall category of potential living spaces, particularly animals such as salmon or sea turtles, which return to particular locations to reproduce. But the claim of a sea turtle to a beach is no more exclusive than the claim of a salmon to a particular stream. If they are homes, they are open communes rather than gated estates. It may well be argued that such a view more closely reflects relational cosmologies, and we accept the point, along with the implication that the land theft taken as characteristic of settler colonialism cannot readily be broadened to include non-humans.

Conclusions

Antarctica is undoubtedly a space in which imperialism of the nineteenth-century European variety was dominant up to the signing of the Antarctic Treaty, and plausibly also afterwards, exemplified by the complaints of Malaysia and other states in the 1980s. This included claims to dominance over lands, seas, and the animals that inhabited the continent and its adjacent oceans. That authority persists to the present, thanks to the architecture of the ATS and in particular the Madrid Protocol, which enforce rigorous control over animals and place. Antarctica's native fauna are a privileged category here – but less because they are considered original inhabitants with sovereign rights, and more because they are original components of ecosystems that the Protocol deems it paramount to protect. The penguins did not reach the conclusion; humans from far away did, even if it aligns with what one would probably consider to be their natural interests (in preserving their right to live their lives undisturbed in their undisturbed habitats). The ATS is *for* Antarctica, not *by* Antarctica.

The case for colonialism having taken place in Antarctica remains problematic, in our view, because it requires an Indigenous human population to be subordinated. The absence of humans could lead to animals (particularly penguins) being enrolled in colonial theatre, and could prompt actions informed by the logic of extractive capitalism with its connections to colonial mindsets, the slaughter of whales and penguins being premised upon their categorisation as resources with no further layers of relationality to the humans who hunted them. But to categorise violence against animals unconnected to a colonised human population as colonialism stretches the meaning of colonialism as an analytical concept to breaking point. We acknowledge and deplore violence toward penguins without placing it in the same category as Australian denial of Indigenous presence, Canadian residential schools or the atrocities in King Leopold's Congo. Cruelty toward animals can surely be fought vigorously without its requiring the label of colonialism. In one sense the point is facile, but in another it is important, because although the processes of decolonisation that took place around the world in the second half of the twentieth century also affected Antarctica, the form it took was ultimately the intensification of human control over animals. The mobilisation of penguins by Greenpeace protesters was necessary because their protests could only ever be *for* the animals and not *by* them.

Here we come to our final point – that of the potentially colonial nature of human relations with Antarctic animals. Although there are no Indigenous human populations directly impacted by harms inflicted upon Antarctic animals, colonialism inflected the attitudes of many humans who engaged with Antarctic animals, and informed an underlying view of them solely as resources for either science, commerce or entertainment. Wehi *et al.* make an important intervention in stressing that different ways of thinking are possible based on relationality and kinship. We are not sure that this would decolonise relations with Antarctic animals. But the presence of such ways of thinking within Aotearoa/New Zealand Antarctic programmes more generally, and thus within the ATS as a whole, cannot be a bad thing.

Colonialism was never intended as a purely intellectual project. Grounded in the material realities of conquest and subjugation, its violent legacies echo into the present. The fundamental act of enforcing dominance over people could also involve dominance over animals. Acts of human dominion over animals might be regarded as infringements upon animal sovereignty – but even if the lands of those animals are also invaded, is the label of colonialism really appropriate? For a term that describes such concrete wrongs we find it a little uncomfortable to ponder its value in conceptual terms. But perhaps Antarctica is a good place to test its boundaries, to ask how the structural inequalities that mark human–animal relations might best be described, addressed – and perhaps eventually remedied.

Notes

1 See, amongst others, William Beinart and Lotte Hughes, *Environment and Empire* (Oxford: Oxford University Press, 2007); Roderick P. Neumann, *Imposing Wilderness: Struggles over Livelihood and Nature Preservation in Africa* (Berkeley: University of California Press, 1998); John Sandlos, *Hunters at the Margin: Native People and Wildlife Conservation in the Northwest Territories* (Vancouver: University of British Columbia Press, 2007); Bernhard Gissibl, *The Nature of German Imperialism: Conservation and the Politics of Wildlife in Colonial East Africa* (New York: Berghahn Books, 2016).

2 For a comprehensive and thoughtful overview, see the first chapter of Jonathan Saha, *Colonizing Animals: Interspecies Empire in Myanmar* (Cambridge: Cambridge University Press, 2022), pp. 28–50.

3 See, for example, Paul Nadasdy, *Hunters and Bureaucrats: Power, Knowledge, and Aboriginal–State Relations in the Southwest Yukon* (Vancouver: University of British Columbia Press, 2003); Peter Keith Kulchyski and Frank J. Tester, *Kiumajut (Talking Back): Game Management and Inuit Rights, 1900–70* (Vancouver: University of British Columbia Press, 2007).

4 Melisa A. Salerno, Jimena Cruz and Andrés Zarankin, 'A Historical Archaeology of the First Antarctic Labourers (Nineteenth Century)', in Adrian Howkins and Peder Roberts (eds), *The Cambridge History of the Polar Regions* (Cambridge: Cambridge University Press, 2023), pp. 407–29.

5 Ben Maddison, *Class and Colonialism in Antarctic Exploration, 1750–1920* (London: Pickering & Chatto, 2014).

6 Peder Roberts, *The European Antarctic: Science and Strategy in Scandinavia and the British Empire* (New York: Palgrave Macmillan, 2011), pp. 31–76.

7 Roberts, *The European Antarctic*, pp. 53–76.

8 On mimicry, see Homi Bhabha, 'Of Mimicry and Man: The Ambivalence of Colonial Discourse', *October* 28 (1984), 125–33.

9 On the complex history of whaling and Anglo-Norwegian relations in this period, see for instance D. Graham Burnett, *The Sounding of the Whale: Science*

and Cetaceans in the Twentieth Century (Chicago: University of Chicago Press, 2012); Roberts, *The European Antarctic.*

10　See, for instance, Pål Thonstad Sandvik and Espen Storli, 'Big Business and Small States: Unilever and Norway in the Interwar Years', *The Economic History Review* 66:1 (2013), 109–31; Patrick Salmon, *Scandinavia and the Great Powers 1890–1940* (Cambridge: Cambridge University Press, 1997); Kristin M. Haugevik, 'Status, Small Powers, and Significant Others: Re-Reading Norway's Attraction to Britain in the 20th Century', in Benjamin de Carvalho and Iver B. Neumann (eds), *Small State Status Seeking: Norway's Quest for International Standing* (Abingdon: Routledge, 2016), pp. 42–55.

11　Jürgen Osterhammel, *Colonialism: A Theoretical Overview* (Princeton, NJ: Markus Wiener Publishers, 2005), p. 58.

12　Osterhammel, *Colonialism*, p. 22.

13　Frederick Cooper, *Colonialism in Question: Theory, Knowledge, History* (Berkeley: University of California Press, 2005), particularly the first chapter.

14　See, for instance, Susan Pedersen, *The Guardians: The League of Nations and the Crisis of Empire* (Oxford: Oxford University Press, 2015).

15　We recognise that certain humans do not have the capacity to take decisions as persons for reasons such as cognitive impairment, and hence require permanent trusteeship arrangements, but this example does not strike us as analogous for making a case regarding colonialism.

16　Sue Donaldson and Will Kymlicka, *Zoopolis: A Political Theory of Animal Rights* (Oxford: Oxford University Press, 2011).

17　Donaldson and Kymlicka, *Zoopolis*, p. 14.

18　Patricia Seed, *Ceremonies of Possession in Europe's Conquest of the New World, 1492–1640* (Cambridge: Cambridge University Press, 1995).

19　Maddison, *Class and Colonialism*, p. 52.

20　Maddison, *Class and Colonialism*, p. 53.

21　Stephen Martin, *Penguin* (London: Reaktion, 2009).

22　Readers may also wonder if it is meaningful that the largest penguins in Antarctica bear the impressive name of 'emperor'. Perhaps, but such attributions of peak position to animals are not unique to the Antarctica: lions are the kings of the jungle, polar bears kings of the Arctic ice and so forth.

23　Michael F. Robinson, *The Coldest Crucible: Arctic Exploration and American Culture* (Chicago: University of Chicago Press, 2006), p. 107. See also the use of this concept in Alexandre Simon-Ekeland, 'Making French Polar Exploration: 1860s–1930s' (PhD thesis, University of Oslo, 2021).

24　Brigid Hains, *The Ice and the Inland: Mawson, Flynn and the Myth of the Frontier* (Carlton: Melbourne University Press, 2002).

25　This did not change with the advent of the Antarctic Treaty. During the 1960s Chile faced difficulties with the Agreed Measures for the Conservation of Antarctic Fauna and Flora (Recommendation III-8, 1964), because Section II-d included the term 'appropriate authority' and Chile could not accept the UK or Argentina issuing permits on the territory it claimed. The official approval of the Agreed Measures in Chile thus stalled, despite the fact that they considered these measures to be a result of their own scientific initiative. Archivo General Histórico, Ministerio de Relaciones Exteriores de Chile 89, 1968, instructions to the Chilean delegation for the Vth ATCM.

26 Saha, *Colonizing Animals*; Rohan Deb Roy, 'Nonhuman Empires', *Comparative Studies of South Asia, Africa and the Middle East* 35:1 (2015), 66–75.

27 On this dark episode, see most famously Adam Hochschild, *King Leopold's Ghost: A Story of Greed, Terror, and Heroism in Colonial Africa* (Boston, MA: Mariner, 1998).

28 Ryan Tucker Jones, *Red Leviathan: The Secret History of Soviet Whaling* (Chicago: University of Chicago Press, 2022). On Soviet extractive ambitions in Antarctica, see the chapter in this volume by Roman Khandozhko.

29 See for instance Ramachandra Guha, 'State Forestry and Conflict in British India', *Past & Present* 123 (May 1989), 141–77.

30 Unni Aas Sandholm, *Sydpolfarerne Per Savio og Ole Must: Liv i grenseland* (Brønnøysund: Temahefter Aas Sandhom, 2013), p. 59.

31 Edward Said, *Orientalism* (New York: Vintage Books, 1979).

32 Priscilla M. Wehi, Vincent van Uitregt, Nigel J. Scott *et al.*, 'Transforming Antarctic Management and Policy with an Indigenous Māori Lens', *Nature Ecology & Evolution* 5 (2021), 1055–9.

33 Pablo Fontana, *La pugna antártica: El conflicto por el sexto continente, 1939–1959* (Buenos Aires: Guazuvirá, 2014); Hugo Schmidt Prado, *¡Base O'Higgins sin novedad!*, 2nd edn (Santiago de Chile: Editorial La Noria, 1992 [1956]), p. 38; Elizabeth Leane and Hanne Nielsen, 'American Cows in Antarctica: Richard Byrd's Polar Dairy as Symbolic Settler Colonialism', *Journal of Colonialism and Colonial History* 18:2 (2017), DOI: 10.1353/cch.2017.0024. We have serious reservations about whether Antarctica can be considered a space for settler colonialism, given the utter dependence of its would-be human colonists on the states from which they came. This view follows Lorenzo Veracini's argument that settler colonialism is always a three-cornered relationship among settlers, Indigenous residents and the mother country – a relationship we do not see in Antarctica. Lorenzo Veracini, *Settler Colonialism: A Theoretical Overview* (New York: Palgrave Macmillan, 2010). For an alternative perspective, see the chapter by Alice Oates in this volume.

34 Elin Andreassen, Hein B. Bjerck and Bjørnar Olsen, *Persistent Memories: Pyramiden – A Soviet Mining Town in the High Arctic* (Totnes: Tapir Academic Press, 2010).

35 Nigel Leader-Williams, *Reindeer on South Georgia: The Ecology of an Introduced Population*, Studies in Polar Research (Cambridge: Cambridge University Press, 1988).

36 Quoted in Nancy Bazilchuk, 'Reining in Reindeer on South Georgia Island', *Frontiers in Ecology and the Environment* 11:4 (2013), 176.

37 Secretariat of the Antarctic Treaty, Protocol on Environmental Protection to the Antarctic Treaty, Annex II, Article 3 (Protection of Native Fauna and Flora), www.ats.aq/e/protocol.html (accessed 13 October 2023).

38 See, for instance, the cetacean studies described in Carl Safina, *Beyond Words: What Animals Think and Feel* (New York: Henry Holt, 2015), pp. 375–82.

39 Donaldson and Kymlicka, *Zoopolis*, p. 194.

40 On the history of Greenpeace, see Frank S. Zelko, *Make It a Green Peace! The Rise of Countercultural Environmentalism* (New York: Oxford University Press, 2013).

41 See the 2014 apology that Greenpeace Canada Executive Director Joanna Kerr posted on the organisation's website, which included a pledge 'to decolonize ourselves'. Joanna Kerr, 'Greenpeace Apology to Inuit for Seal Campaign', 24 June 2014 (accessed 18 September 2022).

42 Mochtar Kusumaatmadja, Mahathir bin Mohamad, S. Rajaratnam and Pham Van Dong, 'Statements by Heads of Delegations from Southeast Asian Countries at the Plenary Meeting of the Seventh Summit Conference of the Non-Aligned Countries in New Delhi, India, on 7–11 March 1983', *Contemporary Southeast Asia* 5:1 (1983), 117–49.

43 The concept of common heritage came from negotiations on the UN Convention on the Law of the Sea. While it has proven inapplicable in legal terms, advocates for a new Antarctic regime in the 1980s regarded it as an alternative foundational principle.

44 On national parks and colonialism, see for instance Bernhard Gissibl, Sabine Höhler and Patrick Kupper, *Civilizing Nature: National Parks in Global Historical Perspective* (New York: Berghahn Books, 2012).

45 These newsletters can be found in most governmental archives on Antarctica. A representative collection is International Institute of Social History, Greenpeace International (Amsterdam) Archives – ARCH02597 (hereafter IISH) 2267.

46 Elizabeth Leane and Stephanie Pfennigwerth, 'Marching on Thin Ice: The Politics of Penguin Films', in Carol Freeman, Elizabeth Leane and Yvette Watt (eds), *Considering Animals* (Abingdon: Routledge, 2011), pp. 29–40 (p. 30).

47 On the negotiations, see Andrew Jackson, *Who Saved Antarctica? The Heroic Age of Antarctic Diplomacy* (Cham: Palgrave Macmillan, 2021).

48 Janet Martin-Nielsen, *A Few Acres of Ice: Environment, Sovereignty, and Grandeur in the French Antarctic* (Ithaca, NY: Cornell University Press, 2023).

49 Michael King, *Death of the 'Rainbow Warrior'* (Auckland: Penguin, 1986).

50 For an example of one group that has consciously worked to address this issue, see Jens Dahl, *IWGIA: A History* (Copenhagen: International Work Group for Indigenous Affairs, 2009). This is not to question the dedication of the people involved in the campaign or that they could also hold anti-colonial views as individuals, nor to claim that it is impossible for science to know what penguins need or that humans should never represent the interests of the Antarctic environment in political and legal contexts.

51 IISH 2251, Mike Bossley, 'Greenpeace and Antarctica: A Personal View', March 1983.

52 IISH 2674, Amsterdam Antarctic Campaign meeting, 6–7 January 1986.

53 IISH 2689, Antarctic Campaign strategy, 13 May 1983.
54 See, for example, internal position papers for SATCM 4-2 in Wellington and SATCM IV-3 in Bonn in 1983; Diplomatic Archives of the Ministry of Foreign Affairs of Japan, 2014–390.

Bibliography

Archives consulted

Chilean Foreign Ministry, General Historical Archives.
International Institute of Social History, Greenpeace International (Amsterdam) Archives.
Japanese Foreign Ministry Diplomatic Archives, Special Antarctic Treaty Consultative Meetings.

Secondary sources

Andreassen, Elin, Hein B. Bjerck and Bjørnar Olsen. *Persistent Memories: Pyramiden – A Soviet Mining Town in the High Arctic*. Totnes: Tapir Academic Press, 2010.
Bazilchuk, Nancy. 'Reining in Reindeer on South Georgia Island'. *Frontiers in Ecology and the Environment* 11, no. 4 (2013): 176.
Beinart, William and Lotte Hughes. *Environment and Empire*. Oxford: Oxford University Press, 2007.
Bhabha, Homi. 'Of Mimicry and Man: The Ambivalence of Colonial Discourse'. *October* 28 (1984): 125–33.
Burnett, D. Graham. *The Sounding of the Whale: Science and Cetaceans in the Twentieth Century*. Chicago: University of Chicago Press, 2012.
Cooper, Frederick. *Colonialism in Question: Theory, Knowledge, History*. Berkeley: University of California Press, 2005.
Dahl, Jens. *IWGIA: A History*. Copenhagen: International Work Group for Indigenous Affairs, 2009.
Deb Roy, Rohan. 'Nonhuman Empires'. *Comparative Studies of South Asia, Africa and the Middle East* 35, no. 1 (2015): 66–75.
Donaldson, Sue and Will Kymlicka. *Zoopolis: A Political Theory of Animal Rights*. Oxford: Oxford University Press, 2011.
Fontana, Pablo. *La pugna antártica: El conflicto por el sexto continente, 1939–1959*. Buenos Aires: Guazuvirá, 2014.
Gissibl, Bernhard. *The Nature of German Imperialism: Conservation and the Politics of Wildlife in Colonial East Africa*. New York: Berghahn Books, 2016.
Gissibl, Bernhard, Sabine Höhler and Patrick Kupper. *Civilizing Nature: National Parks in Global Historical Perspective*. New York: Berghahn Books, 2012.
Guha, Ramachandra. 'State Forestry and Conflict in British India'. *Past & Present* 123 (May 1989): 141–77.
Hains, Brigid. *The Ice and the Inland: Mawson, Flynn and the Myth of the Frontier*. Carlton: Melbourne University Press, 2002.
Haugevik, Kristin M. 'Status, Small Powers, and Significant Others: Re-Reading Norway's Attraction to Britain in the 20th Century'. In *Small State Status*

Seeking: Norway's Quest for International Standing, ed. Benjamin de Carvalho and Iver B. Neumann, pp. 42–55. Abingdon: Routledge, 2016.

Hochschild, Adam. *King Leopold's Ghost: A Story of Greed, Terror, and Heroism in Colonial Africa*. Boston, MA: Mariner: 1998.

Jackson, Andrew. *Who Saved Antarctica? The Heroic Age of Antarctic Diplomacy*. Cham: Palgrave Macmillan, 2021.

Jones, Ryan Tucker. *Red Leviathan: The Secret History of Soviet Whaling*. Chicago: University of Chicago Press, 2022.

Kerr, Joanna. 'Greenpeace Apology to Inuit for Seal Campaign', 24 June 2014, www.greenpeace.org/canada/en/story/5473/greenpeace-apology-to-inuit-for-impacts-of-seal-campaign/ (accessed 18 September 2022).

King, Michael. *Death of the 'Rainbow Warrior'*. Auckland: Penguin, 1986.

Kulchyski, Peter Keith and Frank J. Tester. *Kiumajut (Talking Back): Game Management and Inuit Rights, 1900–70*. Vancouver: University of British Columbia Press, 2007.

Kusumaatmadja, Mochtar, Mahathir bin Mohamad, S. Rajaratnam and Pham Van Dong. 'Statements by Heads of Delegations from Southeast Asian Countries at the Plenary Meeting of the Seventh Summit Conference of the Non-Aligned Countries in New Delhi, India, on 7–11 March 1983'. *Contemporary Southeast Asia 5*, no. 1 (1983): 117–49.

Leader-Williams, Nigel. *Reindeer on South Georgia: The Ecology of an Introduced Population*. Studies in Polar Research. Cambridge: Cambridge University Press, 1988.

Leane, Elizabeth and Hanne Nielsen. 'American Cows in Antarctica: Richard Byrd's Polar Dairy as Symbolic Settler Colonialism'. *Journal of Colonialism and Colonial History* 18, no. 2 (2017). DOI: 10.1353/cch.2017.0024.

Leane, Elizabeth and Stephanie Pfennigwerth. 'Marching on Thin Ice: The Politics of Penguin Films'. In *Considering Animals*, ed. Carol Freeman, Elizabeth Leane and Yvette Watt, pp. 29–40. Abingdon: Routledge, 2011.

Maddison, Ben. *Class and Colonialism in Antarctic Exploration, 1750–1920*. London: Pickering & Chatto, 2014.

Martin, Stephen. *Penguin*. London: Reaktion, 2009.

Martin-Nielsen, Janet. *A Few Acres of Ice: Environment, Sovereignty, and Grandeur in the French Antarctic*. Ithaca, NY: Cornell University Press, 2023.

Nadasdy, Paul. *Hunters and Bureaucrats: Power, Knowledge, and Aboriginal–State Relations in the Southwest Yukon*. Vancouver: University of British Columbia Press, 2003.

Neumann, Roderick P. *Imposing Wilderness: Struggles over Livelihood and Nature Preservation in Africa*. Berkeley: University of California Press, 1998.

Osterhammel, Jürgen. *Colonialism: A Theoretical Overview*. Princeton, NJ: Markus Wiener Publishers, 2005.

Pedersen, Susan. *The Guardians: The League of Nations and the Crisis of Empire*. Oxford: Oxford University Press, 2015.

Roberts, Peder. *The European Antarctic: Science and Strategy in Scandinavia and the British Empire*. New York: Palgrave Macmillan, 2011.

Roberts, Peder and Lize-Marié van der Watt. 'An Environment Too Extreme? The Case of Bouvetøya'. In *Ice and Snow in the Cold War: Histories of Extreme Climatic Environments*, ed. Julia Herzberg, Christian Kehrt and Franziska Torma, pp. 163–88. New York: Berghahn Books, 2019.

Robinson, Michael F. *The Coldest Crucible: Arctic Exploration and American Culture*. Chicago: University of Chicago Press, 2006.

Safina, Carl. *Beyond Words: What Animals Think and Feel*. New York: Henry Holt, 2015.

Saha, Jonathan. *Colonizing Animals: Interspecies Empire in Myanmar*. Cambridge: Cambridge University Press, 2022.

Said, Edward. *Orientalism*. New York: Vintage Books, 1979.

Salerno, Melisa A., Jimena Cruz and Andrés Zarankin. 'A Historical Archaeology of the First Antarctic Labourers (Nineteenth Century)'. In *The Cambridge History of the Polar Regions*, ed. Adrian Howkins and Peder Roberts, pp. 407–29. Cambridge: Cambridge University Press, 2023.

Salmon, Patrick. *Scandinavia and the Great Powers 1890–1940*. Cambridge: Cambridge University Press, 1997.

Sandholm, Unni Aas. *Sydpolfarerne Per Savio og Ole Must: Liv i grenseland*. Brønnøysund: Temahefter Aas Sandholm, 2013.

Sandlos, John. *Hunters at the Margin: Native People and Wildlife Conservation in the Northwest Territories*. Vancouver: University of British Columbia Press, 2007.

Sandvik, Pål Thonstad and Espen Storli. 'Big Business and Small States: Unilever and Norway in the Interwar Years'. *The Economic History Review* 66, no. 1 (2013): 109–31.

Schmidt Prado, Hugo. *¡Base O'Higgins sin novedad!* 2nd edn. Santiago de Chile: Editorial La Noria, 1992 [1956].

Secretariat of the Antarctic Treaty, Protocol on Environmental Protection to the Antarctic Treaty. www.ats.aq/e/protocol.html. Accessed 13 October 2023.

Seed, Patricia. *Ceremonies of Possession in Europe's Conquest of the New World, 1492–1640*. Cambridge: Cambridge University Press, 1995.

Simon-Ekeland, Alexandre. 'Making French Polar Exploration: 1860s–1930s'. PhD thesis. University of Oslo, 2021.

Veracini, Lorenzo. *Settler Colonialism: A Theoretical Overview*. New York: Palgrave Macmillan, 2010.

Wehi, Priscilla M., Vincent van Uitregt, Nigel J. Scott *et al.* 'Transforming Antarctic Management and Policy with an Indigenous Māori Lens'. *Nature Ecology & Evolution* 5 (2021): 1055–9.

Zelko, Frank S. *Make It a Green Peace! The Rise of Countercultural Environmentalism*. New York: Oxford University Press, 2013.

10

Settler colonial mindsets at Halley research station, 1955–present

Alice E. Oates

It is no secret that Britain's Antarctic history is entangled with its colonial history. In the roughly 200 years since Antarctica was discovered, states, including Britain, have explored and made claims to Antarctic territories. They have mapped, traversed, raised flags on and built on Antarctica, declaring their presence and ownership to the world.[1] In 1919, Leopold Amery, Undersecretary at the British Colonial Office, argued that all of Antarctica should be under British rule.[2] '[T]he British Imperial Conference of 1926 [at which time Amery was Colonial Secretary] resolved that the entire Antarctic continent should become a possession of Britain and its dominions, New Zealand and Australia.'[3] States such as Britain have sought to occupy, own and use Antarctica.

In this chapter, I seek to follow those who argue that Antarctica's colonial past has continued into the present, but go a step further and argue that *settler* colonialism is the appropriate term.[4] I do so using original research about Halley station. Between July and November 2020, I conducted one-hour in-depth interviews with 18 individuals who had overwintered at Halley at various times between the 1960s and the present day. These interviews include scientists and operational staff, and reveal insights into how winterers see themselves, their station and their place in Antarctica. The interviews reveal a 'Halley identity', rooted in community, place and shared experience, demonstrating that Halley is specifically a *settled* colonial space, regardless of the presence or absence of colonial intentions among winterers.

Halley research station is a British Antarctic Survey (BAS) research station on the Brunt Ice Shelf on the coast of the Weddell Sea (see Map 10.1). It is the most remote British Antarctic station, established in 1956 by the Royal Society in preparation for the International Geophysical Year (IGY) of 1957–58, a global project of collaboration in geophysical sciences stretching from pole to pole. The IGY saw a massive increase in international scientific activity in Antarctica, and is seen as the point at which Antarctic science 'came of age'.[5] The Royal Society built and ran the base until the end of the IGY, handing it over to the Falkland Islands Dependencies Survey (FIDS)

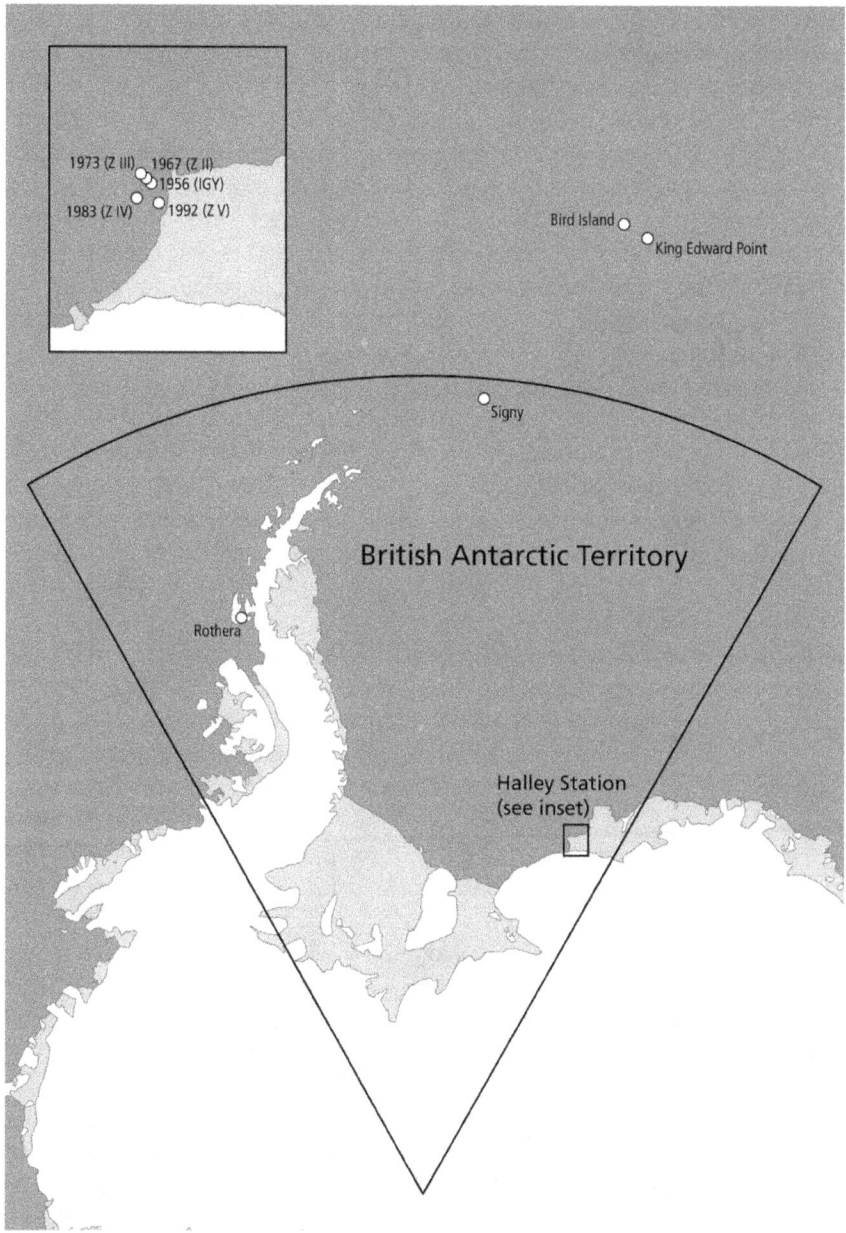

Map 10.1 Key locations mentioned in the chapter

in January 1959.[6] It has been continuously occupied ever since.[7] Halley's scientific portfolio primarily pertains to 'looking up', including meteorology and space weather. Halley's most widely known scientific discovery is that of the hole in the ozone layer, discovered by BAS scientists using records from Halley's Dobson Spectrophotometer.[8] Its origins in the IGY connect Halley to a fundamental turning point in Antarctic geopolitics, culminating in the signing of the Antarctic Treaty on 1 December 1959. Halley bridges the past and present of Antarctic science, connected to the colonial roots of Britain's Antarctic claim through its positioning in space, and to today's peace and science under the Antarctic Treaty by its positioning in time as an IGY station.[9]

In this chapter I argue three things: first, that Halley should be placed in the context of Britain's long and ongoing colonial relationship with the Antarctic continent; second, that stations operate as settlements, despite being scientific workplaces with temporary occupants; and finally, that Halley winterers perform settlement, despite their individually limited time on the ice, primarily in the literal and metaphorical *making* of space/home and the creation of a 'settler' identity at once connected to and independent from state agendas and geographies.

In doing so, I follow the work of Patricia Seed, Barbara Arneil and Cole Harris to build an understanding of how settler colonialism might operate in a continent with no Indigenous inhabitants or permanent settlers, contextualised by British approaches to land and colonisation elsewhere. For the Antarctic context I turn to Adrian Howkins. Howkins presents Antarctica as the 'highest phase' of settler colonialism, in which domination of space is the focus without the 'messy reality of having to rule over colonial peoples'.[10] The question of appropriation of space vs. dispossession of people in settler colonialism is discussed in detail later in this chapter.

The Antarctic context requires different terminology than one might use when discussing settler colonialism elsewhere. While scholars such as Seed commonly refer to colonial appropriation of *land*, I choose to use the word *space* instead for two reasons. First, states made territorial claims in Antarctica without knowing what they were claiming. The question of whether Antarctica was a single continent was part of the scientific profile of the IGY, so at the point Halley was built states were claiming unknown *space*, not known *land*.[11] Second, 'space' is the more appropriate term because of the specific method of delineating claims in Antarctica. Territorial claims in Antarctica worked on the basis of the sector principle, originating in the colonisation of the Canadian Arctic.[12] There, territorial claims were made on a wedge of space between two meridian lines (usually with a northern limit of 60° south and a southern limit of the South Pole) on the basis of having discovered or occupied part of that space.[13] The word 'space' points to states' method of making sweeping claims in Antarctica. The British were first to apply the sector principle to make a claim to Antarctica.[14]

The presence of winterers in Antarctica, and the ways they shape their environment and render it knowable, are central to the idea of Antarctica as a settler colonial space, and the year-round presence of people has historically been one major way in which states defended their sovereign claims, maintaining the right today to a seat at the table in Antarctic governance.[15]

The structure of this chapter is as follows. First, I demonstrate how space and land were at the heart of Britain's colonisation of North America. Second, I use that idea in combination with work from Antarctic scholarship and settler colonial studies to build a conception of settler colonialism driven by domination of space, not people. Third, I apply this to Antarctica to argue that research stations are an expression of this form of settler colonialism. Finally, I explore how interviews with winterers at Halley station evoke mentalities of settler colonialism in the form of a 'Halley identity'.

British colonial philosophies and the question of land

This chapter focuses on the British Antarctic context because the British colonialism discussed here has historically had a philosophy of land and colonisation distinct from that of other colonising European nations.[16] While the practices and mindsets described later in the chapter invoke more of an 'Antarctican' identity than a specifically British one, Halley is a British station, and the context of British colonial practices is relevant. This is central to enabling a conception of settler colonialism founded on appropriation of space, not dispossession of people, as I will demonstrate in the following sections.[17]

In Patricia Seed's work on 'ceremonies of possession' she differentiates the practices of European states in their approach to colonisation of the New World in the seventeenth century. Seed outlines how Europeans' understandings of what constituted a valid ceremony of possession, and a valid basis for the proclamation of colonial rule, were rooted in specific linguistic, cultural, legal and historical norms. For the English, these ceremonies consisted largely of 'employing architectural objects and everyday agricultural activity'.[18] In New England, English settlers claimed spaces by building homes on them, a crucial first step to creating and demonstrating stability and permanence. Once the house was built, the next task was to enclose the surrounding land and plant a garden. Settlers 'improved' land by building fences, claiming land for agricultural or pastoral use.[19] Fences and gardens, so mundane and insignificant to other states, were crucial to English possession of the New World. Other European states had their own ceremonies of possession, resulting in frequent clashes, and the views of Indigenous people were not considered relevant by any.[20]

Understanding this approach to colonisation requires touching on John Locke's *Two Treatises of Government*.[21] Locke was writing at a time when England, among other European states, was concerned with justifying appropriation of land in America. Locke was heavily influenced by his patron, Anthony Ashley Cooper, the Earl of Shaftesbury – zealous colonialist and Lord Proprietor of Carolina – so his work must be understood in the context of a drive to rationalise and justify the English right to possess North America and dispossess its people.[22]

To Locke, the right to possess land derived explicitly from God's command that man must subdue and fill the earth (Genesis 1:28). Locke concludes that it is *labour* that provides the right to land. Indigenous people had no right to possess land because they 'wasted' it and had more than they could make use of. This focus on land and labour is where he differs from other thinkers of the time, justifying colonialism not only as God's will, 'but because each colonist has a natural right within himself, through his labour, to appropriate land'.[23]

Thus, it becomes clear that the English approach to colonisation centred on land and its cultivation through European agrarian labour and 'improvement'. Land and labour form the foundation of English colonial thought, from the specifically English use of manure to 'improve' the land to influential seventeenth-century thinkers and their justification of land appropriation.[24] In the following section, I will draw on scholars from settler colonial studies to argue that settler colonialism can be defined by appropriation of space, tracing that Lockean tradition into present-day Antarctica.

Defining settler colonialism without dispossession

To discuss Antarctica as a settler colonial space, it is necessary to say why the term applies at all. The simplest definition is to say that settler colonialism occurs when members of the colonial state settle in the colonised state. Lorenzo Veracini defines 'settler colonial phenomena' as 'circumstances where colonisers "come to stay" and to establish new political orders for themselves'.[25] It implies permanence, the making of a life in a place that was already home to someone else. On the surface, none of this is true of Antarctica. However, I am not seeking to argue that Antarctica is a settler colony. I argue that stations are settlements, blurring the line between work and home, containing everything from scientific equipment to spaces for relaxation or religious worship. Winterers engage in home-making and place-making practices that persist beyond their individually temporary time on the continent. In any other context a place where people live, eat, work, sleep, even play, could be considered a settlement.[26]

The absence of Indigenous people is the complicating factor. Definitions of settler colonialism within settler colonial studies often involve dispossession of Indigenous peoples. Scott L. Morgensen states that ' "settler" literally signifies the displacement of Indigenous peoples'.[27] Anne Bonds and Joshua Inwood argue that settler colonialism is distinct from colonialism, as 'settler colonialism focuses on the permanent occupation of a territory and removal of indigenous peoples with the express purpose of building an ethnically distinct national community'.[28] Harris refers to settler colonialism as 'that form of colonialism associated with immigrants who became the dominant population in the territories they occupied, and in so doing, displaced the Indigenous peoples who previously had lived there'.[29] In these accounts, dispossession of the Indigenous population of colonised lands is central to the definition of settler colonialism, which would make it inapplicable in Antarctica.

However, this is only one possible definition. Appropriation of space through settlement should be considered central to the operation of British settler colonialism. Although Harris frequently refers to dispossession of people as central, he also argues that 'colonialism and colonisation were about the control of land'.[30] This control was exercised first by making knowable, and then by making use of land, in order to construct a European colonial geography of the colonised space. Settler colonialism may occur on uninhabited land as it does in inhabited space. That a place is inhabited upon 'discovery' by a colonial power, and the subsequent dispossession of those inhabitants, is contingent, not necessary, for settler colonialism to have occurred.

First, colonisers had to understand the space before they could dispossess its original occupants. They had to 'arrange and order the land in terms that Europeans could understand', using 'explorers' reports and maps' to 'possess spaces they hardly knew'.[31] The exercise of mapping and reconfiguring space connects to the English preoccupation with space and land discussed earlier in this chapter. Scholars such as Harris and Elya L. Milner view relations to land and property as central in settler colonialism.[32] In this conception of settler colonialism, the primary impact is the overwriting of existing geographies with new, settler-defined geographies – physical, human and imaginative. Milner views settler colonialism as a 'geographical replacement', in which the colonial project makes land productive according to western norms.[33] Where Europeans went, space became reconfigured in European terms and marked with names and material expressions of ownership.[34]

However, while I argue that the dispossession of Indigenous people is not a necessary theoretical component of settler colonialism, there is a fundamental material difference. It must be made clear that there is no equivalence between colonial contexts where Indigenous peoples have met with violence and oppression for decades, and the Antarctic where there is no human presence. Penguins are not equivalent to people, and possession through science is not equivalent to possession through violent human *dis*possession. To argue otherwise would be to dismiss the past and current experiences of Indigenous communities living with the ongoing impacts of colonialism on their lives.

Settler colonialism in Antarctica

I now turn to the operation of settler colonialism in Antarctica. To assume that Britain did not approach Antarctica in the same way it approached other continents, with a view to colonising and claiming space, would be to speak to an unhelpful form of Antarctic exceptionalism. While the Antarctic context is unique in environment and mode of settlement, it is still the same state – even the same Colonial Office – that lies behind Britain's Antarctic activities. Antarctic science is unquestionably of global value, and the work done at Antarctic stations makes crucial contributions to the study of Antarctica, its place in global systems and other science for which Antarctica is an ideal laboratory. However, there is also political value in having boots on the ice, a visible and unquestionable signal that the host state has invested in Antarctica and has a place there.

Antarctic governance today has been shaped by states such as Britain that have a position of prominence because of their colonial wealth and power from outside Antarctica, and a history of colonial expansion and exploration in Antarctica. Their economic and political motivations should be appropriately contextualised by their pasts in Antarctica and elsewhere. Antarctica is geographically, not geopolitically, isolated. The naturalising of claimant states' privileged position in the Antarctic Treaty System obscures the reasons they were there in the first place, and how those reasons continue to affect the future of Antarctica.

Presenting Antarctic claims as colonial is not a new idea. Writing in 1986, Benedetto Conforti argued that decolonisation would be an appropriate modern principle to apply to the 'old question' of Antarctic territorial claims. He acknowledges that Antarctica is different from other colonial contexts in having no subjugation of Indigenous people, but argues that:

> For several reasons, however, the spirit of territorial claims is clearly a colonial one. First, the claimed areas are far from the homeland. Second, no affinity exists between the claimant states and the claimed territories. Third, no substantial reason exists for asserting national jurisdiction in Antarctica other than prestige and appropriation of natural resources.[35]

Klaus J. Dodds also recognises that the lack of Indigenous people makes Antarctica an unusual context for this kind of analysis, but argues that a critical engagement with colonialism is still possible and necessary despite this absence.[36] The same story described by Harris in North America, of Europeans mapping and making-knowable a space, is true of Antarctica.[37] Claimant states mapped, named and built on the Antarctic in order to claim it and create their own geographies of the continent. In Britain, this work was done by the FIDS.[38]

Mancilla explores the moral element of Antarctic claims, speaking directly to the question of why it is necessary to discuss colonialism and territorial claims in contemporary Antarctica.[39] She argues that 'it is important for these [claimant] countries and their people to have a clearer picture of the foundations that support their claims, and to evaluate them candidly'.[40] Mancilla also identifies 'moral wrongs' in the way that claimant states have engaged with Antarctica:

> [t]he overwhelming and hoarding acquisition of space for economic and strategic reasons (white space); the unequal terms in which the [Antarctic Treaty] was drafted and negotiated, and under which it is maintained (*carte blanche*), and the cloak of innocence under which this was performed (white adventure).[41]

I am also not the first to view research stations as key spaces where Antarctic colonialism is expressed, where broad claims to swathes of territory are maintained by the concrete presence of people and infrastructure. Collis explicitly refers to Australia's Mawson station as a colony, and to the men who built it as colonists.[42] As already discussed, Howkins refers specifically to settler colonialism in Antarctica in his work, arguing that 'people approached the barren, inhospitable continent of Antarctica with a desire to possess, to colonise and to appropriate space'.[43]

Antarctic history is colonial history, and there are moral reasons to investigate the colonial aspects of contemporary Antarctica, but Conforti's colonial situation is not necessarily a *settler* colonial situation. I argue that settler colonialism is the appropriate term here because of the permanence of the bases and the blurring of work and home within them. These scientific 'colonies' are settled, are homes – permanent, albeit unusual among settler colonies for being populated by impermanent inhabitants. And, through the work discussed in the previous section, I have shown that the lack of dispossessed Indigenous people does not preclude Antarctica from being a settler colonial space. Although Bonds and Inwood include dispossession in their definition of settler colonialism, they also include the 'permanent occupation of a territory'. The British state's 'settlement' of the Brunt Ice Shelf has persisted since 1956, despite the transience of specific people, and even specific buildings.

Overall, I would agree with Howkins when he says that while Antarctica's settler colonialism 'could not be wholly derivative of a settler colonial mentality produced elsewhere', Antarctica, 'with its incredibly hostile environment, produced an ideal form of settler colonialism based purely on space'.[44] In summary, British activity in Antarctica is linked to its colonial past and motivations, expressed through permanent occupation, via use of infrastructure that, through the place-making practices of winterers, becomes a settlement. Thus, *settler* colonialism. The British state is not unique in this but is one example of how settler colonialism operates in Antarctica.

I now depart from Howkins's approach – in which the focus on space 'unsettles the assumed centrality of settlers themselves' by recentring the 'settler' winterers – by seeking to understand their experiences of place-making in their own words.[45] In doing so I contribute to scholarship that seeks to connect Antarctica with broader geopolitical processes – beyond 60° south – and scholarship concerned with the micro-level of Antarctic life.

Settler colonialism in practice: Identities and experiences on a research station

In this section I apply these broad principles – of settler colonialism centred on possession of space, and of British Antarctic activity as an expression of that settler colonialism – to the specific context of Halley station.

Halley was established at a key moment in Antarctic history. Halley's position as part of the IGY places it at a turning point in Antarctic governance from (in highly simplistic terms) fights over sovereignty to peaceful international cooperation through the Antarctic Treaty. Halley has therefore been positioned by some, such as Dodds, as part of this 'sea change in British Antarctic policy', in direct contrast with the explicitly colonial activities of the FIDS (which was 'at the heart of imperial defence through its mapping and surveying activities'.[46]

However, it is undeniable that Halley was enmeshed in the same colonial context as any other station. The FIDS, which took over Halley in 1959, was administered by the Colonial Office. Halley's buildings were designed by the Crown Agents, who, according to 1957 Base Commander Joseph MacDowall, had 'become particularly adroit at designing anything for the special needs of the remotest corners of the British Empire'.[47] According to a *Daily Mail* article from 22 November 1955, entitled 'Antarctic Men Take Seed and Soil', the Advance Party took 'one hundredweight of good English potting compost' with them for growing flowers and vegetables, evoking the Lockean idea of 'improvement' described by Seed.[48] Base commanders were issued with instructions informing them that they and their parties would 'be subject to the Colonial Regulations, and the Operational Instructions of the Falkland Islands Dependencies Survey', a reminder that although Halley was a Royal Society base, British activity in Antarctica was firmly under the control of the Colonial Office.[49]

However, although this context is highly relevant, the agendas of the elite men of British Antarctic policy are not necessarily those of the people on the ice. Veracini argues that the settler colonial experience is defined by its transnational, translocal and transcultural characteristics.[50] Settlers experience a tension between 'home' and the settler colony, creating a dynamic relationship between identity and place in which the settler population is simultaneously becoming something new, and remaining 'true to itself in a place that is "other".'[51] I now turn to the settler experience, to how those transnational, translocal lives are expressed at Halley station. In supporting this approach, I draw on scholars from settler colonial studies who attend to the intimate and mundane details of settler life.

Eva Bischoff argues that settler colonial studies has leaned towards macro perspectives, taken from an analytical distance and focusing on theories and concepts.[52] Directing attention towards the micro-scale as well, i.e. individuals or social groups, she argues, enables scholars to gather a fuller picture of actors' roles and experiences, and how these contribute to the 'social and physical (re-)organisation of settler colonial space'.[53] Mark Rifkin also tackles the lives of settlers through 'settler common sense', and addresses how settlers 'renewed' and 'recreated' the structures of colonial governance in their everyday lives 'in ways that do not necessarily affirm settlement as an explicit set of imperatives/initiatives or coordinate with each other as a self-identical programme'.[54] Rifkin's work is particularly useful here, because I seek to argue that my interviewees displayed settler traits or mindsets, but not that they saw themselves as settlers, or were following some colonial agenda, although their presence was made possible partly by exactly such an agenda. My interviewees experienced Antarctica in their own way, according to their own personalities, goals and agendas, and I seek only to identify how that relates to broader questions raised here.

Attention to settler emotions and mundane everyday experiences can illuminate how state motives and actions become re-enacted and naturalised by settlers without them necessarily seeing themselves as colonisers, or as agents of the state. Settlers' actions and daily lives constitute the reality of how the colonial 'system' is expressed on the ground. Governments create physical and legal geographies that structure settlers' lives to a certain extent, but settlers interact with that structure in ways that may reproduce or unsettle it.[55] Attention to both the mundane and the geopolitical is necessary for a complete picture.

Part of this picture is settler identities. Bell talks about authenticity and identity in settler colonies, how 'as people become more mobile – geographically, but especially socially – so too their identities'.[56] Previously, Avril Bell argues, people depended on historical connections to place for identity and authenticity. Without this, not only were settler's identities in flux, but they also had to create new grounding points for 'authenticity', a characteristic attributed to Indigenous cultures by the same Europeans erasing those cultures. They also viewed this authenticity as mobile; as Indigenous people 'disappeared' from the landscape, settlers naturalised themselves, through real or imagined narratives such as adoption by tribes or arguing that settlers had become indigenised.[57]

Harris also considers how migration reconfigured people's lives and identities, as settlers created new places in Canada within which they 'situated their transplanted lives.'[58] While winterer lives are not 'transplanted' to the extent that Harris discusses, several of my interviewees talked about how their experiences shaped their lives post-Halley or how they maintained a connection to winterers past and present long after leaving the ice. The permanence of 'settlement' in Antarctica is therefore present in both the longevity of the station and the long-term effects of Halley on its inhabitants.

Where, in Antarctica, does Rifkin and Harris's sense of identity, of being an authentic 'Antarctican', come from? Halley winterers rarely had more than a year or two's experience on new arrivals, but my interviewees gave a sense of how quickly a person progresses from new and inexperienced to firmly 'in place', experienced and knowledgeable. This process, for one individual, took days or weeks, a very short period.[59] What happens over a winter to build that sense of belonging?

Living in Antarctica is always temporary, but at Halley so is the base itself. Halley is on its sixth iteration. Bases I–IV became buried in snow and were abandoned. Halley V, built on stilts, avoided burial but moved too close to the ice edge. Halley VI, the current station, is raised above the ice, and features skis in order to allow it to be moved. The name, and general location, remain consistent through the decades. Station members are geographically mobile, but also socially mobile because they winter with a different set of people every year, and then experience an influx of new people each summer. Without a stable place or community, the Halley 'identity' seemed to come from four things: a connection to people, past and present; a connection to place; a sense of being unique among Antarctic stations; and connection to a wider Antarctic community. This framework, applied to my interviews with winterers, illustrates how these traits are neither simply settler colonial, nor only a factor of life in the unique Antarctic environment, but a combination of the two: an Antarctic settler colonialism. This is not a specifically British experience, and this section will also explore how the 'Antarctican' identity transcends national identities and agendas.

Identity through community

> When you go south so much of your experience is based around the people that are there, because that's all there is ... you long to go back because of your fond memories. But then you get back and yes it still looks beautiful ... but it's different people and it's almost like it's not yours anymore.[60]

For winterers like this one, the people at Halley were a crucial grounding point for 'their' Halley, creating a sense of place that could not be recaptured. For others, material connections to past Halley winterers created a sense of community through time. Photos of winterers adorn the walls, and there is a memorial to people who have died while at Halley. Post-Halley, there is a kind of 'alumni' community through which people can stay connected and share and revisit stories from Halley.[61]

> Every year it's tradition that the wintering team has a year photo ... the corridors in the dining room at Halley V were covered in all these photos, all past wintering teams going, I mean, not just of Halley V but from the original Halley, so going back into the 1950s.[62]

The ritual of taking an annual photograph helps create a sense of place, and community. It is one of few material continuities between the many iterations of Halley. It's also notable that these are specifically *winterer* photos; summer staff are not given that privileged position in Halley history. With photos and memorials, Halley winterers write their history onto an empty, hostile space. This is a micro-level expression of a macro-level geopolitical trend, in which the British government has promoted the construction of a historical record of British presence in Antarctica, emphasising the longevity of its Antarctic engagement.[63] Similarly, in the Arctic, Richard C. Powell has shown how nation-building and scientific practices are intertwined at the Canadian Polar Continental Shelf Project, creating tension between the IGY vision of global scientific collaboration and persisting nationalism in polar field science.[64] In both instances, the experience of transient visitors to the station can affirm and/or complicate the projection of nationalist power into polar spaces.

Identity through place

Another material 'grounding point' for identity is the station itself. The station buildings are the only place of safety in a very hostile environment. They are home and workplace, where you are both protected and trapped, with little privacy from people you didn't choose and can't escape from. Practices of home-making that turn Halley into more than just a workplace evoke settler homesteading, and are driven by winterers themselves rather than the sponsoring state. Moments of transition between stations demonstrate the connection to place that some interviewees felt:

> It was quite sad actually having wintered at the old Halley V station, to see it the next year ... to see the rooms you'd spent so long in, and the kitchen you'd worked so long in, just kind of abandoned over the winter, and then to take it apart and package it all up for recycling, reuse, disposal.[65]

What is merely wood and metal to one person is layered with meaning for another. This echoes Alison Blunt and Robyn M. Dowling's conception of 'home' as '*both* a place/physical location *and* a set of feelings' (original emphasis).[66] Built forms, material cultures, and feelings of identity and belonging combine to make a place a 'home'.[67] Many of my interviewees had personally been involved in shaping the built environment of Halley, creating not only a scientific observatory but a home.

This was a point of pride for several interviewees, and another way for them to connect with the base and each other very quickly. This evokes a kind of settler homesteading mentality, linked to the historical prioritising of building homes and cultivating land described earlier in this chapter, and enabled winterers to have a sense of self-sufficiency despite being ultimately dependent on the Royal Society/FIDS/BAS. Some practices were polar-specific, and connected winterers to past ways of working in Antarctica, such as passing on the knowledge of how to repair polar equipment.

The ability to demonstrate or develop hands-on skills was often enjoyable as much as it could be a challenge. One winterer preferred to use the time off over midwinter working on projects to make the base more comfortable. He expressed considerable pride during the interview about the work he did building Halley III, in terms of both necessary elements and 'optional extras', such as making the bar into a unique and comfortable space: '[W]e could do most anything, if it was possible to do it we could do it. Very little help and with very little materials and things ... I think we all knew what we were going to do; you had to be self-sufficient at Halley because it is extremely isolated.'[68] One might assume that winterers arrive at fully functional stations and get on with science before returning home. Modern stations such as Halley VI do allow a degree of freedom from the kinds of work described here, but for much of Halley's history the work of winterers has been not only science, but the building and maintenance of their environment. This has been both work and pleasure for the people quoted here, providing challenge, a sense of ownership of their space, connections with past and present winterers, and joyful moments such as the giving of midwinter gifts. Making the base 'homely' was a question not just of preference, but of helping winterers cope with the psychological challenges of a winter in Antarctica. Much like settlers, Halley winterers apply official agendas in ways that write their own wants, needs and histories onto the space.

Identity through uniqueness

All Antarctic stations are remote; challenging to live at; and unique in their environment, the people and the work being done. Halley stands out because it is the most remote of British Antarctic stations and situated on a floating ice shelf. This means the surrounding environment is mostly flat ice, and it is cut off from the outside world in winter. This geographical setting, unique even among British Antarctic stations, was another source of pride for interviewees, particularly those who had experience of multiple stations. I asked one interviewee who had also spent time at Rothera how the two compared, and her answer demonstrated this particularly well:

> Halley was remote, it had much longer winter, we had no rocks ... no plant life, relatively little fauna; the odd penguin would come and visit us. Some of the gulls and petrels. [Rothera] was like a little paradise, lots more people. Much more busy. *It's not the real Antarctic* ... There was a hierarchy, Alice, let me tell you, *there was a hierarchy to this, and Halley was at the top.*[69]

A second interviewee repeated similar sentiments, saying 'once you'd done Halley, that was Antarctica'.[70] Halley's positioning as 'real Antarctica' is another grounding point for the Halley identity and sense of authenticity. However, the remoteness is not uncomplicated in its effects. Although many of my interviewees had very positive experiences at Halley, I am aware of the unspoken gaps of people who did not. Even those who enjoyed their time at Halley still recognised, in many cases, that the darkness, isolation and long months spent with the same few people were challenging. It could also be a kind of badge of honour, or an adventure that stayed with people after their time at Halley was over, influencing their later lives:

> On reflection I learnt lots of my strengths and weaknesses while I was base commander. And it's hard to determine if that's just the age I was at and if I would've been doing that in regular life or if it was some of the impact of the isolation and living in a small team at the time.[71]

This demonstrates that even while there is a sense of play about it – the Antarctic adventure, joking about 'real Antarctica' – the experience of wintering has lasting effects on people's lives, because it is genuinely hard going.

> Once you've done that, nothing fazes me. I'm not scared of anything any-more. You know, I've survived −53° temperatures, blowing a hooley [gale], I've abseiled down cliff faces, flown a plane ... to Rothera ... Nothing since then has fazed me or worried me at all.[72]

The isolated winter season always ended with the arrival of the relief ship at the start of the summer. In some instances, the 'Halley identity' was so well developed that these intrusions from the 'real world' were a difficult adjust-ment. One interviewee spoke strongly of the moment the ship returned, bringing new station members: 'I didn't like the invasion. And the base was invaded. Our home where we lived happily, just the 18 of us, it was invaded by 30 or 40 other people, all crammed in.'[73] He was not alone in finding the return to normal life a challenging adjustment.

Identity through shared experience

Antarctica 'cocoons' winterers from 'real life'.[74] This is a common experi-ence across Antarctic stations. Thus, despite the environmental specificity of Halley, the final aspect of the 'winterer identity' that stands out is how it becomes disconnected from the sponsoring state, and from dynamics 'back home', because of the common experience of wintering in Antarctica:

> The Argentines – it's all ex-military and you think to yourself they're going to be a bit standoff-ish, but they were all lovely, they were like us. Everyone was in the same boat ... to really cope with living in Antarctica, I had to kind of forget the UK, forget my family, forget the other world, and just fully focus myself on living in Antarctica and that became my world.[75]

In a unique, isolated continent completely inhospitable to permanent human settlement, winterers found comfort and identity in shared experience. Far from home, as described by Veracini and Harris, they adapted their new home and their senses of self to their new context, while in other ways holding on to an unchanged sense of self.[76] The 'Halley identity', built from connections to the physical space, other winterers, and the past and present Halley community, evokes settler mentalities in a space not traditionally associated with settler colonialism. The Colonial Office is long gone, but threads of Britain's colonial history have woven themselves inextricably into modern-day Antarctica.

Summary

In this chapter I have drawn together scholarship on settler colonialism, British colonial philosophy and Antarctic humanities to argue that settler colonialism is a relevant issue for understanding Antarctic history and politics. In the earlier sections I identified two potential barriers to this argument: Antarctic settlement does not involve dispossession of Indigenous people, and it is always temporary, with winterers returning to the 'real world' after a season or two.

I have demonstrated that Britain had a specific colonial philosophy centred on making use of land and creating domestic spaces, and that this lends itself to a conception of settler colonialism in which settlement of space is central, not dispossession. In Antarctica, with no Indigenous population, settler colonialism operates through and in service of domination of space. This is not unique to Britain, but is an important context for understanding Halley, a British station.

Regarding the issue of impermanence, I have argued that states permanently occupy Antarctica, which is made home – made settlement – by the practices of winterers and their identity as Antarcticans, creating a community that has permanence beyond the movements of individual members. Moreover, this is not settler colonialism in its whole form, but a settler *mentality* that enables us to find another way of understanding winterers' experiences. I have used interviews with winterers to explore this in practice at Halley research station, where people and place combine to create something that is both unique and connected to a wider Antarctic community.

Beyond the actions of individual winterers, settler colonialism provides a valuable lens for exploring the agendas shaping Antarctic science. Halley is a useful case study for this work. Today, the future of Halley VI station is uncertain. In 2012 BAS identified cracks in the Brunt Ice Shelf that threatened the safety of the station and its staff, with a further major crack identified in 2016, culminating in a major calving event in January 2023. Halley was relocated in a major operation in 2016/17, and became a summer-only station from 2017/18 onwards in recognition of the increased risk.[77]

Following the winter closure of Halley, BAS embarked on a project to automate Halley's core scientific programmes; approximately 90 per cent of Halley's scientific output has been successfully automated.[78] The advantages of automation mix uncomfortably with geopolitical priorities. The Foreign and Commonwealth Office requires BAS to maintain a presence in Antarctica, a requirement that became a particularly explicit part of BAS's mission in 2012, when a debate about a potential merger of BAS with the National Oceanographic Institute prompted scientists and politicians alike publicly to affirm the geopolitical value of BAS presence in Antarctica.[79] The post-2012 agenda prioritised 'boots on the ice' at the same time that ice shelf dynamics began to threaten Halley's ability to fulfil this role. Halley and its residents perform geopolitical, sovereignty-affirming work through their presence alone. Viewing this dynamic through the lens of settler colonialism adds a valuable new perspective to the important question of how, and why, states operate in the frozen continent, and what the future of Antarctic science will look like.

Notes

1　Priscilla M. Wehi, Nigel J. Scott, Jacinta Beckwith *et al.*, 'A Short Scan of Māori Journeys to Antarctica', *Journal of the Royal Society of New Zealand* 52:5 (2021), 587–98, contest this date. They use oral histories to argue that Māori first voyaged to Antarctica as early as the seventh century. The timespan of 200 years refers to the discovery of the continental land mass of Antarctica by Britain and Russia (the exact order has also been contested) in 1819/20.

2　Adrian Howkins, 'Appropriating Space: Antarctic Imperialism and the Mentality of Settler Colonialism', in Tracey Banivanua Mar and Penelope Edmonds (eds), *Making Settler Colonial Space* (London: Palgrave Macmillan, 2010), pp. 25–52.

3　Marcus Haward, 'The Originals: The Role and Influence of the Original Signatories to the Antarctic Treaty', in Klaus J. Dodds, Alan D. Hemmings and Peder Roberts (eds), *Handbook on the Politics of Antarctica* (Cheltenham: Edward Elgar Publishing, 2017), pp. 232–40 (p. 233).

4　Such as Klaus J. Dodds, 'Post-Colonial Antarctica: An Emerging Engagement', *Polar Record* 42:1 (2006), 59–70; and Alejandra Mancilla, 'A Continent of and for Whiteness? "White" Colonialism and the 1959 Antarctic Treaty', *Polar Record* 55:5 (2019), 317–19.

5　Adrian Howkins, 'Emerging from the Shadow of Science: Challenges and Opportunities for Antarctic History', in Peder Roberts, Lize-Marié van der Watt and Adrian Howkins (eds), *Antarctica and the Humanities* (London: Palgrave Macmillan, 2016), pp. 251–72 (p. 251).

6　The Falkland Islands Dependencies (FID) is the prior name for the British Antarctic Territory (BAT), referring to the area of Antarctica claimed by the British state. The BAT is a wedge-shaped area between the longitudes of 20° west and 80° west and running from 60° south to the South Pole. It was administered from the Falklands until 1989, when responsibility passed to the Commissioner of the British Antarctic Territory, and it became the BAT on 3 March 1962 (British Antarctic Territory, 'About the Territory', https://britishantarcticterritory.org.uk/about/about-the-territory/ (accessed

21 January 2023)). British activity in the FID was administered by the FIDS, with a remit to survey and map the FID (Klaus J. Dodds, 'Putting Maps in Their Place: The Demise of the Falkland Islands Dependency Survey and the Mapping of Antarctica', *Ecumene* 7:2 (2000), 176–210). The FIDS was renamed the British Antarctic Survey in 1962.

7 In 2017 Halley had to close in the winter because of a crack in the Brunt Ice Shelf. It is now a summer-only station, with key science programmes becoming automated to preserve long-term observation programmes.

8 Joseph C. Farman, Brian G. Gardiner and Jonathan D. Shanklin, 'Large Losses of Total Ozone in Antarctica Reveal Seasonal ClO_x/NO_x Interaction', *Nature* 315 (1985), 207–10.

9 It remains part of the BAS mission to maintain Britain's presence in Antarctica. Halley's existence and location – it is the only British station in East Antarctica – are part of supporting that mission. British Antarctic Survey, 'Vision and Mission', www.bas.ac.uk/about/about-bas/corporate-aims/ (accessed 24 February 2023).

10 Howkins, 'Appropriating Space', p. 31.

11 Sydney Chapman, 'Scientific Programme of the International Geophysical Year 1957–58', *Nature* 175 (1955), 402–6; Howkins, 'Appropriating Space'.

12 Oscar Svarlien, 'The Sector Principle in Law and Practice', *Polar Record* 10:66 (1960), 248–63. Donat Pharand, 'Canada's Arctic Jurisdiction in International Law', *Dalhousie Law Journal* 7:3 (1983), 315–42, notes that the sector principle was first *systematized* in 1907 by Senator Pascal Poirier to claim sovereignty over all islands north of Canada, but that the use of meridian lines to demarcate territorial claims predates 1907. The Soviet Union then applied the same principle in 1927. Pharand also notes that this 'sector theory' was not generally accepted as a valid legal basis for claims.

13 See Benedetto Conforti, 'Territorial Claims in Antarctica: A Modern Way to Deal with an Old Problem', *Cornell International Law Journal* 19:2 (1986), 249–58; Klaus J. Dodds, 'Governing Antarctica: Contemporary Challenges and the Enduring Legacy of the 1959 Antarctic Treaty', *Global Policy* 1:1 (2010), 108–15; Alejandra Mancilla, 'The Moral Limits of Territorial Claims in Antarctica', *Ethics & International Affairs* 32:3 (2018), 339–60; Janice Cavell, 'The Sector Theory and the Canadian Arctic, 1897–1970', *The International History Review* 41:6 (2019), 1168–93.

14 Svarlien, 'The Sector Principle'; Mancilla, 'The Moral Limits'.

15 The original 12 signatories to the Antarctic Treaty are countries that were active in Antarctica during the IGY and then accepted the invitation to attend the 1959 diplomatic conference in Washington at which the Treaty was negotiated. They are Argentina, Australia, Belgium, Chile, France, Japan, New Zealand, Norway, Russia (then the USSR), South Africa, the United Kingdom and the United States. A further 42 countries have acceded to the Treaty since. Article IX of the Antarctic Treaty allows states to become parties to the Treaty if they are 'conducting substantial scientific research activity there [in Antarctica], such as the establishment of a scientific station or the despatch of

a scientific expedition'. Secretariat of the Antarctic Treaty, Antarctic Treaty (1959), Article IX, available at www.ats.aq/e/antarctictreaty.html (accessed 16 January 2022).

16 Patricia Seed, *Ceremonies of Possession in Europe's Conquest of the New World* (Cambridge: Cambridge University Press, 1995).

17 I also recognise that the 'Antarctic experience' is not homogeneous, and as such do not make generalisations on the basis of interviews with members of a British station. An individual's experience will be shaped by a multitude of factors including their own identity, the location and duration of their stay in Antarctica, and the people and institutions around them.

18 Seed, *Ceremonies of Possession*, p. 14.

19 Seed, *Ceremonies of Possession*.

20 Seed, *Ceremonies of Possession*.

21 John Locke, *Two Treatises of Government* (London, 1689).

22 Barbara Arneil, *John Locke and America: The Defence of English Colonialism* (Oxford: Clarendon Press, 1996).

23 Arneil, *John Locke and America*, p. 166.

24 Seed, *Ceremonies of Possession*; Arneil, *John Locke and America*.

25 Lorenzo Veracini, ' "Settler Colonialism": Career of a Concept', *The Journal of Imperial and Commonwealth History* 41:2 (2013), 313–33 (p. 313).

26 There is a wide body of research exploring how research/field stations are more than workplaces. Examples include Richard C. Powell, *Studying Arctic Fields: Cultures, Practices and Environmental Sciences* (Ontario: McGill-Queen's University Press, 2017); Christy Collis, 'Cold Colonies: Antarctic Spatialities at Mawson and McMurdo Stations', *Cultural Geographies* 14:2 (2007), 234–54; Amy Donovan and Clive Oppenheimer, 'At the Mercy of the Mountain? Field Stations and the Culture of Volcanology', *Environment and Planning* 47:1 (2015), 156–71.

27 Scott L. Morgensen, 'The Biopolitics of Settler Colonialism: Right Here, Right Now', *Settler Colonial Studies* 1:1 (2011), 52–76 (p. 59).

28 Anne Bonds and Joshua Inwood, 'Beyond White Privilege: Geographies of White Supremacy and Settler Colonialism', *Progress in Human Geography* 40:6 (2016), 715–33 (p. 716).

29 Cole Harris, *A Bounded Land: Reflections on Settler Colonialism in Canada* (Vancouver: UBC Press, 2020), p. 3.

30 Harris, *A Bounded Land*, p. 177.

31 Harris, *A Bounded Land*, p. 25.

32 Cole Harris, *Making Native Space: Colonialism, Resistance and Reserves in British Columbia* (Vancouver: UBC Press, 2002); Elya L. Milner, 'Enacting Propriety: Property, Planning, and the Production of Settler Colonial Geographies', *Settler Colonial Studies* 10:2 (2020), 278–93.

33 Milner, 'Enacting Propriety', p. 279.

34 Harris, *A Bounded Land*.

35 Conforti, 'Territorial Claims in Antarctica', p. 257.

36 Dodds, 'Post-Colonial Antarctica'.

37 Harris, *A Bounded Land*; Harris, *Making Native Space*.
38 Dodds, 'Governing Antarctica'.
39 Mancilla, 'The Moral Limits'; Mancilla, 'A Continent of and for Whiteness?'.
40 Mancilla, 'The Moral Limits', p. 340.
41 Mancilla, 'A Continent of and for Whiteness?', p. 317.
42 Christy Collis, 'Mawson and Mirnyy Stations: The Spatiality of the Australian Antarctic Territory, 1954–61', *Australian Geographer* 38:2 (2007), 215–31.
43 Howkins, 'Appropriating Space', p. 48.
44 Howkins, 'Appropriating Space', p. 48.
45 Howkins, 'Appropriating Space', p. 48.
46 Klaus J. Dodds, *Pink Ice: Britain and the South Atlantic Empire* (London: I.B. Tauris, 2002), pp. 85, 15.
47 Joseph MacDowall, *On Floating Ice* (Lancaster: Carnegie House, 1999), p. 9.
48 'Antarctic Men Take Seed and Soil', *Daily Mail*, 22 November 1955, London, Royal Society, EXP/11/1/1/269; Seed, *Ceremonies of Possession*.
49 Instructions to Joseph MacDowall on his appointment as Halley Base Commander, 1957, London, Royal Society, EXP/11/1/1/251.
50 Veracini, 'Settler Colonialism'.
51 Veracini, 'Settler Colonialism', p. 314.
52 Eva Bischoff, 'Experiences, Actors, Spaces: Dimensions of Settler Colonialism in Transnational Perspective', *Settler Colonial Studies* 7:2 (2017), 135–40.
53 Bischoff, 'Experiences, Actors, Spaces', p. 136.
54 Mark Rifkin, 'Settler Common Sense', *Settler Colonial Studies* 3:4 (2013), 322–40.
55 Rifkin, 'Settler Common Sense'.
56 Avril Bell, *Relating Indigenous and Settler Identities: Beyond Domination* (New York: Palgrave Macmillan, 2014), p. 26.
57 Bell, *Relating Indigenous and Settler Identities*.
58 Harris, *A Bounded Land*, p. 146.
59 Base commander/meteorologist, Halley V, interview with Alice Oates, August 2020.
60 Builder, Halley V, interview with Alice Oates, November 2020.
61 This is formalised through the BAS Club, a general club for past employees and associated members of BAS and its precursors, the FIDS and Operation Tabarin. See British Antarctic Survey Club, 'British Antarctic Survey Club', https://basclub.org/ (accessed 14 March 2024); and the Z-fids website: Z-fids, 'Z-fids: Halley Bay, 1956–Present', www.zfids.org.uk/ (accessed 14 March 2024).
62 Chef, Halley V, interview with Alice Oates, September 2020.
63 Klaus J. Dodds and Alan D. Hemmings, 'Britain and the British Antarctic Territory in the Wider Geopolitics of the Antarctic and the Southern Ocean', *International Affairs* 89:6 (2013), 1429–44.
64 Powell, *Studying Arctic Fields*.
65 Chef, Halley V/VI, interview with Alice Oates, September 2020.
66 Alison Blunt and Robyn M. Dowling, *Home* (Oxford: Routledge, 2006), p. 22.
67 Blunt and Dowling, *Home*.

68 Builder, Halley III, interview with Alice Oates, August 2020.
69 Meteorologist, Halley V, interview with Alice Oats, November 2020 (emphases added).
70 Chef, Halley V, interview with Alice Oates, September 2020.
71 Base commander/meteorologist, Halley V, interview with Alice Oates, August 2020.
72 Meteorologist, Halley V, interview with Alice Oates, October 2020.
73 Diesel mechanic, Halley IV, interview with Alice Oates, November 2020.
74 Builder, Halley IV, interview with Alice Oates, November 2020.
75 Meteorologist, Halley V, interview with Alice Oates, October 2020.
76 Veracini, 'Settler Colonialism'; Harris, *A Bounded Land*.
77 British Antarctic Survey, 'Brunt Ice Shelf in Antarctica Calves', www.bas.ac.uk/media-post/brunt-ice-shelf-in-antarctica-calves/, 26 February 2021 (accessed 8 August 2023).
78 British Antarctic Survey, 'Halley Automation', www.bas.ac.uk/project/halley-automation/ (accessed 8 August 2023).
79 Howkins, 'Emerging from the Shadow of Science'.

Bibliography

Arneil, Barbara. *John Locke and America: The Defence of English Colonialism.* Oxford: Clarendon Press, 1996.

Bell, Avril. *Relating Indigenous and Settler Identities: Beyond Domination.* New York: Palgrave Macmillan, 2014.

Bischoff, Eva. 'Experiences, Actors, Spaces: Dimensions of Settler Colonialism in Transnational Perspective'. *Settler Colonial Studies* 7, no. 2 (2017): 135–40.

Blunt, Alison and Robyn M. Dowling. *Home.* Oxford: Routledge, 2006.

Bonds, Anne and Joshua Inwood. 'Beyond White Privilege: Geographies of White Supremacy and Settler Colonialism'. *Progress in Human Geography* 40, no. 6 (2016): 715–33.

British Antarctic Survey. 'Brunt Ice Shelf in Antarctica Calves'. www.bas.ac.uk/media-post/brunt-ice-shelf-in-antarctica-calves/, 26 February 2021. Accessed 8 August 2024.

British Antarctic Survey. 'Halley Automation'. www.bas.ac.uk/project/halley-automation/. Accessed 8 August 2023.

British Antarctic Survey. 'Vision and Mission'. www.bas.ac.uk/about/about-bas/corporate-aims/. Accessed 24 February 2023.

British Antarctic Survey Club. 'British Antarctic Survey Club'. https://basclub.org/. Accessed 14 March 2024.

British Antarctic Territory, 'About the Territory'. https://britishantarcticterritory.org.uk/about/about-the-territory/. Accessed 21 January 2023.

Cavell, Janice. 'The Sector Theory and the Canadian Arctic, 1897–1970'. *The International History Review* 41, no. 6 (2019): 1168–93.

Chapman, Sydney. 'Scientific Programme of the International Geophysical Year 1957–58'. *Nature* 175 (1955): 402–6.

Collis, Christy. 'Mawson and Mirnyy Stations: The Spatiality of the Australian Antarctic Territory, 1954–61'. *Australian Geographer* 38, no. 2 (2007): 215–31.

Collis, Christy. 'Cold Colonies: Antarctic Spatialities at Mawson and McMurdo Stations'. *Cultural Geographies* 14, no. 2 (2007): 234–54.

Conforti, Benedetto. 'Territorial Claims in Antarctica: A Modern Way to Deal with an Old Problem'. *Cornell International Law Journal* 19, no. 2 (1986): 249–58.

Daily Mail. 'Antarctic Men Take Seed and Soil'. *Daily Mail*, 22 November 1955.

Dodds, Klaus J. 'Governing Antarctica: Contemporary Challenges and the Enduring Legacy of the 1959 Antarctic Treaty'. *Global Policy* 11, no. 1 (2010): 108–15.

Dodds, Klaus J. *Pink Ice: Britain and the South Atlantic Empire*. London: I.B. Tauris, 2002.

Dodds, Klaus J. 'Post-Colonial Antarctica: An Emerging Engagement'. *Polar Record* 42, no. 1 (2006): 59–70.

Dodds, Klaus J. 'Putting Maps in Their Place: The Demise of the Falkland Islands Dependency Survey and the Mapping of Antarctica'. *Ecumene* 7, no. 2 (2000): 176–210.

Dodds, Klaus J. and Alan D. Hemmings. 'Britain and the British Antarctic Territory in the Wider Geopolitics of the Antarctic and the Southern Ocean'. *International Affairs* 89, no. 6 (2013): 1429–44.

Donovan, Amy and Clive Oppenheimer. 'At the Mercy of the Mountain? Field Stations and the Culture of Volcanology'. *Environment and Planning* 47, no. 1 (2015): 156–71.

Farman, Joseph C., Brian G. Gardiner and Jonathan D. Shanklin. 'Large Losses of Total Ozone in Antarctica Reveal Seasonal ClO_x/NO_x Interaction'. *Nature* 315 (1985): 207–10.

Harris, Cole. *A Bounded Land: Reflections on Settler Colonialism in Canada*. Vancouver: UBC Press, 2020.

Harris, Cole. *Making Native Space: Colonialism, Resistance and Reserves in British Columbia*. Vancouver: UBC Press, 2002.

Haward, Marcus. 'The Originals: The Role and Influence of the Original Signatories to the Antarctic Treaty'. In *Handbook on the Politics of Antarctica*, ed. Klaus J. Dodds, Alan D. Hemmings and Peder Roberts, pp. 232–40. Cheltenham: Edward Elgar Publishing, 2017.

Howkins, Adrian. 'Appropriating Space: Antarctic Imperialism and the Mentality of Settler Colonialism'. In *Making Settler Colonial Space*, ed. Tracey Banivanua Mar and Penelope Edmonds, pp. 29–52. London: Palgrave Macmillan, 2010.

Howkins, Adrian. 'Emerging from the Shadow of Science: Challenges and Opportunities for Antarctic History'. In *Antarctica and the Humanities*, ed. Peder Roberts, Lize-Marié van der Watt and Adrian Howkins, pp. 251–72. London: Palgrave Macmillan, 2016.

Locke, John. *Two Treatises of Government*. London, 1689.

MacDowall, Joseph. *On Floating Ice*. Lancaster: Carnegie House, 1999.

Mancilla, Alejandra. 'A Continent of and for Whiteness? "White" Colonialism and the 1959 Antarctic Treaty'. *Polar Record* 55, no. 5 (2019): 317–19.

Mancilla, Alejandra. 'The Moral Limits of Territorial Claims in Antarctica'. *Ethics & International Affairs* 32, no. 3 (2018): 339–60.

Milner, Elya L. 'Enacting Propriety: Property, Planning, and the Production of Settler Colonial Geographies'. *Settler Colonial Studies* 10, no. 2 (2020): 278–93.

Morgensen, Scott L. 'The Biopolitics of Settler Colonialism: Right Here, Right Now'. *Settler Colonial Studies* 1, no. 1 (2011): 52–76.

Pharand, Donat. 'Canada's Arctic Jurisdiction in International Law'. *Dalhousie Law Journal* 7, no. 3 (1983): 315–42.

Powell, Richard C. *Studying Arctic Fields: Cultures, Practices and Environmental Sciences*. Ontario: McGill-Queen's University Press, 2017.

Rifkin, Mark. 'Settler Common Sense'. *Settler Colonial Studies* 3, no. 4 (2013): 322–40.

Secretariat of the Antarctic Treaty, Antarctic Treaty (1959). www.ats.aq/e/ antarctictreaty.html. Accessed 16 January 2022.

Seed, Patricia. *Ceremonies of Possession in Europe's Conquest of the New World*. Cambridge: Cambridge University Press, 1995.

Svarlien, Oscar. 'The Sector Principle in Law and Practice'. *Polar Record* 10, no. 66 (1960): 248–63.

Veracini, Lorenzo. '"Settler Colonialism": Career of a Concept'. *The Journal of Imperial and Commonwealth History* 41, no. 2 (2013): 313–33.

Wehi, Priscilla M., Nigel J. Scott, Jacinta Beckwith *et al.* 'A Short Scan of Māori Journeys to Antarctica'. *Journal of the Royal Society of New Zealand* 52, no. 5 (2021): 587–98.

Z-fids. 'Z-fids: Halley Bay, 1956–Present'. www.zfids.org.uk/. Accessed 14 March 2024.

11

Domination as a legacy of the colonial origins and structure of the Antarctic Treaty System

Yelena Yermakova

The unjust beginning of the Antarctic Treaty System (ATS) and its unfair procedures are a common topic of discussion in the Antarctic humanities.[1] However, this discussion lacks a unifying framework to analyse exactly what the problem is. What does unfair and unjust mean in the context of the ATS? To show exactly what the problem is with the ATS I turn to political philosophy and, more specifically, to republican political thought. A central concept in republicanism, the concept of domination, provides a valuable tool to explain the unfairness and injustice of the ATS. Domination, according to the republican tradition, exists when an agent has a power of interference on an arbitrary basis over another agent's range of choices, and justice demands minimisation of domination.[2] Domination at the global level happens when 'states are directly enmeshed in colonial, imperial or post-colonial relations, but also when their integration into the global order operates on terms that are ostensibly non-coercive, yet exhibit features of power imbalance, dependency and arbitrariness'.[3] In this chapter I ask: has the ATS developed through just actions and established a fair regime? I argue for the negative by looking at the problematic nature of the ATS's colonial origins and the subsequent institutional design, which continues to reflect power imbalance. I then offer some strategies to remedy this and to transition toward a more just and postcolonial Antarctic governance.

Antarctica has been part of the colonial legacy since the first territorial claims and the regime that followed, and the fact that it had no Indigenous population does not detract from this legacy. Rather, according to the environmental historian Adrian Howkins, the mentality of settler colonialism is embedded in the origins of the Antarctic regime: 'Antarctica epitomises the elitist, racist and exclusionary mentality of the settler colonial project. "The Great White South" offered imperialists all the glory of empire without the messy reality of having to rule over colonial peoples.'[4] While colonialism did not happen *in* Antarctica in the usual sense because there

were no residents of Antarctica to be the objects of colonialism, it happened *through* Antarctica, i.e. through decisions made *about* Antarctica.
Philosopher Alejandra Mancilla argues that the uniqueness of Antarctic
colonialism lies in the fact that while the unequal power structure is not
enacted territorially (the agents are not there physically), it is embedded in
the institutional structures that govern the territory. The exclusivity of the
regime's initial stages, which left most of the international community out
of the discussion about how to manage the region, was a wrong of colonialism according to Mancilla.[5] This is in line with political theorist Lea
Ypi's account of the wrong of colonialism, which identifies the moral wrong
of colonialism as denying the members of a political association equality
and reciprocity in decision-making.[6] It is not a wrongful occupation of others' land that constitutes the wrong of colonialism, according to Ypi, but
a 'morally objectionable form of political relation'.[7] The twelve original
signatories, the self-appointed guardians of Antarctica, denied participation
to a large group of people in the establishment of the regime (political association), thereby treating them as unequal, as 'wards in need of representation'.[8] They did not just exclude other states, but decided what was in the
interest of all humankind without consulting the rest of the world.[9] It was
a moral wrong of colonialism because one group of agents in a political
association (the Treaty's original signatories) treated another group (the rest
of the states) on unequal terms. The ATS's colonial origins have been maintained to this day through the institutionalisation that followed.

In this chapter, I develop the idea of the origins and the procedures of
the ATS as colonial, relying on republican political thought to highlight the
existence of domination in the ATS. Domination is an integral feature of
colonialism, specifically of the wrong of colonialism identified by Ypi. In the
case of the ATS, focusing on domination rather than discussing colonialism more broadly helps to highlight the exact wrong of colonialism that is
present in Antarctic governance, i.e. a group of states denying participation
in decision-making about Antarctica to the rest of the world. Furthermore,
I use the power-driven path-dependence approach to explain why the ATS's
design reflected hierarchies on the international arena and has reinforced
them through institutionalisation. According to this approach, the initial
stages of institutions reflect the power imbalance of the states involved at
the moment the institution is created, which is further locked in through
institutionalisation.[10] The territorial claims and the emergence of the regime
were colonial and a moral wrong because they exhibited domination,
i.e. the claimant states and original signatories had power of interference
(whether to include or exclude certain states) on an arbitrary basis (lack of
any accountability) over another agent's range of choices (by not including
most of the existing states at the time, the original signatories diminished the
range of choices for those who were left out). The ATS's emergence reflected

pre-existing patterns of interests and the privileged positions of the original 12 signatories (hereinafter, 'the original 12'), who gave themselves the authority of decision-making. This initial advantage was further locked in through Article IX of the Treaty, which created a two-tier system by establishing the science criterion for decision-making and consensus voting that protects the interests of the original 12. The ATS has maintained a regime of power imbalance, dependency and arbitrariness through its procedures.

Before proceeding, a few words on republicanism are in order. Republicans have joined the global justice debate recently, suggesting that the republican ideal of non-domination can contribute to the ongoing discourse on global justice. In the republican view, the problem with the current global order is not necessarily the troubling nature of distributive inequalities across borders, but rather that of domination across borders. The contemporary international legal system masks inequalities of power; more powerful states and other global actors can easily influence the policies of weaker states. More powerful states also shape the global institutions by whose rules the weaker states have to play. A majority of weaker states are 'rule takers' rather than rule makers.[11] Republicanism targets the cause of inequalities in the global order and seeks solutions by focusing on institutional design. Republicanism is a suitable framework to assess the ATS because it sheds light on the problematic institutional design that reflected and reinforced power asymmetries among states. Republican solutions are valuable because the critique starts with looking at existing institutions, identifying their dominating aspects and advocating for transformation.[12]

This chapter is organised as follows. First, I discuss the problematic origins of the regime by looking at the power imbalance present during territorial acquisition. Second, I turn to the development of the negotiations that culminated in Article IV, which reflected existing hierarchies in the international arena. Third, I highlight how the domination was solidified further through Article IX, which established and maintains the two-tier system and protects the interests of the original 12 to this day. I conclude with a brief discussion of republican strategies to minimise the degree of domination and their application to the ATS, which would help to transition toward a postcolonial Antarctic future.

Domination in the Antarctic Treaty System

The territorial claims as unjust origins

The very roots of the regime, i.e. the territorial claims, mirrored the unfair system of the international order. In her assessment of the moral grounds behind the territorial claims, Mancilla highlights their limits and argues that 'there is a vast mismatch between the grounds of the claims and the actual scope they purport to cover'.[13] She breaks down the grounds into connection-based, official documents and geographical doctrines. Some of the activities used to support connection-based grounds were: first exploration and discovery, expeditions, state activity and exploitation of resources. Official documents included the principle of *uti possidetis iuris*, according to which newly independent states inherit the boundaries they had from when they were colonies, and the legal transfer of territory. The geographical doctrines included geographical continuity, contiguity and the sector principle.

There are numerous problems with these arguments, and Mancilla challenges them all. She argues that the connection-based grounds, such as first discovery, exploration and state activity, are not sufficient to justify the extent of the territorial claims. How does state activity such as whaling off the coast justify sovereignty over continuous territory all the way to the South Pole? For example, was Norway justified in claiming a whole sector, and not just the skiing route and the South Pole, as a result of the Roald Amundsen expedition? Or how can a simple ceremony of discovery by a state be a ground for claiming a large territory without any citizens of that state visiting the place for a century after?[14] The criterion of effective occupation, essential for state sovereignty, was impossible to meet in the context of the harsh physical conditions of Antarctica.[15] Only by relaxing this criterion were states able to claim vast territories on the continent, but Mancilla argues for an alternative: 'In a place such as Antarctica, talk of extending the exclusive territorial monopolies of individual states on the basis of their minimal activity and presence should be given up altogether.'[16] As for the Latin American claimants that see themselves as inheritors of historical rights derived from the fifteenth-century division of the 'New World' between Spain and Portugal, the obvious problem here is a lack of fairness in two countries dividing the world between themselves.[17] The issue with the transferring of territory, such as in the case of Great Britain, New Zealand and Australia, is similarly problematic. Only in this case it was one country, Great Britain, that proclaimed transferring a huge territory to others. A transfer of territory is morally justified if the party that transfers it is entitled to do so, but the grounds on which the British claim rests are questionable in themselves. Regarding contiguity, even if we consider the shortest distance between the southern tip of Argentina to the Antarctic Peninsula, it is almost 1,000 km. Although the contiguity theory has been invoked to justify claims to islands outside a state's territorial waters elsewhere, 1,000 km is quite a stretch.[18]

There is one more way of interpreting these claims, of which the origins of the ATS are reminiscent. Before the 1800s elitist claims were a usual practice. According to these claims a particular group had the right or duty to control territories as an elite. Scaling this up to the global level, some nations saw themselves as technologically or culturally superior, and therefore had the right to control territories. Technological ability is the most common ground for the elitist claim; a particular group should have control over territory because it has the ability to develop it.[19] The meaning and greatest potential of development were, of course, left to be decided by the elites. In the Antarctic, the claimants plus the other original signatories had the technological ability to be active in the region whether it was for resource exploitation or science.[20] Although elitist claims are no longer practised in contemporary international law, they are at the base of the ATS regime.[21]

The problematic nature of acquisition of territorial sovereignty is not exclusive to Antarctica; rather, it is characteristic of international law in general in the context of imperial powers claiming territories. Some norms even find a defence in maintaining the international order. For example, the principles of *uti possidetis iuris* might seem unfair from the contemporary point of view, but in international law the usual rule is to interpret treaties not as they exist today, but rather as they existed at the time of signing the treaty. This rule exists in order to ensure the predictability and stability of title in the international system.[22] Yet, laws evolve to reflect changing norms. What was accepted 200 years ago is often accepted no longer; slavery and women's lack of suffrage are just two examples among many that have changed with time and are not considered to be a norm anymore (at least in most of the world). Laws should not be obstacles to progress.

In today's world, where colonialism is recognised as a wrong, the Antarctic presents a unique case to set the precedent for future territorial acquisition and discoveries of *res nullius*, guided by norms of equality and reciprocity. If the grounds for territorial claimants reflected the norms of international law at the beginning of the twentieth century, they should be critically assessed now in light of the prospects of outer-space exploration and the need for international law to lay out rules for governing it. This will not cause instability in the international system, but will rather ensure predictability and stability for future territorial acquisition, whether it be in Antarctica or on Mars. In fact, re-evaluating the Antarctic Treaty will be a positive step toward charting a postcolonial future in which all nations get a say over newly discovered spaces.

Even if we were to accept the foundations of the territorial claims, the development of the Antarctic regime was not characterised by these norms being applicable in the same way to all states. There were states that could produce evidence of activity in the region, such as whaling or participation in expeditions, very similar to the claimants: for instance Belgium (which undertook the first winter expedition in Antarctica in 1897–99), the Netherlands (which had extensive whaling activity in the region), Sweden and Germany (which conducted research in the region), and Japan (which conducted scientific research and engaged in whaling in the region).[23] Additionally, there were countries that had nationals participating in scientific research in Antarctica, such as Czechoslovakia, Hungary, Romania and Poland. Poland, in fact, opened a research station in January 1959.

Furthermore, the claimants were not the only interested parties in the management of Antarctica. India submitted the question of governing Antarctica to the United Nations (UN) General Assembly twice in the 1950s, underlining the importance of the continent to the entire world. Latin American states such as Brazil, Mexico, Peru and Uruguay had interests in the political and legal status of Antarctica. These states were concerned with the governance of Antarctica, and yet they had no control over it, and they were denied participation.

To sum up, the claimants had influence over a range of choices for the rest of the world when they claimed parts of Antarctica driven by resource greed and imperial attitudes at a time when it was already understood that resources in the region were not infinite, whaling being one example.[24] Moreover, they did so on questionable grounds, which should be critically assessed from the standpoint of the evolutionary nature of international law. Evaluating the grounds for these claims presents an opportunity to set a precedent for future discoveries of uninhabited spaces. Antarctica was treated as *terra nullius*, as belonging to no one until appropriated by a first legal taker, where the taker (claimant) was whoever was first, and where what was legal was determined by the taker itself with no accountability. The norms of territorial acquisition were not applicable to all in the same way, excluding states that were interested in the management of the region without any sufficient reasons. Domination, an essential aspect of colonialism, was present at the very origins of the Antarctic regime. The future of Antarctica was to be decided by a small group of countries, which I discuss in the next section.

Power imbalance during the emergence of the Antarctic Treaty System

The original 12 were the historical winners at the time of the development of the ATS. Many states did not get to participate in the negotiations about the future of the Antarctic; during the initial stages of the regime about 30 new states were emerging in the context of decolonisation in Africa and Asia.[25] Who got to participate in the negotiations was largely decided by the United States, the main orchestrating force behind the process.[26] But the exclusion of weaker states, such as Poland, and the inclusion of powerful actors, such as the Soviet Union, highlights how the process of negotiations and the signing of the Treaty reflected hierarchies in the international arena beyond the role of the United States as a hegemon.

The institutionalisation of a power imbalance in the initial stages of the ATS can be explained by the concept of power-driven path-dependence. In this account, institutional structures reflect the actors' power positions. Power-driven path-dependence emphasises that institutions can lock in political power: 'historical winners can preserve initial advantages via institutionalization'.[27] The most notable example of this is the UN Security Council, in which five permanent veto powers still reflect the winning coalition of the Second World War. Political power during the initial stages of institutional design is connected to historical privileges, locked in from the start according to power-driven path-dependence and reinforced later through reforms. In other words, path-dependence means that current outcomes depend on previous outcomes; history matters. The case of the ATS is an example of such a dynamic: the initial stages reflected the actors' power positions, and this was further locked in by the procedures of the scientific research activity requirement and consensus voting.[28] Below I discuss the initial stages of the regime development that culminated in the signing of the Treaty.

Howkins presents the period prior to the International Geophysical Year (IGY) of 1957–58 in Antarctica as a British settler colonial project, with New Zealand, Australia and Norway 'mimicking' the British mentality, while Argentina, Chile and France expressed their interests in Antarctica in opposition to the United Kingdom.[29] In addition to the seven claimants, five other countries conducted research in the Antarctic during the IGY: the United States, the Soviet Union, Japan, Belgium and South Africa. Howkins refers to the IGY as a decisive turning point in Antarctic imperialism. It was not decisive because of the often-idealised story of the IGY as an example of setting aside political differences for the sake of science, but because the results of the IGY showed that there was not much to gain in Antarctica. The IGY was an important moment because it convinced the claimants that fighting for sovereignty was not worth the diplomatic costs, at least in the short term. Internationalisation was the most pragmatic way forward for Britain and the United States to keep their political influence in Antarctica, according to Howkins. Scientific cooperation was a tool to exploit for the sake of political interests.

Legal scholar Shirley Scott suggests that the Treaty itself was a third wave of Antarctic imperialism, following the previous waves.[30] The first one was the fifteenth-century division of the world between Spain and Portugal. In the early twentieth century, the second wave was that of British Antarctic imperialism when European states were concerned with who owned the Antarctic in the manner of the nineteenth-century Scramble for Africa,

while the South American states were concerned with how to delimit the
mutual boundary of the territory to which they saw themselves as the rightful inheritors.[31] The third wave, according to Scott, served the United States'
interests the most. Her account digs deeper than geopolitics scholar Klaus
Dodds's critique of the ATS, which advocates viewing the ATS through a
postcolonial lens. While Dodds argues that Britain, New Zealand, Australia,
Chile, Argentina, and possibly the United States, had engaged in imperial
behaviour in Antarctica, Scott suggests viewing the United States as the
'chief architect of law and policy for the Antarctic'.[32] She argues that Article
IV of the Antarctic Treaty is the cornerstone of American imperialism, as it
reduced the effective sovereignty of claimants while giving the United States
legal basis to access any part of the continent.[33] Setting aside the issue of
territorial claims was in the interest of the United States because it would
ensure its freedom of movement in Antarctica. The United States wanted
to have a position of leadership in the region, and as an orchestrating force
behind the talks the United States had the capacity to interfere without any
effective constraints, i.e. to influence other states' positions and their range
of choices, thus exhibiting domination.

Scott's account, although rightfully highlighting the dominating role
of the United States, misses the dynamics of other states, which point to
a hierarchy in the international arena, reflected in the initial stages of the
regime development. The Soviet government, initially not invited to the
talks on the future of Antarctica, expressed its criticism of the exclusive
nature of the developing discussions. Arguing that Antarctica presented
great value from an economic perspective, as well as for meteorological
studies, to many states aside from those participating in the discussions,
the Soviet government insisted that all interested states should be part of
the conversation. In the 1950 Memorandum to the United States State
Department, the Soviet government wrote that 'in accordance with international practice, all interested countries must be brought into participation in consideration of the regime of any region whatsoever which has
international significance'.[34] And although this might seem like a powerful
state advocating for a more open and democratic regime, a more honest
representation of the Soviet Union's position can be found in the Union of
Soviet Socialist Republics Geographical Society statement a year earlier.
Instead of advocating for the participation of all interested countries, the
position then was that the question of future management of Antarctica
must be decided by 'the states that have the historical rights to participate
in this solution'.[35] The Soviet Union was not much different from the
United States in trying to keep the regime exclusive. It just did not have
enough power to lead the development of the regime as the United States
did, especially in the context of the post-Second World War period. The

Soviet Union did, however, have enough leverage to push against being excluded. This was not the case for less powerful states, such as Poland.

The case of Poland highlights the power hierarchies, characteristic of domination, during the negotiations. Poland expressed its interest in April 1959 in participating in the talks behind the regime development. Poland's request was ignored even though it had undertaken substantial scientific activity in Antarctica: Polish scientists participated in Antarctic expeditions (organised by other states) and was active in the Antarctic waters; and most importantly, in January 1959 (almost a year before the Antarctic Treaty was signed), the Polish scientific station A. B. Dobrowolski was opened (inactive since 1998).[36] This showcases how powerful states from the beginning had an advantage in being part of the decision-making process and the shaping of the regime. The ATS parties in the initial stages of its development had the capacity to decide whom to include and whom to exclude from the negotiations over the Antarctic future. This power was not accountable to anyone, and the excluded states had their range of choices diminished.

The negotiating process, conducted over 60 informal and secret meetings, culminated in the decision to safeguard the status quo of the legal positions on the territorial claims as this was the only way to protect the interests of claimants.[37] What was 'in the interest of all mankind' was decided by a small minority of 'mankind', while in reality only serving the interests of the participating states.[38] While many states were never even given a chance to participate, or did not even exist yet, the powerful states shaped the future of the regime. Thus, the emergence of the ATS regime was driven by domination and reflected the power positions of the states involved, and Article IV was the glue to bind the system.[39] Howkins writes about Article IV: 'The retention of imperial influence into the Antarctic Treaty System is best expressed by Article IV of the Treaty, which suspends (or "freezes" in the official pun of the negotiations) existing claims, rather than renouncing them entirely. All seven claimant countries continue to assert their sovereignty over "their" parts of the continent.'[40] This dynamic was further solidified through scientific imperative and consensus-based decision-making, which I discuss next.

Unfair procedures

While the ATS's emergence mirrored and institutionalised the power imbalance inherited from colonial times and the domination present in the international order, the subsequent procedures reinforced it. Article IX of the Treaty is the foundation of the regime's administration. It locked in the power imbalance by creating a two-tier system, giving a privileged position to the original 12, and establishing consensus-based decision-making.[41] The ATS's institutional design exhibits domination in the following three ways.

1. The consensus rule ensures that no consultative party, the states with a right to participate in decision-making, can be outvoted.
2. The consultative status of the original 12 is unconditional; they do not lose their consultative status regardless of whether they perform substantial scientific activity or not. Instead, the rest of the states that accede to the Antarctic Treaty, and are granted consultative status based on their scientific research activity, retain the status conditionally.
3. Although the ATS is open to anyone in theory, in practice it is a two-tier system that effectively excludes poor countries. The science criterion as an entry ticket to the decision-making group is an obstacle for the states that cannot afford such activity.[42]

First, when measures are recommended at Antarctic Treaty Consultative Meetings (ATCMs), the main decision-making platform of the ATS, they become effective once approved by all consultative parties. This therefore acts as a reinforcement to the legal accommodation in Article IV, as it ensures that a party cannot be outvoted regarding the decisions that might impact the issue of sovereignty.[43] A shift to a majority vote system would be not just more efficient, as I have argued elsewhere, but also more representative.[44] Political scientist Anne-Marie Brady compares the current system to the early stages of the European Union, which was at first consensus-based as well, but later changed to majority rule because consensus-based voting prevented change: 'As it did in the EU, the Antarctic Treaty's current consensus voting system is allowing a minority group of states with vested interests to block change. The seven claimant states, in particular, fear majority rule, but it would be far more democratic and fair and garner greater legitimacy for the Treaty.'[45]

Second, the original 12 are in a superior position compared to the rest of the world as they have consultative status by default. For other states that accede to the Treaty, scientific research activity is required to gain consultative status. A state has consultative status as long as it continues to demonstrate its interest in Antarctica by conducting substantial scientific research activity. Thus, the status is conditional for the states that accede to the Treaty, but it is unconditional for the original 12; they retain consultative status regardless of their presence in the region. Belgium, for instance, one of the original 12, was not present in the Antarctic for almost 40 years, from 1967 until opening a new station in 2009, but this had no impact on its decision-making status, which was kept throughout.[46] If there is a rule that requires scientific activity to have decision-making rights, there should also be a rule, *applicable to all*, including the original 12, that scientific activity must be maintained in order to keep the decision-making status. In practice this could mean that if a state has not been active on the continent it loses its decision-making power for a probational period at least. Why is the performance standard different for those who are 'in' from the beginning versus those who join the system later? Although a minority in the ATS, the 12 original signatories have a special standing in the regime.[47]

Third, the scientific activity requirement is at the core of the two-tier system. It prevents states that cannot afford to do science in the Antarctic from gaining consultative status and having decision-making power. Howkins writes: 'Scientific research in Antarctica did not come cheaply and many countries in the Third World simply could not afford to build expensive scientific bases in Antarctica in order to win a place at Antarctica's political table.'[48] Since the Treaty was signed, only two more states gained consultative status in the first two decades: Poland (1977) and Germany (1981).[49] However, the 1980s had a surge of accessions to the Antarctic Treaty, and 13 more states gained consultative status between 1981 and 2001. The threshold for science performance was lowered, and there was no more requirement to have a permanent wintering station – a summer station was sufficient. Furthermore, when the Netherlands applied for consultative status in 1990, their scientific programmes relying on vessels and stations of other nations were considered sufficient to meet the criterion of substantial scientific research activity.[50]

However, there seems to have been a reverse trend in the last two decades. Since the early 2000s only two more states have gained consultative status: Ukraine (2004) and the Czech Republic (2014). Moreover, since 2017 the guidelines for the procedures to gain consultative status include new details. The examples of the kind of scientific programmes and activities that qualify a state for consultative status include publications in peer-reviewed scientific journals, publications with co-authors from different countries, well-scored citations etc.[51] This makes the path toward consultative status more challenging for countries where the primary academic language is not English. These new rules make the scientific imperative stronger. Moreover, the COVID-19 pandemic showcased the unfair nature of the scientific activity requirement: if the decision-making right is contingent on undertaking science on the continent, then events such as global pandemics have an impact on which countries get to participate in the decision-making. As some of the operations were cancelled, Antarctic science was restricted.[52] According to Brady, poor countries are effectively excluded from Antarctic governance.[53] A similar dynamic is present in the Convention for the Conservation of Antarctic Marine Living Resources (CCAMLR), which followed the Antarctic Treaty two-tier system. Although Japan argued for an open regime during the negotiations of the Convention, the proposal of equal decision-making rights for all contracting parties was opposed by the Soviet Union.[54] The precedent of the Treaty and the consultative parties as a 'club' made it easier for the CCAMLR negotiators to agree on the same model.[55]

Continuing with scientific research as an entry ticket to the decision-making group is an obstacle to postcolonial governance over Antarctica because the requirement to practise science reflects and maintains power imbalance. When states are required to meet the criterion of scientific research activity, essentially they are denied equality and reciprocity in decision-making over Antarctica. But if not science, then what should be the criterion to establish the right to participate in decision-making? Perhaps, the decision-making authority should be more connected to the states affected the most by changes in the Antarctic and diminished for those who contribute the most to the climate change, as historian Peder Roberts has suggested?[56] This is in line with the all-affected principle, according to which those who are affected by the decisions should participate in the making of those decisions. However, changes in the Antarctic are the result of what happens *outside* the continent. So, following the reasoning of the all-affected principle, states affected the most by the Antarctic changes should participate in global climate policy-making to have a real impact.[57] I suggest we should view the right to participate in the Antarctic regime as what political philosopher James Bohman calls 'a basic right to membership'.[58] He asserts that freedom from domination is the most fundamental political human right because non-domination determines who establishes and influences the terms of social cooperation. Social cooperation is dominating when it does not allow for challenging the rules of cooperation and when some members are excluded. This reflects the wrong of colonialism identified by Ypi, when members of the political association are denied equality and reciprocity in decision-making. In the case of the ATS, the consultative parties deny the rights of membership to the rest of the international community. The ATS will become non-dominating if it allows every state to participate in decision-making. Brady has argued that opening up participation in Antarctic governance to all states is needed to make sure that the region is truly managed in the interests of all humankind.[59] Democratisation and opening participation to all states in the ATS is a necessary step toward a postcolonial Antarctica.[60]

Concluding remarks: On a postcolonial path

In this concluding section, I briefly discuss republican strategies to transition away from the power-driven path that the ATS has been on since its beginning, and toward a postcolonial future. These strategies help to achieve the desiderata of republican institutions: to resist the excessive concentration of power; bring informal power under regulation; and further an active, vigilant citizenry. In the case of the ATS, these strategies can right the colonial wrong of domination. I discuss five strategies proposed by Cécile Laborde and Miriam Ronzoni, and suggest what these strategies would look like in the case of the ATS.[61]

The first strategy is power-countering that aims at minimising power imbalance. It envisions alliances of outsiders of the ATS and non-consultative parties to challenge the status quo and the concentration of power among the consultative parties. A coalition of states would enable a higher bargaining power collectively and would be more likely to have effective results compared to a situation in which states try to contest the regime individually. This type of alliance should push the ATS to drop the scientific research activity requirement and open the field for all states to have decision-making rights. Power-countering can also be effected through neutralisation between strong players. For instance, if one of the claimants were open to revising the scientific research activity criterion, it might lead to a domino effect. Considering that New Zealand was open to a UN management of the Antarctic during the development of the regime, this idea is not so far out of reach.[62] The overall long-term goal should be that all states have decision-making rights in the Antarctic regime. However, a high number of members in the decision-making organ have practical difficulties, and finding a balance between inclusion and effectiveness is key to a successful regime.

The second strategy is fair distribution of resources. This strategy is less relevant than others for Antarctica simply because the world does not depend on its resources. However, the future may be different, especially with regard to the value of freshwater reserves and fishing stocks. In the theoretical case of an increased demand for these resources, the distribution strategy would envision equitable access under strict regulation. In the potential case of mineral exploitation certain mechanisms for benefits distribution, equitable access and representation, and reserving areas for exploitation by future generations should be made. The key idea in this strategy, however, is that equitable access and a more inclusive representation in the ATS will ensure that control over the territory, within which there may be some needed resources, is not based on colonial mentality.

The third strategy is democratisation of international institutions, as well as limiting them in scope. Democratisation calls for a more representative, inclusive and accountable ATS with some issues dealt with by area-specific authority placement. Dropping the scientific research activity requirement as an entry ticket to the decision-making club will improve the inclusiveness of the regime. Participation in Antarctic governance should not be earned (at least not through questionable historical activity) but it should be by right, as a basic right to membership in the international community in line with Bohman's account. Furthermore, a shift to a majority vote system would make the ATS more representative. A higher degree of accountability implies external fundamental criticism to contest the rules. This would allow countries that were excluded from the regime, and non-consultative parties, to defend their interests and demand fair terms of interaction in the Antarctic regime. To limit the scope of the ATS, certain issues should be dealt with by separate branches of the ATS, as is currently the case with CCAMLR managing marine living resources. Tourism, for example, can also be managed by a separate agreement and a commission.[63]

The democratisation of international institutions faces an obvious obstacle of how to include individuals. The suggestions above would have a direct impact on states, but less so on individuals. One strategy that is feasible to implement in the case of Antarctica is for the ATS Secretariat to implement a policy of public educational outreach. The Arctic Council is a great example to follow in this regard, as it offers the possibility of signing up for regular informative updates about the Arctic.[64]

The fourth strategy is global constitutionalisation, i.e. international law establishing fundamental rights for individuals, non-state actors and states. This would allow for protection from arbitrary power through global, centralised, judicial powers.

The fifth strategy is a higher degree of regulation globally, which is necessary for the protection of free statehood, as the current domination exists because there is a regulatory vacuum at the global level.

The last two strategies complement each other: a tighter global regulation rests on global constitutional elements. This would require the ATS to be open to external constraints and regulations based on global constitutional rules. Global constitutionalisation and tighter regulation over the global arena will ensure that informal power asymmetries are minimised.

The ATS's origins reflected the power imbalance inherited from the colonial era in the international arena at the time. Territorial claims were made in line with a colonialist mentality and on questionable grounds, and yet they are preserved in Article IV. Later, the future of Antarctica was decided by a small group of states that excluded the rest of the world. While proclaiming that they acted in the interest of all humankind, the reality was that the original 12 were protecting their own interests. This dynamic of domination was only solidified by Article IX, which established the procedures of the scientific activity requirement and consensus-based voting, thus protecting the privileged position of the original 12. Participation in decision-making is limited to states that can afford to conduct scientific research.

The ATS's transition away from domination, an essential aspect of colonialism, requires that decision-making be open to all states and that voting be majority-based. A postcolonial Antarctic regime will need to be more representative, inclusive and accountable. A transition toward a multilevel governance structure and away from an intergovernmental club diplomacy would set the ATS on a postcolonial path.

Notes

1 In addition to the Antarctic Treaty, the ATS includes the Convention for the Conservation of Antarctic Seals; the Convention for the Conservation of Antarctic Marine Living Resources (CCAMLR); the Protocol on Environmental Protection (the Madrid Protocol); and the measures, decisions and resolutions adopted under them. Article IV of the Treaty froze the territorial claims of Argentina, Australia, Chile, France, New Zealand, Norway and the United Kingdom, hereafter referred to as the claimants. The Treaty was signed by the claimants plus Belgium, Japan, South Africa, the Soviet Union and the United States in Washington on 1 December 1959, and entered into force on 23 June 1961. A representative sample of discussion of the unfairness of the ATS can be found in S. V. Scott, 'Ingenious and Innocuous? Article IV of the Antarctic Treaty as Imperialism', *The Polar Journal* 1:1 (2011), 51–62; Klaus J. Dodds, 'Post-Colonial Antarctica: An Emerging Engagement', *Polar Record* 42:220 (2006), 59–70; Alan D. Hemmings, 'Re-Justifying the Antarctic Treaty System for the 21st Century: Rights, Expectations and Global Equity', in Richard C. Powell and Klaus J. Dodds (eds), *Polar Geopolitics: Knowledges, Resources and Legal Regimes* (Cheltenham: Edwar Elgar Publishing, 2014), pp. 55–73; Adrian Howkins, 'Appropriating Space: Antarctic Imperialism and the Mentality of Settler Colonialism', in Tracey B. Mar and Penelope Edmonds (eds), *Making Settler Colonial Space: Perspectives on Race, Place and Identity* (London: Palgrave Macmillan, 2010), pp. 29–52; Alejandra Mancilla, 'Decolonising Antarctica', in Dawid Bunikowski and Alan D. Hemmings (eds), *Philosophies of Polar Law* (Abingdon: Routledge, 2021), pp. 49–61.

2 See Frank Lovett, 'Republican Global Distributive Justice', *Diacritica* 24:2 (2010), 13–30; Cécile Laborde and Miriam Ronzoni, 'What Is a Free State? Republican Internationalism and Globalisation', *Political Studies* 64:2 (2014), 279–96.

3 Laborde and Ronzoni, 'What Is a Free State?', p. 289.

4 Howkins, 'Appropriating Space', p. 31.

5 Mancilla, 'Decolonising Antarctica'. Starting with the assumption of common ownership of the earth's resources, Mancilla also points to another wrong of Antarctic colonialism: the excessive appropriation of territory.

6 Lea Ypi, 'What's Wrong with Colonialism', *Philosophy & Public Affairs* 41:2 (2013), 158–91.

7 Ypi, 'What's Wrong with Colonialism', p. 190.

8 Mancilla, 'Decolonising Antarctica', p. 56.

9 See preamble of the Antarctic Treaty.

10 Tine Hanrieder, 'The Path-Dependent Design of International Organizations: Federalism in the World Health Organization', *European Journal of International Relations* 21:1 (2015), 215–39.

11 The term 'rule takers' is adopted from Andrew Hurrell, 'Global Inequality and International Institutions', *Metaphilosophy* 32:1–2 (2003), 34–57; and Laborde and Ronzoni, 'What Is a Free State?'. For a discussion of how the contemporary interdependent world is connected to growing inequalities in different areas, see Andrew Hurrell and Ngaire Woods (eds), *Inequality, Globalization, and World Politics* (Oxford: Oxford University Press, 1999). For a thorough overview of the debate about globalisation, and specifically how global interdependence is stratified, see David Held, Anthony McGrew, David Goldblatt and Jonathan Perraton, *Global Transformations: Politics, Economics, and Culture* (Stanford, CA: Stanford University Press, 1999). For a systemic analysis of the development of international law and how it failed to be independent from political agendas and rather reflects power asymmetries among states, see Martti Koskenniemi, *The Gentle Civilizer of Nations: The Rise and Fall of International Law 1870–1960* (Cambridge: Cambridge University Press, 2001). On the republican engagement with the issue of how the contemporary global political and legal order brings along increasing possibilities for domination, see James Bohman, 'Republican Cosmopolitanism', *The Journal of Political Philosophy* 12:3 (2004), 336–52; Cécile Laborde, 'Republicanism and Global Justice: A Sketch', *European Journal of Political Theory* 9:1 (2010), 48–69; Lovett, 'Republican Global Distributive Justice'.

12 Laborde, 'Republicanism and Global Justice', p. 50.

13 Alejandra Mancilla, 'The Moral Limits of Territorial Claims in Antarctica', *Ethics & International Affairs* 32:3 (2018), 339–60 (p. 355).

14 No French citizen appeared in the region for a century after Jules Dumont D'Urville's discovery of Adélie Land in 1840; David Day, *Antarctica: A Biography* (Oxford: Oxford University Press, 2013), p. vii.

15 For the principles of territorial acquisition in international law, see James Crawford, *Brownlie's Principles of Public International Law*, 8th edn (Oxford: Oxford University Press, 2012), pp. 215–45. Effective occupation – actual exercise of authority and administration of the territory – is necessary to complete the discovery of territory, which on its own is not sufficient to claim sovereignty over it. And although, in the regions that are remote, uninhabited and inhospitable, a symbolic annexation might be sufficient for a valid title, it still needs to satisfy requirements of effective occupation to demonstrate state activity. For an opposite view, see the position of Soviet jurist W. Lakhtine in Indi Hodgson-Johnston, 'The Laws of Territorial Acquisition as Applied to Claims to Antarctic Territory: A Review of Legal Scholarship', *The Yearbook of Polar Law Online* 7:1 (2016), 556–606.

16 Mancilla, 'The Moral Limits', p. 351. Mancilla concludes that most of the Antarctic continent should be sovereignless, and rights and responsibilities should be assigned according to what states and non-state actors have achieved and what should be achieved. This argument relies on function-based theories

of territorial rights, which justify the right to territory based on important functions that an entity provides. However, assigning rights to some states because they have performed an important function of maintaining peace in Antarctica, for example, is retroactive. They maintained peace because they were there, but I think we should instead ask what goals we want to achieve in Antarctica, what functions must be performed in order to do so and what entity would be the most apt to do so.

17 The division between the two powers and exclusion of other states from navigating the oceans was rejected when Grotius argued for the freedom of the seas; Hugo Grotius and William Welwod, *The Free Sea*, trans. Richard Hakluyt, ed. David Armitage (Indianapolis: Liberty Fund, 2004 [1609]).

18 The distance between the southernmost town, Ushuaia in Argentina, to the Antarctic Peninsula is almost 1,000 km. On the problematic issue of continuity and contiguity, see Hodgson-Johnston, 'The Laws of Territorial Acquisition'.

19 Andrew Burghardt, 'The Bases of Territorial Claims', *Geographical Review* 63:2 (1973), 225–45.

20 It should be noted, though, that without a political will among the original signatories, technological ability is unlikely to be a determining factor in exercising it in the Antarctic. Similarly, political will alone without technological ability would probably fail to secure a seat at the Antarctic decision-making table.

21 It is important to note that not all original signatories fall under the category of elitist claims. New Zealand's claim, for example, was the result of a transfer from Great Britain, as mentioned earlier.

22 Crawford, *Brownlie's Principles*, p. 218.

23 The fact that Germany and Japan did not advance any claims was of course the outcome of the political context following the Second World War. Japan renounced all claims to any right or title to, or interest in connection with, any part of the Antarctic area as per Article 2e of the separatist peace treaty with Japan. See United Nations, 'Treaty of Peace with Japan (with Two Declarations): Signed at San Francisco, on 8 September 1951', *United Nations Treaty Series* 136:1832 (1952), 45–164.

24 Mancilla also makes this point when identifying the wrongs of Antarctic colonialism, but she treats it as a wrongful taking of land, because it robbed the rest of the world of the possibility of claiming territories for themselves. I highlight the same problem but following the concept of domination, i.e. claimants diminished the range of choices for the rest of the world.

25 US Department of State, Office of the Historian, 'Decolonization of Asia and Africa, 1945–1960', https://history.state.gov/milestones (accessed 16 February 2023).

26 Scott, 'Ingenious and Innocuous?'.

27 Hanrieder, 'The Path-Dependent Design of International Organizations', p. 219.

28 This is similar to a concept from biology, *the founder effect*, which legal scholar Alan D. Hemmings uses to describe the ATS: 'the factors in play at the point of creation or codification (whether explicitly recognized then or not) resonate

through the lifetime of that system'. See Alan D. Hemmings, 'Considerable Values in Antarctica', *The Polar Journal* 2:1 (2012), 139–56 (p. 140).

29 Howkins, 'Appropriating Space'.

30 Scott, 'Ingenious and Innocuous?'. While Scott uses the term imperialism and not colonialism, for the purposes of this chapter her account is helpful because it highlights the dominating role of the United States behind the negotiations that led to the signing of the Treaty.

31 Scott's account of this stage is important because it differs from classical historiographical accounts such as Beck's. The latter portrays the territorial claimants as homogeneous – in essence that the South American states were latecomers after Britain claimed a sector, thus giving rise to the establishment of the New Zealand and Australian claims, with France and Norway's claims to follow. Hence, Beck's account is supportive of the British position, as it portrays the South American claims coming after the British; Peter J. Beck, *The International Politics of Antarctica* (London: Croom Helm, 1986). Scott, on the other hand, by separating the European states from those of South America, sheds light on the nuances within the group of claimants. She argues that the British claim pushed Chile and Argentina to justify their position in the framework of the European international law of colonialism; see Scott, 'Ingenious and Innocuous?', p. 56. Latin American claimants do not see themselves as claimants, but rather as inheritors of historical rights. See also Ignacio Cardone's contribution to this volume.

32 Dodds, 'Post-Colonial Antarctica'; Scott, 'Ingenious and Innocuous?', p. 61. Hemmings also referred to the United States as 'the single most significant actor in Antarctic affairs'; Alan D. Hemmings, 'Globalisation's Cold Genius and the Ending of Antarctic Isolation', in Lorne Kriwoken, Julia Jabour and Alan D. Hemmings (eds), *Looking South: Australia's Antarctic Agenda* (Sydney: Federation Press, 2007), pp. 176–90 (p. 184).

33 Scott, 'Ingenious and Innocuous?', p. 61.

34 Union of Soviet Socialist Republics, 'The Embassy of the Soviet Union to the Department of State', in Neal H. Peterson, John P. Glennon, David W. Mabon, Ralph R. Goodwin and William Z. Slany (eds), *Foreign Relations of the United States, 1950*, Vol. I, *National Security Affairs; Foreign Economic Policy* (Washington, DC: United States Government Printing Office, 1977), pp. 912–13.

35 D. Golubev, *Русские в Антарктиде* [*Russians in the Antarctic*] (Moscow: Goskul'tprosvetizdat, 1949), pp. 68–9, as cited in Peter A. Toma, 'Soviet Attitude towards the Acquisition of Territorial Sovereignty in the Antarctic', *The American Journal of International Law* 50:3 (1956), 611–26 (p. 612).

36 Jacek Machowski, *The Status of Antarctica in the Light of International Law* (Warsaw: Office of Polar Programmes and the National Science Foundation, 1977), pp. 31–2.

37 Lorraine M. Elliott, 'Regime Building: The Antarctic Treaty System', in Lorraine M. Elliott (ed.), *International Environmental Politics: Protecting the Antarctic* (London: Palgrave Macmillan, 1994), pp. 25–49.

38 Hemmings, 'Re-Justifying the Antarctic Treaty System'.
39 Gillian Triggs, 'The Antarctic Treaty System: A Model of Legal Creativity and Cooperation', in Paul Arthur Berkman, Michael A. Lang, David W. H. Walton and Oran R. Young (eds), *Science Diplomacy: Antarctica, Science, and the Governance of International Spaces* (Washington, DC: Smithsonian Institution Scholarly Press, 2011), pp. 39–49.
40 Howkins, 'Appropriating Space', p. 47.
41 Non-consultative parties can attend the meetings but do not have any decision-making rights.
42 Antarctic Treaty, Article IX paras 1, 2, 4. Paragraph 2 states tha each Contracting Party that has become a party to the Treaty by accession has a right to appoint representatives to participate in the ATCMs *during such times* as that Contracting Party conducts substantial scientific research activity in Antarctica.
43 Tucker Scully, 'The Development of the Antarctic Treaty System', in Berkman *et al.*, *Science Diplomacy*, pp. 29–38.
44 Yelena Yermakova, 'Legitimacy of the Antarctic Treaty System: Is It Time for a Reform?', *Polar Journal* 11:2 (2021), 342–59.
45 Anne-Marie Brady, 'Opinion: Democratising Antarctic Governance', *The Polar Journal* 2:2 (2012), 451–61.
46 Hemmings, 'Considerable Values in Antarctica', p. 141.
47 Marcus Haward, 'The Originals: The Role and Influence of the Original Signatories to the Antarctic Treaty', in Klaus J. Dodds, Alan D. Hemmings and Peder Roberts (eds), *Handbook on the Politics of Antarctica* (Cheltenham: Edward Elgar Publishing, 2017), pp. 232–40 (p. 236).
48 Howkins, 'Appropriating Space', p. 47.
49 'Secretariat of the Antarctic Treaty', 'Parties', www.ats.aq/devAS/Parties?lang=e (accessed 16 February 2023).
50 Akiho Shibata, 'Japan and 100 Years of Antarctic Legal Order: Any Lessons for the Arctic?', in Gudmundur Alfredson, Timo Koivurova and Julia Jabour (eds), *The Yearbook of Polar Law* 7th edn (Leiden: Brill Nijhoff, 2015), pp. 3–54.
51 Antarctic Treaty Consultative Meeting (ATCM), 'Annex: Guidelines on the Procedure to Be Followed with Respect to Consultative Party Status', https://documents.ats.aq/recatt/att618_e.pdf (accessed 15 March 2024).
52 Jonathan Amos, 'Coronavirus Severely Restricts Antarctic Science', *BBC News*, 7 August 2020, www.bbc.com/news/science-environment-53699681 (accessed 16 February 2023).
53 Brady, 'Opinion', p. 452.
54 Shibata, 'Japan and 100 Years of Antarctic Legal Order', p. 36.
55 John A. Gulland, 'The Antarctic Treaty System as a Resource Management Mechanism: Living Resources', in Gillian Triggs (ed.), *Antarctic Treaty System: An Assessment* (Washington, DC: National Academies Press, 1986), pp. 221–34.
56 Peder Roberts, 'Does the Science Criterion Rest on Thin Ice?', *Geographical Journal* 189:1 (2020), 1–7.

57 On the need for cooperation between the ATS and other global forums, see Donald Rothwell, 'UNEP and the Antarctic Treaty System', *Environmental Policy and Law* 29:1 (1999), 17–24; Shibata, 'Japan and 100 Years of Antarctic Legal Order'.

58 Bohman, 'Republican Cosmopolitanism'.

59 Brady, 'Opinion', p. 460.

60 A possible objection might be that this would have implications for other international treaties, i.e that all states should have a say in all international arrangements. This is not necessarily so because Antarctica presents a unique case, having no Indigenous population, so there is no satisfactory explanation as to why some states get to participate in the decision-making and others do not.

61 Laborde and Ronzoni, 'What Is a Free State?'.

62 Marie Jacobsson, 'Building the International Legal Framework for Antarctica', in Berkman *et al.*, *Science Diplomacy*, pp. 1–16.

63 This was suggested by Kees Bastmeijer, 'Strategic Approaches to Antarctic Protection', paper presented at the 13th Polar Law Symposium, special online session, 2020. Additionally, a commission for Antarctic tourism could help to address regulatory gaps that arise from difficulties of consensus decision-making, if such a commission operates on the basis of majority voting.

64 See Arctic Council, 'About the Arctic Council', https://arctic-council.org/en/about/ (accessed 16 February 2023).

Bibliography

Amos, Jonathan. 'Coronavirus Severely Restricts Antarctic Science'. *BBC News*, 7 August 2020. www.bbc.com/news/science-environment-53699681. Accessed 16 February 2023.

Antarctic Treaty Consultative Meeting [ATCM]. 'Annex: Guidelines on the Procedure to Be Followed with Respect to Consultative Party Status'. https://documents.ats.aq/recatt/att618_e.pdf. Accessed 15 March 2024.

Arctic Council. 'About the Arctic Council'. https://arctic-council.org/en/about/. Accessed 16 February 2023.

Beck, Peter J. *The International Politics of Antarctica*. London: Croom Helm, 1986.

Berkman, Paul Arthur, Michael A. Lang, David W. H. Walton and Oran R. Young (eds). *Science Diplomacy: Antarctica, Science, and the Governance of International Spaces*. Washington, DC: Smithsonian Institution Scholarly Press, 2011.

Bohman, James. 'Republican Cosmopolitanism'. *The Journal of Political Philosophy* 12, no. 3 (2004): 336–52.

Brady, Anne-Marie. 'Opinion: Democratising Antarctic Governance'. *The Polar Journal* 2, no. 2 (2012): 451–61.

Burghardt, Andrew. 'The Bases of Territorial Claims'. *Geographical Review* 63, no. 2 (1973): 225–45.

Crawford, James. *Brownlie's Principles of Public International Law*. 8th edn. Oxford: Oxford University Press, 2012.

Day, David. *Antarctica: A Biography*. Oxford: Oxford University Press, 2013.

Dodds, Klaus J. 'Antarctic Geopolitics'. In *Handbook on the Politics of Antarctica*, ed. Klaus J. Dodds, Alan D. Hemmings and Peder Roberts, pp. 199–216. Cheltenham: Edward Elgar Publishing, 2017.

Dodds, Klaus J. 'Post-Colonial Antarctica: An Emerging Engagement'. *Polar Record* 42, no. 220 (2006): 59–70. DOI: 10.1017/S0032247405004857.

Elliott, Lorraine M. 'Regime Building: The Antarctic Treaty System'. In *International Environmental Politics: Protecting the Antarctic*, ed. Lorraine M. Elliot, pp. 25–49. London: Palgrave Macmillan, 1994.

Grotius, Hugo and William Welwod. *The Free Sea*, trans. Richard Hakluyt, ed. David Armitage. Indianapolis: Liberty Fund, 2004 [1609].

Gulland, John A. 'The Antarctic Treaty System as a Resource Management Mechanism: Living Resources'. In *Antarctic Treaty System: An Assessment*, ed. Gillian Triggs, pp. 221–34. Washington, DC: National Academies Press, 1986.

Hanrieder, Tine. 'The Path-Dependent Design of International Organizations: Federalism in the World Health Organization'. *European Journal of International Relations* 21, no. 1 (2015): 215–39.

Haward, Marcus. 'The Originals: The Role and Influence of the Original Signatories to the Antarctic Treaty'. In *Handbook on the Politics of Antarctica*, ed. Klaus J. Dodds, Alan D. Hemmings and Peder Roberts, pp. 232–40. Cheltenham: Edward Elgar Publishing, 2017.

Held, David, Anthony McGrew, David Goldblatt and Jonathan Perraton. *Global Transformations: Politics, Economics, and Culture*. Stanford, CA: Stanford University Press, 1999.

Hemmings, Alan D. 'Considerable Values in Antarctica'. *The Polar Journal* 2, no. 1 (2012): 139–56.

Hemmings, Alan D. 'Globalisation's Cold Genius and the Ending of Antarctic Isolation'. In *Looking South: Australia's Antarctic Agenda*, ed. Lorne Kriwoken, Julia Jabour and Alan D. Hemmings, pp. 176–90. Sydney: Federation Press, 2007.

Hemmings, Alan D. 'Re-Justifying the Antarctic Treaty System for the 21st Century: Rights, Expectations and Global Equity'. In *Polar Geopolitics: Knowledges, Resources and Legal Regimes*, ed. Richard C. Powell and Klaus J. Dodds, pp. 55–73. Cheltenham: Edward Elgar Publishing, 2014.

Hodgson-Johnston, Indi. 'The Laws of Territorial Acquisition as Applied to Claims to Antarctic Territory: A Review of Legal Scholarship'. *The Yearbook of Polar Law Online* 7, no. 1 (2016): 556–606.

Howkins, Adrian. 'Appropriating Space: Antarctic Imperialism and the Mentality of Settler Colonialism'. In *Making Settler Colonial Space: Perspectives on Race, Place and Identity*, ed. Tracey Banivanua Mar and Penelope Edmonds, pp. 29–52. London: Palgrave Macmillan, 2010.

Hurrell, Andrew. 'Global Inequality and International Institutions'. *Metaphilosophy* 32, nos 1–2 (2003): 34–57.

Hurrell, Andrew and Ngaire Woods (eds). *Inequality, Globalization, and World Politics*. Oxford: Oxford University Press, 1999.

Jacobsson, Marie. 'Building the International Legal Framework for Antarctica'. In *Science Diplomacy: Antarctica, Science, and the Governance of International Spaces*, ed. Paul Arthur Berkman, Michael A. Lang, David W. H. Walton and Oran R. Young, pp. 1–16. Washington, DC: Smithsonian Institution Scholarly Press, 2011.

Koskenniemi, Martti. *The Gentle Civilizer of Nations: The Rise and Fall of International Law 1870–1960*. Cambridge: Cambridge University Press, 2001.

Kriwoken, Lorne, Julia Jabour and Alan D. Hemmings (eds). *Looking South: Australia's Antarctic Agenda*. Sydney: Federation Press, 2007.

Laborde, Cécile. 'Republicanism and Global Justice: A Sketch'. *European Journal of Political Theory* 9, no. 1 (2010): 48–69.

Laborde, Cécile and Miriam Ronzoni. 'What Is a Free State? Republican Internationalism and Globalisation'. *Political Studies* 64, no. 2 (2014): 279–96. DOI: 10.1111/1467–9248.12190.

Lovett, Frank. 'Republican Global Distributive Justice'. *Diacritica* 24, no. 2 (2010): 13–30.

Machowski, Jacek. *The Status of Antarctica in the Light of International Law*. Warsaw: Office of Polar Programmes and the National Science Foundation, 1977.

Mancilla, Alejandra. 'Decolonising Antarctica'. In *Philosophies of Polar Law*, ed. Dawid Bunikowski and Alan D. Hemmings, pp. 49–61. Abingdon: Routledge, 2021.

Mancilla, Alejandra. 'The Moral Limits of Territorial Claims in Antarctica'. *Ethics & International Affairs* 32, no. 3 (2018): 339–60.

Mar, Tracey Banivanua and Penelope Edmonds (eds). *Making Settler Colonial Space: Perspectives on Race, Place and Identity*. London: Palgrave Macmillan, 2010.

Roberts, Peder. 'Does the Science Criterion Rest on Thin Ice?' *Geographical Journal* 189, no. 18 (2020): 1–7.

Rothwell, Donald. 'UNEP and the Antarctic Treaty System'. *Environmental Policy and Law* 29, no. 1 (1999): 17–24.

Scott, Shirley V. 'Ingenious and Innocuous? Article IV of the Antarctic Treaty as Imperialism'. *The Polar Journal* 1, no. 1 (2011): 51–62.

Scully, Tucker. 'The Development of the Antarctic Treaty System'. In *Science Diplomacy: Antarctica, Science, and the Governance of International Spaces*, ed. Paul Arthur Berkman, Michael A. Lang, David W. H. Walton and Oran R. Young, pp. 29–38. Washington, DC: Smithsonian Institution Scholarly Press, 2011.

Secretariat of the Antarctic Treaty. 'Parties'. www.ats.aq/devAS/Parties?lang=e. Accessed 16 February 2023.

Shibata, Akiho. 'Japan and 100 Years of Antarctic Legal Order: Any Lessons for the Arctic?'. In *The Yearbook of Polar Law*, ed. Gudmundur Alfredson, Timo Koivurova and Julia Jabour, 7th edn, pp. 3–54. Leiden: Brill Nijhoff, 2015.

Toma, Peter A. 'Soviet Attitude towards the Acquisition of Territorial Sovereignty in the Antarctic'. *The American Journal of International Law* 50, no. 3 (1956): 611–26.

Triggs, Gillian. 'The Antarctic Treaty System: A Model of Legal Creativity and Cooperation'. In *Science Diplomacy: Antarctica, Science, and the Governance of International Spaces*, ed. Paul Arthur Berkman, Michael A. Lang, David W. H. Walton and Oran R. Young, pp. 39–49. Washington, DC: Smithsonian Institution Scholarly Press, 2011.

Union of Soviet Socialist Republics. 'The Embassy of the Soviet Union to the Department of State'. In *Foreign Relations of the United States, 1950*, Vol. I, *National Security Affairs; Foreign Econimic Policy*, ed. Neal H. Peterson, John P. Glennon, David W. Mabon, Ralph R. Goodwin and William Z. Slany, pp. 912–13. Washington, DC: United States Government Printing Office, 1977.

United Nations. 'Treaty of Peace with Japan (with Two Declarations): Signed at San Francisco, on 8 September 1951'. *United Nations Treaty Series* 136, no. 1832 (1952): 45–164.

US Department of State, Office of the Historian. 'Decolonization of Asia and Africa, 1945–1960'. https://history.state.gov/milestones/1945-1952/asia-and-africa. Accessed 16 February 2023.

Yermakova, Yelena. 'Legitimacy of the Antarctic Treaty System: Is It Time for a Reform?'. *Polar Journal* 11, no. 2 (2021): 342–59.

Ypi, Lea. 'What's Wrong with Colonialism'. *Philosophy & Public Affairs* 41, no. 2 (2013): 158–91.

12

Techno-autochthony: For an ethnography of scientific colonisation in Antarctica

Luís Guilherme Resende de Assis

[F]or archaeology, it is possible to treat South America as a kind of laboratory: it was the last continent occupied on the planet, by a small founding population, but which, after a few millennia, exhibited the whole picture of social and political diversity characteristic of humanity.

(Neves, 2022: 74)[1]

Many Parties stressed that the ATCM's [Antarctic Treaty Consultative Meeting] work for peace, research and environmental protection should not be compromised by the military aggression of one Party against another ... The fact that the Meeting *was able* to adopt Measures, Resolutions and Decisions *in consensus* shows the strength and resilience of the Antarctic Treaty System.

[...]

[T]he meeting considered the decadal synopsis report .. by the Scientific Committee on Antarctic Research as the best available science and acknowledged the advice that *urgent action* is required to *prevent* irreversible *loss of Antarctic values* and consequences for the planet. *All parties* agreed that the ATCM has an *important role in addressing* the threat of global climate change, and decided to focus even more on the subject at the next ATCM.

[...]

In addition the Meeting focused on a specific species: the emperor penguin (...) While a formal decision on Special Protection Status *was blocked by one party*, most Parties indicated that they would nonetheless *implement the draft action plan* that had been developed intersessionally *on a national basis*.

[...]

Though widespread support was declared, *two parties were not ready to decide* on Canada's application at this meeting. The request will therefore be discussed again at ATCM 45, which will take place in Helsinki from 29 May to 8 June [2023].

(Host Country Communiqué,
XLIV ATCM, Berlin, 2022; emphasis added)

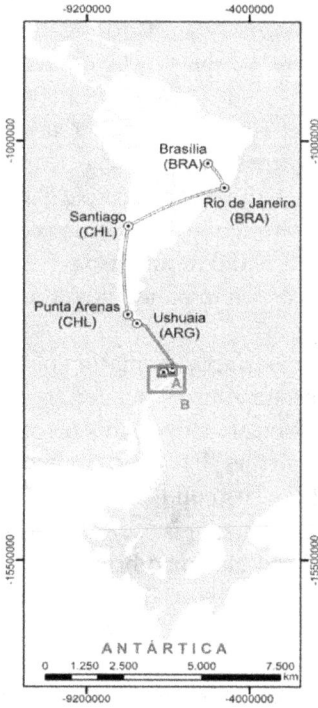

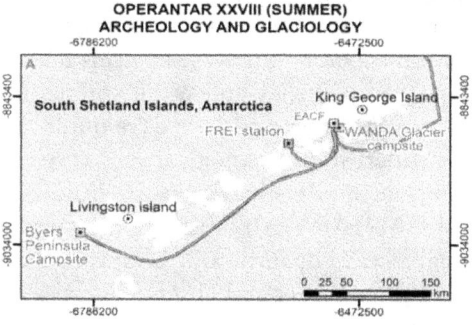

OPERANTAR XXVIII (SUMMER)
ARCHEOLOGY AND GLACIOLOGY

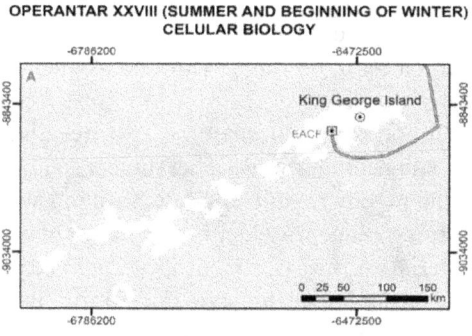

OPERANTAR XXVIII (SUMMER AND BEGINNING OF WINTER)
CELULAR BIOLOGY

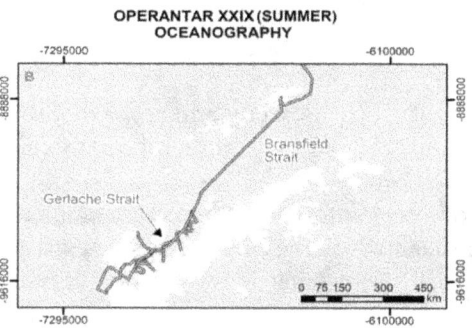

OPERANTAR XXIX (SUMMER)
OCEANOGRAPHY

LEGEND

☐ Studied Area
⊙ Traveled Places
-------- Air Route
~~~~ Sea Route

Datum: WGS 84

Map 12.1 Ethnographic studies area: general lines of movement (RT Raquel HF Costa, CREA / PA – 151.660.501).

'I think it is textile.' Quiet and crouched, suddenly Andrés Zarankin disengages himself from work and looks at me: 'We dig up trash, we have to be careful.' He rises and approaches, transversely transposing three quadrants. Along the way, he leans his torso 'out' of the perimeter string, suspended 6 inches above the surface layer – 'inside': 4 inches, maybe. We have been working for days outdoors under the clear summer sky of the 'Sealer 3' archaeological site: atypical brightness for tropical people. Night, in the Brasilia time zone: Andrés reaches the preferred spatula in a PROANTAR's 'Marfinite™', precipitating its function.[2] Technical coupling, tactical operation ... he approaches me: 'I will continue from here.' I give him my spot and observe him at a distance: pen in hand, gloves with cut-out fingers.

The delicate gestures flow, and there follows a perfect exhumation of the coarse textile imperfections, which had at some stage been mended by the user – a man, for sure. Required as an archaeological artifact, this piece of material obliged accostumed motor-perceptive virtues. This was a textile's condition to reveal dirtiness, textures and fashion. Its conditions to reveal the subject's gestures. The subject's, not the archaeologist's. Recognised in the precinct, Andrés's veteran hand wielded the esteemed brick trowel, scraping diligently. He, better than anyone, could bring to the surface the material culture as it is, or as it emerged from soil. Nothing more, nothing less: no signature, no style imposition, no tears, no carelessness. No marks that were not there already. 'Looks like a bonnet.' Metropolises feed on colonial silence: a typical clarity for tropical people.

Scarcity and *separateness*: Archaeologies of autochthonous colonisations[3]

For this chapter, 'autochthonous colonisation'[4] is the set of operative chains through which the specific pioneer experience – i.e. relative to the species – initially evanescing and wandering, is resolved, individuated, concretising a set of gestures, praxis, territorialities and anthropologically discrete traditions.[5] The vehicle of autochthony is motor perceptive virtues at the same time performed and resulting from integration operations, not always harmonic, between bodies, tools, architectures and magnitudes.[6] It is not particularly human beings who establish themselves as autochthonous, but rather the pedagogies of the itinerant experience, which insist on guiding them as contexts of demanding worlds. Humans: contexts of demanding worlds. Successful, we bipeds will soon use praxeogenetic functionalities as diacritical marks and segment ourselves socially.[7] The homogeneity without an 'Other' terrifies us. Differentiating oneself is the universal human practice, says anthropology. It can be noted, then, that function and meaning become together within the technical operations of individuation: the functioning is constituted of significant performances.[8] On the other hand, the becoming cannot be confused with interest – or even with consciousness. Once instantiated, the powers of praxis continue accomplishing performances beyond desire, beyond intention. Efficacy and success are unconfused in the specific autochthonous functioning. If a technical performance makes an operation work, then there is effectiveness. Effectiveness drives the meaning of the operation. The 'stony' concretions of human technical effectiveness, intentional or not, are called by the geosciences 'technogenes'.[9] Anthropological and (geo)archaeological questions about the 'morphology' and 'syntax' of technogenes give the opportunity for legitimate investigation of the techniques – of autochthonous colonisations.

It is important, then, to collate the technogenic records of the last successive human 'autochthonous colonisations': Amazon ($\approx$ 12,000 BP) and Antarctica ($\approx$ 250 BP).[10] Quite true, observed chronological interpositions of the phenomenon in Polynesia and Scandinavia do not reach the scale and continental impact of the tropics and the pole. The technogenic records of the archaeosphere are like praxeogenetic secretions in the new environments, witnessing colonial senses that literally *occurred* in the processing of (geo)forms, functions, landscapes, architectures, bodies, ethology, taphonomy and social segmentations.[11] In other words, the 'autochthonous colonisations' evidence successful or functional technical transformations over the medium of human bodies, architectures, artifacts and tools, which were forged and 'installed' in their turn within the very operatory chains demanded of the art of 'frequently' being or living there, connecting the Antarctic as part of the living territory for humans of a particular kind: for those transformed bodies, architectures, artifacts and tools. They are cosmopolitical celebrations that fixed primeval anthropic features, including – or markedly – in engaged humans.[12] Archaeologists find them in resolutives for everyday problems embedded in materiality and in their unintentional strands. Therefore, materiality is the semiotic medium where archaeological reflections unfold, denouncing different conceptual colonialisms about the unprecedented processes of human participation within the earth-system.[13]

Here predicated as techno-autochthonies, the primeval technical transformations are arranged as privileged 'objects' of archaeo-anthropological studies of the colonisation of Antarctica, within Antarctica (*sic*). Its statute attracts a 'contrast control' with the 'autochthonous colonisation' of the Amazon, consubstantiating technogenic records or memories, such as, for example, 'Amazonian dark earth', fat-derived char, carbon dioxide, black carbon, methane, microplastics.[14] Prudently, we do not lose sight of the superposition of modern colonial processes related to continental annexations by the world-system.[15] However, the 'colonial encounter' is replaced among cosmopolitan meanings of the concept of 'colonisation' itself, in the light of autochthonies that, in turn, shuffle the durations, in a Bergsonian sense.[16] The shuffling of geological, evolutionary and historical durations is what they call the 'Anthropocene'.[17]

To a large extent, 'dithering', this inability to make decisions in the metropolitan political bosom – notably in the Antarctic Treaty System (ATS) – derives from the ostracism of techno-autochthonies in the political theories of colonisation.[18] In them, the criticism of people domination by the managers of the world-system does not find correspondence with the modern-colonial cosmopolitanisms involved in the production of a geobiological history of the earth – and of autochthony itself. Consequently, the sense of 'novelty' and 'necessity' of the Anthropocene obnubilates technogenic segmentations within the 'autochthonous colonisations', moralising the duration.[19] Its morality is the generic human action giving negative results on nature, not the diachronic contrast of cosmographies recorded in technogenes, here thematised.[20]

Contrast control: Amazon and scarcity

The 'autochthonous colonisation' prior to the Antarctic is that of the Amazon. The archaeological interpretation of its technogenic records provincialises the scarcity as an explanatory element of 'white colonisation', centred, since the Comte de Buffon, on stratigraphic synchrony.[21] Synchronisation was the obsession of the Anthropocene Working Group (AWG) in search of a 'bottom' technogenic element, before its recent scientific denial by the stratigraphic community.[22] In the synchronic stratigraphic perspective, the 'autochthonous colonisation' of the Amazon is part of the past, owing nothing to the epoch placed before, even when referring to it – either as wilderness or as an identical 'fitting' to the global process of 'evolution to agriculture'.[23] Neither one nor the other will say the autochthonous 'Amazonian dark earth', brought into being by Brazilian archaeology.

First, because the 'Amazonian dark earth' – i.e. the autochthonous sedentarism – is recent ($\approx$ 2,500 BP), while the occupation in the Amazon dates back to the end of the Pleistocene ($\approx$ 12,000 BP), synchronous to all America, thus demonstrating, therefore, that it had never been a barrier for the human species. Second, its characteristic is why the successive concatenation of techno-autochthonous abandonments was explained only by ostensive abundance, not scarcity. The ancient Amerindians chipped stones. They stopped. Ceramics: they stopped. Fertile soil: they did not farm. What they did, diachronically, was to undertake a non-domestication cultivation of forest diversity, today called the Amazon ($\approx$ 9,000–8,000 BP), in consonance with the inconstancy of the soul that is today called 'Amerindian'.[24] Domestication or transition to agriculture has never occurred. The 'autochthonous colonisation' of the Amazon is an opening to alterity: a present, current, contemporary transition concurrent with 'white colonisation'. It is also coetaneous with the 'autochthonous colonisation' of Antarctica, just as the Amazon, right now while you are reading this, is working for earth-systems, as it has been since $\approx$ 9,000–8,000 BP, as an Amerindian technological device, not a pristine and imagined 'wilderness' – or, worse, 'nature' itself. Day after day, this device is corrupted ideologically by 'white' and 'developmental'-oriented devices.

A relevant archaeological doubt, which impacts what has been written about the Anthropocene, is whether or not the techno-autochthonous cultivation of the Amazon contributed to the extinction of the megafauna of the Pleistocene: eventually the only systematic *continuum* on a scale other than geological between the 'autochthonous colonisation' and the 'white colonisation'. Moreover, it is settled in the literature that the 'Amazonian dark earth' resulted from the habits of living in abundance. The social rupture, the technological transitoriness, and the Amazonian agroforestry cultivation demonstrate that 'autochthony' refers much more to cosmographic knowledge, opened to the circumstances of a today and a tomorrow, against that sedentarism that evolved into the national state, incorporating fear of tomorrow – and today. The Amazonian case impacts evolutionists' and economists' habits of thinking about the earth's history. I believe Antarctica does the same with the stratigraphic synchrony intended – and denied by scientists – by the AWG.

It is within this contrasting phenomenal framework that we, the social scientists, must think of the 'autochthonous colonisation' of Antarctica without allowing ourselves to be confused by the metropolitan colonisation of the signatories of the ATS. 'Before western history', human colonisation is a deep-time anthropological phenomenon engraved in the earth-system's material culture – the archaeosphere. We will find its relevancies by contrasting technical and, if available, historical processes of transformation of bodies, objects and ecologies within colonial sites. In this sense, the Amazon is a living and pungent archaeological site of technogenic records, similar to Antarctica. Some technogenic records are techno-autochthonous – such as Amazonian dark earth or Antarctic fat-derived char concretions and domestic black carbon. Others are not – such as high diachronic or regional soil concentrations of Amazonian mercury, or the hole in the Antarctic ozone layer. Identifying these 'regional' technogenic processes and their segmentations is fundamental to perceiving how power games are played within the earth-system, not – only – within the world-system of Wallerstein. If the Amazon is a techno-autochthonous

Amerindian device of undeniable positive global climate performance, hydro-electricity, mining, mineral pipeline routes, roads, transmission lines, gas pipelines and the like are techno-allochthonous white devices of undeniable negative global performance. Moralising a geological era by homogenising and emptying the civilisational technogenic diacritics is another form of barbarity, as it was – and is – the 'white colonisation' itself. The moderns need other means of absolving their guilt. The stratigraphic synchrony pursued by AWG seems useless, even if it was achieved – which was not the case.[25]

The study of 'autochthonous colonisations' must identify diachronic technogenic strata (intentional and unintentional) resulting from the recording and memorisation of human knowledge (nomadic or sedentary) within the archaeosphere. The secrets of cohesion or rupture between these strata are what we seek when performing ethnographies of the technique, including those of the archaeology, or of 'deep time's' tangible elements.[26] Intentional actions, such as 'non-domestication cultivation' and cosmographic agroforestry knowledge, characterise the Amazon as techno-autochthony. Its unintended effect in the 'open question' of the Pleistocene also made to the researcher: does the 'dark earth' or 'organised dispersion' of Holocene Amazonian hyper-dominant trees display – and explain – the synergy or rupture with white colonisation technological devices, concerning the Pleistocene's megafauna extinction? Likewise, intentional actions within Antarctica, such as the scientific methodological performances reiterated in the research, cosmograph diacritical signs regarding other techno-autochthonous segments: logistics operators, hunter-fishermen, tour operators, bio-geo-prospectors. Its unintended performances in the 'open question' of the Anthropocene also made to the researcher: 'Do the autochthonous technogenes (produced in the 'Great Acceleration' discovery process by Antarctic scientists) have effects synergistic or concurrent to those promoted by allochthonous technogenes, which dragged to Antarctica from other regions of the earth-system?' Such are the strong anthropological interrogations made of the shuffled durations of 'Deep-Time'.

Precolonial Antarctic cosmopolitanism: The separation

In Antarctica, the study of techno-autochthonies restores the Separation of colonial social segmentations equally indebted to the world-system and the earth-system. With this, it highlights the Anthropocene as a late metropolitan experience of coloniality. The diplomatic-imperial hesitation creatively imprinted in Article IV and in the cosmopolitan principles of 'peace, cooperation and science' of the ATS, the last refuge of colonial-modern hope, is a vivid example of this experience.

To understand the referred coloniality it is necessary first to distinguish the social segmentations that the ATS produced: on the one hand, scientists who settle methodological techno-autochthonies within Antarctica; on the other, remote managers of the enclave. The first glossed over the bad news from 'Geopolitics' to offer a tin ear to the latter: interested in 'geo-Politics' – in the singular. In other words, the political impositions of earth (the ones translated by geoscientists and climatologists) do not find an echo in the diplomatic encounters of the ATS, consolidating its vocation to systemic geopolitical inaction or hesitation in the inter(trans)national context. They are different humanities because the scientists, as such, are born and become autonomous in the architectures of the methods, becoming bibliographic surnames cited in other articles. And the meanings of the methods result from their functioning in the world – in this case, in Antarctica. Every model is before, modelled – so taught me the oceanographers who work with statistics, during my fieldwork research. And the methodological models are organisations of procedures from the relationship between scientific doubts and possibilities of satisfying them in interaction with the magnitudes of interest. The frequency with which this or that methodological arrangement is updated, forming recognised PhDs and authors, evidences techno-autochthonous traditions of recognisable features within Antarctica – whence the possibility of an ethnography of scientific colonisation. They are not to be confused, I repeat, with metropolitan colonists.

Although I postulate the sealer's period as 'precolonial', since its techno-autochthonies did not maintain a distinct tradition in Antarctica, the processes of social segmentation and related technogenic records converge with the contemporary colonial process established by the ATS. The debunked metropolitan Separation, still in force, originates with the sealers. This origin is perceived in the seminal discovery of the sealers' Antarctic pyrotechnology by geoarchaeology from samples collected in 2010 on the southern side of the Byers Peninsula, Livingston, at the 'Sealer 3' and 'Sealer 4' sites.[27]

At that time, the archaeological collection counted on diversified artifacts of the sealers' praxeological autochthony: pipes, furniture, board games, shoes, patches, sticks. They contrasted with the allochthonous material culture: sugar, coffee, barley, nails, textiles, cattle and pig bones. The interpretation of the artifacts positioned the Separation proper to the annexation of Antarctica to the world-system in the eighteenth and nineteenth centuries. This ideological frame of the 'wilderness' is a nobleman motif of (natural) history writing.

Anchored in the market's demand, the Separation satisfied pockets and 'Sino-Euroyankee' tastes, aiming to finance more and more 'sporadic' rounds of pinniped carnage. Explorations never undressed exploitations in the three sealers' cycles and beyond.[28] We disregarded the technogenic messages, which said a lot about the production of man's autochthony by man, in the cosmopolitan theatre of scarcity – a habit of ancestral thought of the contemporary Anthropocene, although less acedious and melancholic.[29] 'Living in the Cold', by Ximena S. Villagran, Carlos E. G. R. Schaefer and Bertand Ligouis, became a landmark for anthropological thinking about the autochthonous colonialisation of Antarctica, by proving the predominance of fat-derived char concretions at the sealer sites, as well as postdepositional and unintended taphonomic characteristics.[30] The fat-derived char typified the autochthonous energetic homeostasis in terrestrial space, contradicting previous archaeological interpretations, when charcoal was considered allochthonous, thus carrying substantive consequences. Note it.[31]

If allochthonous, then the archaeological debunking of Separation would be evidenced by the exposition of absolute metropolitan economic management of colonial scarcity. Counterfactually, social segmentation in Antarctica would figure as a true class design so that the subtraction of the historical protagonism of the sealers would also be of the technical experience within the environment itself. In other words, the sealers would be incapacitated for the intestinal (trans)individuation, homeostatic – the one that emanates from the need to solve themselves in the circumstances of everyday life.[32]

When setting sail, the writers of history would have planned all the possible resolutives for the sealers' subordinates. When docking, they performed the possible resolutives passively. Consequently, autochthonous techniques and artifacts would be ephemeral, even anecdotal, imposing metropolitan structural supplies' planning as the interpretative treadmill of material culture. Antarctica, the perfect colony, a blank slate, a true annex of social relations and differentiation processes identical to those observed in the world-system out there.

In this counterfactual vein, the archaeological site would present itself as a design of the method, and the archaeological interpretation, as spontaneity born and created in the university environment of the metropolises. The archaeologists would be transcendent, apt to deal with the immanence of the sites without any affection.[33] I shall speculate further. If the fat-derived char was allochthonous, the Antarctic scientific colonisation understanding based on the ATS would waive the 'anthropology of technique'.[34] The ethnography of symbolic and classificatory systems would be sufficient to illustrate the social segmentations, imperceptibly colonial, given that the scientists would be 'metropolitans in travel' in the service of a national Antarctic programme. Its segmentation owed nothing exactly to Antarctica but was due to the cultural diversity and power relations found in the geopolitics of knowledge and the transnational problems of national management of 'peace, cooperation and science'.

The Anthropocene, in turn, would be admitted as an entity or deity, or geological epoch, which finally 'arrived' in Antarctica, indicating, only now, the end of the Separation.[35] It would never be what it is: a feeling. The feeling of coloniality experienced in the metropolises in the form of failure of attempts to homogenise man – i.e. humanism. The feeling that we have never been a 'We', let alone humans. You have always been Others who have submitted everyone to Your Nature. And the objects of astronomy, as well as those of geology, are as indifferent to 'us' as the organisms that inhabit our guts. The metropolitan colonisers never listened to the autochthonous colonisers, spokesmen of the perennial austral revolt and, therefore, of the bad news: the *Pax Antarctica* has always been a cosmopolitan illusion, a colonialist vehicle. Well, then, char is autochthonous.

As fat-derived char concretions indicate, labour relations were crueller than once imagined in the human annexation of Antarctica to the world-system. The productivity of the business was associated with spontaneous solutions in the control of fire by workers, and, therefore, their energetic homeostasis. Not only did they feed partially on the Antarctic fauna but they heated themselves in it by reusing bones and fat, probably blubber. No metropolitan colonial capitalist design had been planned for the afterlife of the sealers who descended and remained on land. Thus, Antarctic pyrotechnology constitutes a techno-autochthony, extrapolating social segmentation beyond the class structure.[36]

The technogenic concretion was, at the same time, praxeogenetic: humans coalesced distinct from those who did not have the motor-perceptive virtues for pyrotechnology. These concretions, as soon we will see, incorporate the very same capacity of concentrating chemical elements as those concentrated in soils, because of birds' ethology. They also reproduce the very same pre-existing autochthonous taphonomic and pedologic activity. From the purposeful fuel shortage, we comprehend scarcity as a metropolitan colonial project, with no view to permanent occupation, whence the alleged Separation. From pyrotechnology, we see technical successes, the duration of the piecework and the permanence that played the role timidly. The workers received their wages from the productivity of each expedition, so they were interested in ensuring their stay while they could extract fur and fat. Would this be the superstructural calculation materialised in fat-derived char and operationalised in pyrotechnology?

Then, what to say about the labour relations in which the dominated had some autonomy to designate their journey? After all, the availability of fuel was much more abundant than was known, and its production was defined by the sealers' moods and pinniped colonies, not only by the provisional trial balances. Could they organise riots if the 'bosses' invited them to set sail, contrary to expectations of delay? Did the occupants of the highest ranks of the hierarchy depend on the production of fuel by the workers? Did all equally dominate pyrotechnics? What was the teaching and learning process like? What was the repercussion of the pyrotechnology for the already loosened hierarchical relations on land? Geoarchaeological findings inform us that the highest concentrations of fat-derived char were in the housing and living precincts, not in those destined for work. This means that the manufacture of autochthonous fuel impacted not only the speed of production of furs and oil but also competed for the use of the same craved-for resources for profit generation. What did these evidences deliver to the management of the production chain and human resources by traders?

At the metropolises and ports demanded by the ship's track, there arose the problem of the selection of workers. Were recidivists favoured for mastering pyrotechnics? What were the characteristics of the places and the nature of the hustle and bustle by which a novice became acquainted with the technique? Did Antarctic pyrotechnology produce typical architectures and convivialities in cities and ports? In other words, how did coloniality, the dark side of modernity, present itself in the metropolises?[37] What kind of humans, techniques, slynesses, foibles, needs, contingencies and implications did Antarctica itself regurgitate to cosmopolitan colonisers, transcendental men and national heroes?

Evidently, from the sealers to the present, such enquiries provide opportunity to anthropological imaginations of the autochthonous colonisation of Antarctica substantiated by the ethnography of techniques, replacing the design of scarcity with the circumstantial spontaneity of functional celebrations. Undoubtedly, the Separation has never made sense, but for reasons distinct from what we have imagined.

Archaeological performances in Antarctica are not tacit or explicit reproductions of exclusively methodological metropolitan cultures. The success of a methodological 'round' is its demonstrated ability to produce meaning in a given context, where functioning is meaning: the technical core affirmation. Consequently, from an anthropological perspective, there is hardly any such thing as 'deductive knowledge', as every element of the world is to be known within – or purified from – its context in a meaningful way. The world is sedentary, the theory is nomadic, and the methods are means to take one as if it was the other.[38] Note the architectonic parallel. Concrete, bricks and ironmongery do not in themselves have any signatures. But joined together by Oscar Niemeyer in Brasilia, they are sedentarised in the 'Brutalism' typical of the city. Similarly, chemical multielement processing and micromorphology are taken as generalised methods to study the formation of prehistoric technogenic soils. But its association with petrology, in

'Living in the Cold', refers to the previous experience of archaeologists, who invariably found 'coal' at the sites.[39]

The convocation and organisation of methods were obligations dictated by Antarctica through the archaeological requirement for clues of human settlement strategies on the Byers Peninsula.[40] And it is not just that. The methodological circumstances were derived from logistical determinisms, as every Brazilian polar scientist knows well. For the samples to be collected, the archaeologists undertook negotiations to book a coveted room for the team's geoarchaeologist in the Brazilian navy of the XXVIII OPERANTAR.[41] In an addendum, they had to sign interinstitutional agreements to process the three intertwined methods, multiplying the authorship of the knowledge produced.

Thus, at once, that methodological arrangement, in that OPERANTAR, resulted from Antarctica, guaranteeing, for another couple of years, the presence of archaeologists in Livingston. This is the reason why the contemporary sense of colonisation occurred – and occurs – in the technical performance of methodological functions, which, in Antarctica, are autochthonous – unequally competing with native heirs of nautical knowledge, logistics, fisheries, hunters and prospectors. They contrast with all these assiduous Antarctic regular frequenters, the metropolitan colonisers ensnared in the remote management of the enclave, generally studied by sociology, history, geopolitics, law and international relations.[42] The necessary revision of the mythical Separation is due to this social segmentation, whose technogenic and praxeogenetic ancestors are the fat-derived char and the sealers' pyrotechnology, respectively.

Additionally, the processes of production of technogenic records derived from pyrotechnology and, therefore, from sealers' social segmentation, resemble, on a minute scale, those of the current scientific colonisation of Antarctica. The indelible Anthropocene emerges there as another metropolitan cosmopolitanism, which sees in the colony a blank slate for the confirmation of its own contradictions. This was the case when the speed of fur production was affected by the purposeful invention of fuel shortages, providing the sealers with resolutives in the management of energetic homeostasis. It is the case now that the speed of scientific verifications, brought about by the invention of the ATS, buries the *Pax Antarctica* in the ashes of domestic production of black carbon, microplastics and other technogenes derived from scientific techno-autochthonies, tourism, fishing and others.[43] Techno-autochthonous social segmentation is still to be characterised ethnographically.

The acceleration of carbon concentration in the pedology of the sealer is notable. The geoarchaeologists carried out chemical analyses of soil elements from samples collected inside and outside the sites. From the point of view of the formative elements, they found little variation in the higher, lower and trace concentrations, which suggests parent sediments. However, in the combustion features, there are fewer local sediments and a higher concentration of technogenic particles. Only one of the insider sample units of the sites was characterised as typical Antarctic soil, even because it was extracted from the layer prior to the occupation layer. All the others – and herein lies the neuralgic point – had carbon concentrations comparable with ornithogenic soils. As there is no penguin area, the authors conclude that 'the enrichment would be anthropic'.[44]

Retranslating. There were 'episodic' sealers' settlements, characterising the first movements of the annexation of Antarctica to the world-system. There were three cycles: the shortest and bloodiest, from 1819 to 1825; the one from 1830 to 1850; and, finally, the one from 1870 to 1890. From the first to the third, resources and ships decreased, since the pinnipedspopulations could not recover from the initial slaughter throughout the century. In this perspective, the time of seals, wolves and elephants invaded the time of the sealers, gradually extruding them, until their final replacement by heroes – by-products of steam, electricity and imperialism.

Eventually, the precincts and camping sites could be reused in successive summers. Eventually! Ximena S. Villagran _et al._ state: 'In all cases, the stratigraphy is quite simple, with only one occupation layer with artifacts and combustion features.'[45] Thus, the technogenic soil, shy and little but present and autochthonous, took a couple of years to reach carbon concentrations similar to ornithogenic soils on the Byers Peninsula. The same peninsula is the largest ice-free extension of the Southern Shetlands, with 25 archaeological sites identified and 12 excavated. Well, currently, the area of scientific and logistical facilities in Antarctica is equivalent to the entire ice-free area below the 60° parallel.[46]

Is it not precisely the acceleration in carbon concentrations in elements of the earth-system and the occupation of ice-free areas that characterise the current scientific colonisation of Antarctica initiated by the ATS? Where is the Separation? And the rupture? Finally, we find the intransigently continuous effect of the annexation of Antarctica to the world-system that no postcoloniality, decoloniality or 'Shout of Independence' elucidates. Nor could it be because the political successions of metropolitan colonial ideologies never found correspondents in the autochthonous colonisation that persists and follows. Therefore, it is necessary to investigate the lineage and praxeological ruptures conducive to strata and technogenic successions in Antarctica – from fat-derived char to geoengineering projects still in the phase of dystopian hallucination, a mockery of 'new humanism' (_sic_).[47]

Finally, as the authors hypothesise, the sealers' site may be functioning as a technogenic means of fungal activities in the present, similar to
what occurs in natural soils where there are hairs or keratin. In general,
the production of microtissues is influenced by lithology and cryoturba-
tion, promoting a keratinophilic taphonomic process. Fungi degrade fur
by secreting structures nicknamed 'ghost hair'.[48] In this context, the geoarchaeology differs little from the study of soils, since the site is much more
soil in activity. The past is present, and the refution of Separation: technogene. We saw a similar effect in the control contrast of the Amazon. The
sealers' segmentation in the context of the annexation of Antarctica to the
world-system is taken to current social and material 'phenomenology'. It
is, therefore, available to the ethnography of social segmentations resulting from the technogenic settlement of scientific methods to which I have
been pleading for the techno-autochthony predication or, simply, scientific
colonisation.

In the case of sealers, the pyrotechnology supposes the praxeogenetics
in the control of fire, and the unintentional autochthonous concretion of
pedological characters. In the current colonisation, archaeology supposes
the praxeologics of excavation in the multidisciplinary manoeuvre of the
sealers' materiality. At the same time, it suggests the not-so-intentional vola-
tilisation, as aesthetic, of technogenic records of our own camping site: the
colonial character of remote management of the enclave by the ATS, via the
national state. I refer to the pile of stones used as windbreaks in our tents
and the mischaracterisation of any trace or garbage that could denounce
'unintentional' techno-autochthonous archaeological features.[49]

In these times of persistent denial of coloniality in the metropolises
– renowned for the supposed geological epoch of humans, because the
moderns were never to blame – it is symptomatic that when we unpiled
'our' stones, stones remained piled up by European researchers who territorialised that site – where we camped, not where we excavated. It is
symptomatic, too, that the aesthetic removal of our tracks took place as
we expected the approaching ship, followed by dozens of aircraft 'slings'
for equipment removal. Following orders, we erased the contradiction of
Antarctic scientific colonisation, without much certainty as to the effectiveness of those gestures. Would our legal obedience, PROANTAR's positive
etiquette in the ATS, somehow be contributing to the amelioration of metropolitan coloniality?

There were other concerns in mind: when would we return? Would it
be possible for Brazilian humanities to continue participating in the programme? What would be of the sealers' silence? What about contemporary
autochthonies? Can subaltern sciences speak?[50]

Yesterday there was another controversy initiated by C. Again, logistics tried to intervene in scientific practice, even here, where we are seven humans on an island. The civilian representative of the Brazilian navy said that today, we should not work in any of the periods of the day, given the meteorological information provided by the ship via radio. We have been digging for a few days, and it is tiring. Maybe C. is really tired of accompanying us. The work is monotonous for a climber; everything is flat and risk-free. Carry Marfinites™ plastic boxes every day, prepare food to take … I don't know. It is tiring. In any case, I packed the backpack with food because Zarankin is the one who defines if we are going to work; and there is no sign of a storm. A little later, S. arrived at the kitchen tent to organise the food as well. Let's go to the site, I think.

We arrived at the 'Sealer 4'. I sat down exhausted from the journey. I slept badly last night. I've been writing over time until now. I had only a couple of hours of sleep. Zarankin and F. went to the 'Sealer 3' to remove the vertebrae left in the centre of the excavation. They will then cover the area and the annex. I felt useless in the '4' and went to help in the '3'. When I arrived, the vertebra was already accommodated as an archaeological object. Some buckets of earth were poured into the covering and Zarankin asked me and F. to leave the grid E2 uncovered. It was the last excavation – and also the deepest, reaching the bottom of the debris of the stone wall. 'Let's leave a note', he said. I wrote, following the dictation of the archaeologist: 'Site excavated in February 2010 by the archaeology team of the Federal University of Minas Gerais – UFMG, Brazil. The situation of the Sealer Site 3: 60% excavated. Byers, February 23, 2010'. I wrapped the note so it wouldn't get wet. I was going to bury it, laughing 'inside', because of the archaeological joke. C. suggested leaving the note in evidence with a stake in the surface layer. He didn't seem to understand what was going on. Sometimes logisticians don't understand scientists; sometimes they don't want to. They have other concerns. They need to articulate the campsites with the ship, the station and – Brasilia. Zarankin smiled and ordered the burial, explaining: 'They'll have to read our articles, C., it's a joke with other archaeologists.' This is amazing for my research. In addition to the humour that makes the ethnography cool, it shows the circulation of scientific references on the site itself, not only in the virtual world of publications. I imagine the face of a hypothetical archaeologist of the future, who had not read the work of the team and excavated the 'Sealer 3', finding the note …

Zarankin planted our team, territorialised us. What a formidable demonstration of scientific colonisation! Irreverently, we are now part of the 'material culture' of the 'Sealer 3'. The Federal University of Minas Gerais (UFMG) is the 'bottom sediment' upon which any other archaeological production will have to rise. We have become necessary. Ignoring us will be a joke.[51]

The technogenic vortex and the colonial mirror

Before an interesting dialogue with the scientist Heitor Evangelista, the anthropological coherence between social segmentations and the autochthonous and allochthonous technogenic distinctions in Antarctica was not clear to me. It is curious how, recursively, after verifying that the references 'were already there', we seem naive in the first rounds of publication. Although aware of the phenomenon of autochthonous scientific colonisation – the ethnographic period from 2009 to 2021, with expeditions in 2010 and 2011 – I hesitated to foretell it this way.

Earlier, I used to deal with the cosmopolitical variations involved in Brazilian Austral praxeogenetics: a multi-methodological mashwork performing a game of physical forces, traction, movements, prehensions and energetic flows – wages and labour. The colonial architectures of the campsites, ships and station were stages of 'reciprocal co-captures' between military logistics and civil science, whence emanated technical celebrations of seven discrete human groupings: archaeologists, glaciologists, biologists, oceanographers, 'land' military, 'ship' military and civilian mountaineers.[52]

At that time, for the knowledge I had accumulated, only the structures and archaeological methods became techno-autochthonous insofar as they studied technogenic records and artifacts of the archaeosphere. The other techno-autochthonies did not seem to relate to technogenic records per se in that they did not objectively 'belong' to the archaeosphere. I had faith in the limits of the 'spheres'.[53] I did not perceive, for example, that the ontological motricities and overshadowings of the Wanda Glacier, identified by women geomorphologist glaciologists with sticks, balls, buckets, shovels and campsite, were technogenic records of the archaeosphere within the cryosphere: material culture in the southern vortex. I knew that those researches took place in the context of military logistics, in response to the historical context of the establishment of the ATS, resulting, through scientific performance, in the possibility of Brazil's diplomatic presence in Antarctica. I knew that the data would travel to laboratories and would be 'sanitised', i.e. standardised for disciplinary recognition and, therefore, for valid publication. I knew, evidently, that climate change and the Anthropocene are 'humans producing effects and beings in the world' and that Antarctica is the vortex of the earth-system. But that was it.

All this is entangled in the ATS, a characteristic device of the colonial hesitation of the Cold War, which structured, from the signatory metropolises, the human hierarchies worthy of entry and permanence. The ATS established that the academic elites of the elite countries would territorialise Antarctica at the whim of national interests travestied as scientific doubts in a transnational arena. The installation of the 'Nukey Poo', the affectionate nickname of a nuclear reactor, at McMurdo station, and the establishment of the Scott–Amundsen base at the South Pole, at the time of the signing of the Treaty, evidenced, from the outset, the kind of effort that a country such as Brazil would need to make in order to 'cooperate', i.e. to make itself known in polar scientific progress.

The scientific progress derived from austral praxeology has functioned as a pretext for national positionings in international relations. It rarely finds any echo within the colonial-metropolitan management of the enclave at a distance, otherwise by the Scientific Committee on Antarctic Research (SCAR). The political mark of war hesitation, the one aimed at containing sovereignties, and nuclear bellicose fencing, led to an institutional arrangement that depends on Separation to configure Antarctica as the most protected place on earth. As the Separation is a colonial metropolitan virtuality, the existent Antarctic colony really configures the most regulated and least protected place. The protective precepts of the 'public sphere' of the ATS are translated into structured institutions for hesitation in the icy 'public space', under penalty of 'jurisdictional' interference accusation on other international regimes and themes linked to the United Nations (UN).[54] Isn't it such an almost contradictory hesitation we read with added emphasis in the German 'Host Country Communiqué', to the XLIV ATCM, 2022, in the epigraph?[55] Such is the 'transnational' political condition of the Antarctic metropolitan colonisation – experienced nationally.

Within this framework, my research has shown that the metropolitan colonisation contrasts and competes with the social segments elected to represent it in the colony. In the colony, the scientific colonisation is that of sedimentation of the species in perennial technical transformation with the environment: praxeogenetics, a transition and distant opening but potentially similar to the 'autochthonous colonisation' of the Amazon. On other hand, the colonisation by the ATS represented a political dispute for meanings of the annexation of Antarctica to the world-system from metropolises, or candidates for metropolises differently disposed in a postcolonial diplomatic background (*sic*).[56] The scientific colonisation glossed over the reality of Antarctica as a vortex of the earth-system to which garbage from the world-system flows, whence the Anthropocene. The metropolitan colonisation originates the celebration of Separation in the form of international political hesitation.

At this point occurred the conversation with Heitor, which had an effect on me similar to the discovery of the fat-derived char for the archaeologists.

We were talking about the possibilities of my participation with his team in 'Ipanema', in the vicinity of the Brazilian Comandante Ferraz Antarctic Station (EACF), in the forthcoming expeditions. As before, I would try to comprehend the praxeologics of the activities, discerning in the functional methodological successes the meanings of the research – and, in these senses, to explore Brazilian participation in the scientific colonisation. Shrewd, jury-rigged solutions have always been dear to me because they mark operational foibles, distinctive of this or that laboratory, practising this or that method. Whenever I discovered some kind of foible, such as, for example, the trans-individual binocular system by which Brazilian oceanographers understand the demography of whales in the Gerlache Strait, I would study it as I would the publications of the group. I would understand the correspondence of the work with the methodological and technical canons, would comprehend the controversies that the academic world, aims solve and, then, would reconfigure, at different scales, the praxeologics of the austral scientific *intelligentsia*. I would thus demonstrate that the types of knowledge produced are, first, functional technical resolutions or, as I prefer, shrewd jury-rigged solutions – senses of tthe humanities within Antarctica that cannot be captured without ethnographic fieldwork research.

I also commented on the impossibility for any social scientist of my generation to be able to ignore the notion of the Anthropocene. I told Heitor that, in my opinion, if there was no scientific research in Antarctica, they would not have retranslated the Soviet Technogene as Anthropocene, associated with climate change ... that the colonisation of Antarctica coincided with the history – or with the possibility of history – of something called the Anthropocene. And that the Anthropocene was the feedback from scientific colonisation, overabundantly ignored by metropolitan colonisation. My perspective was still celebratory of the debutant concept – albeit tragic. The idea of Antarctica as a vortex of the earth-system was central and, I used to believe, there too, humans were propelled, dragged toward this polar vortex to Antarctica. They could rehearse modes of association more collaborative with the moods of the resurrected Gaia.[57] I used to believe ...

Through the lens of the anthropology of techniques, I recount here the story that disconcerted me. Heitor agreed with what I had suggested but made more or less evident my excessive use of the term 'Anthropocene' ... something foreign to his science (*sic*), and, therefore, preferred to speak in the terms he was more accustomed to using. I will admit this exclusion but, ending the present effort, I will resume other lexicons alluded to. Well then.

It was 1987. The Comandante Ferraz Antarctic Station – EACF – had a container module with construction foundations on display: southern Tupiniquim architecture.[58] Concrete discs balanced on the container with people. Scientists. One was Heitor. And he climbed a rudimentary ladder, one of those ladders for 'bricklayers', against the metal wall. Jeans and a coat were enough for summer on King George Island. He wanted to reach structures similar to pre-digital TV antennae.

Apparatus in hand, he measured the concentration of the magnitude of interest in the Antarctic vortex, the carbon dioxide. It was the time that the hole in the ozone layer over Heitor's head was made public by the operation of austral techno-autochthonies,[59] the time when the fires in the Amazon made the headlines. Heitor wrote down 'CO_2: 350 ppm'. Curiosities increased about other vortex technogenes, such as black carbon, even if their austral concentrations barely met Greenland's pre-Industrial Revolution patterns. This facilitated foreign technogenic identification: Amazon, Indonesia, Africa, Andes, Patagonia …

2007, Detroit Plateau, Antarctic Peninsula. The article of Heitor's most widely read by peers, around the world, was celebrating a year.[60] It had become famous for being the first real-time monitoring of Amazonian particles landing in Antarctica, including in the winter of 1993. Invariably, the black carbon increased in September, coinciding with the feats of spontaneous burning, or derived from the 'white colonisation' of the techno-autochthonous Amazon. Heitor's body now wore special clothes, even an 'astronaut' helmet. The plateau was 1,900 metres high and had low temperatures. It was expected that the extraction of the testimony of a 20-metre ice core would reverse the last 50 years of Amazonian burning. Meanwhile, taken to Nevada, to the famous 'Desert Research Institute', the testimony betrayed Heitor. Twice. The organic volatiles were technogenic, not derived from nature's activities. Heitor even cogitated that he would have ruined everything in the collection, contaminating the sample. That was uncommon. But his colleague denied that possibility. Even worse, the testimony told the story of only five years of black carbon. Frustration.

Shrewd jury-rigged solutions: 'classify what we have in terms of the seasons of the year', he said to his colleagues. The dative precision would be high, as well as the fright of the results, secreted in the performance of the techno-laboratorial function: 60 per cent of black carbon did not correspond to months of burning in any continent in the world. And Heitor searched well. But it didn't 'match'. Shrewd jury-rigged solution: 'correlate concentrations with all the navigations and flights on the Peninsula in the period. Tourism, fishing and research: everything'. Bingo! The black carbon was technogenic, explaining, in tow, the aerosols of similar origin. Techno-autochthonies are unevenly productive of the elements and particles: tourism, fishing and science. It brought about a paradigm shift. It brought about the anthropological necessity of comprehending the social segmentations in Antarctica by technogenes, not just by praxeological and cosmopolitical ones. The question of autochthony as colonisation has gained concreteness. The vortex, mirror of coloniality.

2022. Heitor no longer climbs rudimentary ladders to measure carbon dioxide. He receives the data on screens of the 'Ipanema', his austral laboratory. The display shows 420 ppm. The 70 ppm of difference captured by hand in 1987 corresponds to the integrality of an interglacial period: ≈ 10,000 years. Today, the problem in the austral colony is grievously serious. Very grievous. The secrets of the circumstances that led the western sector to melt down blatantly were not whispered to scientific techno-autochthonies. The despair of the coloniality that presents itself in the Antarctic metropolises is such that carbon dioxide has already been set aside as something that can be 'fought' in a timely manner.

The metropolitans have given up on hesitation. They need to buy time. They elected battles and possible enemies so as not to lose hope in the humanity that they chose to be. 'Attack methane and black carbon', says the Intergovernmental Panel on Climate Change (IPCC) of the United Nations – not the ATS. Over the western sector lay the most robust techno-autochthonies of tourism, fishing and science. There is the black carbon, a technogenic 'lexicon' to be considered in the semiotic web of scientific colonisation, which needs to keep going. Or you will not know how you are being defeated.

The contradictions of coloniality perceived by Heitor are a spark of disorientation caused in the Antarctic metropolises that, by establishing hesitation as a means of waging the Cold War, seems to have nothing to do with the non-powers it has created. It has never been so urgent to study anthropologically the technical transformations within Antarctica and the relations between techno-autochthonies and scrambles in the duration.[61] As denounced by the sealers' fat-derived char concretions, the colonial situation is more dramatic than imagined. The vortex vomits the image and resemblance of the world-system. It no longer synthesises allochthonous aggressions to pristine autochthonies. How will the colonial metropolises hear the colony if they barely know what's going on anthropologically in it?

Separation? None. Scarcity? What does this mean? Peace? The Peace … perhaps one day nature will abandon circumstantial spontaneity and return to the designs of obscurantism.[62] The politics of scientific denial long for this day when the Promise will be reached of a 'land flowing with milk and honey'. Until then, we know the settlers, there will be a cosmopolitical war. Against or through the ATS.

Acknowledgements

This chapter was translated by Aniky Martins de Freitas Barros.

Notes

1 Eduardo Neves, *Sob os tempos do equinócio: Oito mil anos de história na Amazônia Central* (São Paulo: Ubu Editora, 2022), p. 74. Free translation.
2 The Brazilian Antarctic Programme.

3 Julian Steward, 'Culture Areas of the Tropical Forests', in Julian Steward (ed.), *Handbook of South American Indians* (Washington, DC: Bureau of American Ethnology, Smithsonian Institute, 1948), pp. 883–903; Jeffrey McGee, 'Frozen Eden Lost? Exploring Discourses of Geoengineering Antarctica', in Elizabeth Leane and Jeffrey McGee (eds), *Anthropocene Antarctica* (Abingdon: Routledge, 2020), pp. 56–72; Thomas Headland and Robert Bailey, 'Have Hunter-Gatherers Ever Lived in Tropical Rain Forest Independently of Agriculture?', *Human Ecology* 19:2 (1991): 115–22; Rosivach, 'Autochthony and the Athenians'.

4 Why autochthonous and not Indigenous? Over 13,000 years ago, the 'original' people's ancestors colonised the Amazonian plains, yet to be proven the Neolithic phenomenon and the agricultural revolution at that time. Yet to be confused with the natives of India by two successive and related mistakes in the mythical 'discovery of America – and of Brazil': (i) ethnocidal racism, typical of the Nautical School of Sagres in the fifteenth and sixteenth centuries, and (ii) the reinvented 'navigation mistake' would have led to the American 'discoveries'. To be an Indian, in the seventeenth-century European sense, was a terminative condition: not to be human. That is, not having a soul, not recognising Christ; kings; and, the greatest of gods, money. It took 500 years to complete the anthropophagy and positive politicisation of the term 'Indigenous' by social movements, which exorcised the systematic decimation and rape of entire populations, implied in the white sense of the word. Therefore, borrowing the term to define the human colonisation of Antarctica, disassociated from its conceptual history, is temerarious. Even more so because the autochthonous colonisation of Antarctica is performed hegemonically by cis-, non-Indigenous men from the upper and middle classes, coming from the signatory countries of the ATS. Let it be said, by the way, that the same temerarious use is observed in unthinking borrowings, irrespective of the historical meaning of the term 'postcolonial', arduously incorporated into the dated grammar of African and Indian resistance. The ordinary usage of the term 'Indigenous', in the English-speaking world, to refer to non-human things or species, even in the biological sciences, needs to be rethought, as it is deeply misleading and, without a doubt, racist. The terms 'autochthonous' and 'allochthonous' occur frequently in geosciences. Furthermore, 'autochthonous' is how the ancient Greeks, awardees of the title of citizens, self-referenced their belonging to the ground, the nativity of the *polis* and the exclusivity of access to the world of political decisions. Carlos Fausto and Eduardo G. Neves, 'Was There Ever a Neolithic in the Neotropics? Plant Familiarization and Biodiversity in the Amazon', *Antiquity* 92:366 (2018), 1604–18; Klaus J. Dodds and Christy Collis, 'Post-Colonial Antarctica', in Klaus J. Dodds, Alan D. Hemmings and Peder Roberts (eds), *Handbook on the Politics of Antarctica* (Cheltenham: Edward Elgar Publishing, 2017), pp. 50–68; Vincent J. Rosivach, 'Autochthony and the Athenians', *Classical Quarterly* 37:2 (1987), 294–306.

5 Marcel Mauss, 'Techniques of the Body', *Economy and Society* 2 (1973): 70–88; André Leroi-Gourhan, *Gesture and Speech* (Cambridge, MA: MIT Press, 2018); Gilbert Simondon, *Individualization in Light of Notions of Form and Information*, 2 vols (Minneapolis: University of Minnesota Press,

2020); Gilbert Simondon, *On the Mode of Existence of Technical Objects* (Minnesota: University of Minnesota Press, 2016); Ludovic Coupaye, 'Ways of Enchanting: Châines Opératoires and Yam Cultivation in Nyamikum Village, Maprik, Papua New Guinea', *Journal of Material Culture* 14:4 (2009): 433–58; Nathan Schlanger, 'The Chaîne Opératoire', in Colin Renfrew and Paul Bahn (eds), *Archaeology: Key Concepts* (London: Routledge, 2005).

6 Isabelle Stengers, 'Introductory Notes on an Ecology of Practices', *Cultural Studies Review* 11:1 (2005): 183–96; Isabelle Stengers, 'The Cosmopolitical Proposal', in Bruno Latour and Peter Wibel (eds), *Making Things Public* (Cambridge, MA: MIT Press, 2007), pp. 994–1006. Isabelle Stengers, *Cosmopolitics I* (Minnesota: University of Minnesota Press, 2010); Isabelle Stengers, *Cosmopolitics II* (Minnesota: University of Minnesota Press, 2011); Luc Ferry, *A revolução do amor: Por uma espiritualidade laica* (Rio de Janeiro: Objetiva, 2012); Vladimir Safatle, 'O ato para além da lei: "Kant com Sade" como ponto de viragem do pensamento lacaniano', in Vladimir Safatle (ed.), *Um limite tenso: Lacan entre a filosofia e a psicanálise* (São Paulo: Editoria UNESP, 2002), pp. 189–232; Reginaldo O. Silva, 'Kant e Sade na alcova: Sobre os paradoxos da ética moderna', *Princípios revista de filosofia* 21:36 (2014), 177–98.

7 Carlos E. Sautchuk, 'Técnica e/em/como transformação', in Carlos E. Sautchuk (ed.), *Técnica e transformação* (Rio de Janeiro: ABA Publicações, 2017), pp. 11–36; Carlos E. Sautchuk, 'The Pirarucu Net: Artefact, Animism and the Technical Object', *Journal of Material Culture* 24:2 (2018), 1–18; Jean-Pierre Warnier, 'A Praxeological Approach to Subjectivation in a Material World', *Journal of Material Culture* 6:1 (2001), 5–24; Jean-Pierre Warnier, 'Technology as Efficacious Action on Objects ... and Subjects', *Journal of Material Culture* 14:4 (2009), 459–70.

8 Bryan Pfaffenberger, 'Social Anthropology of Technology', *Annual Review of Anthropology* 21:1 (1992), 491–516; François Sigaut, 'Technology', in Tim Ingold (ed.), *Companion Encyclopedia of Anthropology: Humanity, Culture and Social Life* (London: Routledge, 1994), pp. 420–59.

9 George Ter-Stepanian, *Beginning of the Quinary or the Technogene: An Engineering Geological Analysis*, Laboratory of Geomechanics IGES, Ac. Sc. Communication 5 (Yerevan: Armenian Academy of Sciences Press, 1985); George Ter-Stepanian, 'Beginning of the Technogene', *Bulletin of the International Association of Engineering Geology/Bulletin de l'Association internationale de géologie de l'ingénieur* 38 (1988), 133–42. George Ter-Stepanian, 'Did the Quinary Start?', *XI Congress of the International Union for Quaternary Research: Abstracts* (1983), 260; Antonio M. S. Oliveira and Alex U. G. Peloggia, 'The Anthropocene and the Technogene: Stratigraphic Temporal Implications of the Geological Action of Humankind', *Quaternary and Environmental Geosciences* 5:2 (2014), 103–11.

10 Neves, *Sob os tempos do equinócio*; Fausto and Neves, 'Was There Ever a Neolithic in the Neotropics?'; Paulo Tavares, 'The Geological Imperative: On the Political Ecology of the Amazonia's Deep History', in Etienne Turpin (ed.), *Architecture in the Anthropocene* (Detroit, MI: Open Humanities

Press, 2013), pp. 209–40. Cf. Andrés Zarankin, Fernanda Codevilla Soares, Melisa A. Salerno *et al.*, 'Paisagens em branco: Balanço após 10 anos de existência no Brasil', in Andrés Zarankin, Luiz H. Rosa, Rosa M. E. Arantes and Fernanda Codevilla Soares (eds), *Antártica em Minas Gerais* (Belo Horizonte: Imprensa Universitária da UFMG, 2021), pp. 23–62; Andrés Zarankin, Sarah Hissa, Melisa A. Salerno *et al.*, 'Paisagens em branco: Arqueologia e antropologia antárticas – avanços e desafios', *Vestígios: Revista Latino-Americana de Arqueología Histórica* 5:2 (2011), 9–51; Melisa A. Salerno, María Jimena Cruz and Andrés Zarankin, 'A Historical Archaeology of the First Antarctic Labourers', in Adrian Howkins and Peder Roberts (eds), *The Cambridge History of the Polar Regions* (Cambridge: Cambridge University Press, 2023), pp. 407–29; Michael Pearson, Andrés Zarankin and Melisa A. Salerno, 'Exploring and Exploiting Antarctica: The Early Human Interactions', in Marc Oliva and Jesus R. Fernandez (eds), *Past Antarctica: Paleoclimatology and Climate Change* (London: Elsevier Academic Press, 2020), pp. 259–77.

11 Chosen as a concept that highlights material culture's 'deep time' mode of existence (inscription, memorisation or 'sedimentation') side by side with other relevant 'spheres' of the earth-system (bio-, crio-, pedo-, litho- and atmo-) whose magnitudes are relevant to characterise as 'critical zones'. See Tim Ingold, 'Beyond Art and Technology: The Anthropology of Skill', in Michael B. Schiffer (ed.), *Anthropological Perspectives on Technology* (Albuquerque: University of New Mexico Press, 2001), pp. 17–32; Pfaffenberger, 'Social Anthropology of Technology'; Sigaut, 'Technology'; Etienne Turpin, 'Who Does the Earth Think It Is, Now?', in Etienne Turpin (ed.), *Architecture in the Anthropocene* (Detroit, MI: Open Humanities Press, 2013), pp. 3–10; David G. Anderson , Jan Peter Laurens Loovers, Sara Asu Schroer and Robert P. Wishart, 'Architectures of Domestication: On Emplacing Human–Animal Relations in the North', *Journal of the Royal Anthropological Institute* 23 (2017), 398–418; Sautchuk, 'Técnica e/em/como transformação'; Sautchuk, 'The Pirarucu Net'.

12 Cf. Stengers, *Cosmopolitics I*; Stengers, *Cosmopolitics II*.

13 Lucien Lévy-Brühl, *Primitive Mentality* (London: Allen & Unwin, 1923); Pedro Paulo Pimenta, 'Antropoceno: Apontamentos para a história de uma ideia', in Stelios Marras and Renzo Taddei (eds), *O Antropoceno* (São Paulo: Fino Traço, 2022), pp. 1–16.

14 Neves, *Sob os tempos do equinócio*; Ximena S. Villagran, Carlos E. G. R. Schaefer and Bertrand Ligouis, 'Living in the Cold: Geoarchaeology of Sealing Sites from Byers Peninsula', *Quaternary International* 315 (2013), 184–99; Raúl R. Cordero, Edgardo Sepúlveda, Sarah Feron *et al.*, 'Black Carbon Footprint of Human Presence in Antarctica', *Nature Communications* 13 (2022), 984; Enio B. Pereira, Heitor Evangelista, Kely Cristine Dalia Pereira, Iracema F. A. Cavalcanti and Alberto W. Setzer, 'Apportionment of Black Carbon in the South Shetland Islands, Antarctic Peninsula', *Journal of Geophysical Research* 111 (2006), D03303, DOI: 10.1029/2005JD006086; Daniel Sigman and Edward Boyle, 'Glacial/Interglacial Variations in Atmospheric Carbon Dioxide', *Nature*

407:19 (2000), 859–69; William J. Collins, Christopher P. Webber, Peter M. Cox *et al.*, 'Increased Importance of Methane Reduction for a 1.5 Degree Target', *Environmental Research Letters* 13:5 (2018), 054003, DOI: 10.1088/1748-9326/aab89c; Clara Leistenschneider, Patricia Burkhardt-Holm, Thomas Mani, Sebastian Primpke , Heidi Taubner and Gunnar Gerdts, 'Microplastics in the Weddell Sea (Antarctica): A Forensic Approach for Discrimination between Environmental and Vessel-Induced Microplastics', *Environmental Science and Technology* 55:23 (2021), 15900–11.

15 Walter Mignolo, 'The Geopolitics of Knowledge and the Colonial Difference', *The South Atlantic Quarterly* 101:1 (2002), 57–96; Walter Mignolo, *The Darker Side of Modernity* (Durham, NC: Duke University Press, 2011); Immanuel Wallerstein, *World Systems Analysis* (Durham, NC: Duke University Press, 2006).

16 Talal Asad (ed.), *Anthropology and the Colonial Encounter* (London: Ithaca Press, 1973); Bruce Robbins, 'Really Existing Cosmopolitanism', in Pheng Cheah and Bruce Robbins (eds), *Cosmopolitics* (Minneapolis: University of Minnesota Press, 1998), pp. 1–19; Henri Bergson, *Duration and Simultaneity* (Manchester: Clinamen Press, 1999).

17 Pimenta, 'Antropoceno'; Paul J. Crutzen, 'Geology of Mankind', *Nature* 415 (2002), 23, DOI: 10.1038/415023a; Paul J. Crutzen and Eugene F. Stoermer, 'The "Anthropocene"', *IGBP Global Change Newsletter* 41 (2000), 17–18; Jan Zalasiewicz, Colin N. Waters, Colin P. Summerhayes *et al.*, 'The Working Group on the Anthropocene: Summary of Evidence and Interim Recommendations', *Anthropocene* 19 (September 2017), 55–60; Phillip L. Gibbard, Michael Walker, Andrew Bauer *et al.*, 'The Anthropocene as an Event, not an Epoch', *Journal of Quaternary Science* 37:3 (2022), 395–9.

18 Juan F. Salazar, 'The Anthropocene Melt: Antarctica's Geologic Politics', in Elizabeth Leane and Jeffrey McGee (eds), *Anthropocene Antarctica* (Abingdon: Routledge, 2020), pp. 73–83.

19 Ben Maddison, *Class and Colonialism in Antarctic Exploration, 1750–1920* (London: Pickering & Chatto, 2014); Mignolo, *The Darker Side of Modernity*; Mignolo, 'The Geopolitics of Knowledge'; Aníbal Quijano, 'Coloniality of Power, Eurocentrism and Latin America', *Nepantla* 1:3 (2000), 533–80; Asad, *Anthropology and the Colonial Encounter*; Pimenta, 'Antropoceno'.

20 Paul Little, *Amazonia: Territorial Struggles on Perennial Frontiers* (Baltimore, MD: Johns Hopkins University Press, 2001); Ter-Stepanian, 'Did the Quinary Start?'; Ter-Stepanian, *Beginning of the Quinary or the Technogene*; Ter-Stepanian, 'Beginning of the Technogene'; Oliveira and Peloggia, 'The Anthropocene and the Technogene'.

21 Neves, *Sob os tempos do equinócio*; Pimenta, 'Antropoceno'.

22 Gibbard *et al.*, 'The Anthropocene as an Event'.

23 Fausto and Neves, 'Was There Ever a Neolithic in the Neotropics?'.

24 Eduardo Viveiros de Castro, *A inconstância da alma selvagem* (São Paulo: Cosac & Naify, 2002).

25 Gibbard *et al.*, 'The Anthropocene as an Event'.

26 Colin Tudge, *The Time before History: 5 Million Years of Human Impact* (New York: Touchstone, 1996).

27 Villagran *et al.*, 'Living in the Cold'.

28 Pearson *et al.*, 'Exploring and Exploiting Antarctica'.

29 In the Anthropocene, medieval feelings such as 'Acedia' and 'Melancholia' returned to westerners. Addressing these feelings, I say that the Anthropocene is the coloniality lately felt by the ex-coloniser. These 'new-old' feelings of Acedia and Melancholia, due to the Anthropocene, are 'just' coloniality. The moderns say 'We have never been moderns' because they probably did not know that, unlike 'modernity', coloniality is not something one can choose or discard. It is concrete and perceived by people. Mignolo says that modernity-coloniality (or vice versa) is a one-word concept, but he did not reach this point of showing coloniality in modern territories. He just showed that modernity and coloniality constitute the same historical, political and epistemic process. People from ex-colonies should know this. And I say that people from metropolises should feel it. And they do. (Cf. Pimenta, 'Antropoceno'.)

30 Villagran *et al.*, 'Living in the Cold'.

31 Zarankin *et al.*, 'Paisagens em branco: Balanço após 10 anos de existência no Brasil'; Zarankin *et al.*, 'Paisagens em branco: Arqueologia e antropologia antárticas'; Andrés Zarankin, María Ximena Senatore and Melisa A. Salerno, 'No Man's Land: Landscape Archaeology in South Shetlands Islands, Antarctica', in Andrés Troncoso and Felix Acuto (eds), *South America Landscape Archaeology* (Oxford: British Archaeological Reports, 2009); Andrés Zarankin and Melisa A. Salerno, 'The Anthropocene in Antarctica: Considering "Fixed" and More "Fluid" Perspectives of Analysis', in Marcos A. T. Souza and Diogo M. Costa (eds), *Historical Archaeology and Environment* (Cham: Springer International, 2018), pp. 253–65; Andrés Zarankin and Melisa A. Salerno, 'The Wild Continent? Some Discussion on the Anthropocene in Antarctica', *Journal of Contemporary Archaeology* 1:1 (2014), 116–20; Salerno *et al.*, 'A Historical Archaeology'; Andrés Zarankin and María Ximena Senatore, *Histórias de um pasado en blanco* (Belo Horizonte: Argumentum, 2007); Andrés Zarankin and María Ximena Senatore, 'Archaeology in Antarctica', *Cuartas jornadas de investigación antárticas/Fourth Conference on Antarctic Research* 2 (1997), 7–10; Pearson *et al.*, 'Exploring and Exploiting Antarctica'; M. Pearson and María Ximena Senatore, 'Conserving the Oldest Historical Sites in the Antarctic', *Polar Record* 46 (2009), 57–64 (p. 57).

32 Simondon, *Individualization*.

33 Jeanne Favret-Saada, 'Ser afetado', *Cadernos de campo* 13:13 (2005), 155–61.

34 Mauss, 'Techniques of the Body'; Leroi-Gourhan, *Gesture and Speech*; Simondon, *Individualization*; Ingold, 'Beyond Art and Technology'; Pfaffenberger, 'Social Anthropology of Technology'; Sigaut, 'Technology'.

35 Cf. Elizabeth Leane and Jeffrey McGee, 'Anthropocene Antarctica: Approaches, Issues and Debates', in Leane and McGee, *Anthropocene Antarctica*, pp. 1–14; McGee, 'Frozen Eden Lost?'; Salazar, 'The Anthropocene Melt'; Tim Stephens, 'Governing Antarctica in the Anthropocene', in Leane and McGee,

Anthropocene Antarctica, pp. 17–32; Ben Maddison, 'Indigenising the Heroic Era of Antarctic Exploration', in Leane and McGee, *Anthropocene Antarctica*, pp. 136–55.

36 Cf. Maddison, *Class and Colonialism*.

37 Mignolo, *The Darker Side of Modernity*.

38 Stengers, 'Introductory Notes'; Stengers, 'The Cosmopolitical Proposal'.

39 Villagran *et al.*, 'Living in the Cold'; Ximena S. Villagran and Carlos E. G. R. Schaefer, 'Geoarqueologia das primeiras ocupações humanas na Antártica', *Vestígios: Revista Latino-Americana de Arqueología Histórica* 5:1 (2011), 115–36.

40 Stengers, *Cosmopolitics I*.

41 The 28th Antarctic Operation of the Brazilian Antarctic Programme.

42 Little, *Amazonia*.

43 Cordero *et al.*, 'Black Carbon Footprint'; Leistenschneider *et al.*, 'Microplastics in the Weddell Sea'; Pereira *et al.*, 'Apportionment of Black Carbon'.

44 Villagran *et al.*, 'Living in the Cold', p. 195.

45 Villagran *et al.*, 'Living in the Cold', p. 189 (italics added).

46 Shaun T. Brooks , Julia Jabour, John van den Hoff and Dana M. Bergstrom, 'Our Footprint on Antarctica Competes with Nature for Rare Ice-Free Land', *Nature Sustainability* 2 (2019), 185–90 (p. 185).

47 McGee, 'Frozen Eden Lost?'.

48 Villagran *et al.*, 'Living in the Cold', p. 196.

49 Zarankin and Salerno, 'The Anthropocene in Antarctica'; Zarankin and Salerno, 'The Wild Continent?'.

50 Cf. Rosalind. C. Morris and Gayatri C. Spivak (eds), *Can the Subaltern Speak? Reflections on the History of an Idea* (New York: Columbia University Press, 2010).

51 Fieldwork Diary, Notebook 02, 23 February 2010.

52 Stengers, 'Introductory Notes'; Stengers, 'The Cosmopolitical Proposal'; Stengers, *Cosmopolitics I*; Stengers, *Cosmopolitics II*; Sautchuk, 'Técnica e/em/como transformação'; Sautchuk, 'The Pirarucu Net'.

53 Raquel G. Aguilar, Rebecca Owens and John R. Giardino, 'The Expanding Role of Anthropogeomorphology in Critical Zones Studies in the Anthropocene', *Geomorphology* 366:1 (2020), 1–25.

54 Cf. Luís R. Cardoso de Oliveira, *Direito legal e insulto moral* (Rio de Janeiro: Relume Dumará, 2002).

55 Stephens, 'Governing Antarctica in the Anthropocene'; Leane and McGee, 'Anthropocene Antarctica'.

56 Dodds *et al.*, *Handbook on the Politics of Antarctica*.

57 Salazar, 'The Anthropocene Melt'.

58 This term characterises the Brazilian way of inhabiting Antarctica, native Brazilians or a synonym for anything related to the Brazilian people, similar to 'Yankees' as the United States inhabitants or US natives.

59 Dasan M. Thamattoor, 'Stratospheric Ozone Depletion and Greenhouse Gases since the International Geophysical Year: F. Sherwood Rowland and

the Evolution of Earth Sciences', in Roger D. Launius, James R. Fleming and David H. DeVorkin (eds), *Globalizing Polar Sciences* (New York: Palgrave Macmillan, 2010), pp. 355–72.

60　Pereira *et al.*, 'Apportionment of Black Carbon'.
61　Bergson, *Duration and Simultaneity*.
62　Pimenta, 'Antropoceno'.

Bibliography

Aguilar, Raquel G., Rebecca Owens and John R. Giardino. 'The Expanding Role of Anthropogeomorphology in Critical Zones Studies in the Anthropocene'. *Geomorphology* 366, no. 1 (2020): 1–25.

Anderson, David G., Jan Peter Laurens Loovers, Sara Asu Schroer and Robert P. Wishart. 'Architectures of Domestication: On Emplacing Human–Animal Relations in the North'. *Journal of the Royal Anthropological Institute* 23 (2017): 398–418.

Asad, Talal (ed.). *Anthropology and the Colonial Encounter*. London: Ithaca Press, 1973.

Bergson, Henri. *Duration and Simultaneity*. Manchester: Clinamen Press, 1999.

Brooks, Shaun T., Julia Jabour, John van den Hoff and Dana M. Bergstrom. 'Our Footprint on Antarctica Competes with Nature for Rare Ice-Free Land'. *Nature Sustainability* 2 (2019): 185–90.

Cardoso de Oliveira, Luís R. *Direito legal e insulto moral*. Rio de Janeiro: Relume Dumará, 2002.

Collins, William J., Christopher P. Webber, Peter M. Cox *et al.* 'Increased Importance of Methane Reduction for a 1.5 Degree Target'. *Environmental Research Letters* 13, no. 5 (2018): 054003. DOI: 10.1088/1748-9326/aab89c.

Cordero, Raúl R., Edgardo Sepúlveda, Sarah Feron *et al.* 'Black Carbon Footprint of Human Presence in Antarctica'. *Nature Communications* 13 (2022): 984. DOI: 10.1038/s41467-022-28560-w.

Coupaye, Ludovic. 'Ways of Enchanting: Châines Opératoires and Yam Cultivation in Nyamikum Village, Maprik, Papua New Guinea'. *Journal of Material Culture* 14, no. 4 (2009): 433–58.

Crutzen, Paul J. 'Geology of Mankind'. *Nature* 415 (2002): 23. DOI: 10.1038/415023a.

Crutzen, Paul J. and Eugene F. Stoermer. 'The "Anthropocene"'. *IGBP Global Change Newsletter* 41 (2000): 17–18.

Dodds, Klaus J. and Christy Collis. 'Post-Colonial Antarctica'. In *Handbook on the Politics of Antarctica*, ed. Klaus J. Dodds, Alan D. Hemmings and Peder Roberts, pp. 50–68. Cheltenham: Edward Elgar Publishing, 2017.

Dodds, Klaus J., Alan D. Hemmings and Peder Roberts (eds). *Handbook on the Politics of Antarctica*. Cheltenham: Edward Elgar Publishing, 2017.

Fausto, Carlos and Eduardo G. Neves. 'Was There Ever a Neolithic in the Neotropics? Plant Familiarization and Biodiversity in the Amazon'. *Antiquity* 92, no. 366 (2018): 1604–18.

Favret-Saada, Jeanne. 'Ser afetado'. *Cadernos de campo* 13, no. 13 (2005): 155–61.

Ferry, Luc. *A revolução do amor: Por uma espiritualidade laica*. Rio de Janeiro: Objetiva, 2012.

Gibbard, Phillip L., Michael Walker, Andrew Bauer *et al.* 'The Anthropocene as an Event, not an Epoch'. *Journal of Quaternary Science* 37, no. 3 (2022): 395–9.

Headland, Thomas and Robert Bailey. 'Have Hunter-Gatherers Ever Lived in Tropical Rain Forest Independently of Agriculture?'. *Human Ecology* 19, no. 2 (1991): 115–22.

Ingold, Tim. 'Beyond Art and Technology: The Anthropology of Skill'. In *Anthropological Perspectives on Technology*, ed. Michael B. Schiffer, pp. 17–32. Albuquerque: University of New Mexico Press, 2001.

Leane, Elizabeth and Jeffrey McGee. 'Anthropocene Antarctica: Approaches, Issues and Debates'. In *Anthropocene Antarctica*, ed. Elizabeth Leane and Jeffrey McGee, pp. 1–14. Abingdon: Routledge, 2020.

Leistenschneider, Clara, Patricia Burkhardt-Holm, Thomas Mani, Sebastian Primpke, Heidi Taubner and Gunnar Gerdts. 'Microplastics in the Weddell Sea (Antarctica): A Forensic Approach for Discrimination between Environmental and Vessel-Induced Microplastics'. *Environmental Science and Technology* 55, no. 23 (2021): 15900–11.

Leroi-Gourhan, André. *Gesture and Speech*. Cambridge, MA: MIT Press, 2018.

Lévy-Brühl, Lucien. *Primitive Mentality*. London: Allen & Unwin, 1923.

Little, Paul. *Amazonia: Territorial Struggles on Perennial Frontiers*. Baltimore, MD: Johns Hopkins University Press, 2001.

Maddison, Ben. *Class and Colonialism in Antarctic Exploration, 1750–1920*. London: Pickering & Chatto, 2014.

Maddison, Ben. 'Indigenising the Heroic Era of Antarctic Exploration'. In *Anthropocene Antarctica*, ed. Elizabeth Leane and Jeffrey McGee, pp. 136–55. Abingdon: Routledge, 2020.

Mauss, Marcel. 'Techniques of the Body'. *Economy and Society* 2 (1973): 70–88.

McGee, Jeffrey. 'Frozen Eden Lost? Exploring Discourses of Geoengineering Antarctica'. In *Anthropocene Antarctica*, ed. Elizabeth Leane and Jeffrey McGee, pp. 56–72. Abingdon: Routledge, 2020.

Mignolo, Walter. *The Darker Side of Modernity*. Durham, NC: Duke University Press, 2011.

Mignolo, Walter. 'The Geopolitics of Knowledge and the Colonial Difference'. *The South Atlantic Quarterly* 101, no. 1 (2002): 57–96.

Morris, Rosalind C. and Gayatri C. Spivak (eds). *Can the Subaltern Speak? Reflections on the History of an Idea*. New York: Columbia University Press, 2010.

Neves, Eduardo. *Sob os tempos do equinócio: Oito mil anos de história na Amazônia Central*. São Paulo: Ubu Editora, 2022.

Oliveira, Antonio M. S. and Alex U. G. Peloggia. 'The Anthropocene and the Technogene: Stratigraphic Temporal Implications of the Geological Action of Humankind'. *Quaternary and Environmental Geosciences* 5, no. 2 (2014): 103–11.

Pearson, Michael and María Ximena Senatore. 'Conserving the Oldest Historical Sites in the Antarctic'. *Polar Record* 46 (2009): 57–64.

Pearson, Michael, Andrés Zarankin and Melisa A. Salerno. 'Exploring and Exploiting Antarctica: The Early Human Interactions'. In *Past Antarctica: Paleoclimatology and Climate Change*, ed. Marc Oliva and Jesus R. Fernandez, pp. 259–77. London: Elsevier Academic Press, 2020.

Pereira, Enio B., Heitor Evangelista, Kely Cristine Dalia Pereira, Iracema F. A. Cavalcanti and Alberto W. Setzer. 'Apportionment of Black Carbon in the South Shetland Islands, Antarctic Peninsula'. *Journal of Geophysical Research* 111 (2006): D03303. DOI: 10.1029/2005JD006086.

Pfaffenberger, Bryan. 'Social Anthropology of Technology'. *Annual Review of Anthropology* 21, no. 1 (1992): 491–516.

Pimenta, Pedro Paulo. 'Antropoceno: Apontamentos para a história de uma ideia'. In *O Antropoceno*, ed. Stelios Marras and Renzo Taddei, pp. 1–16. São Paulo: Fino Traço, 2022.

Quijano, Aníbal. 'Coloniality of Power, Eurocentrism and Latin America'. *Nepantla* 1, no. 3 (2000): 533–80.

Robbins, Bruce. 'Really Existing Cosmopolitanism'. In *Cosmopolitics*, ed. Pheng Cheah and Bruce Robbins, pp. 1–19. Minneapolis: University of Minnesota Press, 1998.

Rosivach, Vincent J. 'Autochthony and the Athenians' *Classical Quarterly* 37, no. 2 (1987): 294–306.

Safatle, Vladimir. 'O ato para além da lei: "Kant com Sade" como ponto de viragem do pensamento lacaniano'. In *Um limite tenso: Lacan entre a filosofia e a psicanálise*, ed. Vladimir Safatle, pp. 189–232. São Paulo: Editoria UNESP, 2002.

Salazar, Juan Francisco. 'The Anthropocene Melt: Antarctica's Geologic Politics'. In *Anthropocene Antarctica*, ed. Elizabeth Leane and Jeffrey McGee, pp. 73–83. Abingdon: Routledge, 2020.

Salerno, Melisa A., María Jimena Cruz and Andrés Zarankin. 'A Historical Archaeology of the First Antarctic Labourers'. In *The Cambridge History of the Polar Regions*, ed. Adrian Howkins and Peder Roberts, pp. 407–29. Cambridge: Cambridge University Press, 2023.

Sautchuk, Carlos E. 'The Pirarucu Net: Artefact, Animism and the Technical Object'. *Journal of Material Culture* 24, no. 2 (2018): 1–18.

Sautchuk, Carlos E. 'Técnica e/em/como transformação'. In *Técnica e transformação*, ed. Carlos E. Sautchuk, pp. 11–36. Rio de Janeiro: ABA Publicações, 2017.

Schlanger, Nathan. 'The Chaîne Opératoire'. In *Archaeology: Key Concepts*, ed. Colin Renfrew and Paul Bahn, pp. 25–31. London: Routledge, 2005.

Sigaut, François. 'Technology'. In *Companion Encyclopedia of Anthropology: Humanity, Culture and Social Life*, ed. Tim Ingold, pp. 420–59. London: Routledge, 1994.

Sigman, Daniel and Edward Boyle. 'Glacial/Interglacial Variations in Atmospheric Carbon Dioxide'. *Nature* 407, no. 19 (2000): 859–69.

Silva, Reginaldo O. 'Kant e Sade na alcova: Sobre os paradoxos da ética moderna'. *Princípios revista de filosofia* 21, no. 36 (2014): 177–98.

Simondon, Gilbert. *Individualization in Light of Notions of Form and Information*. 2 vols. Minneapolis: University of Minnesota Press, 2020.

Simondon, Gilbert. *On the Mode of Existence of Technical Objects*. Minnesota: University of Minnesota Press, 2016.

Stengers, Isabelle. 'The Cosmopolitical Proposal'. In *Making Things Public*, ed. Bruno Latour and Peter Wibel, pp. 994–1006. Cambridge, MA: MIT Press, 2007.

Stengers, Isabelle. *Cosmopolitics I*. Minnesota: University of Minnesota Press, 2010.

Stengers, Isabelle. *Cosmopolitics II*. Minnesota: University of Minnesota Press, 2011.

Stengers, Isabelle. 'Introductory Notes on an Ecology of Practices'. *Cultural Studies Review* 11, no. 1 (2005): 183–96.

Stephens, Tim. 'Governing Antarctica in the Anthropocene'. In *Anthropocene Antarctica*, ed. Elizabeth Leane and Jeffrey McGee, pp. 17–32. Abingdon: Routledge, 2020.

Steward, Julian. 'Culture Areas of the Tropical Forests'. In *Handbook of South American Indians*, ed. Julian Steward, pp. 883–903. Washington, DC: Bureau of American Ethnology, Smithsonian Institute, 1948.

Tavares, Paulo. 'The Geological Imperative: On the Political Ecology of the Amazonia's Deep History'. In *Architecture in the Anthropocene*, ed. Etienne Turpin, pp. 209–40. Detroit, MI: Open Humanities Press, 2013.

Ter-Stepanian, George. *Beginning of the Quinary or the Technogene: An Engineering Geological Analysis*. Laboratory of Geomechanics IGES, Ac. Sc. Communication 5 (Yerevan: Armenian Academy of Sciences Press, 1985).

Ter-Stepanian, George. 'Beginning of the Technogene'. *Bulletin of the International Association of Engineering Geology/Bulletin de l'Association internationale de géologie de l'ingénieur* 38 (1988): 133–42.

Ter-Stepanian, George. 'Did the Quinary Start?'. *XI Congress of the International Union for Quaternary Research: Abstracts* (1983): 260.

Thamattoor, Dasan M. 'Stratospheric Ozone Depletion and Greenhouse Gases since the International Geophysical Year: F. Sherwood Rowland and the Evolution of Earth Sciences'. In *Globalizing Polar Sciences*, ed. Roger D. Launius, James R. Fleming and David H. DeVorkin, pp. 355–72. New York: Palgrave Macmillan, 2010.

Tudge, Colin. *The Time before History: 5 Million Years of Human Impact*. New York: Touchstone, 1996.

Turpin, Etienne. 'Who Does the Earth Think It Is, Now?'. In *Architecture in the Anthropocene*, ed. Etienne Turpin, pp. 3–10. Detroit, MI: Open Humanities Press, 2013.

Villagran, Ximena S. and Carlos E. G. R. Schaefer. 'Geoarqueologia das primeiras ocupações humanas na Antártica'. *Vestígios: Revista Latino-Americana de Arqueología Histórica 5*, no. 1 (2011): 115–36.

Villagran, Ximena S., Carlos E. G. R. Schaefer and Bertrand Ligouis. 'Living in the Cold: Geoarchaeology of Sealing Sites from Byers Peninsula'. *Quaternary International* 315 (2013): 184–99.

Viveiros de Castro, Eduardo. *A inconstância da alma selvagem*. São Paulo: Cosac & Naify, 2002.

Wallerstein, Immanuel. *World Systems Analysis*. Durham, NC: Duke University Press, 2006.

Warnier, Jean-Pierre. 'A Praxeological Approach to Subjectivation in a Material World'. *Journal of Material Culture 6*, no. 1 (2001): 5–24.

Warnier, Jean-Pierre. 'Technology as Efficacious Action on Objects … and Subjects'. *Journal of Material Culture* 14, no. 4 (2009): 459–70.

Zalasiewicz, Jan, Colin N. Waters, Colin P. Summerhayes *et al.* 'The Working Group on the Anthropocene: Summary of Evidence and Interim Recommendations'. *Anthropocene* 19 (September 2017): 55–60.

Zarankin, Andrés and Melisa A. Salerno. 'The Anthropocene in Antarctica: Considering "Fixed" and More "Fluid" Perspectives of Analysis'. In *Historical Archaeology and Environment*, ed. Marcos A. T. Souza and Diogo M. Costa, pp. 253–65. Cham: Springer International, 2018.

Zarankin, Andrés and Melisa A. Salerno. 'The Wild Continent? Some Discussion on the Anthropocene in Antarctica'. *Journal of Contemporary Archaeology* 1, no. 1 (2014): 116–20.

Zarankin, Andrés and María Ximena Senatore. 'Archaeology in Antarctica'. *Cuartas jornadas de investigación antárticas/Fourth Conference on Antarctic Research* 2 (1997): 7–10.

Zarankin, Andrés and María Ximena Senatore. 'Archaeology in Antarctica: Nineteenth-Century Capitalism Expansion Strategies'. *International Journal of Historical Archaeology* 9 (2005): 43–56.

Zarankin, Andrés and María Ximena Senatore. *Histórias de um pasado en blanco.* Belo Horizonte: Argumentum, 2007.

Zarankin, Andrés, Sarah Hissa, Melisa A. Salerno *et al.* 'Paisagens em branco: Arqueologia e antropologia antárticas – avanços e desafios'. *Vestígios: Revista Latino-Americana de Arqueología Histórica* 5, no. 2 (2011): 9–51.

Zarankin, Andrés, Fernanda Codevilla Soares, Melisa A. Salerno *et al.* 'Paisagens em branco: Balanço após 10 anos de existência no Brasil'. In *Antártica em Minas Gerais*, ed. Andrés Zarankin, Luiz H. Rosa, Rosa M. E. Arantes and Fernanda Codevilla Soares, pp. 23–62. Belo Horizonte: Imprensa Universitária da UFMG, 2021.

Zarankin, Andrés, María Ximena Senatore and Melisa A. Salerno. 'No Man's Land: Landscape Archaeology in South Shetlands Islands, Antarctica'. In *South America Landscape Archaeology*, ed. Andrés Troncoso and Felix Acuto. Oxford: British Archaeological Reports, 2009.

Postscript: Antarctica and colonialism: A historian's reflections

Rebecca Herman

This volume probes the limits of critical Antarctic studies' quest to debunk Antarctic exceptionalism. Excellent scholarship in recent years has demonstrated that our planet's vast uninhabited continent does not sit above the fray of geopolitics and, in fact, can best be understood with an eye toward some of the same formative dynamics that have shaped the rest of the world: imperialism, nationalism and capitalism.[1] The conveners of this volume ask: must we stop there? What about that other big '-ism' that so fundamentally reordered the globe over the last 500 years? What is the relationship between Antarctica and colonialism? In the volume's introductory chapter and the contributions that follow, the potential link between Antarctica and colonialism manifests largely along two tracks of reflection. The first considers whether and how Antarctica can contribute meaningfully to global histories of colonialism, and the second considers whether it makes sense to talk about colonialism *in* Antarctica.

I confess that my own reaction when I first heard the question of whether we can use colonialism to describe human activities in Antarctica was uneasiness. Perhaps conservative in this regard, I tend to err on the side of caution when it comes to invoking colonialism outside unambiguous instances of formal colonial rule. My concern is that sometimes 'colonialism' in other contexts serves as shorthand for 'bad', and is a short cut to critique that bypasses too much. In dedicating an entire volume to the question, the contributors here take no short cuts, but instead offer a thoughtful series of meditations on whether the conceptual framework is a productive one for understanding the Antarctic past and, if so, in what ways and during which periods. Contemplating my own uneasiness with the question prompted reflection on disciplinary differences and the stakes of scholars' linguistic choices, proving the volume's provocation a useful one for me, even as it may well conclude without consensus.

My intellectual background is probably responsible for my resistance to liberal uses of the word colonialism. A relative newcomer to Antarctic studies, by training I'm a historian of Latin America. In that field, colonialism is not just an important conceptual frame, but is also a key marker of periodisation that organises our understanding of the region's past into 'colonial' and 'modern' chapters. Of course, the legacies of colonialism that were deeply embedded in Latin American societies in all sorts of ways by the end of those three centuries of colonial rule were hardly erased when power shifted, with independence, from one set of elites to another. But rather than proclaim it all colonialism, or declare independence an insignificant turning point, we dedicate ourselves to understanding the mechanisms that, after independence, sustained inequalities that colonialism created. After all, parsing continuity and change over time is historians' bread and butter.

Colonialism, its attendant vocabulary and its limits are also a concern in my second field of study, which is the history of US foreign relations. Scholars in this field examine the many ways that the United States has exerted cultural, political, economic and military power abroad. The scholarship includes histories of colonialism, as in Puerto Rico and the Philippines, but it is necessarily more expansive than that, and recognises colonial rule as but one tool in Washington's toolkit. United States policy in Antarctica, in fact, offers an excellent illustration of some of the other signature methods by which the USA has asserted and maintained disproportionate power and access around the world.

Critics may say that historians are just bad at theory. But we're not devoted to precision merely for precision's sake. If we call all US foreign policy colonial, we lose explanatory power. Allowing for differences between US assertions of authority in Antarctica and in the Marshall Islands enables us to see how essential the employment of different practices in different contexts was to the rise of US global power. By honing all sorts of imperialist techniques in addition to formal empire, the United States managed to forgo some of the expense, burden and moral obstacles that complicated the maintenance of formal colonies in the second half of the twentieth century.

In short, I'm committed to the idea that we need a robust and carefully calibrated vocabulary that can adequately describe the many forces that create and sustain inequality alongside colonialism, after its decline, or in its absence where it never existed, while signalling the through-lines and commonalities between them.

One reservation about the suitability of colonialism to the Antarctic context that even those scholars more comfortable with treating colonialism as a portable lens might share is what I've come to think of as the 'people problem'. When I contemplate the aspects of Antarctic governance that bear the most resemblance to my narrow view of colonial history, such as Argentine and Chilean efforts to settle the Antarctic peninsula, I struggle to make the leap from colonisation to colonialism in the absence of any Indigenous population. What work does colonialism do if it doesn't tell us something about power relations between people? And is whatever payoff one gains from it worth the trouble one must go through to explain away the people problem? Imperialism seems only to require people asserting authority, while colonialism seems to require people subordinated to the authority of imperialists. Put another way, if you hand me two books, one on Spanish imperialism and one on colonial Latin America, I'll have a sense right away for how they differ and whose agency they foreground. Who are the protagonists in a book about colonial Antarctica?

The most compelling case for resolving the people problem is one that I don't think many historians are yet prepared to make, but that may well become more mainstream in the coming years as climate change renders larger swathes of the planet uninhabitable to humans and countless other species: an insistence that our discipline is unacceptably anthropocentric and that by calling governance in Antarctica colonial we are shifting toward an understanding of power and violence that elevates non-human animals and landscapes. This line of argument is not centred in this volume, but it invites further contemplation.

If I remain uneasy about employing the word colonialism in scholarly analysis of the Antarctic past, I am very interested in the ways that historical actors have used anti-imperial and anticolonial language in popular discourse to advance their agendas in Antarctic governance during different moments in the twentieth century. Just as our word choices are powerful, so too are those of the people we study. My disciplinary inclination is to historicise those instances rather than take them as a cue that we should employ the same vocabulary ourselves. These episodes add further evidence to the case made by scholarship in this volume that suggests that there is plenty to say about colonialism *and* Antarctica, whatever one thinks of colonialism *in* Antarctica.

Argentina and Chile have long employed anticolonial and anti-imperialist rhetoric in advancing their claims to national sovereignty on the Antarctic peninsula.[2] Their Antarctic bases bear the names of heroes from their wars for independence with Spain, and the British territorial claim that overlaps with theirs imbues the mission to defend claims to Antarctic territory with an anti-imperialist rhetorical power that effectively summons nationalist sentiment. After the signing of the Antarctic Treaty, the two countries managed to continue to celebrate nationalist claims to the territory with anti-imperialist credentials, even as they defended the Antarctic Treaty System (ATS) from anticolonial challenges arising elsewhere in the global community.[3]

Anti-imperialist and anticolonial critiques of Antarctic governance experienced a second wave during the legitimacy crisis in the ATS in the 1980s. With decolonisation, humans reached a striking consensus that the nation-state was the gold standard for governing people, but the question of how to think about nature and natural resources in the places beyond state sovereignty remained somewhat less resolved. As various actors on the global stage asserted alternative ways of ordering the world, decrying Antarctic governance as imperialist or colonial was a way to delegitimise it.

Various critiques along these lines came from voices in the so-called Third World. India's criticism of the ATS as elitist marked an early move to tie the ATS to the legacies of colonialism. When that torch was taken up again later by Malaysia and other members of the Non-Aligned Movement, the thrust was similar. The notion that the wealthiest powers in the world might hoard for themselves the natural resources of Antarctica that were not rightfully theirs was easy to tie to the colonial past. Argentina and Chile, the earliest champions of anti-imperialism in Antarctica as far as their own claims were concerned, were also among the most important defenders of the ATS from critiques originating elsewhere in the Third World. The concept that the deep seabed and Antarctic continent composed a category entirely apart from the nation-state – a common heritage of mankind – is part of this broader global story of decolonisation and its limits.[4]

Finally, there was yet another move to reframe understandings of the world and Antarctica's place in it that dabbled in anti-imperialist rhetoric during these years: a rising transnational environmental movement. Environmentalists from Greenpeace and the Antarctic and Southern Oceans Coalition advocated transforming the Antarctic into humanity's first 'World Park'.[5] In the 1970s, environmental activists had begun to view environmental problems in increasingly global terms, and environmental activism became more common around the world. The Stockholm Conference on the Human Environment drew international attention to questions of environmental governance, and linked the problems of global inequality, economic development and environmental devastation. In the 1980s the language of 'sustainable development' became more commonplace, and today's headlines that perpetually remind the public that those countries poised to suffer the greatest consequences from climate change have done the least to cause it have intellectual roots in this period.

In this context, environmentalists from the north had to walk a fine line between cultivating allies in what was then called the developing world and appearing to be constraining poorer nations' development strategies, denying them the methods pursued freely by wealthier countries in order to slow down a problem that wealthier nations were mostly responsible for. Observers and activists used the term 'ecological colonialism' to describe the polluting behaviours of wealthier countries that impacted poorer ones, and they used the same term to describe a dynamic that environmentalists from the developing world guarded against in their collaborations with North

American and European partners.[6] Once again, mobilising the language of colonialism at the height of decolonisation proved a powerful means to criticise the status quo and stake out one's politics in a new vision for the planet.

It can be tricky for historians to remain clear-eyed about what we mean when we use a word, and how that might differ from the meaning our historical actors invest in the same language. This is trickier still because the language historians use to describe the past isn't static – indeed, the way we imbue the past with new meaning is often by rethinking the words we use to describe it. That robust vocabulary for inequality that I described earlier has included a number of terms that have come in and out of fashion over the years – informal empire, hegemony, neocolonialism, postcolonialism and internal colonialism. The practice of considering and reconsidering the language we use is a productive one in any field, as this volume has proven it to be here. My concern for language is the reason I so enjoy the provocation that this volume presents.

On a history exam, I know I've written a good essay question when it's one that allows students with opposing viewpoints to make a compelling case in either direction. In those instances, the practice of considering the question and surveying the points that might be made in favour or in opposition is more valuable than the conclusion itself. Such is the case, I believe, with the questions posed in this volume, which are sure to prompt conversation that will continue beyond these pages. Is colonialism the one -ism that just doesn't reach Antarctica? Wherever readers of this volume land, to get there they will have to refine their own understandings of the nature of Antarctic exceptionalism, the nature of colonialism and what can properly be done with either concept.

Notes

1 For a sampling of some of this scholarship, see Klaus J. Dodds, Alan D. Hemmings and Peder Roberts (eds), *Handbook on the Politics of Antarctica* (Cheltenham: Edward Elgar Publishing, 2017).
2 For two perspectives on this, see the chapters by Alejandra Mancilla and Ignacio Cardone in this volume.
3 For a recent introduction to Latin American activities in and claims to Antarctica, see Pablo Fontana, 'The Antarctic Extension of Latin America', in Adrian Howkins and Peder Roberts (eds), *The Cambridge History of the Polar Regions* (Cambridge: Cambridge University Press, 2023), pp. 672–701.
4 On India's critique, see Adrian Howkins, 'Defending Polar Empire: Opposition to India's Proposal to Raise the "Antarctic Question" at the United Nations in 1956', *Polar Record* 44:1 (2008), 35–44; Sanjay Chaturvedi, 'Rise and Decline

of Antarctica in Nehru's Geopolitical Vision: Challenges and Opportunities of the 1950s', *The Polar Journal* 3:2 (2013), 301–15. For an overview of Malaysia's Antarctica policy from 1982 to 2011, see B. A. Hamzah, 'Malaysia and the 1959 Antarctic Treaty: A Geopolitical Interpretation', *The Polar Journal* 1:2 (2011), 287–300. For a brief introduction to the common heritage principle in relation to Antarctica, see Rüdiger Wolfrum, 'Common Interest and Common Heritage in Antarctica', in Dodds *et al.*, *Handbook on the Politics of Antarctica*, pp. 142–51; for a brief overview of 'the Antarctic question' at the United Nations, see Peter J. Beck, 'Antarctica and the United Nations', in Dodds *et al.*, *Handbook on the Politics of Antarctica*, pp. 255–68.

5 Greenpeace International, 'The World Park Option for Antarctica: Background for a Fourth UN Debate', Antarctic and Southern Oceans Coalition Archive, Washington, DC.

6 For an example of both uses of the term, see 'Primera entrevista concedida a un medio: Greenpeace Argentina (Paz Verde)', *Pulso* (March 1986), p. 3.

Bibliography

Beck, Peter J. 'Antarctica and the United Nations'. In *Handbook on the Politics of Antarctica,* ed. Klaus J. Dodds, Alan D. Hemmings and Peder Roberts, pp. 255–68. Cheltenham: Edward Elgar Publishing, 2017.

Chaturvedi, Sanjay. 'Rise and Decline of Antarctica in Nehru's Geopolitical Vision: Challenges and Opportunities of the 1950s', *The Polar Journal* 3, no. 2 (2013): 301–15.

Dodds, Klaus J., Alan D. Hemmings and Peder Roberts (eds). *Handbook on the Politics of Antarctica*. Cheltenham: Edward Elgar Publishing, 2017.

Fontana, Pablo. 'The Antarctic Extension of Latin America'. In *The Cambridge History of the Polar Regions*, ed. Adrian Howkins and Peder Roberts, pp. 672–701. Cambridge: Cambridge University Press, 2023.

Hamzah, B. A. 'Malaysia and the 1959 Antarctic Treaty: A Geopolitical Interpretation'. *The Polar Journal* 1, no. 2 (2011): 287–300.

Howkins, Adrian. 'Defending Polar Empire: Opposition to India's Proposal to Raise the "Antarctic Question" at the United Nations in 1956'. *Polar Record* 44, no. 1 (2008): 35–44.

Pulso. 'Primera entrevista concedida a un medio: Greenpeace Argentina (Paz Verde). *Pulso*, March 1986, p. 3.

Wolfrum, Rüdiger. 'Common Interest and Common Heritage in Antarctica'. In *Handbook on the Politics of Antarctica*, ed. Klaus J. Dodds, Alan D. Hemmings and Peder Roberts, pp. 142–51. Cheltenham: Edward Elgar Publishing, 2017.

Index

EU authorised representative for GPSR:
Easy Access System Europe, Mustamäe tee 50,
10621 Tallinn, Estonia
gpsr.requests@easproject.com

www.ingramcontent.com/pod-product-compliance
Lightning Source LLC
Chambersburg PA
CBHW050627280326
41932CB00015B/2549